PERGAMON INTERNATIONAL LIBRARY
of Science, Technology, Engineering and Social Studies

The 1000-volume original paperback library in aid of education,
industrial training and the enjoyment of leisure

Publisher: Robert Maxwell, M.C.

BRITISH CITIES
An Analysis of Urban Change

BRITISH CITIES
An Analysis of Urban Change

NIGEL SPENCE
*Department of Geography,
London School of Economics and Political Science*

ANDREW GILLESPIE
*Centre for Urban and Regional Development Studies,
University of Newcastle upon Tyne*

JOHN GODDARD
*Department of Geography,
University of Newcastle upon Tyne*

STEPHEN KENNETT
*Inner Cities Directorate,
Department of the Environment*

STEVEN PINCH
*Department of Geography,
University of Southampton*

ALAN WILLIAMS
*Department of Geography,
University of Exeter*

PERGAMON PRESS
OXFORD · NEW YORK · TORONTO · SYDNEY · PARIS · FRANKFURT

U.K.	Pergamon Press Ltd., Headington Hill Hall, Oxford OX3 0BW, England
U.S.A.	Pergamon Press Inc., Maxwell House, Fairview Park, Elmsford, New York 10523, U.S.A.
CANADA	Pergamon Press Canada Ltd., Suite 104, 150 Consumers Rd., Willowdale, Ontario M2J 1P9, Canada
AUSTRALIA	Pergamon Press (Aust.) Pty. Ltd., P.O. Box 544, Potts Point, N.S.W. 2011, Australia
FRANCE	Pergamon Press SARL, 24 rue des Ecoles, 75240 Paris, Cedex 05, France
FEDERAL REPUBLIC OF GERMANY	Pergamon Press GmbH, 6242 Kronberg-Taunus, Hammerweg 6, Federal Republic of Germany

First edition 1982

Library of Congress Cataloging in Publication Data

British cities: an analysis of urban change
(Urban and regional planning series ; v. 26)
(Pergamon international library of science, technology, engineering, and social studies)
Includes bibliographical references.
1. Cities and towns—Great Britain—History—
20th century. 2. Social change—Great Britain—
History—20th century. 3. Urban policy—Great
Britain—History—20th century. I. Spence,
Nigel. II. Series. III. Series: Pergamon inter-
national library of science, technology, engineering,
and social studies.
HT133.B72 1982   307.7'6'0941   81-19178
AACR2

British Library Cataloguing in Publication Data

Spence, Nigel
British cities: an analysis of urban
change. — (Urban and regional
planning series; v.26). — (Pergamon
international library)
1. City planning—Great Britain
2. Great Britain—Social policy
I. Title II. Series
307.7'6'0941   HT169.G7
ISBN 0-08-028931-2

In order to make this volume available as economically and as rapidly as possible the authors' typescripts have been reproduced in their original forms. This method unfortunately has its typographical limitations but it is hoped that they in no way distract the reader.

The reports and research upon which this work is based were commissioned by the Department of the Environment for its (currently titled) Inner Cities Directorate. The views expressed are not necessarily those of the Department. Some of the material in this work is " © Crown Copyright 1981" and is reproduced with the permission of the Controller of Her Majesty's Stationery Office.

Printed in Great Britain by A. Wheaton & Co. Ltd., Exeter

Preface and Acknowledgements

It seems ironic but somehow appropriate that these opening remarks are being written minutes after completing my Census 1981 return. This is a study of the 1971 Census. It came about through the commissioning of a Department of the Environment research contract extending over several years in the middle seventies. The basic objective was to provide a descriptive snapshot of urban change in Britain since the nineteen fifties. Various demographic and economic themes were to be emphasised in the description but the whole study was intended to be integrated by its common set of functionally defined areas. The research was commissioned at around the time much detailed research on inner city areas was being undertaken by the Department of the Environment and their consultants and it was hoped that the present study research would provide a national urban systems context into which such detailed studies could be placed. This general context focusing mainly on trends of population and employment change in aggregate was published by the Department of the Environment in 1976 as British Cities: Urban Population and Employment Trends, 1951-1971. Research Report 10. (QMW Lib: HT133 GRE)

The research continued however after this to disaggregate the demographic and economic variables under analysis. Employment trends were analysed by sex, by occupational and industrial groups, and were linked to population through studies of activity rates. Population trends were analysed by birthplace groups, by age structure and were linked to employment through studies of socio-economic groups. Furthermore considerable research effort was expended analysing two sources of fundamental interaction in the urban system-migration and worktravel. In all the project issued some 52 working reports as well as a dozen or so conference papers. In a way this present publication came about because it became impossible to satisfy the repeated requests for working papers and information now long out of print. Such requests came from academics and professionals in a variety of fields both in Britain and abroad. Many a geographical or urban planning studies text or planning or commercial information base has used the information and material generated by the project. Thus, although now history by exactly one decade, the detailed research undertaken by the project has proved its use. The period that it considers is an important one for a variety of reasons as will be explained. This book will make the findings more widely known and provide a well surveyed benchmark against which to measure and subsequently monitor future change.

The research was directed by Roy Drewett, John Goddard and Nigel Spence and was based at the London School of Economics and Political Science. Six research officers were employed by the project, Caroline Connock, Robert Pinkham, Steven Pinch, Alan Williams, Stephen Kennett and Andrew Gillespie. Numerous other research assistants were also employed and all were well served by Stephen Thorton as computer programmer.

This book reflects a selection of the research undertaken for the project and is based on original drafts prepared by Nigel Spence, John Goddard, Steven Pinch and Alan Williams (demographic and economic), Andrew Gillespie (worktravel) and Stephen Kennett (migration). Nigel Spence selected and edited the material. With so many researchers over such a lengthy period of time consistency and depth of treatment inevitably varies. The aim of the book is to provide detailed coverage of the disaggregated population and employment trends previously only made available in the aggregate. These detailed research findings are introduced after a brief consideration of trends in urban change going on elsewhere in the world, and are concluded with a brief consideration of their implications for planning.

Many persons in addition to those mentioned contributed much to the present study.

The enthusiasm and encouragement of Mr. Burnett and his team at the Department of the Environment was much appreciated. The administrative staff of the London School of Economics and particularly the Department of Geography made for speedy resolution of problems. Cartographic services were most ably provided by the Drawing Office at the London School of Economics under the watchful supervision of Mrs. E. Wilson. Barbara Glover prepared the illustrations for the selection of research presented in this volume. Several generations of secretaries have helped in the production of the familiar red covered working reports. Mrs. E. Diamond skilfully typed this final version of the research. To all these hardworking people the team extend their grateful thanks.

                                                    Nigel Spence
                                                    5 April 1981

Contents

List of Tables and Figures

Figures

PART ONE

British Urban Systems in Context

1.1   INTERNATIONAL URBAN SYSTEMS

Counter urbanisation - the converse of urbanisation - is the main theme of this
research. It is a process which has become to characterise the urban systems evolution of a number of the world's nations especially in the west. In some countries
the switch from urbanisation processes to counter urbanisation processes has been
dramatic and pronounced, in others the rate of change has been less significant,
and in others there seems to have been little change if any. Berry's important
collection of essays on Urbanisation and Counterurbanisation (1976) well illustrate
these trends in a wide ranging international context. Where the trend reversals
have taken place there will be clear problems of adjustment in the functions that
the urban system has evolved to perform. But leaving aside the planning implications for the moment the basic task of this introductory section is to provide an
international context into which to place the detailed research on Britain which
is to follow. It will be seen that there are fundamental lessons of urban systems
evolution that Britain can both take and give in such an international context. It
has progressed further towards counter urbanisation than most countries but has not
yet experienced some of the advanced stages like some others.

The lessons from the United States

That, of all countries in the world, counter urbanisation trends in the United
States are most advanced cannot be doubted. A considerable body of detailed research has been developed on the trends in the United States' urban system. Perhaps
the most useful and thoughtful compilation of such research is that provided by
Sternlieb and Hughes' collection of essays on Post Industrial America (1975), and
this will provide the focus of this review. Having the benefit of post-1970 data,
some of which is presented in Table 1.1, the major trendlines of the evolution of
the United States' urban system are presented under three headings. First, trends
in the overall metropolitan profile are considered, and six basic conclusions
drawn:-

(1) Metropolitan area growth rates have been substantially reduced,
     1971-74.

(2) Non metropolitan areas grew faster than metropolitan areas,
     1971-74.

British Cities

TABLE 1.1 Population, Change and Components of Change for Selected Groups of Metropolitan and Nonmetropolitan Counties 1960-1970 and 1970-1973 (thousands)

| | Population | | | Population change | | | |
| | | | | 1970-1973 | | 1960-1970 | |
	July 1 1973	April 1 1970	April 1 1960	Number	Percent	Number	Percent
UNITED STATES	209,851	203,300	179,323	6,551	3.2	23,997	13.4
Inside SMSAs	153,350	149,093	127,348	4,258	2.9	21,744	17.1
Metropolitan areas over 1,000,000	91,894	90,083	76,260	1,811	2.0	13,823	18.1
Metropolitan areas over 3,000,000	56,189	55,635	47,763	544	1.0	7,872	16.5
New York area	16,657	16,701	15,126	-45	-0.3	1,576	10.4
Los Angeles area	10,131	9,983	7,752	147	1.5	2,231	28.8
Chicago area	7,689	7,611	6,794	78	1.0	817	12.0
Philadelphia area	5,653	5,628	5,024	25	0.4	604	12.0
Detroit area	4,691	4,669	4,122	22	0.5	547	13.3
San Francisco area	4,544	4,423	3,492	121	2.7	932	26.7
Boston area	3,783	3,710	3,358	73	2.0	352	10.5
Washington area	3,042	2,910	2,097	132	4.5	813	38.8
Metropolitan areas of 1-3,000,000	35,705	34,448	28,497	1,257	3.6	5,951	20.9
Northeast	3,720	3,751	3,712	-30	-0.8	38	1.0
North Central	12,427	12,381	10,868	46	0.4	1,513	13.9
Florida	3,376	2,976	2,078	400	13.4	898	43.2
Other South Atlantic	3,845	3,677	2,973	178	4.9	694	23.2
South Central	5,930	5,675	4,305	255	4.5	1,370	31.8
West	6,406	5,998	4,561	408	6.8	1,438	31.5
Other SMSAs	61,456	59,009	51,088	2,447	4.1	7,921	15.5
Northeast	13,517	13,225	11,828	292	2.2	1,397	11.8
North Central	14,761	14,447	12,820	313	2.2	1,627	12.7
Florida	3,072	2,735	2,015	338	12.3	720	35.7
Other South Atlantic	7,556	7,317	6,285	238	3.3	1,032	16.4
South Central	14,458	13,753	12,178	705	5.1	1,575	12.9
West	8,093	7,532	5,962	561	7.4	1,570	26.3
Outside SMSAs	56,500	54,207	51,975	2,293	4.2	2,232	4.3
171 counties with 20% or more commuters to SMSAs	4,099	3,848	3,474	251	6.5	373	10.7
315 counties with 10-19% commuters to SMSAs	9,683	9,269	8,636	414	4.5	633	7.3
Other counties	42,719	41,091	39,865	1,628	4.0	1,226	3.1
Northeast	3,823	3,673	3,490	150	4.1	183	5.2
North Central	13,493	13,101	12,919	392	3.0	182	1.4
Florida	868	767	617	100	13.1	150	24.4
Other South Atlantic	7,585	7,347	7,183	239	3.2	164	2.3
South Central	10,021	9,723	9,718	298	3.1	5	0.1
West	6,929	6,481	5,938	449	6.9	542	9.1

Source: Barabba (1975)

(3)   Net out-migration from metropolitan areas is the prime
      determinant of change.

(4)   The heaviest declines are in the largest metropolitan
      areas (above 3 million population).

(5)   Metropolitan areas of intermediate size (between 1 and 3
      million population) although still growing have reduced
      rates of growth. The actual rate depends on regional
      location with stagnation typifying the North East and North
      Central, heavy declines in growth rates in the West, and
      declines in growth rates in the South. Those areas in the
      South and West which are growing through net in-migration
      are the recreational and retirement centres.

(6)   The smaller metropolitan areas (less than 1 million popul-
      ation) have experienced increased rates of in-migration,
      1970-74.

Second, change within the confined of metropolitan areas are considered and some
eight basic conclusions drawn:-

(1)   The suburban areas are housing an ever increasing share of
      metropolitan area population.

(2)   Central cities lost some 10% of their 1970 population through
      net out-migration, a figure which reduces to a 5% loss when
      net natural increase is accounted for.

(3)   Two thirds of net out-migration to non metropolitan areas
      came from the central cities.

(4)   The heaviest central city declines are in the largest metro-
      politan areas.

(5)   Metropolitan area growth is located mainly in the suburbs,
      all in the case of the North and South, only in the West
      there being any increase in the central city.

(6)   There has been no proportionally large movement of blacks
      from cities to suburbs, 1970-74. The black population of
      the central cities increased by about 6%, 1970-74 mainly
      through net natural increase.

(7)   Substantial flux of movement into and out of central cities
      continued. The net loss of aggregate personal income of
      those in-migrating and those out-migrating was about $30
      billion, 1970-74.

(8)   Metropolitan job growth is fastest in the suburbs. Profess-
      ional employment in the central city, traditionally a growth
      sector, was also in decline, although modestly.

Lastly, regional growth patterns are reviewed with ten fundamental points to be
made explicit:-

(1)   The North East lost population through substantial net out-
      migration, especially of whites but also significantly of
      blacks, 1970-74.

(2)   The South is in receipt of about as many blacks as leave.
      A marked trend reversal.

(3)   The South has received a major increase in net in-migration.

(4) Employment growth rates were five times greater in Southern
     Atlantic states compared to Middle Atlantic states 1967-1972.
     (Typically reflecting North-South differences).

(5) The prime determinant of the growth rate differentials in the
     Southern and Middle Atlantic states was in manufacturing.
     (7% growth in the former and 12% decline in the latter).

(6) Related to manufacturing growth in the South was growth in
     most other employment sectors.

(7) Employment growth rates were nine times greater in Georgia
     compared to New York State, 1967-1972.(Typically reflecting
     North-South differences).

(8) The Bureau of Economic Analysis predict a pronounced shift
     of income away from the North East and North Central parts of
     the country to Southern and Western Regions, at least to 1990.
     This income shift will be based on a wide range of manufactur-
     ing and service industries.

(9) The metropolitan housing stock of the South is increasing one
     and a half times faster than in the North East.

(10) The housing stock in the South is younger and reflects a more
     rapidly changing mix of units, built at a much lower cost
     threshold than in the North East.

Without doing full justice to the impressive analysis contained in this volume,
these are some of the main findings reflecting the ongoing trends in the evolution
of the United States' urban system. Dramatic and interesting though they are, the
lessons to be learned from them for the British context must also depend on an
understanding of why these processes are taking place.

Not unexpectedly the cause, of course, seems to be multivariate in character. In
the words of Sternlieb and Hughes 'The changes taking place, or at least those
which have suddenly become visible, are the cumulative result of a number of small
scale events and innovations, acting in concert with long-standing cultural predispositions and accumulating market forces, which have finally congealed into the
dynamic that now confronts us'. The reasons for post war suburbanisation that
have been described are many and varied. They include unsatisfied central city
housing demand, increased affluence, increased car ownership, and increased mort-
gage funds. Prior to this of course the improved technologies of public utilities,
such as in electricity, sewerage and water supply, made a less centralised form of
urban life possible. The transportation revolution is a further important dimension facilitating urban change. The central city focussed rail system became sup-
erceded by developments in air transport and goods distribution by road. Improvements in metropolitan road networks permitted an ever increasing separation of home
and workplaces. Furthermore improvements in inter-state road linkages have permitted decentralisation of small manufacturing plants previously restricted in terms
of accessibility. Manufacturing industry in general has itself undergone a major
revolution in its locational preferences. The major central cities grew and
developed because of the continuous cycle of manufacturing innovation and development that took place there. Such innovation and development now seems to be lacking. Instead the locational preference for such activity now appears to be in
decentralised, often non metropolitan and high amenity, locations. The production
process itself is also seeking decentralised locations, capitalising on lower land
values, cheaper power sources, and low wage - poorly organised labour.   It should
not be surprising that light manufacturing activity is migrating south.   All
these reasons then may be posited to account for the counter urbanisation trends
without even drawing upon the exciting implications of the telecommunications
revolution or suffering a description of the forces of decline, decay, crime and

poverty extant in the inner cities.

Although clearly not yet as advanced, the early stages of these trends, so dramatic in the United States, are becoming apparent in Britain. The spatial scales are of course different, the important and distinctive ethnic components are not the same, and perhaps the cultural predispositions of the populations can be contrasted. Notwithstanding these differences there are many respects in which the trends that are currently being experienced by the United States will be those of the not too distant future in Britain.

The lessons for Europe

That of all the continents of the world, counter urbanisation trends in Europe are the most diverse also cannot be doubted. Much detailed research effort recently has gone into specifying this diversity of experience in the evolution of European urban systems. Of several studies which could have been chosen perhaps the most detailed and comprehensive is the research provided by Hall and Hay on Growth Centres in the European Urban System (1980) and as such this will provide the focus of this short review.

Some fourteen countries of western and central Europe were included in this study involving the analysis of 539 individual urban systems and some 351 non-metropolitan areas. Population and employment were the principal variables under analysis, these for 1950, 1960 and 1970. To facilitate summary the research aggregates the results of individual nations to arbitrary but conventional groupings of countries. Atlantic Europe is made up of Great Britain and Ireland. This group is heavily dominated in size terms by Britain and provides the control comparison with the rest of Europe which is of interest to this review. Northern Europe comprises Sweden, Norway and Denmark. Western Europe includes the Netherlands, Belgium (with Luxembourg) and France. Southern Europe is made up of Spain, Portugal and Italy. Finally, Central Europe comprises West Germany, Switzerland and Austria. Table 1.2 presents details of the evolution of European urban systems since 1950 for these national groupings in terms of population change. What conclusions can be drawn from this impressive statistical exercise? First, European urbanisation in total can be considered:-

(1) Europe is a highly urbanised nation and furthermore it is
     increasingly becoming so. Some 86% of its population lived
     in metropolitan areas in 1950, with a further 2.3% added by
     1970.

(2) European urbanisation is essentially core focussed and again
     this is on the increase. Some 35.9% of its population lived
     in the core areas of the urban system in 1950, with a further
     2.4% added by 1970.

(3) The urban zones immediately surrounding the core areas have
     moved from a position of below average growth to above average
     growth, the fifties compared to the sixties. Furthermore, by
     the second decade growth in this area exceeded, in both absol-
     ute and percentage terms, the growth in the core areas.

(4) In contrast to the metropolitan rings, the non-metropolitan
     areas moved from a position of modest growth in the fifties
     to heavy decline in the sixties. Almost a million people were
     lost from this zone in the second decade.

(5) The concentration of employment in the metropolitan areas of
     Europe has been higher than that of population. If anything
     (the data are rather uncertain being drawn from a number of
     different sources) this concentration of employment seems to

TABLE 1.2   European Urban Change 1950, 1960 and 1970 (thousands)

	1950 Total	%	1960 Total	%	1970 Total	%	1950-1960 Absolute Change	% Change	% of Total	1960-1970 Absolute Change	% Change	% of Total
Atlantic Europe												
Core	27322	10.10	27833	9.56	27160	8.60	511	1.87	2.46	-673	-2.42	-2.72
Ring	22556	8.34	24531	8.42	28163	8.91	1975	8.75	9.52	2632	14.80	14.69
Non-Met	3419	1.26	3267	1.12	3340	1.06	-153	-4.47	-0.74	73	2.25	0.29
Total	53298	19.71	55631	19.10	58663	18.57	2333	4.38	11.24	3032	5.45	12.26
Northern Europe												
Core	4959	1.83	5554	1.91	5950	1.88	594	11.99	2.86	396	7.14	1.60
Ring	6274	2.32	6589	2.26	7403	2.34	315	5.02	1.52	814	12.35	3.29
Non-Met	3378	1.25	3485	1.20	3536	1.12	107	3.17	0.52	51	1.45	0.21
Total	14612	5.40	15628	5.37	16889	5.34	1016	6.95	4.89	1261	8.07	5.10
Western Europe												
Core	22744	8.41	26719	9.17	30761	9.74	3976	17.48	19.16	4042	15.13	16.35
Ring	27711	10.25	29807	10.23	32839	10.40	2096	7.56	10.10	3032	10.17	12.26
Non-Met	9648	3.57	9810	3.37	10245	3.24	164	1.70	0.79	435	4.43	1.76
Total	60101	22.22	66336	22.78	73845	23.38	6235	10.38	30.04	7508	11.32	30.36
Southern Europe												
Core	22801	8.43	27821	9.55	33346	10.55	5020	22.02	24.19	5575	19.86	22.54
Ring	37747	13.95	38696	13.29	41267	13.06	949	2.51	4.57	2572	6.65	10.40
Non-Met	21045	7.78	20927	7.19	19405	6.14	-118	-0.56	-0.57	-1522	-7.27	-6.15
Total	81593	30.17	87444	30.03	94018	29.75	5851	7.17	28.19	6575	7.52	26.59
Central Europe												
Core	19256	7.12	22719	7.80	23632	7.48	3463	17.98	16.68	914	4.02	3.70
Ring	41240	15.29	43066	14.79	48453	15.34	1825	4.43	8.79	5387	12.51	21.78
Non-Met	329	0.12	360	0.12	408	0.13	31	9.28	0.15	48	13.38	0.19
Total	60825	22.49	66144	22.71	72493	22.94	5319	8.74	25.63	6349	9.60	25.67
Europe												
Core	97082	35.89	110646	37.99	120850	38.25	13564	13.97	65.35	10203	9.22	41.26
Ring	135529	50.11	142689	48.99	158124	50.05	7160	5.28	34.50	15436	10.87	62.42
Non-Met	37852	13.99	37883	13.01	36972	11.70	31	0.08	0.15	-911	-2.40	-3.68
Total	270460	100.00	291218	100.00	315946	100.00	20755	7.67	100.00	24728	8.49	100.00

Source: Hall and Hay (1980)

be slightly increasing over the whole continent. However for
the more urbanised nations in Europe the proportion of employment in metropolitan areas remained static over the two decades.

(6)   Core area employment in the more urbanised countries (the only
set with information back to 1950) seems to have increased pro-
portionately up to 1960 and then decreased its share. The interpretation is that the movement off the land to the large cities
had been reduced and a decentralisation process to the surrounding rings started. The picture for the less urbanised countries
is unavailable and would indeed have provided an interesting comparison.

Second, European urbanisation analysed by regional national aggregates can be
considered:-

(1)   Atlantic Europe (trends dominated by those in Britain) is a
highly urbanised region and becoming more so. The fraction of
the population dwelling in core areas is continuously falling,
with corresponding increases being felt in the ring zones.
Significantly non-metropolitan areas were beginning to achieve
some growth in the later decade of the sixties. This is therefore a region of considerable population decentralisation. Such
decentralisation was only relative in the fifties because the
cores were still growing. The sixties brought absolute decentralisation as the core zones moved into absolute decline.

(2)   Northern Europe is much less urbanised than Europe in general.
Only 79.1% of the population lived in metropolitan areas in
1970, a figure which had only been slowly increasing since 1950.
Core population proportions were also less than the European
average. A somewhat dispersed metropolitan settlement pattern
typifies this urban system and it would seem that this subur-
banised pattern of life is on the increase.

(3)   Western Europe, being a mixed urban and rural, regional national aggregate is not so metropolitan as might be expected
from its title. In fact the proportion of population living
in metropolitan areas is slightly less than in Europe in general.
The proportion living in urban cores is around the European average, if perhaps a little higher, but what is significant is
that it is increasing. Population centralisation is the overall
effect with ring population shares on the decline and the major
growth being felt in the central core areas. (The results for
this regional aggregate seem to be heavily influenced by France,
for if anything the Benelux countries exhibit opposite trends
and for the most part feature population decentralisation).

(4)   Southern Europe, like Northern Europe, seems to be much less
urbanised than Europe as a whole. Low proportions of population live in both metropolitan areas and the core zones therein.
However, there the similarity ends, for unlike Northern Europe
Southern Europe seems to be showing marked concentration trends.
The proportion of population living in metropolitan areas and
their cores has increased markedly since 1950. The highest
growth rates were being achieved in the urban cores compared
to the rings and the non-metropolitan areas were in absolute
decline.

(5)   Central Europe seems to have moved from a decade of centralisation in the fifties to a decade of decentralisation in the sixties.

The core areas at first increased their share of total population and achieved by far the largest element of growth.
Then these areas decreased their share of total population
and recorded only modest growth.

(6) In Britain, Switzerland and Austria decentralisation of both
people and jobs is apparent. In Germany, like much of Northern and Western Europe decentralisation of population is
clear but jobs seem to be still centralising. In general
terms, then, it is apparent that the decentralisation of employment does seem to lag the decentralisation of population.
In the rest of Europe both population and employment continued
to centralise.

(7) Population change by size of urban area is a further interesting feature of change. In Atlantic and Northern Europe it
appears that the medium sized metropolitan areas are the main
growth centres. In the rest of Europe, and especially in those
areas still highly centralising population, the large metropolitan areas achieved the highest gains.

(8) Irrespective of national boundaries several distinct growth
zones can be identified in Europe. The economic core of
Europe – the Golden Triangle bounded by Amsterdam, Paris and
Milan – was particularly dynamic and contained some ten major
growth zones. These were the East Randstad – North Rhine area,
the Paris Basin, the Geneva-Lausanne area, the Lyon-Grenoble
area, Provence and the Cote d'Azur, Milan, Turin, Munich, the
Lorraine, and the Upper Rhine – Central Switzerland region.
The regions based on Stockholm, Rome, and the North West fringe
of London provided three further growth zones. And four more
could be identified in Spain: the Basque Coast, Madrid,
Barcelona and Valencia. In total these seventeen regions accounted for about 54% of the total population growth (net) in
Europe from 1950 to 1970. These, by no means peripheral areas,
then, well illustrate that the industrial heartland of the continent seems to be still thriving, even if there appears to be
developing a particularly vital growth dynamic in the south of
the continent.

So without doing justice to this impressive study some features of European urbanisation should be clear. Europe, in aggregate an urbanised continent, shows considerable variation in the degrees of urbanisation across its nations. Even greater
variation is apparent in the changes in urbanisation taking place. Britain seems to
be most advanced down the centralisation to decentralisation urbanisation path.
Nations in Northern and Central Europe and the Benelux countries seem to be not too
far behind, with their populations beginning to decentralise, although in some cases
not yet their jobs. In France and in Southern Europe centralisation trends are
still dominant, although there are some signs that in certain parts of some of these
countries decentralisation tendencies are likely to follow. Is Europe then likely
to follow the advanced decentralisation trends, with all of the associated planning
problems, that have occured in the United States? An evolutionary interpretation
of metropolitan change would indicate that this might be so. If so, the lessons
which should be apparent for Britain from the United States concerning likely fut-
ures are perhaps equally transmissible from Britain to the rest of Europe in time,
cultural differences always notwithstanding.

1.2 BRITISH URBAN SYSTEMS

It should be apparent that all of the detailed empirical conclusions previously
considered in an international context have been dependent on functionally sensible
definitions of the metropolitan areas under analysis. Before attempting to point
up some of the main features of the evolution of the British urban system, detailed
consideration of the definition of metropolitan areas in a British context is necessary. Such definition will lay the foundation for the whole of this work and it
is crucial that these definitions are carefully reviewed.

Metropolitan area definition

Curiously any serious contemporary consideration of British urban systems must start
in the United States. The United States has been fortunate in having a set of consistently applied definitions of urban areas since 1940. The Census then produced
data for Standard Metropolitan Regions, subsequently referred to as Standard Metropolitan Areas in 1950 and Standard Metropolitan Statistical Areas (SMSA) in 1960.
The American definition recognises that in functional terms an urban area consists
of a core municipal area linked by journey to work movements to a commuting hinterland. The basic building block of the SMSA is the administrative county - generally
much smaller in population than the British county. 'Central cities' or urban cores
are defined as counties with at least a 50,000 population. Linked to the central
city is a 'metropolitan ring' composed of contiguous minor civil divisions with at
least 75% of their economically active population in non-agricultural occupations
and 15% commuting to the core and finally a population density of at least 150 persons per square mile. A modified version of the SMSA concept has been applied to
Britain by Political and Economic Planning (Hall et al, 1973) using 1961 Census data,
and a similar basic methodology was adopted for this study using updated information.
The basic building blocks were local authorities (Metropolitan Boroughs, County
Boroughs, Urban Districts and Rural Districts) of which there were 1,765 in 1971.

The modifications firstly involved the dropping of the non-agricultural occupations
and population density criteria from the ring definitions as those were considered
irrelevant to Britain. Secondly, the definition of the 'central city' or urban
core was based upon density of employment rather than total population since central workplaces are the obvious focus for inward commuters. Density figures were
used as these reduced the problem of over or underbounding that can result from the
use of administrative areas as the basic building blocks. A density criteria of
five jobs per acre was selected as being most relevant for major cities. But as
this criteria would have excluded a number of free-standing towns with a large
number of central jobs but at low density, an alternative criteria was added in the
identification of urban cores, namely a minimum of 20,000 jobs. Unlike the American definition, several administrative areas could form a single urban core providing that they were contiguous and together met the employment criteria. Finally
a minimum population for the core plus ring of 70,000 was set.

The criteria of functional integration with the urban core used in the definition
of SMSAs, namely 15% of the economically active population commuting to the core,
was adopted without modification by PEP. This is clearly an arbitrary threshold on
a continuous fall-off of commuting intensity with distance from the core. In a
partial attempt to overcome this criticism PEP introduced a third urban zone, the
outer metropolitan ring, composed of all local authorities sending more commuters
to the core in question than to any other core.

The urban core plus the 15% commuting hinterland was given the title Standard Metropolitan Labour Area (SMLA) to indicate the inclusion of an employment criteria in
the definition. The SMLA plus its outer ring was termed the Metropolitan Economic
Labour Area (MELA). The MELAs were designed to approximate the Metropolitan Economic

Area designed for the United States by Berry as a result of criticism of the arbitrary commuting threshold used in defining SMSAs. (Berry, 1968 and 1973)

In summary then the concept of the local labour market, focussed on an employment core forms the basis of the definitions. Jobs are unevenly distributed throughout the country and tend to be concentrated in specific nodes which are the focal points of in-commuting. At the same time, the vast majority of people still tend to live close to their work. The local labour market area therefore provides a valuable linkage between the economic environment from the point of view of business, commercial and public organisations (for example, in terms of potential employees and service suppliers) and the social environment for the individual and household (for example, in terms of potential job opportunities that can be reached without changing home). The labour market area should not be confused with the labour market in a non-geographic sense. In terms of recruitment, the labour market for different occupations may vary geographically, from the nation for the most specialised jobs, to the very local area for the most ubiquitous. Also in terms of journey to work patterns, higher occupational groups will be able to afford to travel longer distances and therefore reside in more spatially extensive areas. Although in practice it is only feasible to use non-overlapping labour market areas, in reality such definitions will be imposed on a more complex reality.

In practical terms the first step involves the identification of urban cores. These are usually defined as single or contiguous local authorities (pre 1974 CBs, MBs and UDs) with an employment density of over 5 workers per acre (12.5 per hectare) or a total employment of over 20,000 jobs. In 1971, 126 such cores were identified.

To be included in an urban core's immediate commuting hinterland or metropolitan ring a local authority must be contiguous with the core and send at least 15% of its economically active population to that core for employment purposes. The urban core plus the metropolitan ring is referred to as the Standard Metropolitan Labour Area (SMLA). In order to qualify for this status, the combined population of the core and the ring should normally exceed 70,000 people. Beyond the 15% threshold, the number of commuters to a core tends to decline less rapidly with distance. Small but significant numbers of commuters are, however, likely to be found. In order to take account of this fact a third zone or outer metropolitan ring is defined as all local authority areas from which at least some commuters move to a particular core. (In the case of commuters going to one or more cores, the local authority is assigned to that to which the maximum number of workers travel.) The SMLA plus the outer metropolitan ring is referred to as the Metropolitan Economic Labour Area (MELA). While in theory the division of each MELA suggests three concentric zones (Fig. 1.1), in practice a much more complex picture emerges. It is clearly indicated in Figs. 1.2 and 1.3 which delimit the 126 SMLAs and MELAs of Britain and is especially apparent in Fig. 1.4 which shows the local authority components of the cores, rings and outer rings of the Million Cities of Britain. These maps are worthy of comment since they illustrate important points concerning the definition. (A full specification of the local authority components of all the areas is provided in the Appendix).

(1) Urban cores, which consist of one or more whole local authority areas, must not be equated with the often deprived inner areas. The latter form a compact area around the central business district. These inner areas would need to be defined on a range of socio-economic criteria of urban deprivation rather than simply employment density. Also, because the basic building blocks are large and frequently heterogeneous local authorities, urban cores can contain within them districts which should not be classified as being deprived (e.g. Hampstead is included in the London urban core).

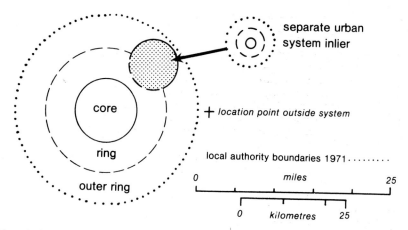

Fig. 1.1   Constituent zones of Metropolitan Economic Labour Areas

Metropolitan Labour Areas by 1971 Economic Planning Regions

1 Northern

23	Carlisle
33	Darlington
47	Hartlepool
70	Newcastle
97	Sunderland
101	Teesside
112	Workington

2 Yorkshire & Humberside

4	Barnsley
35	Dewsbury
36	Doncaster
42	Grimsby
44	Halifax
46	Harrogate
52	Huddersfield
53	Hull
58	Leeds
87	Scunthorpe
88	Sheffield
105	Wakefield
115	York

3 East Midlands

29	Corby
34	Derby
59	Leicester
62	Lincoln
68	Mansfield
72	Northampton
74	Nottingham

4 East Anglia

20	Cambridge
41	Great Yarmouth
54	Ipswich
56	King's Lynn
73	Norwich
76	Peterborough

5 South East

1	Aldershot
2	Ashford
3	Aylesbury
6	Basildon
7	Basingstoke
9	Bedford
14	Bournemouth
15	Brighton
21	Canterbury
24	Chatham
25	Chelmsford
28	Colchester
31	Crawley
37	Eastbourne
43	Guildford
45	Harlow
48	Hastings
49	Hemel Hempstead
51	High Wycombe
61	Letchworth
64	London
65	Luton
66	Maidstone
69	Milton Keynes
75	Oxford
78	Portsmouth
81	Reading
84	St. Albans
90	Slough
91	Southampton
92	Southend
95	Stevenage
102	Thurrock
104	Tunbridge Wells
106	Walton & Weybridge
108	Watford
110	Woking
113	Worthing

6 South West

8	Bath
16	Bristol
26	Cheltenham
39	Exeter
40	Gloucester
77	Plymouth
86	Salisbury
99	Swindon
100	Taunton
103	Torquay
114	Yeovil

7 Wales

22	Cardiff
71	Newport
79	Port Talbot
82	Rhondda
98	Swansea

8 West Midlands

10	Birmingham
18	Burton on Trent
30	Coventry
50	Hereford
55	Kidderminster
89	Shrewsbury
94	Stafford
96	Stoke
111	Worcester

9 North West

5	Barrow-in-Furness
11	Blackburn
12	Blackpool
13	Bolton
17	Burnley
19	Bury
27	Chester
32	Crewe
38	Ellesmere Port
57	Lancaster
60	Leigh
63	Liverpool
67	Manchester
80	Preston
83	Rochdale
85	St. Helens
93	Southport
107	Warrington
109	Wigan

10 Scotland

116	Aberdeen
117	Ayr
118	Dundee
119	Dunfermline
120	Edinburgh
121	Falkirk
122	Glasgow
123	Greenock
124	Kilmarnock
125	Motherwell
126	Perth

Fig. 1.2   Standard Metropolitan Labour Areas
(See below Fig. 1.1 for key)

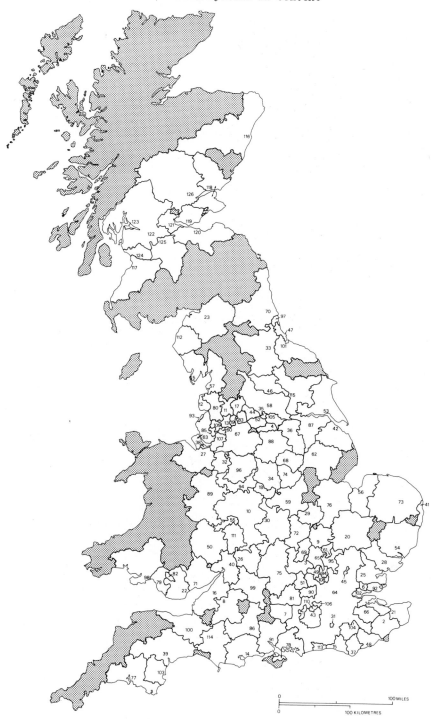

Fig. 1.3   Metropolitan Economic Labour Areas
(See below Fig. 1.1 for key)

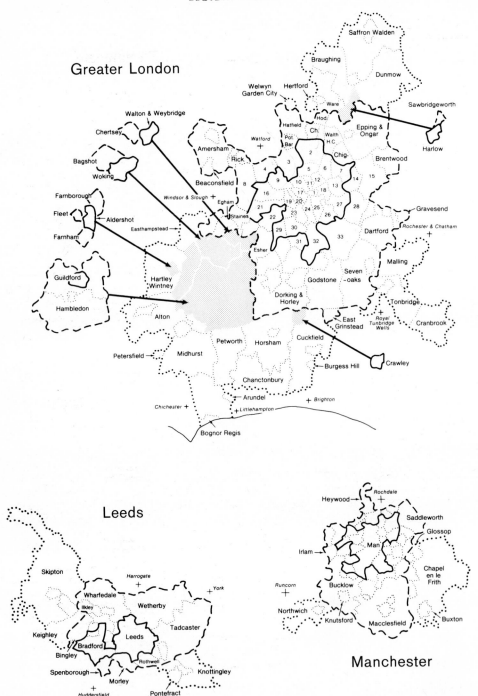

Fig. 1.4(a)   Definitions of Million City MELAs

Fig. 1.4(b)   Definitions of Million City MELAs

(2) Metropolitan rings include but also extend well beyond the continuously built-up areas of the larger cities. In the case of London, the metropolitan ring stretches from Amersham in the north west to Gravesend in the south east and Epping in the north east to Dorking in the south west. In a limited number of cases, a city may be composed only of an urban core without a metropolitan ring.

(3) Several cities either do not possess an outer metropolitan ring or if they do this may not completely encircle the SMLA. This may be due to the close juxtaposition of other towns, for example, Watford is a core in its own right and breaks into London's outer metropolitan ring. The same can be said of Coventry vis-a-vis Birmingham.

(4) In the case of London a number of places within the outer metropolitan ring qualify as employment cores (e.g. Aldershot and Guildford) and are therefore 'inliers' of the London MELA. In these cases, while the majority of journeys to work are local, significant numbers of commuters leapfrog the intervening centres and travel long distances into London. At the same time outer metropolitan rings may contain within them employment nodes which just fall short of qualifying for urban core status in their own right.

(5) Residual areas remain unclassified. These are by and large upland or deep rural areas although in certain parts of the country, notably in north Devon and Cornwall they include employment centres which do not cross the urban core threshold.

These then are the 126 functional urban areas as used by this study. Sometimes analysis will refer to these areas individually. Other tabulations will refer to aggregations of areas to the 10 Standard Regions of Britain. A convention of locating each MELA in the region wherein its core lies is adopted. In other parts of the research especially when examining characteristics of migration and worktravel a functional group classification of British cities has been adopted. This classification has the advantage that labour markets are aggregated to a level which is functionally meaningful in its own right. As with any classification of this kind there is inevitably a certain amount of heterogeneity within the derived groups. Nevertheless within group variation is considerably less than variation between groups.

It is important to emphasise that the roots of the classification are multifaceted. The groups have been selected to achieve a wide ranging 'utility'. They are thus formed using pragmatic solutions, and not an optimum procedure, derived on the basis of operations conducted on an individual variable or collection of variables. The quasi-objective approach adopted provides a compromise framework whereby both past and present components of analysis may usefully be reviewed and, hence, their results compared.

The classification of labour markets was primarily determined by two independent grouping strategems: one principally a selection of 1971 socio-economic structure variables derived from the Census for whole Metropolitan Economic Labour Areas; the other relating solely to internal dynamics of population and employment change within MELAs for the 1951-61 and 1961-71 decades. The grouping strategy adopted in both instances was hierarchical (Ward, 1963). Providing variables are standardised to avoid bias toward those variables with physically greater volumes, but not necessarily greater significance, the data may be inputed direct into a hierarchical algorithm.

In the case of the socio-economic classification, bias had been considerably diminished, although not entirely eliminated, by the choice of a similar number of variables from different aspects of areal attributes, together with the elimination of one of any pair of variables correlating highly.

Whilst the majority of MELAs fell into similar groups in both procedures, a number of labour areas proved difficult to order as they revealed apparently different associations or affinities. These MELAs were subsequently studied in greater depth with regard to migration data (both net and flow) and work-travel characteristics. They were then allocated to the class which appeared most similar on the basis of these new attributes.

Additionally, from the class containing large industrial areas, the seven labour markets with SMLA population sizes exceeding one million were extracted. The rationale for this decision is that size has clearly played a most important role in determination of both work-travel and migration trends and thus the monitoring of the largest systems must be considered useful as well as possibly providing indication of future developments.

From the procedure outlined above a total of nine groups were derived. (Fig. 1.5). This was the smallest number which could satisfactorily distinguish unlike areas in a functional sense and maintain relatively small numbers of labour areas in each class. Any increase in the total would, of course, fail to meet the purpose of the grouping - to produce a manageable number of discrete combinations of labour areas.

The resulting classification of labour markets is outlined below. It is important to emphasise that in a number of cases whilst the grouping has resulted in distinct classes it is not always possible to provide short labels for these combinations which can relate to all the groups' members and yet to none outside of the class. The provision of such names or labels is thus purely to facilitate easy recognition within the tables. With the classes that are outlined below a brief description of some of the common within group characteristics is provided.

Group 1   The Million Cities   Total 7

            London, Birmingham, Manchester, Glasgow, Liverpool,
            Newcastle, Leeds.

Group 2   Major Industrial Centres   Total 13

            The remaining 20 top MELAs in population size, other
            than the Million Cities.

            Sheffield, Bristol, Cardiff, Edinburgh, Coventry,
            Nottingham, Leicester, Stoke, Portsmouth, Hull,
            Teesside, Derby, Southampton.

Group 3   Secondary Industrial Centres   Total 26

            MELAs concentrated in Long Established Industrial
            Regions. Variety of Size Ranges.

            Workington, Barrow, Sunderland, Darlington, Preston,
            Blackburn, Burnley, Crewe, Huddersfield, Doncaster,
            Mansfield, Burton, Corby, Northampton, Luton, Chatham,
            Swansea, Port Talbot, Newport, Plymouth, Ellesmere
            Port, Rhondda, Kilmarnock, Greenock, Hartlepool,
            Motherwell.

Group 4   Small Labour Markets dependent on the Lancashire-   Total 11
            Yorkshire Conurbations.

            Distinct from Group 3 in that these areas are contig-
            uous to one of the Yorkshire/Lancashire Million Cities.

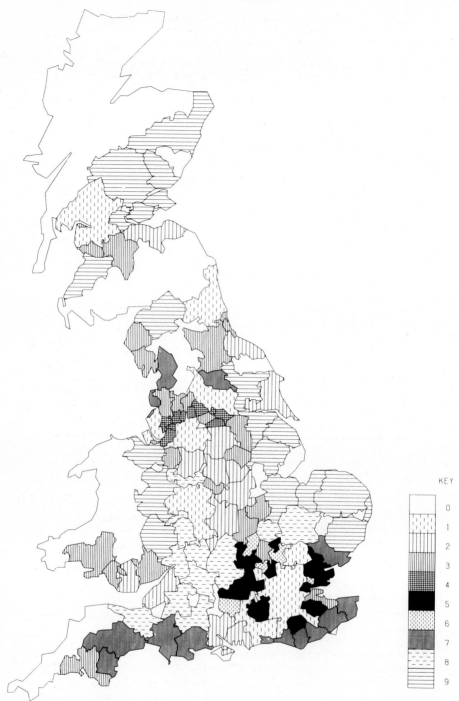

KEY

Fig. 1.5   A functional classification of MELAs
            (see text for key)

Each reveals strong commuting links, and receives more
than 25% of in-migrants from Manchester, Liverpool or
Leeds (Barnsley case = Sheffield).

Warrington, Leigh, St. Helens, Wigan, Bolton, Bury,
Rochdale, Halifax, Dewsbury, Wakefield, Barnsley.

Group 5   London Periphery Labour Markets   Total 16

Relatively small in terms of population sizes (except
Reading). All strongly linked to London in terms of
commuting and migration. Principal destinations for
London out-migrants.

Aldershot, Aylesbury, Guildford, High Wycombe, Letchworth,
Maidstone, St. Albans, Reading, Slough, Thurrock, Walton
& Weybridge, Watford, Woking, Southend, Tunbridge Wells,
Chelmsford.

Group 6   The New Towns   Total 7

MELAs whose core areas broadly coincide with designated
New Towns or Expanded Areas. All fall in lowest size
quartile.

Basildon, Crawley, Harlow, Hemel Hempstead, Milton Keynes,
Basingstoke, Stevenage.

Group 7   Resort/Retirement Centres   Total 15

Two types: (a) MELAs with coastal resort (except Harrogate)
cores incurring retirement migration in their own right.
(b) MELAs with inland cores not experiencing high rates of
retirement migration but with large rings and outer rings
(probably coastal) experiencing retirement migration.

(a) Blackpool, Southport, Harrogate, Torbay, Bournemouth,
     Worthing, Brighton, Eastbourne, Hastings.
(b) Lancaster, Exeter, Yeovil, Ashford, Canterbury,
     Colchester.

Group 8   Southern Free Standing Labour Markets   Total 12

Located on periphery of main industrial axis. Mainly
County towns with very large outer rings relative to core
population. All located in south (only Stafford is north
of Birmingham). SMLAs and MELAs tend to be quite advanced
in terms of decentralisation and all rings and outer rings
receiving net in-migration. (Element of retirement migration to some outer rings.)

Stafford, Kidderminster, Worcester, Gloucester, Cheltenham,
Oxford, Swindon, Bath, Salisbury, Taunton, Bedford, Cambridge.

Group 9   Peripheral Free Standing Labour Markets   Total 19

Lowest levels of integration with the main industrial areas.
Very large outer rings relative to core populations in
systems with the low rates of internal decentralisation or
continued centralisation. Cores tend to fare better than
rings in extreme North/Scotland and OMRs everywhere in terms
of net in-migration.

Shrewsbury, Hereford, Chester, Ipswich, Great Yarmouth, Norwich,

                King's Lynn, Peterborough, Lincoln, Grimsby, Scunthorpe, York,
                Carlisle, Aberdeen, Dundee, Perth, Ayr, Falkirk, Dunfermline.

British cities: urban population and employment trends

A preliminary analysis of the principal urban population and employment trends in
British cities has already been made available by the sponsors of the research
(Department of the Environment, 1976). This provides a full context into which
this presentation can be set. However a short and summary contextual perspective
might usefully be provided in this introduction both to compare with what is going
on elsewhere in the world and to set the scene for the detailed British study.

During the 1950s and 1960s the economy and society of Britain both underwent fundamental changes. It is therefore not surprising that the nation's cities also experienced a massive transformation both in their internal structure and in the distribution of population and economic activity between cities in different parts of
the country. Whether this process of transformation has continued with the same
magnitude and direction into the less prosperous 1970s will not be revealed until
the evidence of the 1981 Census is available. Whatever the outcome there can be no
denying that many of today's urban problems are the consequences of past trends
that need to be understood, not just in terms of the experience of individual cities, but as an expression of significant forces at work throughout the nation's
urban areas.

What have been the principal patterns of change? The most well known are those in
the internal structure of the largest cities resulting from the substantial shift
of people and latterly jobs from inner to outer urban areas, a process widely referred to as metropolitan decentralisation. Although decentralisation is most advanced and has contributed to the most undesirable consequences in the form of
inner city problems in the largest urban areas, the evidence suggests that this
process has come to characterise most British cities. Generally, decentralisation,
especially to the outer metropolitan zones, has been most rapid in the more prosperous parts of the country, a situation which tends to suggest that this spatial
process is related to underlying economic forces, notably the ability of people
to turn preferences for lower density living conditions into actual residential
choices and for industry which is expanding to seek out more extensive sites. On
the other hand decentralisation from the decaying very innermost areas of British
cities is not a prosperous area phenomenon, with the inner cities in development
areas well represented.

Metropolitan decentralisation has not been confined within the bounds of the larger
cities or even to their immediate commuting hinterlands. The out movement of jobs
as well as people over ever increasing distances has resulted in significant changes in the status of frequently smaller settlements peripheral to the largest cities; many of these having become significant employment centres in their own right.
The effect of this combined out movement of population and employment from large
cities, most of which are concentrated in the main axial belt of urban England
stretching from Manchester to London, has been a net shift of population and employment away from this older heartland into intermediate and smaller sized settlements in previously less industrial parts of the country, notably in East Anglia
and the South West. Environmental amenity is clearly becoming a consideration in
the inter as well as intra urban transfer of population. Many smaller towns both
within and outside this axial belt have experienced rapid growth in the 60s.
Industry, which has become increasingly footloose, has frequently followed population, seeking out locations in the inter-metropolitan periphery.

It is under these relatively recent inter-urban trends that the long established
shift of population and economic activity from northern to south regions of the

country has continued to operate. Many of the problems of Britain's traditionally declining regions appear now also to be urban problems exacerbated by changes in the intra regional distribution of population and economic activities, changes which in a number of respects have heightened intra-regional differences relative to those at the inter-regional scale. The decline of large cities in once more prosperous regions, notably London in the South East and Birmingham in the West Midlands contributed to further dampening down these inter-regional contrasts.

Population and employment shifts within and between cities in the past two decades have therefore led to a fundamental restructuring of the settlement system of the country, a restructuring which may prove as significant as that occurring during the nineteenth century when industrialisation and urbanisation went hand in hand to produce large concentrations of population in particular parts of the country endowed with certain natural resources. At both the urban and regional scales, once peripheral areas have now become the locus of growth, while previously core cities and regions have faced problems of stagnation and decline.

As a context for what follows and in order to provide some substantive support for these generalisations about urban change in Britain the findings of the earlier report are summarized here.

(a)   Taking a broad definition of cities, Britain is not only an urban nation, but the nation's city regions are gaining population at the expense of non-urban areas. Thus 95.7% of the nation's population lived within the sphere of influence of a city as defined in 1971 compared with 93.1% as defined using the same criteria in 1961.

(b)   In addition to the outward extension of the commuting hinterland of established cities, urban growth has resulted in the rise to urban status of free-standing settlements in rural areas or in the outer commuting hinterland of London. In the South East the decentralisation of jobs from London has contributed towards the growth to urban status of former dormitory areas.

(c)   The dominant trend for population is accelerating decentralisation, initially from urban cores to their inner commuting hinterland, but subsequently spilling over in the 1960s into the outer commuting hinterlands, areas which are only weakly connected to the urban cores. While population was decentralising in the 1950s, jobs were growing most rapidly in the urban cores where the bulk of employment was concentrated. In the period 1961-71, however, job formation occurred more rapidly in the commuting rings than in the urban cores. Just as the national employment growth in the previous decade had chiefly benefited urban cores, so the effect of slower employment growth in the next decade was felt most strongly in these areas of the nation's cities which in aggregate experienced a net loss of 439,000 jobs (-3.1%). In contrast, metropolitan rings experienced a net employment gain of 707,000 jobs (15%) during the same period. However, since employment has decentralised less than population, the cores, which still contain the main mass of employment, have become more dependent upon the supply of labour commuting from the outer zones. The immediate inference is that there has been an increase in the separation of homes and workplaces in urban Britain, with a consequent increase in the length of the journey to work.

(d)   Decentralisation of population and latterly of jobs is a process which is coming to characterise most British cities, regardless of their size, region or relative location. (See Figs. 1.6, 1.7,

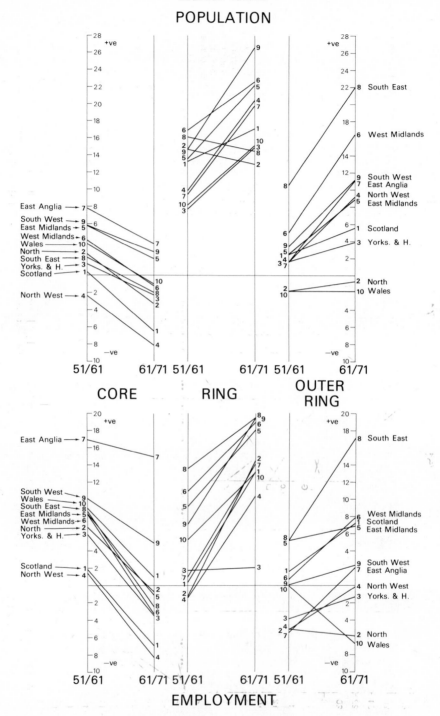

Fig. 1.6   Relative population and relative employment change for
the constituent zones of MELAs averaged for Economic
Planning Regions, 1951-1961 and 1961-1971.

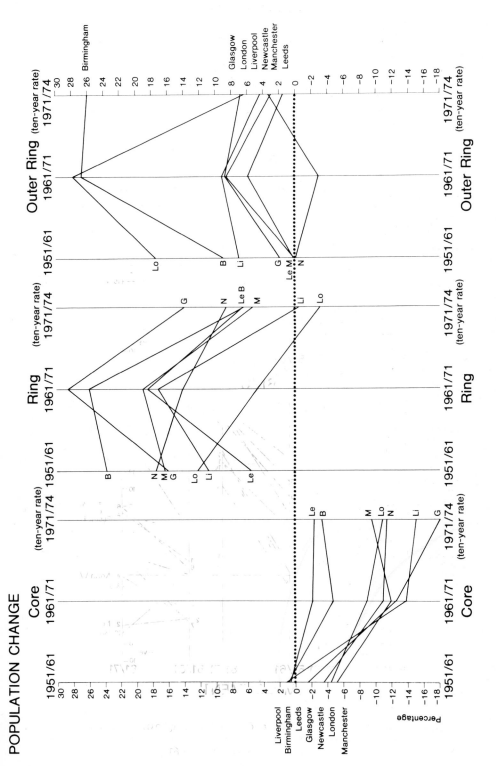

Fig. 1.7   Relative population change for the constituent zones
of Million Cities, 1951–1961, 1961–1971 and 1971–1974

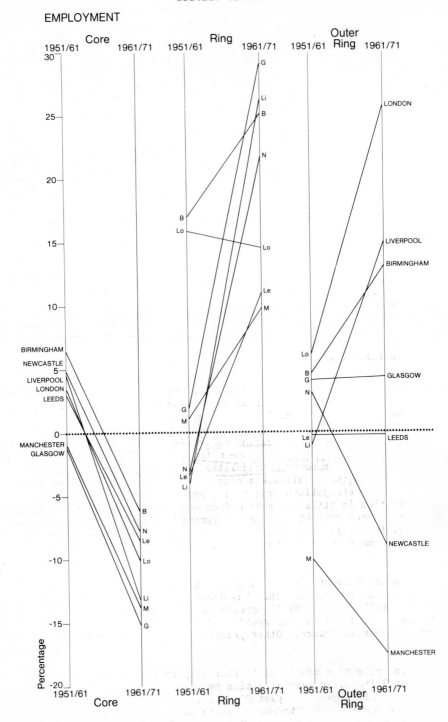

Fig. 1.8   Relative employment change for the constituent zones
of Million Cities, 1951-1961 and 1961-1971

1.8, 1.9 and 1.10). What does vary is the rate at which this
process is operating and the stage it has reached. Cities in
the older industrialised regions are decentralising more rapidly than freestanding towns in less populated regions, suggesting that there is a relationship between economic growth and the
rate of change in the internal structure of a region's cities.
Size of city is also an important factor in explaining rates of
decentralisation, principally because it is related to the density of jobs and people at the urban core. Density may in turn
be related to the stage a city has reached in its life cycle.
Large cities, generally with an old stock of buildings, have
progressed most towards rapid decentralisation. This has partly
been a response to widespread central urban renewal aimed at
lowering overall densities. Smaller cities, especially new towns,
have had space to grow at the core.

(e) Differential net migration has been the principal cause of the
     varying rates of population growth in the constituent zones of
     British cities (See Figs. 1.11 and 1.12). Net migration loss
     has been the normal experience of urban cores although there is
     considerable variation. Conversely, high rates of net migration
     gain have occurred in the commuting hinterlands of most British
     cities. While rates of natural change vary less dramatically
     between and within urban zones, natural increase is significant-
     ly higher in the metropolitan rings than in the urban cores of
     the nation's cities. Even if migration into the rings of British
     cities is curtailed in the future, higher levels of population
     increase due to natural change are likely to be maintained by a
     demographically young population.

(f) The processes of change within the urban areas of Britain suggests
     an evolution of daily urban systems or a type of life cycle through
     which most of the cities in the system pass. The cycle has a num-
     ber of stages. After initial growth to urban status, and a period
     of consolidation, involving centralisation of people and jobs in
     the urban core vis-a-vis the metropolitan ring and in this ring
     vis-a-vis the outer metropolitan ring, a process of decentralis-
     ation begins. This takes place, initially from the urban core
     to the metropolitan ring during which it is likely that central-
     isation is still proceeding from the outer ring. After a period,
     the decentralisation movement spreads even to the outer metrop-
     olitan ring. Testing of this sequence for Britain indicates
     that most cities do relate to the cycle and can be classified
     accordingly.

In a densely settled country like Britain, intra- and inter-urban changes are difficult to separate. It is clear that the decentralisation of population and latterly jobs has contributed towards the growth to urban status of settlements in the
commuter ring of London. The designation of new towns has also supported this
process of inter-urban change. Other principal findings on inter-urban change are
set out below.

(a) In spite of a considerable stability in the urban size hierarchy
     of Britain, individual cities have experienced dramatic growth
     or decline over the past 20 years. The most striking feature is
     the continuity of trends established during the period 1951-61
     into the 1961-71 period. (See Figs. 1.13, 1.14 and 1.15). In
     the main, cities that were either growing or declining relative
     to the nation in the 1950s continued this trend in the 1960s.

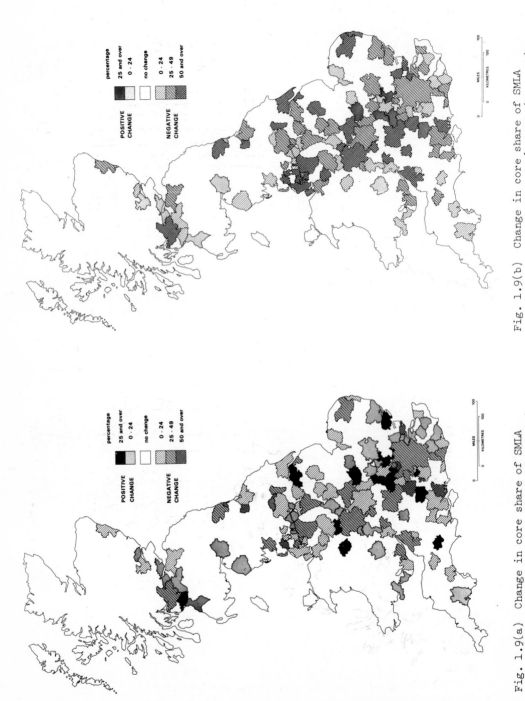

Fig. 1.9(b) Change in core share of SMLA
             population, 1961-1971 (Percent)

Fig. 1.9(a) Change in core share of SMLA
             population, 1951-1961 (Percent)

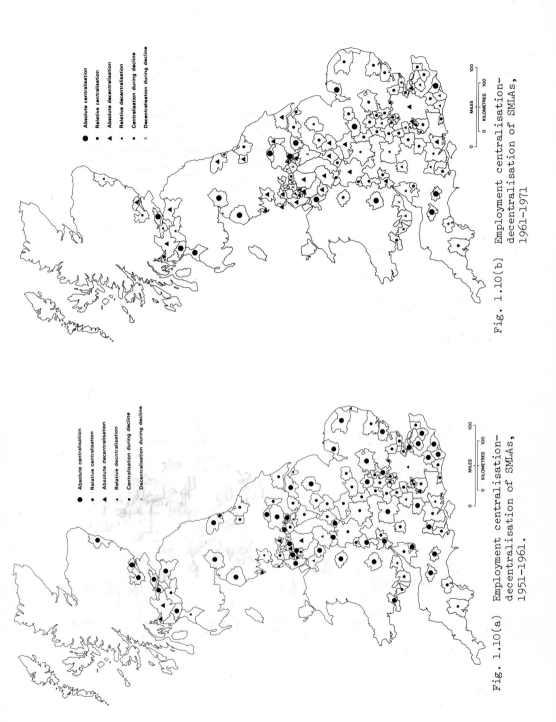

Fig. 1.10(b) Employment centralisation–
             decentralisation of SMLAs,
             1961–1971

Fig. 1.10(a) Employment centralisation–
             decentralisation of SMLAs,
             1951–1961.

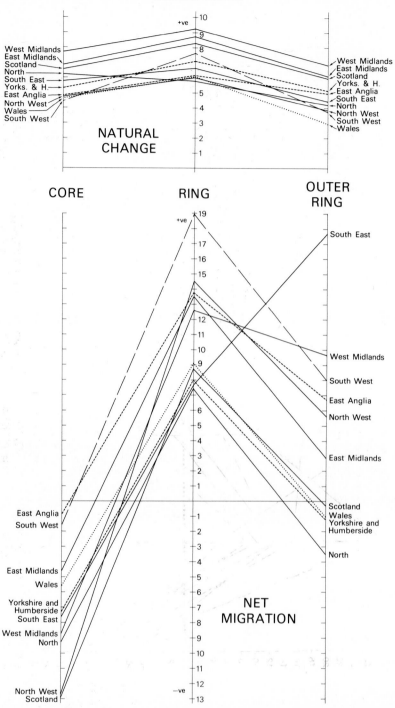

Fig. 1.11   Relative natural change and relative net migration for
            the constituent zones of MELAs averaged for Economic
            Planning Regions, 1961-1971.

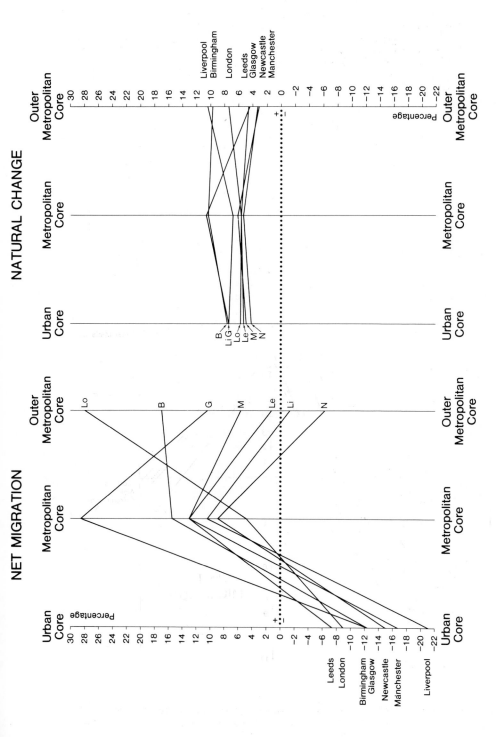

Fig. 1.12   Relative net migration and relative natural change
for the constituent zones of Million Cities, 1961–1971

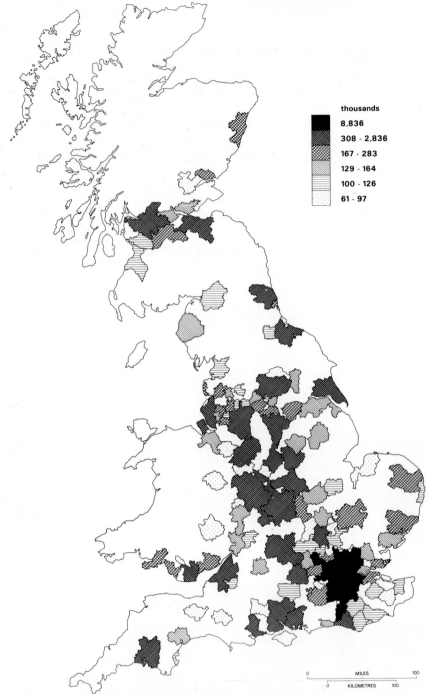

thousands

8,836

308 - 2,836

167 - 283

129 - 164

100 - 126

61 - 97

Fig. 1.13   Standard Metropolitan Labour Area Populations, 1971.
             (Class 1 = London ranked 1;   class 2 = places ranked 2-26;
             class 3 = places ranked 27-51;   class 4 = places ranked
             52-76;   class 5 = places ranked 77 - 101;   class 6 =
             places ranked 102 - 126)

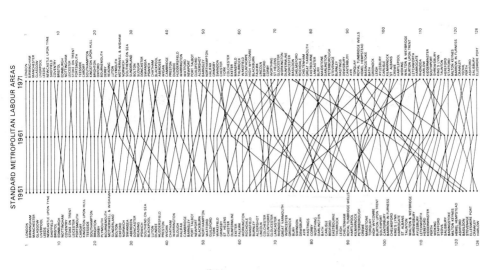

Fig. 1.15   Change in population rank order of
Standard Metropolitan Labour Areas,
1951, 1961 and 1971

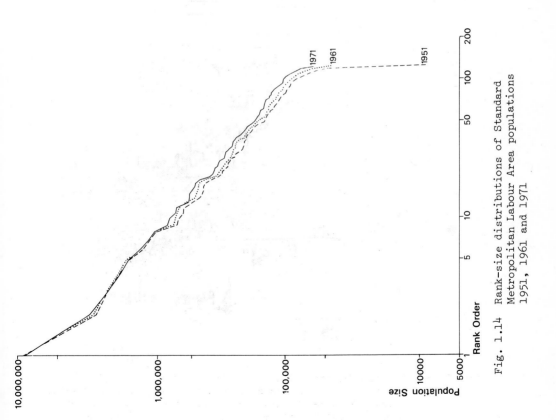

Fig. 1.14   Rank-size distributions of Standard
Metropolitan Labour Area populations
1951, 1961 and 1971

(See Figs. 1.16 and 1.17). Some of the largest cities which
experienced substantial absolute population gains 1951-61 were
nevertheless exhibiting growth rates well below the national average; in several instances this was followed in the next decade
by absolute population losses. Many towns in the assisted areas
had below average population growth rates in both the 1950s and
1960s while most towns in the southern half of the country (excepting London) had consistently increasing growth performances. The
exceptions to this continuity of trends across the two decades are
principally provided by certain free-standing towns on the periphery of urban Britain (notably in the South-West, East Anglia and
the Welsh Marches) and by towns adjacent to the large cities of
Midland and Northern Britain. These provide examples of improved
population growth performance in 1961-71.

(b) During the period 1961-71 a number of major cities in the West
     Midlands and Yorkshire and Humberside regions, notably Birming-
     ham, Coventry and Leeds, grew more slowly in employment than in
     population. This is in marked contrast to the previous decade
     when these towns recorded some of the highest employment gains.
     London had above average employment growth in the 1950s, follow-
     ed by below average growth in the 1960s. In the cores of several
     cities it would seem that urban employment growth in the 1950s
     attracted in-migration of population: high population growth
     rates were sustained by natural increase but were not matched
     by continued employment growth in the 1960s. Relative to other
     British cities, those of the Northern Region had a marked loss
     of population and jobs in the 1950s; however, the 1960s showed
     some slowing in the rate of job losses whilst the population
     continued to decline.

(c) In addition to regional situations, city size is an important
     factor in explaining urban population and employment growth.
     The nature of the overall relationship between city size, and
     population and employment growth was markedly reversed across
     the decades. In the period 1951-61 there was a positive relat-
     ionship between absolute change and city size with the larger
     cities in 1951 recording the greater absolute population and
     employment gains in the next decade. The period 1961-71 was
     in contrast characterised by an inverse relationship with the
     larger cities in 1961 recording the smaller population and em-
     ployment increments. So over the period under investigation
     there has been a significant shift in the pattern of urban
     growth in Britain, away from the largest cities and in favour
     of intermediate sized and smaller cities.

(d) Net migration is much more important than natural change in
     explaining variation in the population growth rates of British
     cities. Generally, rates of net migration are closely related
     to overall population change rates. There are a few predict-
     able deviations, notably new and expanded towns which have
     generally high rates of natural increase, and retirement towns,
     which often have a natural decrease in population. Cities with
     high rates of net in-migration follow a clear regional pattern;
     above average rates of net in-migration characterise all southern
     cities outside London; exceptions to this pattern are retirement
     centres and certain towns adjacent to the largest northern cities.
     In contrast above average rates of natural change characterise
     urban areas in a much wider tract of Southern and Midland England.
     A number of Midland cities, notably Birmingham and Coventry, have

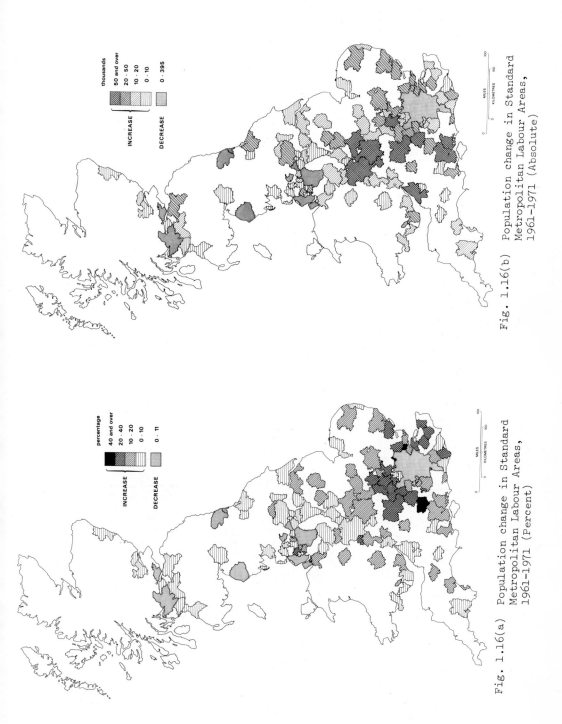

Fig. 1.16(b) Population change in Standard
Metropolitan Labour Areas,
1961–1971 (Absolute)

Fig. 1.16(a) Population change in Standard
Metropolitan Labour Areas,
1961–1971 (Percent)

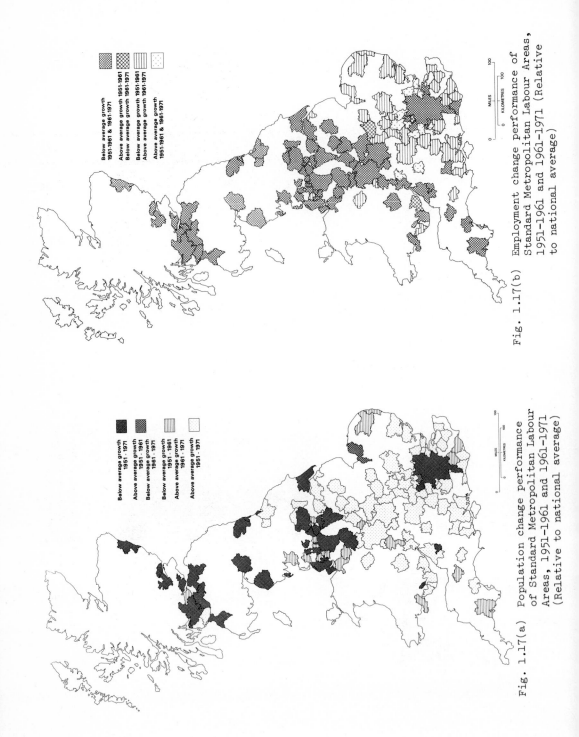

Fig. 1.17(b) Employment change performance of
Standard Metropolitan Labour Areas,
1951-1961 and 1961-1971 (Relative
to national average)

Fig. 1.17(a) Population change performance
of Standard Metropolitan Labour
Areas, 1951-1961 and 1961-1971
(Relative to national average)

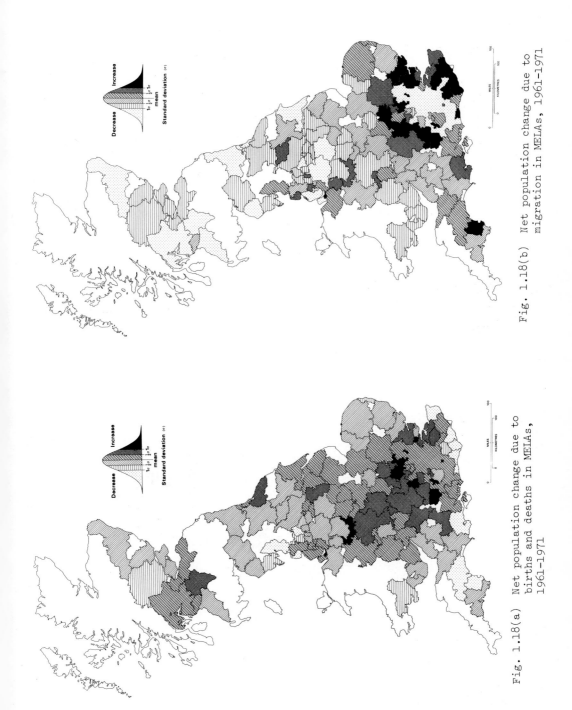

Fig. 1.18(b) Net population change due to
             migration in MELAs, 1961-1971

Fig. 1.18(a) Net population change due to
             births and deaths in MELAs,
             1961-1971

high rates of natural population increase. Indeed most of
the large cities, including London, Liverpool, Glasgow,
Newcastle and Teesside, have above average rates of natural
change which given their population size implies a considerable absolute population increase. Thus London, Birmingham,
Glasgow, Manchester and Liverpool together accounted for a
total natural increase in the urban population of 1.1 million
in the ten years 1961-71. So although the large cities have
been losing population through net migration, this has been
partially offset by natural increase. (See Fig. 1.18).

British cities: an analysis of urban change. Study outline.

The population and employment shifts that have been described above reflect in aggregate the outcome of myriads of individual decisions. These decisions have in turn
been influenced by fundamental, social and economic forces. The analysis of Census
data on which this research is based can say little directly about these processes.
However, disaggregation of the population and employment data provides a valuable
reflection of the basic components of social and economic change at work in the
nation during the 1960s.   Part 2 of this study examines these changes in detail.

In terms of the demand for labour perhaps the most important change has been the
continual shift from manual to non-manual employment, part of the transformation
of Britain into a so-called 'post-industrial society'. There are many facets to
this change; those that will be examined here include the growth of the service
sector relative to manufacturing and primary industry and of clerical, managerial
and professional occupations relative to those involving physical production. Associated with these changes has been a growing demand for female labour, an important contribution to increased female activity rates. These changes have been translated on the supply side into a changed social economic composition of the work
force. Rising family income and changed social values have followed from new patterns of employment opportunities. A process frequently referred to as the 'en-
bourgeoisification' of the workforce has been associated with higher incomes, greater mobility and new aspiration. This process has been reflected in the pattern of
demand for housing both by type and location and for services of all categories -
notably education, health, welfare and retail services.

These long term secular trends have been superimposed upon events and situations
which were perhaps unique to the 60s. Amongst these should be included a massive
influx of immigrants from overseas to meet pressing labour demands. These demands
were not only a response to the state of the economy but a reflection of basic
demographic conditions which will not perhaps be repeated in the foreseeable future
- namely a large number of young people and rising numbers entering the above pensionable age groups relative to those of working age. The comprehensive redevelopment of large sections of the inner parts of many cities, involving significant
lowering of housing densities and the elimination of much small scale industry is
another feature that perhaps will in a longer term perspective probably prove to be
unique to the early part of the sixties.

But however unique the situation in the 60s, the consequences of the changes that
same about in this period will remain for decades to come, not least because of the
transformation they wrought in the spatial structure of the British economy and
British society at both the urban and regional scales. National trends, however,
formulated, had differential impacts from place to place according to the variations
in initial conditions. It is therefore important to specify the exact magnitude and
location of the various changes that have been touched upon. A number of questions
immediately spring to mind. What types of industry have been decentralising from
British cities? What have been the consequences of the shift towards office employ-

ment in terms of the intra- and inter-urban distribution of managerial, clerical and professional jobs? How has the national trend towards higher female activity rates affected individual cities and their constituent urban zones? Has the shift from manual to non-manual socio-economic groups been associated with differential rates of population decentralisation from inner to outer urban areas? What implications has population decentralisation for the age structure profiles of the population in different localities?   To what extent has the influx of overseas immigrants been confined to certain cities and have various immigrant groups been able to decentralise more or less rapidly than the indigenous population?

Not least amongst the groups of decisions mentioned before as underlying the aggregate statistics are those resulting from the fundamental question of where to live. Of course these decisions are influenced by basic social and economic forces and many would legitimately argue that choice only occurs within fairly narrow bounds. Again the analysis of Census data on which this research is based indicates little directly about these processes. However a detailed description of migration movements is valuable in a number of ways and is the prime objective of Part 3 of this study.

These longer term movements of population of course involve a change in residence. The description of migration patterns in a sense focusses attention not on the cause of the movement nor on the ultimate outcome at either the sending or receiving end, but on the stage in between. In fact it is a snapshot of the actual movement, articulating the cause and effect. There are a range of interesting questions that can be asked about the nature of such migrations, such as who migrates and how far? Which parts of the urban system receive or send short or long distance migrations and do they vary with who is moving? To these can be added equally valid questions concerning the effect in net terms of migrations on the socio-economic structure of areas. After all the diffusion process which is migration is the prime mechanism by which population change takes place.

Equally fundamental, and not unrelated to the decision about residential location, is the question of where to work. The usual provisos about understanding decision making processes and Census data have of course to be made but nevertheless a detailed account of worktravel movements is again valuable and may be considered as the principal purpose of Part 4 of this study.

These short term movements of population are of course many in number and daily occurences. Indeed these data were the basis of the functional urban area definitions underlying the whole study. The daily flow and ebb of people within cities as they move from one environment to another is familiar enough. Such movements articulate the supply of labour with the mostly central city demand for it. But the situation is not as static as might be thought when examining population and employment change in aggregate. Decentralisation of course is the main process of internal urban change clearly affecting patterns of worktravel. But is the process quickening or slowing? Do more people, nation wide, commute longer and longer distances? What about the decrease in the numbers of people residing centrally? Is it quickening? Where do these people work? Does the process occur in all cities? All these questions affect and involve the important balance of jobs and people, an issue crucial in the current economic climate. Planning for worktravel is one of the few items which can affect this balance other than the most difficult creation of new jobs.

The last part of the study reviews the empirical conclusions of the research within a planning context. It will be argued that some form of national urban policy is essential if the significant trends outlined in this research are to be regulated or harnessed.

PART TWO

Population and Employment in British Cities

2.1   URBAN CHANGE AND SOCIO-ECONOMIC TRENDS

An impressively wide variety of aspects of population and employment characteristi
potentially could be considered under this heading, especially when the full resources of the census tapes are thought of. Clearly some selectivity is necessary.
The basic objective of the research which forms the basis of this part was to take
the outline trends in population and employment (considered previously and summarised in part one) and attempt to elaborate on the basic components of them. This
would involve some understanding of employment change by industrial or occupationa
type; or for population some understanding of age or birthplace structure. An
overall view of socio-economic group trends was also an objective. In terms of th
census provision perhaps the most notable omission was the consideration of the
built form characteristics of the urban system, primarily reflected in housing.
This was not selected for a number of reasons, most notably those involving the
difficulty of defining consistent variables suitable for the analysis of change.
The selection, then, was made simply to add further understanding to the dimension
of urban change in the characteristics of the British people themselves.

The approach will be to move from the national to the local urban scales. The fir
section describes social and economic trends in British cities as a whole, disaggregated into their constituent urban zones (urban cores, metropolitan rings and
outer metropolitan rings). The national pattern is then broken down into its regional components when inter regional variations in rates of intra urban change are
considered. Next attention is switched to inter-urban change between cities considered individually. This makes it possible to specify, for example, the cities
with the highest rate of change in managerial and professional socio-economic grou
Additionally, at the most detailed level, trends within individual urban areas are
considered.

At each level of scale the analysis first focusses on the economic or employment
aspects of the urban areas moving to specifically demographic features via a treatment of socio-economic group characteristics. Some emphasis in the consideration
of total employment will be given to the changing contribution made by females, an
the way this is reflected in the trends in activity rates. For operational purpos
here an activity rate is defined as the proportion of men or women who are in employment (including the unemployed), or the economically active population, compare
to the total resident population (male or female) over the age of 15. No retireme
age cut-off was adopted here because of data difficulties and also because a sur-

prising number of people over retirement age do actually have gainful employment.

Occupational and industrial trends are considered in detail next and in this analysis much selectivity had to be undertaken. A full Standard Industrial classification consideration at the order level was prepared for industry but for occupational trends office occupations were singled out for detailed treatment. Difficulty
of presentation was perhaps the main reason why industrial trends were not considered at the minimum list heading level but also classification changes have more
ramifications at this scale. Office occupations were chosen primarily because they
are the most dynamic sector, but also because they are some of the few occupational
classes which say something about the levels of skill used rather than membership
of industrial group. Some problems were nevertheless encountered as usual in making
the industrial classifications compatible for the ends of the time period under
analysis; specifically this meant making the 1968 SIC used in the 1971 Census comparable to the 1958 version used five years previously. This was necessary because
it was only for the terminal date that the fine industrial detail necessary to
undertake the task was readily available. The result is then a comparable five
year change period 1966-71 based on the 1958 SIC at the order level. It must be
stressed that no account has been taken of the varying levels of unemployment at
each Census date. In June of the Census years 1966 and 1971 the unemployment levels
in Britain were 261,000 and 687,000 respectively. Regional variations in unemployment are likewise ignored.

The changing socio-economic structure is treated next introducing the analysis of
the more demographic variables. For this analysis it was necessary to define
social groups which were relatively homogeneous in terms of their income, status
and lifestyles. The most widely available and commonly used data on social status
is provided by the Registrar General's socio-economic groups. These are occupational groupings based on employment, status and occupation which 'ideally ... should
contain people whose social cultural and recreational standards and behaviour are
similar ...' (Census of England and Wales, 1961). There are 17 socio-economic
groups and for analytic purposes it was necessary to aggregate these into broader
categories. Within the constraints of maintaining within group homogeneity, the
main concern of the aggregation was to isolate the two extremes in the hierarchy
of social status and to differentiate the middle along manual and non-manual lines.
Four groups were chosen which were interpreted as (A) 'managerial and professional',
(B) 'intermediate non-manual', (C) 'skilled manual', and (D) ' semi- and unskilled
manual'. The socio economic groupings used here and detailed in the Appendix are
based on numbers of economically active males (numbers of females economically
active by socio-economic group not being available in 1961). Occupations of males
are assumed to be a useful indicator of the status and lifestyles of households as
a whole, although the much increased female participation rates during the sixties
have to be kept in mind.

For the analysis of age structure it was necessary to define age groups which were
relatively homogeneous in terms of the mobility and lifestyle associated with different stages in the individual's life cycle. Four groups have been selected; those
aged 0-14, aged 15-29, aged 30 to pensionable age, and those above pensionable age.
Pensionable age is 65 for males and 60 for females. The first group approximates
to those below school leaving age. Mobility and status for this group is dependent on parents. Birth rate variations are quickly transmitted into changes in
this group. The second group includes those who are usually considered to be most
mobile. This is an important stage in the life cycle during which most individuals
leave the parental home to establish separate households and families. The 30 to
pensionable age group are usually considered to be a more stable group both in
terms of spatial and social mobility. The final group, those above pensionable
age, represents another stage in the life cycle. Employment comes to an end,
children have usually left home and movement to pleasanter surroundings or to be

near relatives results in increased mobility.

However the use of these groups does impose a limitation on the analysis. Changes in the composition of the population between 1961 and 1971 reflect outcomes of natural change and migration. Changes in the particular age groups during this period are also dependent of the previous age group in 1961. For example, the number aged 40 to 50 in 1971 is partly dependent on the number aged 30 to 40 in 1961. To analyise such cohort changes over the ten years between 1961 and 1971 requires the use of 1, 5 or 10 year age groups. Instead 15 and 30 year age groups have been chosen. Consequently it is possible that large changes within age groups may not be reflected in changes between groups. Therefore in interpreting changes between 1961 and 1971 inference cannot be made from the age structure as it existed in 1961. Instead the emphasis is on describing the changes in age structure and relating these both in this part and the next to the major migration patterns in the urban system.

Within constraints of the available data the birthplace groups were selected to represent the broad sub-continents which have been the main origins of immigration to Great Britain in recent years. These criteria, together with the need for maximum comparability of definitions between 1961 and 1971 produced some six categories. (1) Irish: includes persons born in Northern Ireland since the composite group only was supplied in 1961. (2) Indian sub-continent: India, Pakistan and Ceylon. (3) African: Ghana, Kenya, Malawi, Nigeria, Rhodesia, Sierra Leone, Tanzania, Uganda, Zambia and other African Commonwealth. (4) Americas: Barbados, Guyana, Jamaica, Trinidad and Tobago, and other and unspecified Americas New Commonwealth. (5) Other Commonwealth: Australia, Canada, New Zealand, Gibralter, Malta and Gozo, Hong Kong, Malaysia, Singapore, and other New Commonwealth in Asia and Oceania. (6) Other Immigrants: other non-commonwealth, excluding Eire, and not stated. The remainder of the population is composed of those born in Britain, and therefore excluding Northern Ireland.

Some cautionary remarks might be appropriate to reduce ambiguity and grounds for misinterpretation of the following empirical analysis of birthplaces. The census data refer to the country of birth and not to nationality or race. This means that those categoried under some countries will include persons whose descent was not native to these countries. As a result birthplace cannot be strictly equated with colour. The lack of any necessary relationship between birthplace and colour is also intensified by the fact that these data take no account of children born in this country to immigrants of a previous generation. Nevertheless, despite these necessary reservations, it can be reasonably assumed that the majority of the immigrants from the Americas, Africa and the Indian sub-continent are coloured and that the majority of children born to these immigrants in Great Britain are resident with or near their parents. A more important limitation of these data as an index of the distribution of coloured immigrants is the likely under-enumeration of certain immigrant groups. Peach (1966) has suggested that in some areas, the 1961 Census under-enumerated the West Indian immigrant population by as much as 20%. Furthermore it is known that mistakes were made by some enumerators in the categorisation of birthplace groups. In 1961 many were under the impression that the Republic of South Africa was part of the Commonwealth and wrongly coded persons to the African New Commonwealth, so over stating this coloured immigrant group. Nevertheless, like the other sources of error described above, this limitation is not likely to radically undermine the usefulness of the data as an index of which areas have received the largest increases in immigrant groups in recent years.

As context for these more detailed aspects of socio-economic change which follow in the remaining sections of this part, it might be useful to review major population and employment trends for national totals. Since these totals are strongly influenced by trends in the largest cities, thus possibly concealing different tendencies elsewhere in urban Britain, separate data are presented here at MELA level for the seven SMLAs with a 1971 population in excess of one million. These seven MELAs account for some 40% of the urban population of Britain in 1971.

What was the impact of population trends on the structure of urban areas? Table 2.1 shows that although urban cores recorded population growth in the 1950s this was well below the national average. Relative decentralisation had therefore already begun in this period to be followed in the next decade by an absolute loss of population in urban cores. The effect of the decline of the birth rate in the 1971-74 period resulted in further population decline in urban cores, but at the same time halved the rate of population growth in metropolitan rings. In outer metropolitan rings population growth in the 50s had been below the national average, but the position was dramatically reversed in the next decade as population decentralised beyond the SMLAs. This rate of growth was sustained into the early 1970s.

TABLE 2.1   Population Change by Urban Zone 1951-61; 1961-71;
             1971-74 Absolute (000's) and Percent

Urban Cores

		1951 - 61		1961 - 71		1971 - 74*	
Britain	Abs	500		-719		-459	
	%		1.9		-2.7		-5.9
Million cities	Abs	-363		-1199		-473	
	%		-3.7		-9.0		-13.2
Rest of Britain	Abs	863		480		19	
	%		6.9		3.5		0.3

Metropolitan Rings

Britain	Abs	1708		2503		442	
	%		13.6		17.5		8.6
Million cities	Abs	783		828		53	
	%		10.2		13.1		2.3
Rest of Britain	Abs	925		1675		389	
	%		16.4		21.0		13.2

Outer Metropolitan Rings

Britain	Abs	245		788		292	
	%		3.1		9.8		10.6
Million cities	Abs	101		220		49	
	%		7.2		14.7		9.2
Rest of Britain	Abs	144		568		243	
	%		2.2		8.6		10.9

* Ten year % rate of change based on Registrar General's Annual
  Population Estimates

While this was the overall picture, Table 2.1 suggests that there were marked contrasts between the largest cities and the rest of urban Britain. In the 1950s there was an absolute decline of population in the urban cores of the million cities (London, Birmingham, Manchester, Liverpool, Newcastle, Glasgow and Leeds). This was in marked contrast to a rate of population growth above the national average in

urban cores elsewhere. So where the largest cities were absolutely decentralising
during the 50s, in the rest of Britain urban cores were faring relatively well.
In the 60s the rate of decline in the urban cores of the million cities increased
but levelled out somewhat in the early 70s, while relative decentralisation from
urban cores became a feature of cities throughout the rest of Britain. These figures possibly suggest population decentralisation from the million cities may now
have levelled out, with rehabilitation replacing redevelopment;   probably what remains is for this process to work its way down the urban hierarchy. At the same
time, population growth in the metropolitan rings and outer metropolitan rings of
the million cities has also slackened off as the MELAs themselves begin to decline
and growth is transferred to neighbouring systems and to smaller free standing
towns in the rest of Britain. In this group, the development of metropolitan rings
has continued apace.

Decentralisation of employment has in general lagged behind the outward movement of
population (Table 2.2). During the 1950s urban cores which contained 60.5% of all
employment, received the lion's share of employment growth in the period. The rate
of growth in metropolitan rings was similar to that of the cores, while employment
in the outer rings declined absolutely. However, the 1960s witnessed a dramatic
reversal. During a period of low overall employment growth (1.7%), jobs in metropolitan rings increased by 15.0% and declined in urban cores by -3.1%. The problem
of the 60s was therefore essentially one of the rapid turn around from employment
centralisation to rapid decentralisation.

TABLE 2.2   Employment Change by Urban Zone 1951-61;   1961-71.
Absolute (000's) and Percent

Urban Cores

		1951 - 61		1961 - 71	
Britain	Abs	902		-439	
	%		6.7		-3.1
Million cities	Abs	231		-793	
	%		3.1		-10.4
Rest of Britain	Abs	671		354	
	%		11.2		5.3

Metropolitan Rings

Britain	Abs	293		707	
	%		6.6		15.0
Million cities	Abs	164		347	
	%		8.9		17.3
Rest of Britain	Abs	129		360	
	%		5.0		13.4

Outer Metropolitan Rings

Britain	Abs	-14		130	
	%		-0.4		3.9
Million cities	Abs	15		45	
	%		2.6		10.5
Rest of Britain	Abs	-29		85	
	%		-3.3		2.5

The contrast in national employment levels between the first and second half of the
sixties has already been noted. What was the effect of the recession at the end of
the decade on employment decentralisation? Table 2.3 clearly indicates a slowing
down of the rate of decentralisation in the 1966-71 period. Employment growth in
metropolitan rings fell from 10.8% during 1961-6 to 3.8% between 1966 and 1971.
Outer metropolitan rings also experienced a reduction in growth rate from 5.3% to
1.1%. However, the net effect of the reductions in ring growth on the structure
of urban areas was offset by massive job losses in urban cores, losses which only
became of major significance after 1966. Indeed up until this date employment had
continued to grow, in urban cores as a whole. These figures suggest that employment decentralisation during the 60s was dominated by new employment opportunities
created during the boom years of the early 60s in metropolitan rings and job losses
arising in the less bouyant latter half of the decade. In fact if anything the
figures quoted understate the case. There are two reasons for this; first, the
base total is of course larger in 1966 and second, the base total according to the
Census is likely to be undernumerated.

TABLE 2.3   Employment Change by Urban Zone 1961-66; 1966-71*
Absolute (000's) and Percent

Urban Cores

		1961 - 66	1966 - 71
Britain	Abs	145	-591
	%	1.0	-4.1
Million cities	Abs	-243	-550
	%	-3.2	-7.4
Rest of Britain	Abs	387	-41
	%	5.8	-0.6

Metropolitan Rings

Britain	Abs	512	197
	%	10.8	3.8
Million cities	Abs	276	71
	%	13.8	3.1
Rest of Britain	Abs	236	125
	%	8.7	4.2

Other Metropolitan Rings

Britain	Abs	175	-39
	%	5.3	-1.1
Million cities	Abs	41	6
	%	6.8	1.0
Rest of Britain	Abs	134	-45
	%	4.9	-1.6

*
Slight discrepancies exist between these two five year period statistics and those
for the same ten year period. Rounding error is of course a problem but it should
also be remembered that the 1971 and 1966 statistics used here do not come from
the same source (worktravel tables) as those used previously (industry tables).
Employment in the former excludes residents with workplaces abroad and non residents with workplaces in Britain.

Further examination of Table 2.3 reveals that employment growth in urban cores in
the early part of the 60s was taking place only outside the million cities. Not
surprisingly, it was the urban cores of the million cities that experienced the
most significant job losses in the latter five years of the decade. At the same
time employment growth rates in metropolitan rings and outer rings of these cities
were also much reduced. Evidence so far presented suggests a pattern of population decentralisation followed by job decentralisation, a process beginning in the
largest cities and then spreading down the urban hierarchy. Has this meant an
increasing imbalance in jobs and population between urban zones and therefore an
increase in commuting as these differences are reconciled within the labour market
area?

In order to answer this question it is necessary to relate the distribution of the
economically active population, not the total population, to the distribution of
jobs. Evidence is available only for the periods 1961-66 and 1966-71 and it suggests that in the first half of the decade the decline of the economically active
population in urban cores and its growth in metropolitan rings and outer rings was
largely in line with the employment trend. However, in the next five years, it
would seem that the decentralisation of the economically active population continued unabated, while the rate of decentralisation of jobs appeared to have declined.
While the employed population in urban cores fell by nearly 900,000 between 1966
and 1971 and the number of jobs dropped by less than half this figure, in metropolitan rings, the reverse was the case, with economically active population increasing much more rapidly than employment.

2.2   NATIONAL, REGIONAL AND LOCAL PERSPECTIVES ON URBAN CHANGE

2.2.1 Socio-economic Trends at the National Urban Scale.

This section seeks to summarise the impact of significant social and economic trend
on the internal structure of British cities as a whole. National trends are described and broken down to the level of the constituent zones of Metropolitan Economic Labour Areas (cores, rings and outer rings).

Changes in the structure of a city system may be viewed in terms of shifts in the
pattern of demand for labour generated by public and private employers and in the
supply of labour emanating from the household or residential sector. In each city
these changes will depend upon the way in which national trends interact with the
conditions in that particular urban labour market area and its constituent zones.
The most fundamental national changes relate to population and employment trends
since these obviously impose limits on rates of urban development. Thus it is
reasonable to assume that rapid population growth in a period of prosperity is
likely to lead to pressure for low density living in metropolitan rings; a period
of economic expansion will also result in a higher demand for green field sites
and therefore employment decentralisation. Population oriented service employment
will also follow the outflow of people.

The above consideration in mind it is important to note that in the period under
investigation in this study, principally 1961-1971, but with backward looks to 1951
there have been significant differences in national rates of population and especially employment change as the previous section shows. Population grew at around
5% in both the 50s and the 60s, but in the early 70s, due primarily to a significant fall in the birth rate a decennial population increase of only 2.2% was being
recorded. During the 1950s employment growth kept pace with that of population,
but in the 60s fell well behind increasing by only 1.7%. This poor employment
growth may in part be attributed to the recession that was at its peak for the

period in 1971, when 1.3 million or 5.2% of the working population were unemployed, compared with 2.8% in both 1966 and 1961. So employment increased in line with population up until the mid-60s and then lagged behind in the second half of the decade.

Male and female employment trends

One of the most striking national changes in the 50s and 60s was the growth of employment opportunities for women. It would be surprising, given the tendency of women to work nearer their homes and in population orientated service industries, if this trend had not had a significant impact on the distribution of total employment between urban zones.

During the period 1951-1961 female employment increased by 11.4%, but male employment by only 2.9%. In the next decade, the contrast was even more pronounced with a 14.3% increase of female jobs compared with a -6.4% decline of male employment. Table 2.4 suggests employment decentralisation, especially during the 1960s, could be caricatured in terms of male employment losses in urban cores and the growth of new job opportunities for women in metropolitan rings. Between 1951 and 1961, female employment increased by 205,000 in metropolitan rings compared with only an 88,000 increase of male employment. In the next ten years 514,000 extra female jobs compared with 195,000 male jobs were recorded in metropolitan rings. Female employment was growing in the urban cores, but the increase between 1961 and 1971 of 266,000 was insufficient to offset a 705,000 loss in jobs for men.

TABLE 2.4   Male and Female Employment Change by Urban Zone
            1951-61; 1961-71. Absolute (000's) and Percent

		1951 – 61		1961 – 71	
		Male	Female	Male	Female
Urban Cores					
Britain	Abs	461	441	-705	266
	%	5.2	9.7	-7.6	5.3
Million cities	Abs	91	141	-661	-132
	%	1.9	5.4	-13.4	-4.8
Rest of Britain	Abs	370	301	-44	398
	%	9.1	15.4	-1.0	17.7
Metropolitan Rings					
Britain	Abs	88	205	195	514
	%	2.8	16.9	5.9	36.3
Million cities	Abs	66	98	129	217
	%	5.3	16.7	9.8	31.9
Rest of Britain	Abs	22	107	66	297
	%	1.1	17.1	3.3	40.4
Outer Metropolitan Rings					
Britain	Abs	-118	104	-136	265
	%	-4.8	12.6	-5.7	28.4
Million cities	Abs	-9	24	-10	54
	%	-2.1	15.4	-2.3	30.2
Rest of Britain	Abs	-109	80	-126	211
	%	-5.3	11.9	-6.4	28.0

The largest contrast between urban zones in rates of male and female employment change can be found in the million cities. There are also marked differences between these and other cities in every zone. For example, during the 50s, male employment was growing most rapidly in the cores of the non-million cities (9.1%) followed by the rings of the million cities (5.3%). By the 60s this pattern had changed considerably with the highest rates of male employment growth occurring in the rings of the million cities while the cores of other cities began to experience a small loss of male jobs. By this decade, female employment was also declining in the cores of the million cities (-132,000), but growing dramatically in their inner and outer rings. However, in urban cores elsewhere there were significant increase in female employment opportunities.

Changes in the pattern of demand for labour will be reflected in changes in supply, although not necessarily emanating from the same urban zones. One measure of supply is the activity rate, expressed as a proportion of men and women living in each urban zone who are in employment. So while employment data referred to places of work activity rates refer to places of residence. In 1961 male activity rates declined outwards from urban cores: however, the loss of male employment in cores in the next ten years meant that by 1971, male activity rates were lower in urban cores than in metropolitan rings (Table 2.5). Female activity rates also declined outward from urban cores both in 1961 and 1971. However, between 1961 and 1971 female activity rates increased by 19.9% in metropolitan rings and 21.0% in outer metropolitan rings, but by only 8.9% in urban cores. The result was a convergence of female activity rates between urban zones.

The contrast between the million cities and the rest of Britain was not great in either male or female participation in the labour force in 1961 or subsequent changes in these levels. The only exception to this generalisation was that female activity rates in the urban cores of the million cities were 7.9% higher in 1961 than elsewhere; by 1971 this difference had been significantly reduced. In individual cities the rates of change of female activity rates has largely been in line with that of female employment, which tends to support the view that women tend to live nearer their workplace than males.

Occupational and industrial trends

The growth of female employment has not surprisingly been associated with the expansion of office jobs in the national economy. In 1971, 30.9% of all economically active women were in office occupation, compared with 20.2% of economically active men. During the previous decade office employment had continued to grow nationally while manual employment continued to decline. In 1971 office occupations accounted for 25.2% of local MELA employment compared with 22.7% in 1966. Between 1966 and 1971 office employment in urban Britain increased by 11.4% and total employment declined by -1.8%. This period also saw substantial changes in the composition of the office workforce. Clerical occupations in 1966 accounted for 61.5% of total office employment, reflecting significant increases during the previous fifteen years. Managerial and professional occupations made up a further 14.0% and 24.2% respectively. However, in the next five years these latter groups increased by 19.1%, this being half the rate of the previous five years.

Clerical employment is predominantly a female occupation; in 1971 79.9% of clerical jobs were filled by women, a proportion which has increased considerably since 1966. By contrast, managerial and professional employment is chiefly a male preserve, with 90.0% of all such jobs being occupied by them.

Before examining the impact of these trends on the distribution of office jobs between urban zones, two points should be noted. First, office employment is an occupation that can be found across all sectors of the economy including manufact-

TABLE 2.5   Changes in Activity Rates by Urban Zone 1961-71

Male activity rate	1961	1971	% change 1961-71
Urban Cores			
Britain	87.5	81.3	-7.1
Million cities	88.6	82.2	-7.2
Rest of Britain	86.3	80.6	-6.6
Metropolitan rings			
Britain	86.3	82.5	-4.4
Million cities	86.8	81.8	-5.8
Rest of Britain	85.9	83.1	-3.3
Outer Metropolitan Rings			
Britain	85.8	79.4	-7.5
Million cities	85.1	80.6	-5.3
Rest of Britain	85.9	79.1	-7.9
Female activity rate			
Urban Cores			
Britain	41.6	45.3	8.9
Million cities	45.5	48.2	5.9
Rest of Britain	37.6	42.8	13.8
Metropolitan rings			
Britain	34.6	41.5	19.9
Million cities	37.3	43.7	17.2
Rest of Britain	32.5	39.8	22.5
Outer Metropolitan Rings			
Britain	31.4	38.0	21.0
Million cities	33.0	39.9	20.9
Rest of Britain	31.0	37.5	20.6

uring industry, services and central and local government. Office employment is not just a feature of the financial and business services sector, although in these sectors it admittedly accounts for the majority of employment. As will be shown later many of these sectors have different distributions within and between urban areas and have exhibited different patterns of locational change. Furthermore, employment data give no indication as to the organisational status of the workplace concerned; an office manager as recorded in the Census may work in a detached city centre head office of a manufacturing organisation or at the production site itself, in a branch office or the headquarters of a building society and so on.

The second point to note is that urban cores as defined for this study cover a much wider area than the central business district. In most large cities the urban core contains large inner industrial areas as well as the central business district. As a consequence contrasting trends for these two zones may be concealed.

In spite of these caveats it is not surprising that office jobs are more important in the occupational structure of employment in the urban core than in all other zones. In 1966 they accounted for 26.5% of all employment in cores; by 1971 this figure had risen to 29.1%. This increase can largely be attributed to the decline in non-office employment in the urban cores. Table 2.6 shows that while total employment in urban cores fell by -4.1% between 1966 and 1971 office employment increased by 4.9%. This increase of office jobs was most pronounced in the urban cores

British Cities

TABLE 2.6   Office Employment Change by Urban Zone 1966-71
Absolute (000's) and Percent

	Britain		Million Cities		Rest of Britain	
Urban Cores	Abs	%	Abs	%	Abs	%
Total employment	-591	-4.1	-550	-7.4	-41	-0.6
Total office	190	4.9	8	0.4	174	10.8
Clerical	25	1.0	-64	-4.5	89	8.9
Managerial	79	15.6	32	10.7	46	22.8
Other office	86	9.2	40	7.5	46	11.4
Metropolitan Rings						
Total employment	197	3.8	71	3.1	125	4.2
Total office	197	21.5	94	19.9	103	23.3
Clerical	95	18.0	47	16.7	48	19.4
Managerial	44	28.7	21	26.7	24	30.7
Other office	58	24.9	27	23.1	31	26.7
Other Metropolitan Rings						
Total employment	-39	-1.1	6	1.0	-45	-1.6
Total office	68	13.3	13	11.8	61	15.2
Clerical	33	10.5	9	14.6	23	9.5
Managerial	19	23.2	4	22.4	15	23.5
Other office	17	13.5	-0	-0.3	17	18.1

in the rest of Britain outside the million cities. So in these cities the loss of jobs in other types of employment was not compensated for by gains in the office sector. In fact clerical jobs declined absolutely in the cores of the million cities compared with significant increases in urban cores elsewhere. While there was a growth of managerial jobs in the cores of the million cities, the rate of increase was less than half that recorded in other urban cores.

Table 2.6 shows that office employment accounted for virtually all employment growth in metropolitan rings - a 21.5% increase between 1966 and 1971 compared with a 3.8% increase of total employment. Increases in clerical jobs were absolutely the most important component of this growth; however, in relative terms, the growth of managerial employment in metropolitan rings was more than 10% higher than the growth of clerical employment. Broadly similar trends are apparent in the metropolitan rings of the million cities as compared with cities elsewhere, although the growth rates of both clerical and managerial employment were higher in the rings of smaller cities. Even in the outer metropolitan rings, office employment was growing while total employment declined.

Clearly then, in a period of considerable decline in total employment, office jobs have been a dynamic component of intra-urban change. Although office occupations have in aggregate contributed to offsetting the loss of other jobs in urban cores, this has been chiefly true of the smaller cities. In the million cities only managerial jobs have been increasing in urban cores but even then at a less rapid rate than elsewhere. Thus throughout urban Britain both clerical and managerial jobs have been decentralising from urban cores to outer metropolitan rings.

These conclusions are reinforced by the results of a shift share analysis. This shows that total office employment in urban cores grew less than might have been expected if it had increased at the same rate as nationally (total shift negative or -3.69%). This negative total shift can only be attributed in small degree to

TABLE 2.7   Employment Change by Urban Zone, 1966-1971 (Absolute 000's and Percent)

	Urban Cores		Metropolitan Rings		Outer Metropolitan Rings		Britain	
	Abs	%	Abs	%	Abs	%	Abs	%
Agriculture, forestry, fishing	-10	-22.5	-43	-15.6	-46	-15.7	-127	-16.6
Mining and quarrying	-24	-33.1	-68	-29.0	-69	-29.7	-169	-30.1
Food, drink and tobacco	-31	-6.2	4	2.8	9	10.1	-13	-1.7
Chemicals and allied industries	8	2.9	6	4.5	16	21.6	34	6.8
Metal manufacture	-34	-8.6	10	9.0	-15	-20.2	-38	-6.4
Engineering and electrical goods	-96	-6.5	45	9.6	36	16.3	-5	-0.2
Shipbuilding and marine engineering	-0	-0.0	4	28.3	-2	-17.1	2	0.9
Vehicles	-25	-4.7	7	3.8	-4	-4.1	-20	-2.4
Metal goods	-55	-13.5	8	7.6	5	10.1	-41	-7.3
Textiles	-89	-23.6	-24	-13.4	-15	-11.1	-130	-17.9
Leather, leather goods and fur	-5	-15.1	0	0.2	-1	-12.7	-6	-9.9
Clothing and footwear	-51	-14.2	1	1.0	3	4.4	-45	-8.6
Bricks, pottery, glass, cement etc.	-16	-9.6	-5	-5.2	-1	-1.5	-22	-6.8
Timber, furniture etc.	-16	-8.7	10	16.4	6	15.9	3	0.8
Paper, printing and publishing	-19	-4.4	10	9.0	3	4.9	-4	-0.6
Other manufacturing industries	-23	-11.5	13	18.8	5	0.1	-1	-0.4
Construction	-143	-14.1	-34	-7.0	-26	-9.4	-211	-11.2
Gas, electricity and water	-40	-15.0	-2	-2.2	-6	-11.6	-48	-11.6
Transport and communications	-56	-4.8	18	7.2	-1	-0.5	-44	-2.7
Distributive trades	-219	-10.3	16	2.7	-17	-4.2	-229	-7.0
Insurance, banking and finance	51	9.1	18	17.7	11	17.7	82	11.2
Professional and scientific services	228	15.4	112	19.3	51	14.8	402	16.0
Miscellaneous services	-81	-5.5	11	1.8	-8	-2.1	-77	-3.0
Public administration and defence	96	12.2	46	14.3	14	5.7	164	11.6
Industry inadequately described	59	139.7	25	167.0	14	195.9	104	156.2
Total in employment *	-592	-4.0	191	3.6	-38	-1.1	-441	-1.8

* Rounding differences

the occupational structural office employment in the urban cores - that is a greater
specialisation in the slow growing clerical group. (Proportionality shift -0.14%).
Far more important is the negative differential shift of -3.5% which suggests that
all components of the office work force have grown less rapidly in urban cores than
nationally. Conversely, in metropolitan rings a total shift of 12.9% is largely
attributable to a higher rate of growth in all types of office employment in this
zone than elsewhere, rather than to the occupational structure favouring the more
rapidly growing managerial and professional groups. Finally, in the outer metropolitan rings the growth of office employment is greater than expected although
less so than in the inner rings. This suggests that the wave of decentralisation
has yet to reach this outer zone.

The magnitude of total employment change especially the decline in the urban cores
of the nation has already been discussed. The purpose next is to attempt to disaggregate such change by industrial sector. Throughout, the analysis is concerned
only with the total number of jobs so the important implications of the differential growth of male and female jobs described previously has to be kept in mind.

Table 2.7 shows the remarkable absolute and relative changes that took place in
employment in British industries over the five year period. Out of the 25 orders
of the Standard Industrial Classification only five managed to record growth in
urban cores. The three most important were in the service sector, trends in financial, professional and administrative services mentioned before in the context of
occupation change being substantiated. Some 375,000 new jobs were created in these
three sectors with in addition individual sectors undergoing massive relative
growth, for example, professional and scientific services by 15.4%. Only one manufacturing activity, chemicals, grew in employment in core areas, and then only
modestly, the other growth industry relating to the inadequately described.

In total, urban cores lost close on 600,000 jobs. It was two other service sectors,
distributive trades and miscellaneous services, which made a principal contribution
to this loss with a decline of around 300,000. Before considering the important
underlying cause of this non-basic employment change some mention should be made
here of the drift from primary activity, with really quite substantial absolute
and relative decline occuring even in urban cores of the nation. In manufacturing
almost all industries declined, making up around 450,000 jobs in all. In absolute
terms the main components were engineering and electrical goods and textiles, with
the latter individually managing to record the highest relative manufacturing decline. Related industries such as metals, metal goods and leather goods, clothing
and footwear augmented this decline. Summarising the dismal fortunes of the nation's central cities a large decline could be expected in the well known sectoral
indicator, construction, and expectations are confirmed.

The picture in the nation's metropolitan rings, although mirroring national industrial trends in general, is not by any means the same. As might be expected much
greater absolute decline in the primary sector can be seen due to its location
characteristics. For manufacturing the situation although not rosy is not as
gloomy. At least most manufacturing employment grew, with only refractory and
leather products declining. This growth is modest in absolute terms but for individual sectors does represent a major relative growth initiative, for example,
in timber products or in paper and printing. So at least some of the massive
declines in the manufacturing sectors of the nation's core areas were finding
their way into manufacturing in the rings. Probably the more important trend
though was the switch to the service sector, even more so the growth generated in
metropolitan rings. All service sectors grew in the rings with the exception of
utilities. Distributive trades of course are directly influenced by population
change and even with the clear implications of changing technology and scale in
the industry, this sector records growth in the rings. However it is again the

professional, administrative and financial sectors, joined to a lesser extent by the transport and communications group, which recorded the highest growth rates. In all of the first three sectors listed above the relative growth rates were higher than for the core areas. The absolute numbers involved are important too, with close on 200,000 new jobs being created in these sectors. The expected link with the growth in female activity rates in these areas can only be hinted at for the present, but clearly there is a link. The overall result of all of these trends was a growth of around 200,000 in the total employment in the metropolitan ring areas of Britain - a 3.6% improvement to put alongside a 4.0% deterioration in the nation's cores. Although the outer ring areas of the country lost employment in total - some 38,000 or 1.1% in fact - they lie intermediate between cores and rings in terms of their change composition. Again decline was heavily dominated by the primary sectors with well over 100,000 jobs lost which in relative terms must have had an important impact. The fortunes in manufacturing sectors were mixed; seven achieved growth and six declined. On balance it was the growing sectors which dominated at a rate of over two to one in terms of jobs. Interestingly it is the important engineering and electrical goods sector (as was the case in the metropolitan ring areas) which was achieving the best performance in absolute terms, making a 16.3% growth. The fortunes of the service sectors were also mixed, three gained and four lost. The former not unexpectedly were the principal growth industries discussed previously with the 51,000 extra jobs in professional and scientific services being particularly noteworthy.

The million cities/rest of Britain split in the composition of these industrial trends is instructive. Consider the example of industries chosen in Table 2.8. Here it can be seen that for engineering it is the performance of the million cities' cores which turns growth elsewhere in the cores into massive decline. Similar trends can be seen for the other manufacturing sector with important absolute and relative declines apparent for the large cities although the rest of Britain in this case also did not manage to grow. With textiles the situation was not the same. Declines in the centres of small textile towns of northern England ensured important declines in the rest of Britain - to more than match those in the million cities. Distributive services, again a useful reflection of population change, were far more drastic in their declines from million cities' cores than elsewhere. On the other hand the two growth service sectors dealing in activities traditionally thought of as million city based achieved a much better performance in the other towns of Britain.

Much the same was true for financial and professional services in the metropolitan rings of the million cities and the rest of Britain. Distribution was however different. Here growth was occurring; what is more, it was faster in the rest of Britain than in the inner commuting hinterlands of the big cities. Similarly with the other manufacturing sector and even more significantly with engineering and electrical manufacturing sectors it was the ring areas of the rest of Britain which were providing the growth impetus. Textiles of course were ubiquitously in decline.

Textiles were also in decline in the outer metropolitan rings, but interestingly neither engineering nor other manufacturers recorded declines in this zone no matter the city set. At this outer ring scale some decline in distributive trades for cities in the rest of Britain was apparent, perhaps reflecting some centralisation of employment consistent with increasing scale in this sector. The other service sectors, being nationally growing, performed well at this scale throughout Britain.

Socio-economic structure

Residential segregation of socio-economic groups is a long established process. This section considers whether the process also occurs in the centralisation-

British Cities

TABLE 2.8   Selected Employment Change by Urban Zone, 1966-1971
(Absolute 000's and Percent)

Urban Cores	Million cities		Rest of Britain	
	Abs	%	Abs	%
Engineering and electrical goods	-112	-14.5	16	2.3
Textiles	-37	-30.1	-52	-20.4
Other manufacturing industries	-20	-17.3	-3	-3.4
Distributive trades	-163	-15.0	-56	-5.4
Insurance, banking and finance	28	8.5	23	13.3
Professional and scientific services	82	11.2	147	19.8
Metropolitan Rings				
Engineering and electrical goods	-9	-3.7	55	25.3
Textiles	-9	-14.4	-15	-12.9
Other manufacturing industries	3	7.9	11	29.9
Distributive trades	6	2.1	10	3.4
Insurance, banking and finance	3	20.7	8	22.9
Professional and scientific services	49	18.5	63	20.0
Outer Metropolitan Rings				
Engineering and electrical goods	4	7.8	33	18.7
Textiles	-4	-15.7	-12	-10.1
Other manufacturing industries	2	18.5	4	8.3
Distributive trades	-1	-1.8	-16	-4.8
Insurance, banking and finance	10	-31.6	7	18.7
Professional and scientific services	12	18.3	38	14.0

decentralisation of socio-economic groups between urban zones, and therefore, across local authority boundaries. As commuting ability varies between socio-economic groups it would be surprising if it were otherwise, even though the large scale of the zones tends to even out differences. As is the case with age groups, it will be seen that interpretation of intra-urban changes is made more difficult by the different changes, nationally in the sizes of these groups.

The national changes are summarised in Table 2.9. These were dominated by the large absolute and percentage decrease in the number in semi- and unskilled manual occupations (649,000 and 15.1%) and by a large increase in the number in managerial and professional occupations (496,000 and 20.5%). There was a smaller increase in the number in intermediate non-manual occupations and a smaller decrease in the number in skilled manual occupations. Therefore, both absolute and percentage changes were greatest at the extremes and least in the middle of the social structure. Even taking into account the effects of unemployment and of any retitling of occupations which may have occurred, these changes are so large that it is unlikely they are misrepresentative in either direction or magnitude. As a result, there were changes in the composition of the workforce with an increase in the proportion employed in non-manual occupations from 30.5 to 34.8% and a decrease in the proportion employed in manual occupations from 66.0 to 61.8%. The greatest restructuring was in the extremes with the proportion in managerial and professional occupations increasing from 14.1 to 17.3%, and the proportion in semi- and unskilled manual occupations decreasing from 26.6 to 23.0%.

The changes between urban zones reveal a certain symmetry. The lowest status group, semi- and unskilled manual occupations, experienced decreases in all zones,

TABLE 2.9 Male Socio-Economic Group Change in Britain,
1961-1971

National Change (Absolute 000's and percent)	1961		1971		1961-1971	
Professional and managerial	2,288	14.1	2,757	17.3	469	20.5
Intermediate non-manual	2,661	16.4	2,785	17.5	124	4.7
Skilled manual	6,398	39.4	6,182	38.8	-217	-3.3
Semi- and unskilled manual	4,311	26.6	3,661	23.0	-649	-15.1
Armed forces and inadequately described	575	3.5	533	3.4	-41	-7.1
Total	16,232	100.0	15,920	100.0	-314	-1.9

Zonal Change (Absolute 000's and percent)	Urban Cores 1961-1971		Metropolitan Rings 1961-1971		Outer Metropolitan Rings 1961-1971	
Professional and managerial	87	8.7	305	38.1	74	21.3
Intermediate non-manual	-99	-6.6	162	20.8	60	20.1
Skilled manual	-457	-13.2	152	9.0	75	7.6
Semi- and unskilled manual	-353	-15.6	-125	-11.6	-143	18.6
Total	-806	-9.5	480	10.6	30	1.2

Zonal Structure (Percent)	1961	1971	1961	1971	1961	1971
Professional and managerial	44.5	40.2	35.0	40.1	15.1	15.2
Intermediate non-managerial	56.3	50.2	29.2	33.7	11.3	13.0
Skilled manual	54.3	48.8	26.4	29.9	15.3	17.1
Semi- and unskilled manual	51.9	52.0	25.4	26.0	17.9	17.1
Total	52.2	48.2	27.8	31.4	15.7	16.1

with the largest decrease being -353,000 in the cores. In contrast, the highest status group, professional and managerial occupations, increased in all zones, with the largest gain, 305,000 in the rings. These figures suggest that intra-urban changes were leading to polarisation of these groups. The other groups experienced a decrease in the cores and increases in the rings and outer rings. However, there was a large decrease in the number of skilled manual occupations in the cores of -457,000 and this was so great that the number in this group in both SMLAs and MELAs also declined. In contrast, there was only a relatively small decrease in the number of intermediate non-manual occupations in cores so that the numbers in SMLAs and MELAs increased.

The percentage changes give a further perspective on these patterns. Although the number of professional and managerial occupations grew in number in all zones, the largest percentage increases were in the rings and outer rings, especially the former (38.1%). The changes in semi-skilled and unskilled manual occupations were more uniform but the smallest decrease was in the rings, that is, in the same zone as there was the largest relative increase in the professional and managerial occupations. For the intermediate non-manual (20.8 and 20.1%) and the skilled manual (9.0 and 7.6%) there was little difference in the increases in the rings and outer rings.

In the SMLAs there was absolute decentralisation of all economically active males - in line with the pattern for total population. This was also the case for the middle status groups, the skilled manual and the intermediate non-manual. For professional and managerial occupations, however, there was relative decentralisation and for the semi- and unskilled manual there was relative decentralisation in decline. There was, therefore, a tendency to increased polarisation of the highest and lowest status groups between cores and rings.

Interpretation of these intra-urban variations, however, is difficult because of the predominance of overall changes in the sizes of the groups. Shift and share analysis assists the interpretation of the changes.

The shifts reveal a different pattern to the absolute and percentage changes. All groups had a negative shift in the cores and a positive shift in the rings. Thus, all groups experienced the same underlying decentralisation trend. However, professional and managerial occupations displayed the largest negative shift in the cores and the largest positive shift in the rings, while semi- and unskilled manual occupations displayed the smallest negative shift in cores and the smallest positive shift in the rings. The other two socio-economic groups displayed similar, if somewhat weaker decentralisation trends than the highest status group.

What do these results indicate about the polarisation of socio-economic groups? (Harris, 1973). The percentage changes revealed some polarisation of the semi- and unskilled manual in the cores because all the other groups were increasing at a considerably faster rate in the rings. The shifts strengthen the evidence on this for while there were only relatively small shifts in the semi- and unskilled manual in the cores and rings, the other groups had large positive shifts in the rings and large negative shifts in the cores. This applies to the professional and managerial despite the absolute increase of this group in cores. Therefore, there is evidence that intra-urban changes in the period 1961-1971 were leading to the increased polarisation of the semi- and unskilled manual from the other economically active males. This reflects on a larger spatial scale the process known to occur in the inner cities. (Department of the Environment, 1977).

Finally, the distribution of these groups between zones is summarised in Table 2.9. The changes in the intra-zonal distributions between 1961 and 1971 underline the absolute and percentage trends. There was relatively little change in the distribution of the semi- and unskilled manual but there was some centralisation in the SMLA as the proportion in the outer rings decreased. For all the other groups there is the expected shift from cores to rings with the proportion in the former decreasing and in the latter increasing.

The extent of the concentration in the cores at either date also illustrates some of the differences between the socio-economic groups. The professional and managerial were the least concentrated in cores, there being approximately 40% both in cores and rings in 1971. For all the other groups, at least 48% were in cores in 1971 and, in fact, the semi- and unskilled manual were only slightly more concentrated in the cores than the two middle status groups. Even more surprising is the fact that in 1961 the semi- and unskilled manual (51.9%) were _less_ concentrated in the cores than the middle status groups, (56.3 and 54.3%).

In summary, it is clear that changes were leading to an increased polarisation of the lowest status groups but that intra-urban differences were complicated by the predominance of the national decrease in this group. However, there is no evidence that the lowest status groups were concentrated in the cores to any greater extent than the middle status groups. Yet, the considerable reversal of their position in the 1960s indicates that this could occur in the future.

TABLE 2.10   Age Group Change in Britain, 1961-1971

National Change (Absolute 000's and percent)	1961		1971		1961-1971	
0 - 14	11,924	23.3	12,930	24.0	1,006	8.4
15 - 29	9,959	19.4	11,335	21.0	1,376	13.8
30 - pensionable age	21,861	42.6	20,902	38.7	-959	-4.4
Over pensionable age	7,542	14.7	8,810	16.3	1,268	16.8
Total	51,287	100.0	53,978	100.0	2,691	5.3

Zonal Change (Absolute 000's and percent)	Urban Core		Metropolitan Rings		Outer Metropolitan Rings	
0 - 14	-4	-0.1	761	22.4	224	11.8
15 - 29	313	5.9	739	27.2	275	18.1
30 - pensionable age	-1,411	-12.4	485	7.9	3	0.1
Over pensionable age	383	10.0	519	25.8	289	22.7
Total	-719	-2.7	2,503	17.5	788	9.8

Zonal Structure (Percent)	1961	1971	1961	1971	1961	1971
0 - 14	51.0	47.0	28.5	32.2	16.0	16.5
15 - 29	53.2	49.5	27.3	30.5	15.3	15.9
30 - pensionable age	51.9	47.6	28.2	31.8	15.4	16.2
Over pensionable age	51.0	48.0	26.6	28.7	16.9	17.8
Total	51.8	47.9	27.9	31.1	15.8	16.4

Age structure

Demographic age groups can be expected to mirror clearly the population changes in and between zones, that is, the decentralisation which occurred in 1961-1971. The distributions of the age groups are not independent for the co-residence of persons of different ages is a consequence of family organisation. By and large, there is indeed little difference in the static distributions of the age groups. However, the actual changes observed are greatly influenced by the national changes in the sizes of these groups.

The national changes are summarised in Table 2.10. The dominant feature was the large decrease in the 30 to pensionable age group of almost a million (-959,057), while the combined increases in the other groups totalled just over a million. The percentage changes, however, reveal differences in the relative magnitude of these trends; there were considerably larger percentage increases in the above pensionable age groups (16.8) and the 15-29 group (13.8) than in the 0-14 group (8.4). As a result, the age composition of the population altered between 1961 and 1971, with a decrease in the percentage of 30 to pensionable age, and large increases in the percentage above pensionable age and aged 15-29. There was also a smaller increase in the percentage aged 0-14. The net result of the decline of the 30 to pensionable age cohort was a younger population by 1971 (the percentage aged under 30 increased from 42.7 to 45.0) although the percentage of the elderly increased by 16.8%.

The national changes tend to dominate the absolute and percentage changes in the urban zones. The 0-14 and 30-pensionable age groups decreased in cores and had the smallest increases in the rings and outer rings. In contrast, the 15-29 and greater than pensionable age groups increased in all zones, exceeding the increase in the outer two groups in all cases. This accords with the overall (national) changes in these groups. The decrease in the 30-pensionable age group in the cores (-1,411,000) was so great that there were also decreases in the number in this group in the SMLAs (-926,000) and the MELAs (-923,000). The small absolute decrease in the 0-14 group (-4,000) was cancelled out by the increases in the other zones so there are increases in both SMLAs and MELAs.

These figures are important because they show that the net loss of population of 719,000 in the cores was attributable mainly to the large decrease in the number of 30 to pensionable age. The decline in this group was partly offset by the increase in the 15-29 and above pensionable age groups. In the rings and outer rings, however, the increases in the 30-pensionable age group complemented the changes in the other groups.

The results, in terms of the age composition of each zone, were predictable. The 30-pensionable age group decreased and all the other groups increased as proportions of the total population of each zone. Consequently, the populations of all zones became relatively younger. However, there were not great differences between zones. Thus, in 1971 the percentage aged under 30 was 45.2 in cores, 45.4 in rings and 44.3 in outer rings. The differences between zones were greatest in the changes and not in age composition.

It is evident that the changes observed in the urban zones are greatly influenced by the national changes in age composition. For example, the overall increase in those above pensionable age would be expected to lead to increases in this group in all zones, while the large overall decrease in the 30-pensionable age group would be expected to lead to a decrease in cores and only small increases in the rings. These figures, therefore, do not reveal the extent of the underlying cent- ralisation-decentralisation which was occurring if the overall changes in the size of the groups was controlled for. Shift and share analysis does provide a persp- ective on these underlying trends.

These shifts reveal a remarkable uniformity, particularly for the three younger age groups. The shifts for these groups ranged between only -8.0 and -8.7 in cores, 12.3 and 13.8 in rings and 3.1 and 4.5 in outer rings. The group over pensionable age did not differ greatly from this pattern but did exhibit a smaller negative shift in the cores, a smaller positive shift in the rings and a larger positive shift in the outer rings. The similarity of the shifts does suggest there was underlying uniformity in the decentralisation of all the groups.

Finally, Table 2.10 summarises the distribution of the age groups between urban zones in 1971. Again there is considerable uniformity. The percentages of the four age groups resident in the cores and rings ranged only between 47.0 and 49.5%, and between 28.7 and 32.2% respectively. The two groups which deviated most from the pattern for total population were those aged 15-29, being relatively more con- centrated in cores, and those over pensionable age, being relatively more concent- rated in the outer rings and relatively less important in the rings. The changes in these intra-zonal distributions since 1961 are also uniform; the proportion in the cores decreased and the proportions in the rings and outer rings increased for all groups.

The distribution of the age groups, therefore, showed relatively small differences between zones. This is as expected, given the general lack of independence in these distributions. The underlying trends in the changes were also uniform, indicating the same basic decentralisation trend was influencing all age groups. The absolute and percentage changes were, however, different and were dominated, especially in the cores, by the decrease in the 30 to pensionable age group. In the rings the largest increase was in those aged 15-29, which is the expected outcome of high rates of immigration to this zone and the age specific nature of migration.

Birthplace structure

Between 1961 and 1971 although the largest absolute change in the size of any of the birthplace groups was in those born in Britain, there were large percentage increases in the number of immigrants. As this decade was characterised by decent-ralisation of the British born, the important question is whether there was cent-ralisation or lesser rates of decentralisation for the immigrants and, hence, pol-arisation in the cores. Evidence from previous studies, (Peach, 1975), on a smaller spatial scale, suggests that there may be relative decentralisation of the West Indians, and centralisation of the Indian Sub-Continent (S.C.) immigrants.

The absolute and percentage changes present different pictures. Nationally, the largest absolute increase was in the number born in Britain, followed by the Other Migrants group rather than by any of the New Commonwealth immigrants (see Table 2.11). In contrast, the percentage changes were greatest for the New Commonwealth immigrants from the Indian Sub-Continent (125.2), Africa (296.4) and the West Indies (71.3). However, this does not mean that immigrants formed a large propor-tion of the population; even in 1971, the largest immigrant group was the Other Migrants who were 2.1% of the total population. Over the decade, the percentage born in Britain did decrease but only from 95.3 to 93.8%. Those of non-British birth in 1971 totalled 3,353,000.

As expected, the absolute changes for the British born reveal decreases in the cores and increases in the rings and outer rings. The same pattern is observed for the Irish born. For all the New Commonwealth immigrants, however, there were in-creases in all zones and the largest, in fact, were in the cores. As a result, the large decrease in the number of British born in the cores, -1,335,000, was partly cancelled out by the increase in the number of New Commonwealth immigrants so that the total population decrease was only -719,000 in this zone. The increase in the number born in Britain dominated the changes in the rings and outer rings.

The percentage changes reveal another aspect of these patterns and, in particular, the differences among the New Commonwealth immigrant groups. Only for the Indian Sub-Continent and the Africa-born were the largest percentage increases in the cores; for the West Indians the largest increase was in the rings. Therefore, at a time when there was absolute decentralisation of the British and Irish born, there was relative decentralisation of the West Indians and relative centralisation of those born in Africa or the Indian Sub-Continent. It seems that polarisation of the British born and the New Commonwealth immigrants occurred in this period. As there was also absolute decentralisation of jobs in this period, this has import-ant implications for the employment opportunities for these immigrant groups.

These changes are further illustrated by examining the distribution of the groups between the urban zones. Of the British born, in 1971, 46.7% were in cores, 31.7% were in rings and 16.9% were in the outer rings. This reveals an increase in the proportion in rings and outer rings and a decrease in the proportion in cores since 1961, that is, the expected decentralisation of this group. There is a similar pattern for the Irish born. The difference between New Commonwealth immigrants is also underlined. The proportion of West Indians resident in the cores decreased, while the proportions of the Africa and Indian Sub-Continent born increased con-

TABLE 2.11   Birthplace Group Change in Britain, 1961-1971

National Change (Absolute 000's and percent)	1961		1971		1961-1971	
Ireland	925	1.8	960	1.8	35	3.9
Indian S-C	207	0.4	467	0.9	260	125.2
Africa	39	0.1	156	0.3	116	296.4
West Indies	173	0.3	296	0.6	123	71.3
Other Commonwealth	273	0.5	331	0.6	58	21.3
Other Migrants	803	1.6	1,143	2.1	340	42.3
Great Britain	48,867	95.3	50,625	93.8	1,759	3.6
Total	51,287	100.0	53,978	100.0	2,691	5.3

Zonal Change (Absolute 000's and percent)	Urban Cores 1961-1971		Metropolitan Rings 1961-1971		Outer Metropol- itan Rings 1961-1971	
Ireland	-9	-1.4	38	18.4	10	12.8
Indian S-C	224	160.6	27	60.6	8	46.8
Africa	89	344,7	20	242.7	6	149.4
West Indies	111	70.1	10	96.3	2	58.5
Great Britain	-1,353	-5.3	2,269	16.5	725	9.3
Total	-719	-2.7	2,503	17.5	792	9.8

Zonal Structure (Percent)	1961	1971	1961	1971	1961	1971
Ireland	70.0	66.6	19.9	22.7	8.2	8.9
Indian S-C	67.4	78.0	21.8	15.6	8.6	5.6
Africa	65.7	73.7	21.2	18.4	10.1	6.4
West Indies	91.4	90.7	5.9	6.7	2.4	2.3
Great Britain	51.1	46.7	28.2	31.7	16.1	16.9
Total	51.8	47.9	27.9	31.1	15.8	16.4

siderably from 65.7 to 73.7%, and 67.4 to 78.0%, respectively. Again, there is apparently polarisation of those born in the Indian Sub-Continent and Africa.

To concentrate only on the changes in the distribution would be misleading. Certainly the direction of the changes in the West Indian group are more similar to the British than to the other New Commonwealth groups. However, in terms of the zonal distribution at any one point in time, the West Indians were the most dissimilar to the British born. At both dates over 90% of this group were resident in cores compared with only 46.7% of the British in 1971. In contrast only 78.0% of the Indian Sub-Continent and 73.7% of the African groups were resident in cores even in 1971.

However, to place these figures in perspective, none of the immigrant groups form- ed more than 2.5% of the total population of any zone and, in combination, all the non-British born did not exceed 9% of the total population of any zone in 1971.

It is possible, therefore, to distinguish three categories of birthplace groups.

The British and Irish born were decentralising absolutely from cores to rings and
had relatively small proportions of their totals in the cores in 1971. The West
Indians also experienced decentralisation, albeit relatively, but were heavily concentrated in the cores. Finally, the African and Indian Sub-Continent groups were
the most polarised in terms of changes - experiencing relative centralisation - but
were far less concentrated in cores in 1971 than the West Indians.

How can the differences in the changes experienced by the New Commonwealth groups
be explained? Other research has suggested a number of reasons for the increased
segregation of the Indians and Pakistanis observed within the cities of Birmingham,
Coventry and London. (Peach, 1975). On the one hand, strong community links and a
desire for owner-occupation rather than local authority housing encouraged concentration. On the other hand, their relatively short length of residence, and therefore, their low position on the local authority housing waiting lists combined with
racial discrimination in jobs and housing discouraged dispersal.   Perhaps even
more fundamental was the change in the composition of this group. In 1961 many of
the Indian Sub-Continent group were white, being the children born to parents working abroad, but most of the immigrants from the Sub-Continent in 1961-1971 were
non-white and, therefore, more likely to reside in cores. Here accommodation was
cheaper, ties with friends likely to be stronger and more suitable work opportunities available. This would appear to explain satisfactorily the centralisation of
this group and the same argument may apply to those born in Africa. Decentralisation of the West Indians within cities may be due to their greater access to
local authority housing as a result of their more favourable position on housing
waiting lists; this itself, is the result of their longer residence in the United
Kingdom. Greater access to local authority housing allows greater decentralisation
because of the existence of peripheral local authority housing estates. This may
be the case within cities but the decentralisation from cores to rings occurs
across local authority boundaries and, therefore, largely without the assistance
of local authority housing. The reasons for this are not yet clear, although
length of residence is surely a factor.

2.2.2 Regional Variations in British Urban Socio-economic Change

Inter-regional contrasts in social and industrial structure are a well established
feature of the British space economy. However, in the post-war period, significant
inter-regional shifts in the distribution of population and economic activity have
occurred. For example, under the influence of significant regional policy controls
and incentives a considerable net movement of manufacturing activities toward the
peripheral areas has taken place although established manufacturing industries in
these areas have continued to decline. At the same time office activity has grown
rapidly, especially in the South East - although there has been some intra-regional
decentralisation away from London. In terms of social structure, this has implied
a continuing contrast between a core region where managerial and professional occupations predominate and peripheral regions with an emphasis on manual jobs. The
balance of these forces has sustained a rapid growth of population in the South
East although this has to some extent been off-set by industrial movement and retirement migration from this region to East Anglia and the South West.

These broad regibnal trends have been superimposed on contrasting intra-regional
urban structures. The mix of small and large settlements varies significantly between regions and, as has already been established, there have been marked contrasts
in the growth and decentralisation rates of towns of different size. Moreover, a
connection between the regional context and rates of intra-urban decentralisation
has also been suggested with the most rapid out-movement occurring in the more
prosperous regions.

To demonstrate regional variations in urban change, SMLAs and MELAs have been

assigned to the Economic Planning Regions wherein their cores are located, irrespective of whether parts of their metropolitan rings or outer metropolitan rings
fall into other regions. In view of these regional considerations this section
will attempt to disaggregate some of the intra-urban trends already identified at
the national level to the ten planning regions of the country. The analysis will
seek to highlight inter-regional differences in urban structure and change for a
range of employment and population characteristics. As far as possible the same
order of presentation will be adhered to as before, that is moving from employment
disaggregated by sex, occupation and industry, and population disaggregated by
socio-economic group, age and birthplace.

Male and female employment trends

At the national level the growth of female employment in metropolitan rings and th
decline of male employment in urban cores has been identified as a key process in
the net decentralisation of employment from the inner parts of British cities.
Female employment is characteristic of certain industries such as textiles and ser
vices, industries which are known to have distinctive regional and intra-urban dis
tribution patterns. The same can be said of male employment in respect of industries like metal manufacturing and engineering. It would therefore be reasonable t
anticipate variations between regions in rates of male and female employment chang
at the intra-urban scale.

Table 2.12 indicates that the significant contrast already noted between urban
zones in the distribution of female opportunities is superimposed on a parallel bu
less distinct regional pattern. Broadly speaking, female employment is most impor
tant in the South East, the North West and Scotland and the least important in
Wales and the South West. These contrasts prevail across all urban zones. Nevertheless, it is important to note that the intra-urban contrasts (a range of approx
imately 4% in the proportion of jobs held by women) are as great as the inter-
regional contrasts.

The pattern described in Table 2.12 is the outcome of significant shifts in the
distribution of male and female employment between urban zones and regions.

TABLE 2.12   Proportion in Female Employment by Urban Zone and Region, 1971 (Percent)

	Urban Cores	Metropolitan Rings	Outer Metropolitan Rings
South East	39.5	35.8	35.0
West Midlands	37.2	34.7	34.6
East Midlands	37.9	34.8	34.4
East Anglia	37.6	32.5	31.8
South West	36.9	33.8	33.5
Yorkshire and Humberside	37.7	34.3	33.5
North West	39.1	36.9	36.0
North	36.7	34.8	34.3
Wales	35.1	33.1	32.5
Scotland	40.1	36.1	35.3
Britain	38.5	35.4	34.2

Table 2.13 shows that during the 1950s male employment was growing in urban cores in all regions, with the highest rates of growth in the southern half of the country. Female employment increased in cores at a higher rate but with a broadly similar pattern of inter-regional variations. In peripheral regions the lower average male employment growth in urban cores was associated with an absolute loss of male jobs in metropolitan rings. In nearly all regions except the South East and East Midlands, outer metropolitan rings were characterised by absolute losses of male employment. In contrast, female employment growth was strong in metropolitan rings and outer rings in all regions; in several instances the rate of growth exceeded that in urban cores.

The reasons for these trends are not difficult to ascertain, although the specific factors clearly vary from region to region. The loss of male employment in outer rings and even rings in certain regions was a reflection of the declining importance of dispersed primary industry, particularly agriculture, while heavy manufacturing industry was still growing in urban core areas. In certain regions, notably Yorkshire and Lancashire, the textile industry, dispersed amongst many small settlements in the hinterlands of larger cities, was also in decline. Female employment, while growing in certain service industries in the cores, was also following the outward push of population in services such as education.

In the 1960s a significant change came about particularly in the distribution of male employment. While female jobs continued to grow in all urban zones - but especially in metropolitan rings and outer rings - male employment experienced an absolute decline in urban cores in all regions except East Anglia. Not surprisingly, the highest rates of decline were experienced in the peripheral regions especially the North West and Scotland. In contrast, metropolitan rings in most regions experienced either an increased rate of male employment growth (South East and East and West Midlands) or a turn about from absolute loss to significant growth (all other regions except Yorkshire and Humberside and the North where woollen textiles and coal-mining respectively continue to decline). Thus in peripheral areas inter-regional industrial mobility, coupled with local decentralisation reversed a previous decline of employment opportunities in metropolitan rings. However, in all regions except the South East and Scotland, male employment continued to decline in outer metropolitan rings. The South East situation may be attributed to outward movement of industry into London's outer metropolitan ring and in the case of Scotland could be associated with the beginnings of North Sea oil exploration, highland forestry and other primary industry in remote areas.

The growth of female and the decline of male jobs represent only part of the employment equation. On the supply side demographic factors and the increasing willingness of women to enter employment have been important considerations, while on the demand side unemployment has clearly had a differential effect on male and female employment opportunities. Male and female activity rates, here defined as the proportion of men and women above 15 years actually in employment are one reflection of the balance of these demand and supply considerations in individual urban zones.

Table 2.14 re-emphasises the regional and urban contrasts outlined in the previous table. Thus during the 1960s male activity rates were declining most rapidly in urban cores and outer metropolitan rings, but especially in peripheral areas, notably Scotland and the North, and less rapidly in metropolitan rings, again with a pronounced contrast between core and peripheral regions. Taking account of both intra-urban and inter-regional contrasts the range of activity rate change is quite dramatic from -2.3 decline in the proportion of men in employment in metropolitan rings in the West Midlands to -11.4 in outer metropolitan rings in the North. In contrast, the growth of female activity rates while occurring in all regions was most important in those urban zones in peripheral regions which experienced the

TABLE 2.13 Male and Female Employment Change by Urban Zone and Region 1951-61 and 1961-71 Absolute (000's) and Percent

Males 1951-61 and Females 1951-61

	Males 1951-61						Females 1951-61					
	Urban Cores		Metropolitan Rings		Outer Metropolitan Rings		Urban Cores		Metropolitan Rings		Outer Metropolitan Rings	
	Abs	%	Abs	%	Abs	%	Abs	%	Abs	%	Abs	%
South East	226.50	6.9	97.77	8.0	5.31	1.3	191.05	11.6	118.40	24.0	26.75	17.8
West Midlands	73.79	7.3	14.89	4.6	-5.77	-3.2	52.55	10.4	32.73	27.9	7.78	11.5
East Midlands	31.77	7.8	10.08	5.9	2.17	1.4	21.09	9.4	9.97	20.0	8.61	15.7
East Anglia	24.60	16.5	-4.23	-3.4	-15.68	-8.6	12.67	17.8	3.63	11.8	5.61	11.9
South West	23.42	6.0	9.00	6.4	-13.50	-4.4	33.54	19.4	3.51	8.4	13.71	14.4
Yorkshire and Humberside	35.46	4.1	-7.52	-2.1	-14.47	-5.4	41.87	9.4	15.71	13.8	13.09	15.7
North West	9.43	0.7	-12.20	-2.5	-26.42	-8.9	20.57	2.8	3.06	1.3	1.96	1.6
North	18.70	3.7	-7.70	-4.7	-25.19	-10.0	25.85	12.0	8.00	19.4	10.00	15.7
Wales	13.22	6.1	1.71	1.6	-11.39	-4.9	13.37	16.5	5.61	17.2	11.13	18.9
Scotland	1.79	0.2	-10.99	-4.2	-12.41	-5.9	22.32	5.2	8.96	10.6	6.49	8.4

Males 1961-71 and Females 1961-71

	Males 1961-71						Females 1961-71					
	Urban Cores		Metropolitan Rings		Outer Metropolitan Rings		Urban Cores		Metropolitan Rings		Outer Metropolitan Rings	
	Abs	%	Abs	%	Abs	%	Abs	%	Abs	%	Abs	%
South East	-178.31	-5.2	85.90	7.0	29.49	7.1	119.46	6.5	181.99	29.7	73.47	41.6
West Midlands	-67.99	-6.3	30.03	8.9	-3.49	-2.0	12.67	2.3	59.72	39.8	23.09	30.6
East Midlands	-23.30	-5.3	12.51	6.9	-2.89	-1.9	15.75	6.4	30.83	51.5	18.08	28.5
East Anglia	11.90	6.8	2.83	2.4	-16.60	-9.9	26.44	31.6	18.70	54.3	17.38	33.0
South West	-7.05	-1.7	14.57	9.8	-21.68	-7.4	43.97	21.3	23.11	51.1	29.83	27.4
Yorkshire and Humberside	-75.68	-8.4	-18.88	-5.3	-22.82	-9.0	26.87	5.5	29.40	22.6	18.29	18.9
North West	-145.00	-11.3	24.31	5.2	-17.35	-6.4	-28.68	-3.8	48.61	20.6	15.39	12.1
North	-40.57	-7.7	-2.59	-1.7	-43.14	-19.0	36.32	15.1	32.41	65.8	26.36	35.8
Wales	-18.13	-7.9	3.42	3.1	-37.72	-16.9	21.08	22.3	15.62	40.7	18.00	25.7
Scotland	-108.68	-13.2	3.67	1.4	2.57	1.3	20.12	4.5	43.01	45.8	26.38	34.1

TABLE 2.14   Male and Female Activity Rates Change by Urban
Zone and Region, 1961-1971

Urban Cores

	Males		Change	Females		Change
	1961	1971	1961-71	1961	1971	1961-71
South East	87.2	81.7	-5.5	43.2	47.4	4.1
West Midlands	89.2	84.2	-5.0	44.7	47.1	2.4
East Midlands	88.6	81.8	-6.8	42.8	45.4	2.6
East Anglia	82.6	76.2	-6.4	35.0	42.0	7.0
South West	84.7	78.3	-6.4	35.0	40.5	5.5
Yorkshire and Humberside	87.2	80.8	-6.4	40.6	43.6	3.0
North West	87.0	80.8	-6.2	44.1	45.6	1.4
North	87.8	81.3	-8.3	34.6	41.6	7.0
Wales	86.3	79.4	-6.9	31.2	38.5	7.3
Scotland	89.3	81.2	-8.1	40.1	44.8	4.7
Britain	87.5	81.3	-6.2	41.6	45.3	3.7

Metropolitan Rings

	Males		Change	Females		Change
South East	85.2	82.8	-2.4	35.1	41.9	6.8
West Midlands	87.1	84.8	-2.3	36.9	43.2	6.3
East Midlands	88.4	82.8	-5.6	35.8	42.3	6.5
East Anglia	86.2	80.9	-5.3	28.7	37.1	8.4
South West	83.3	79.8	-3.5	28.9	37.8	8.9
Yorkshire and Humberside	89.3	82.4	-6.9	34.9	40.0	5.0
North West	86.8	82.3	-4.5	38.3	42.7	4.4
North	86.1	81.3	-4.8	29.7	39.9	10.2
Wales	84.6	80.4	-4.2	28.1	36.7	8.6
Scotland	86.9	82.5	-4.4	31.1	42.3	11.2
Britain	86.3	82.5	-3.8	34.6	41.5	6.9

Outer Metropolitan Rings

	Males		Change	Females		Change
South East	82.2	78.1	-4.1	30.0	36.9	6.9
West Midlands	88.2	82.7	-5.5	34.9	41.4	6.5
East Midlands	87.5	81.5	-6.0	34.5	41.3	6.8
East Anglia	85.8	80.7	-5.1	27.3	36.3	9.0
South West	84.1	76.7	-7.4	29.7	34.8	5.1
Yorkshire and Humberside	87.3	80.3	-7.0	32.6	38.1	5.5
North West	86.2	80.4	-5.8	37.8	41.0	3.2
North	88.5	77.1	-11.4	28.3	38.3	10.0
Wales	86.2	78.7	-7.5	27.6	35.7	8.1
Scotland	87.4	81.2	-6.2	31.8	39.2	7.4
Britain	85.9	79.1	-6.8	31.0	37.5	6.5

greatest decline in male activity rates. Thus the female activity rate in outer
metropolitan rings in the North increased by ten points between 1961 and 1971 (28.3
to 38.3) raising it to above the national average for this zone. At the same time
regions and urban zones with relatively high female activity rates in 1961 (for
example, urban cores in the North West) experienced the lowest subsequent increases
Intra-urban convergence of female activity rates already noted at the national
level was therefore also occurring at the regional scale. This was in marked contrast to male activity rates where peripheral regions in 1971 still appeared to be
at a lower level than those in the southern half of the country.

Occupational and industrial trends

The association between the increase of female activity rates and the growth of
tertiary sector employment opportunities, particularly office jobs, in metropolitan
rings at the national level has already been illustrated. To what extent have ther
been regional variations in this process? Data on disaggregated employment trends
are only available for the period 1966-71; in view of possible differences between the earlier and later parts of the 1960s total employment change figures broke
down by urban zone and region are presented in Table 2.15 as a context for the subsequent more detailed examination of occupational and industrial trends.

TABLE 2.15   Total Employment Change by Urban Zone and Region
1966-71. Absolute (000's) and Percent

	Urban Core		Metropolitan Ring		Outer Metropolitan Ring	
	Abs	%	Abs	%	Abs	%
South East	-178.90	-3.3	96.53	4.8	28.30	4.2
West Midlands	-93.27	-5.1	28.06	5.1	12.28	4.8
East Midlands	-26.04	-3.7	12.04	4.4	4.52	1.9
East Anglia	11.07	4.0	9.92	6.1	-13.05	-5.6
South West	-4.80	-0.7	10.28	4.6	-5.30	-1.3
Yorkshire and Humberside	-127.31	-8.6	-6.74	-1.3	-27.59	-7.6
North West	-126.30	-6.3	25.39	3.4	-33.88	-7.6
North	-33.63	-4.4	6.69	3.0	10.29	3.7
Wales	-3.21	-1.0	23.56	16.4	-8.18	-2.9
Scotland	-71.00	-5.7	54	0.1	5.93	1.9

In addition to the intra-urban contrasts, pronounced regional variations are apparent in Table 2.15. With the notable exception of Wales, the highest rates of job
losses in urban cores, were in the assisted areas, with Yorkshire and Humberside
topping the list with a -8.6% decline. East Anglia, the region with in aggregate
the best overall employment performance during this period, was the only region to
record an employment increase in the cores of its urban areas. With the exception
of Wales, and Yorkshire and Humberside regional variations in metropolitan ring
employment growth were less pronounced. Metropolitan rings in all the regions
clearly benefitted during this period from the local decentralisation of jobs while
in peripheral regions job losses were further offset by inter-regional industrial
movement which in most instances was directed towards this zone rather than urban

cores. However, the same cannot be said about the outer metropolitan rings.
Employment declined in this zone in all the regions except the South East, the East
and West Midlands and the North and Scotland.

Office employment, which was the only growth sector during this period, has clearly
been the important element in this pattern of change. Table 2.16 shows that this
activity became more important in the overall employment structure of all urban
zones in all regions. The growth of office employment relative to other types of
jobs was therefore a ubiquitous process at both the urban and regional scales.
Nevertheless, pronounced regional variations in the relative importance of office
employment remain. In urban cores the contribution of office employment ranged
from 36.1% in the South East to 22.3% in the North in 1971. The West Midlands is
particularly noticeable for its low proportion of office workers, a position which
worsened relative to the national average between 1966 and 1971. Significantly,
regions which experienced the most rapid total employment growth during this period
(the South West and East Anglia) by 1971 ranked second and third behind the South
East in terms of the relative importance of office jobs in the employment structure
of urban cores.

TABLE 2.16   Proportion in Office Employment by Urban Zone
and Region, 1966 and 1971

	Urban Core		Metropolitan Ring		Outer Metropolitan Ring	
	1966	1971	1966	1971	1966	1971
South East	33.1	36.1	21.7	25.2	19.0	21.0
West Midlands	23.1	23.9	16.8	19.3	14.4	16.4
East Midlands	22.3	25.5	13.3	15.3	14.2	16.6
East Anglia	24.3	27.3	11.6	14.8	11.8	15.3
South West	25.3	28.1	17.1	20.1	15.3	17.4
Yorkshire and Humberside	20.5	23.5	13.4	14.9	12.6	14.2
North West	23.6	25.7	16.8	19.6	15.6	18.3
North	21.0	22.3	13.8	18.4	11.7	14.4
Wales	24.1	25.7	17.0	17.3	13.2	14.2
Scotland	22.8	25.5	12.7	15.4	13.3	14.5

While office employment became relatively more important in metropolitan rings
during this period the contrast between the South East and other regions in this
zone remained, while in outer rings outside the South East the variation in office
employment proportions between regions remained relatively small. In fact in several regions the contrast between metropolitan rings and outer rings in office employment in proportions is small but with both levels sometimes ten percentage points
below that in urban cores. Limited regional variations in these proportions in the
outer urban zones suggest there is possibly a minimum level of office employment
necessary to support the residential and industrial activities of these areas with
regional variations being more typical of urban cores where higher order functions
tend to be located.

Differential growth rates in office employment over the period 1966-1971 need to
be seen in the light of the above observations, (Table 2.17). Urban cores in

TABLE 2.17   Office Employment Change by Urban Zone and
          Region, 1966-71. Absolute (000's) and Percent

	Urban Core		Metropolitan Ring		Outer Metropolitan Ring	
	Abs	%	Abs	%	Abs	%
South East	93.83	15.2	93.25	21.4	19.59	15.5
West Midlands	8.39	2.3	19.42	21.1	7.12	19.2
East Midlands	15.74	10.0	7.07	19.4	4.86	14.4
East Anglia	12.67	18.7	6.49	34.0	6.26	22.6
South West	15.15	9.0	8.71	22.9	8.67	13.8
Yorkshire and Humberside	14.45	4.8	6.24	9.2	3.46	7.6
North West	11.15	2.3	26.19	20.7	5.51	7.9
North	2.69	1.7	11.64	37.4	6.21	19.0
Wales	4.37	5.5	4.49	18.5	1.77	4.8
Scotland	15.06	5.3	10.81	22.1	4.70	11.6

assisted areas, already with the lowest proportions of their employment in office
jobs in 1966, experienced the smallest relative increases during the next five
years. Thus urban cores in the North recorded only a 1.7% increase in office employment compared with a 15.2% increase in urban cores in the South East. The West
Midlands is again noticeable for a low growth of core office employment (2.3%).
In part, this relatively poor growth in urban cores in regions like the North and
North West was compensated for by major increases in office employment in metropolitan rings (37.4% and 20.7% amounting to 11,640 and 26,190 extra jobs in each
region respectively). The West Midlands also gained 19,000 additional office jobs
in metropolitan rings. So even in parts of the country with a relatively poor
overall employment growth during the latter part of the 1960s major increases in
office employment were occurring, but significantly in metropolitan rings rather
than urban cores.

In considering industrial structure, even at the order level, at scales less than
the national the sheer volume of data is difficult to present and comprehend. Some
selectivity is essential. Tables 2.18 and 2.19 list the regional employment change
undifferentiated by urban zone for the full list of industrial classification orders
The heavy declines in primary employment (agriculture and mining), specified previously nationally, are apparent across all regions. Scotland's absolute and relative decline in the agricultural workforce is particularly noteworthy. The decline
in mining and quarrying is significant for all regions save the three most southern,
but the North with a loss of 41 thousand jobs, roughly 40% of the mining workforce,
has been especially significant.

Manufacturing employment change regionally must again reflect national performance
in the main. Employment in chemicals and allied industries grew in all regions but
it was only in the South East that an impressive relative gain of 8.5% reflected
important absolute growth (13,000). In Wales and the South West only 4,000 and
3,000 jobs respectively increased employment in this activity by 20 and 30%. The
regional performances of employment in engineering and electrical goods are interesting for they show the regional concentration of decline into the North West, the

TABLE 2.18   Employment Change by Economic Planning Region, 1966-1971   (Absolute 000's)

	Scotland	North	North West	Yorkshire & Humberside	East Midlands	West Midlands	Wales	East Anglia	South East	South West
Agriculture, forestry, fishing	-15	-3	-9	-9	-7	-8	-2	-14	-22	-8
Mining and quarrying	-14	-41	-17	-30	-17	-16	-22	-0	-0	-2
Food, drink and tobacco	4	4	-2	-2	1	-2	-3	2	-20	-0
Chemicals & allied industries	0	1	4	2	1	0	4	1	13	3
Metal manufacture	-4	-1	-6	-10	0	-8	-9	-0	-3	1
Engineering & electrical goods	3	2	-17	1	3	-8	12	3	-21	10
Shipbuilding & marine engineering	-7	-4	-0	-0	-1	2	-1	0	9	4
Vehicles	-4	-1	3	-2	-3	2	6	4	-20	-3
Metal goods	-0	0	-3	-8	1	-19	-3	1	-11	-1
Textiles	-15	0	-51	-41	-10	-7	-1	-0	-5	-2
Leather, leather goods & fur	-0	2	-2	0	0	-1	-0	0	-3	-1
Clothing and footwear	2	0	-12	-4	-6	-2	0	-1	-23	-2
Bricks, pottery, glass, cement etc.	-0	1	-4	0	-2	-6	-1	0	-1	-1
Timber, furniture etc.	1	1	-4	-1	2	-1	2	3	-9	2
Paper, printing and publishing	-6	0	2	-0	1	1	1	2	-6	1
Other manufacturing industries	-2	1	-1	2	1	3	-0	1	-4	2
Construction	-22	-11	-25	-22	-10	-23	-0	-1	-78	-11
Gas, electricity and water	-4	-3	-7	-4	-1	-4	-0	-1	-18	-4
Transport and communications	-10	-5	-18	-7	-1	-4	-5	0	14	-2
Distributive trades	-30	-17	-41	-23	-7	-14	-8	0	-78	-2
Insurance, banking and finance	7	3	7	2	3	4	3	2	45	4
Professional and scientific services	31	23	47	42	23	36	16	17	133	23
Miscellaneous services	-3	-4	-15	2	2	-5	1	0	-50	-3
Public administration and defence	20	10	27	9	6	18	6	0	58	1
Industry inadequately described	5	4	12	7	5	10	3	2	45	5
Total in employment*	-63	-36	-137	-95	-16	-56	-1	21	-63	14

* Rounding differences

TABLE 2.19 Employment Change by Economic Planning Region, 1966-1971 (Percent)

	Scotland	North	North West	Yorkshire & Humberside	East Midlands	West Midlands	Wales	East Anglia	South East	South West
Agriculture, forestry, fishing	-24.4	-10.7	-8.8	-4.3	-20.7	-13.2	-13.4	-17.5	-13.4	-12.3
Mining and quarrying	-28.1	-39.9	-42.7	-22.7	-23.5	-32.8	-32.2	8.1	-1.5	-23.4
Food, drink and tobacco	4.9	13.2	-2.3	-2.1	2.0	-3.7	-17.9	6.9	-9.8	-0.5
Chemicals & allied industries	0.7	1.4	3.4	4.6	6.3	1.9	20.8	13.6	8.5	30.0
Metal manufacture	-7.4	-1.1	-10.6	-8.2	0.8	-6.0	-12.1	-4.2	-5.9	17.4
Engineering & electrical goods	1.8	1.3	-5.6	0.6	2.3	-2.8	25.2	5.0	-2.7	10.6
Shipbuilding & marine engineering	-14.5	-10.7	-0.6	-1.1	-69.4	186.3	-48.9	13.0	28.8	44.6
Vehicles	-8.7	-10.6	2.9	-4.1	-5.3	-1.0	37.8	30.2	-8.2	-5.3
Metal goods	-1.7	0.1	-3.6	-10.6	6.6	-9.8	-13.5	33.8	-8.3	-6.7
Textiles	-21.1	11.5	-23.9	-23.8	-9.6	-13.7	13.3	-1.0	-13.8	-16.0
Leather, leather goods & fur	-11.1	11.6	-16.2	0.7	3.8	-15.3	-22.6	0.9	-15.1	-23.7
Clothing and footwear	5.4	2.9	-12.3	-7.2	-9.1	-6.1	0.9	-4.0	-15.0	-10.7
Bricks, pottery, glass, cement etc.	-1.4	4.4	-8.0	1.6	-12.5	-7.8	-18.7	5.0	-11.4	-12.8
Timber, furniture etc.	3.0	1.1	5.6	-3.2	17.7	-5.0	31.3	30.0	-7.1	10.5
Paper, printing and publishing	-10.5	6.7	-1.3	-1.1	6.2	2.3	15.9	13.9	-2.1	2.3
Other manufacturing industries	-12.4	20.0	-14.7	17.1	3.7	5.2	-3.2	20.1	-3.4	11.5
Construction	-12.8	-10.5	-10.9	-13.5	-12.0	-13.8	-0.7	-2.1	-12.5	-10.0
Gas, electricity and water	-12.3	-13.1	-13.8	-11.1	-3.5	-10.2	-15.0	-5.7	-12.8	-13.1
Transport and communications	-7.5	-6.1	-8.2	-5.4	-1.4	-3.7	-9.2	0.9	2.2	-2.9
Distributive trades	-11.0	-9.9	-9.1	-7.7	-4.6	-5.0	-8.6	-0.1	-6.9	-1.2
Insurance, banking and finance	15.5	15.7	9.6	5.8	15.5	9.3	21.6	13.7	13.2	12.2
Professional and scientific services	13.8	18.7	15.5	20.4	22.6	16.9	21.4	25.1	14.2	15.6
Miscellaneous services	-1.7	-3.4	-4.8	1.0	1.6	-2.4	1.5	0.2	4.7	-1.8
Public administration and defence	19.9	13.9	21.3	9.7	10.6	19.1	13.4	0.2	10.1	1.0
Industry inadequately described	202.9	105.7	81.0	82.4	260.5	46.1	45.8	46.8	28.1	52.0
Total in employment*	-3.2	-2.8	-4.3	-4.2	-1.3	-2.3	-0.1	3.1	-0.8	1.1

* Rounding differences

West Midlands and the South East. Elsewhere in the country and especially Wales
and the South West some important gains in these activities are clear, perhaps indicating some evidence of successful regional policy inducements. Wales is similarly
successful in gaining employment in vehicles manufacture. Other features of manufacturing employment change include the useful gains, although small, in all industries except clothing and footwear in East Anglia. Manufacturing performance in the
South East can be similarly compared to the dismal performance in the industrial
heartland of England - the West and East Midlands, the North West and Yorkshire and
Humberside. Engineering, vehicles and clothing all recorded significant losses in
the South East, the decline of metal goods employment was particularly important in
the West Midlands, and heavy losses in textiles (over 100,000 jobs in total) dominated the other three regions. The employment change in Scottish manufacturing industry was not dissimilar to these last group of regions, the 21% decline in textiles,
(15,000 jobs) being particularly important. The construction industry declined in
all regions of the country, with only two regions, Wales and East Anglia, having
losses of employment lower than 10%.

The growth of the office sector has already been detailed and Tables 2.18 and 2.19
show this well by industrial classification order. Almost ubiquitous regional employment losses are shown in non office based services such as the utilities, transport, distribution and miscellaneous services. Ubiquitous employment gains on the
other hand are found in insurance, banking and finance, professional and scientific
services and public administration. In absolute terms for this latter office based
group of services, the largest gains of course accrue to the South East but in relative terms most of the regions do equally as well if not better.

To illustrate some of the intra urban trends at the regional scale a selection of
orders from the industrial classification are shown in Table 2.20. The core areas
of the nation being the prime employment centres of course reflect both the aggregate national and regional dimensions of change. If anything it would be expected
that they would exhibit more pronounced trends, especially for certain of the selected industries. In engineering and electrical goods the job losses from urban
cores in the North West and West Midlands were well over 20,000 in each, rates of
decline approximating 10%. In these two regions as a whole the overall decline
amounted to only 25,000 jobs reflecting change rates of -5.6% and -2.8% in each
respectively (Tables 2.18 and 2.19). In the South East the trend of decline in
this sector in the urban core is even more intense with a loss of 40,300 jobs
(-7.7%). Recall that the total comparable regional figures amounted to only half
this loss, at much less than half the rate of decline. The picture of decline for
textiles indicates that the location of this activity was not solely in the core
areas. Declines of almost 26,000 jobs in each of the North West, and Yorkshire and
Humberside core regions leaves considerable job losses to come from the other urban
zones to make up the regional totals of over 50,000 and 40,000 respectively. In
other manufacturing employment core employment performance, although not everywhere
in decline, has usually been inferior to the aggregate regional performance. Turning
next to selected service activity in core areas. Distribution being traditionally
a core located service has suffered drastic losses in core areas and in the main
these have usually accounted for almost the whole of the total regional decline.
The converse picture is illustrated by the pattern of employment change in insurance,
banking and finance. This is a traditional core located service, but a fast growing
one. In the South East and Scotland the cores have achieved the major slice of the
total regional growth. Elsewhere the core areas seem to have gained no more than
their share of growth in this activity. Lastly, employment in professional and
scientific services, although in the main core located over all regions, and growing
in this zone, rarely achieves more than about 60% of total absolute regional growth.

The pattern of change in the metropolitan rings of the regions complements the above
trends described for urban cores. While only two core zones in the regions actually

TABLE 2.20 Selected Employment Change by Economic Planning Region and Urban Zone, 1966-1971
(Absolute 000's)

Urban Cores	Scotland	North	North West	Yorkshire & Humberside	East Midlands	West Midlands	Wales	East Anglia	South East	South West
Engineering & electrical goods	-4.7	-9.1	-23.9	-0.6	-0.7	-21.3	3.3	-1.2	-40.3	2.3
Textiles	-11.9	-3.1	-25.9	-25.9	-10.3	-6.0	0.3	-0.4	-4.3	-1.4
Other manufacturing industries	-4.4	0.7	-11.9	0.8	-0.2	-1.6	-1.4	1.8	-7.7	0.9
Distributive trades	-29.2	-13.6	-39.6	-20.1	-6.9	-19.1	-6.3	-0.2	-79.7	-4.5
Insurance, banking & finance	5.2	1.2	3.5	1.4	2.4	1.4	1.5	1.1	32.1	1.7
Professional & scientific services	21.8	12.4	27.3	27.1	11.2	21.9	8.4	10.1	75.4	12.9
Metropolitan Rings										
Engineering & electrical goods	2.2	5.7	3.6	3.2	1.8	8.3	3.3	2.7	9.9	4.3
Textiles	-1.4	1.4	-12.1	-11.5	1.1	-0.7	0.1	0.0	-1.0	-0.0
Other manufacturing industries	2.0	1.7	2.5	1.5	0.7	2.9	1.0	-0.9	1.2	0.9
Distributive trades	0.8	0.4	3.3	-0.0	1.1	5.0	0.2	-0.1	3.8	1.7
Insurance, banking & finance	0.5	0.5	3.1	0.8	0.5	1.5	0.6	0.3	9.5	0.6
Professional & scientific services	5.6	6.2	13.5	9.5	6.6	11.8	3.4	4.0	47.3	4.1
Outer Metropolitan Rings										
Engineering & electrical goods	5.4	4.9	3.4	-1.6	1.7	4.6	3.8	1.1	9.4	3.7
Textiles	-2.0	3.6	-12.8	-3.8	-0.8	0.0	0.7	0.3	0.3	-0.8
Other manufacturing industries	0.5	0.1	0.6	0.2	0.1	1.2	-0.1	0.5	2.7	-0.5
Distributive trades	-1.5	-3.8	-4.9	-2.8	-0.9	0.2	-2.7	0.2	-2.1	1.0
Insurance, banking & finance	0.9	1.5	0.3	0.3	0.3	1.0	0.8	0.6	3.9	1.0
Professional & scientific services	3.6	4.2	6.2	5.7	5.2	2.7	3.9	3.0	10.8	5.2

gained employment in engineering industries, all ring zones achieved growth. Additionally all regional ring zones, save for East Anglia, grew in other manufacturing industry employment. The situation as expected was not the same for textiles, with metropolitan ring zones contributing important dimensions of decline to regional totals. Employment in distributive trades is interesting in the metropolitan rings for in all regions, except again for East Anglia and marginally in Yorkshire and Humberside, job gains were recorded. This runs counter to aggregate regional trends and is in complete contrast to the massive job losses in core areas. Distribution certainly seems to have followed the decentralisation of the urban population. Job growth in insurance banking and finance, and professional and scientific services is clearly apparent in the metropolitan rings of all regions. In absolute terms (as well as percentage terms) the gains made by the latter order in the rings of the regions are especially impressive.

No less impressive are the total employment gains in professional and scientific services in the outer metropolitan rings. The same can be said for job growth in this zone in the engineering industry, except for Yorkshire and Humberside. In general the same sort of trends which are being experienced by the metropolitan rings are also taking place in the outer zone. The notable exception is of course employment in distribution which is for the most part in decline in this zone across the nation.

Overall then it can be seen in this short section that the total employment trends that characterise urban change in British regions reflect the outcomes of the changing fortunes of a variety of economic activities in a variety of locations.

Socio-economic structure

The principal determinant of changes in the socio-economic composition of the British Economic Planning Regions is the changing occupational structure of the regions. The analysis at the national scale indicated an overall decline in the numbers and proportions of economically active males in the semi- and unskilled manual occupations and a considerable increase in the professional, managerial and non-manual occupations. These changes reflect the growth of technologically based industries and the service sector of the British economy at the expense of heavy industrial manufacturing. In consequence, those regions which experienced general increases in employment should also display increases in these rapidly growing high status occupations; alternatively, those regions which experienced declines in employment should display the greatest losses in the rapidly declining low status occupations.

The percentage changes of the four socio-economic groups within MELAs summed to Economic Planning Region level (Table 2.21) provide striking confirmation of these expectations. In the case of professional and managerial occupations all the regions with above average increases - the South East, South West, East Anglia and West Midlands - experienced percentage increases in employment between 1961 and 1971, while the regions with below average increases in professional and managerial occupations, - Yorkshire and Humberside, North West, the Northern region, Wales and Scotland - all experienced either declines or small increases in employment. Scotland, however, has a larger percentage increase in professional and managerial occupations than might be expected given the general employment fortunes of the region between 1961 and 1971.

The percentage changes of the intermediate non-manual occupations broadly conform with the 'north-south' division but the dispersions from the national average are not as clear cut as in the case of the professional and managerial occupations. The North and Yorkshire and Humberside both have above average increases in this group (8.7 and 5.4% respectively) while the increase in the South East (4.6%) is just below the national average. The outstanding percentage increase of intermediate non-manual occupations was in East Anglia (16.2%) and this may reflect decen-

TABLE 2.21 Socio-Economic Group Change by Region, 1961-1971.
Absolute (000's), Percent and Extreme Percentage Increase by
Urban Zone - Cores (C), Rings (R) and Outer Rings (OR).

	Professional and Managerial		Intermediate non-manual		Skilled Manual		Semi and unskilled manual	
	Abs	%	Abs	%	Abs	%	Abs	%
South East	230	26.3 OR	49	4.6 OR	-81	-4.4 OR	-177	-14.7 OR
West Midlands	47	22.7 R	21	9.6 R	-19	-2.7 OR	-36	-8.4 R
East Midlands	24	24.9 R	13	11.8 R	3	0.8 R	-32	-15.5 C
East Anglia	15	22.7 R	10	16.2 R	16	10.2 OR	-14	-9.8 C
South West	33	26.4 R	15	10.4 R	6	1.9 R	-26	-11.8 R
Yorkshire & Humberside	23	12.2 R	11	5.4 R	-22	-3.3 R	-84	-18.7 C
North West	44	15.8 R	-2	-0.5 R	-54	-6.2 R	-86	-14.2 R
Northern	14	13.9 R	11	8.7 R	-17	-4.3 R	-65	-23.0 C
Wales	7	11.1 R	3	3.8 R	-3	-1.4 R	-43	-23.7 C
Scotland	30	18.5 R	-9	-4.0 R	-58	-10.3 R	-60	-15.3 R
Britain *	467	20.5	124	4.7	-217	-3.7	-649	-15.1

* includes unclassified areas

ralisation policies which have attempted to divert office growth from the congested
South East region.

The percentage changes in skilled manual workers are again differentiated along a
north-south continuum and range from -10.3% in Scotland to an increase of 10.2% in
East Anglia. Regions of poor economic performance experienced declines in skilled
manual workers while the relatively prosperous regional economies of the South experienced increases or only small percentage declines in this group. The major exception to this pattern is the South East which has a relatively large decrease
(-4.4%) below the national average. Once again, this seems likely to reflect decentralisation policies which have diverted growth into the surrounding regions of
East Anglia and the South West.

All the regions display percentage decreases in semi- and unskilled manual workers.
Nationally,there was a decrease of -15.1% and this varied from -23.7% in Wales to
-8.4% in the West Midlands. With the exception of the North West, all the regions
with decreases less than the national average are located in 'southern' regions
while regions with decreases above the national average are in the 'northern'
regions. This pattern should be interpreted carefully for unemployment was much
greater in 1971 than 1961. Nevertheless, the strength and consistency of the
patterns would suggest that the differential impact of unemployment is unlikely to
be a complete explanation for the regional patterns of change. Furthermore, since
much of this unemployment would seem to reflect a long term decline in the heavy
industrial base of the northern regions, rather than merely the temporary effects
of a recession, it does signify important structural changes in the British economy
and its social status structure.

The absolute magnitude of these changes within the four socio-economic groups within Economic Planning Regions are also shown in Table 2.21. The most striking feature of the professional and managerial group is the enormous increase of 230,000 in the South East, which represents almost half of the total national increase in this group during the period 1961 to 1971. All the other regions have much smaller increases, the largest being in the industrial regions of the West Midlands, and the North West. The increases are much smaller in the case of intermediate non manual workers but the South East again has the largest increase in this group. The North West and Scotland are the only two regions to experience declines in this group. In direct contrast to the previous groups, the South East has the largest decline in skilled manual workers. Scotland and the North West also recorded large declines in this group but, in sharp contrast to its neighbours, the Northern region experienced a relatively large increase in skilled manual workers. Semi- and unskilled manual workers declined rapidly in all regions. The largest decrease in this group was again in the South East but the remainder of the large decreases are concentrated in the regions of relatively high unemployment and poor economic performance.

Finally, this section considers regional variations in social group structure. The proportions in the four socio-economic groups within MELAs aggregated into Economic Planning Regions reveal a consistent pattern (Table 2.22). The southern regions of the South East, South West, East Anglia, West Midlands and East Midlands all tend to have larger proportions of professional, managerial and intermediate non-manual workers and smaller proportions of skilled, semi-skilled and unskilled manual workers. The northern regions of Yorkshire and Humberside, the North West, North, Wales and Scotland have smaller proportions of the high status groups and relatively larger proportions of lower status occupations.

If this information structure is combined with the data concerning changes, then clear relationships emerge. The higher status professional and managerial groups have grown most rapidly, in both relative and absolute terms, in the regions in which they were already most prevalent - the South East and southern England in general. Conversely, the low status semi- and unskilled manual occupations have declined at the fastest rate in the northern or 'peripheral' regions in which they were most numerous. The major exception to this second pattern is the South East for, despite a relatively high status social structure, this area has the largest absolute (though not relative) decline in manual occupations. This is likely to reflect considerable intra-regional variations amongst urban areas within the South East region and these are examined later.

The aggregate intra-urban changes revealed a pattern of decentralisation; absolutely for the skilled manual and intermediate non-manual and relatively for the professional and managerial. There was a more uncertain pattern of decentralisation in decline for the semi- and unskilled manual. The aggregate regional changes have shown the importance of the north-south distinction with the largest increases or smallest decreases in the south, with the exception of the South East. These two themes also dominate the regional intra-urban changes which are considered here.

Table 2.21 also summarises the centralisation - decentralisation trends by highlighting the zone in each area for each group with the largest percentage increase 1961-1971. For the professional and managerial and intermediate non-manual occupations there are simple patterns; the largest percentage increases are in the rings in all regions except the South East, where the increase in the outer rings is greater. Decentralisation of these two groups therefore occurs in all regions. This is relative decentralisation of the professional and managerial in all regions except the North West and Yorkshire-Humberside, where there is absolute decentralisation. Decentralisation of the intermediate non-manual group is absolute in all cases for there are not increases in this group in the cores of any region. The same applies to the skilled manual for whom there is also absolute decentralisation

TABLE 2.22   Socio-Economic Group Structure by Region, 1971.
Percent and Extreme Proportions by Urban Zone - Cores (C),
Rings (R) and Outer Rings (OR)

	Professional and managerial		Intermediate non-manual		Skilled manual		Semi and unskilled manual	
South East	21.3	R	21.3	C	33.7	OR	19.8	C
West Midlands	15.6	R	14.8	R	43.4	C	23.9	C
East Midlands	15.2	R	15.8	R	44.3	OR	21.7	C
East Anglia	17.0	R	14.9	C	36.4	C	25.6	OR
South West	17.9	R	17.7	C	37.0	C	21.8	OR
Yorkshire & Humberside	14.4	R	14.9	C	43.9	OR	24.4	C
North West	15.7	R	16.7	R	39.9	OR	25.4	C
Northern	12.9	R	15.3	R	43.8	OR	25.2	C
Wales	13.1	R	15.2	C	43.5	OR	25.4	OR
Scotland	14.9	R	16.6	C	39.7	R	25.9	OR
Britain	17.3		17.7		38.8		22.9	

Range of Percentages in	) Cores) Rings) Outer Rings	11.1 - 17.8 16.3 - 27.3 10.3 - 21.2	34.7 - 45.0 31.8 - 44.5 35.4 - 47.4	34.7 - 45.0 31.8 - 44.5 35.4 - 47.4	22.0 - 28.7 16.3 - 25.1 21.2 - 28.0

in all regions. However, the greatest percentage increases for this group are in
the outer ring in the West Midlands, East Anglia and the South West. Therefore, at
least in terms of cores and rings, the national patterns of decentralisation are
repeated in the individual regions for these three groups.

For the semi- and unskilled manual there is a more diverse pattern with centralisation and decentralisation observed although with decreases in number in all the
zones. The centralisation - decentralisation pattern does not follow a simple
north-south regional distinction. Note, also, that in the South West and South
East the smallest percentage decrease was in the outer rings.

There was certainly uniformity in the decentralisation of all socio-economic groups
except the semi- and unskilled manual. Do the differences in the strength of decentralisation vary according to the north-south regional distinction? Consider
the percentage changes in the two most different groups, the professional and managerial, and the semi- and unskilled manual. For both groups in both cores and
rings the largest increases or smallest decreases are in the southern regions of
East Anglia, South West, West Midlands, East Midlands and, to a lesser extent, the
South East. The smallest increases or largest decreases are in Wales, the North
and Yorkshire-Humberside. The changes in the outer rings are more varied but, as
expected, the increase in the South East outer rings is of a similar magnitude to
that of the rings in the other regions. Also, the largest decreases or smaller
increases in the outer rings are in Wales, Scotland, the North and Yorkshire-
Humberside.

Therefore, in terms of the changes between 1961 and 1971 two dominant themes can be identified. There is decentralisation from cores to rings in all regions for the three higher status groups, but the largest increases or decreases are in the south, reflecting the known regional distinction in employment and wealth in Britain. The South East region is the main exception having relatively large increases in the outer rings, which is in accordance with the known population decentralisation in Britain.

Are these intra-urban and regional patterns repeated in the socio-economic compos-ition of zones? These features are summarised in Table 2.22. The summary range statistics indicate that, as with age groups, the greatest difference in composition is in the rings. In this zone, professional and managerial and, to a lesser extent, intermediate non-manual occupations are relatively more important, and the manual groups are relatively less important than in the cores and outer rings. This con-firms the higher status composition of this zone in the individual regions. It also confirms that, overall, there were no startling differences in the social com-position of the urban zones of regional level.

What are the patterns within individual regions? For professional and managerial occupations the largest percentages are in the rings and the smallest percentages are in the cores in all regions. Certainly for the highest status group, the rings are relatively the most important residential areas. There is a more diverse patt-ern for intermediate non-manual occupations with the largest proportions being in the cores or rings (with no adherence to the north-south regional distinction). For the manual occupational groups the most distinctive feature is that the smallest proportion in most regions is in the ring, that is, the expected corollary of the large proportion of non-manual groups in these zones. Otherwise, the largest prop-ortions are in the cores or outer rings but not in conformity with a north-south or any other simple regional distinction.

In terms of polarisation, therefore, there is little evidence that by 1971 regions had become greatly polarised by zones. Certainly the proportions in the highest status groups were greatest in the rings in all regions but this was not yet greatly different from the levels in other zones and was also not matched by the lowest status groups consistently having the largest proportions in the cores in all reg-ions. The changes between 1961 and 1971, however, did indicate a tendency towards polarisation with the increases in the highest status groups in all regions being greatest in the rings. However, although the lowest status groups were decreasing in number in all the cores the evidence for polarisation was not clear. This group fell in number in all zones and regions and only in some regions were the decreases in the cores greater than in the rings. The South East was an exception to this pattern for the largest increases in all zones were in the outer rings – further evidence of the decentralisation of population to the outer zone rather than to the rings in this region.

Age structure

This section considers patterns of change in the four age groups within MELAs agg-regated to Economic Planning Regions. Changes in the distribution of age groups at this scale will result from two main factors; natural change (the net outcome of births and deaths in a region) and net migration (the net effect of inmigration and outmigration in an area). However while regional variations in rates of natural increase are relatively small, there are considerable differences in rates of net migration. Scotland, Wales, the Northern region and Yorkshire and Humberside all recorded an average net loss of population due to migration while other regions gained population through net migration. Conventional wisdom asserts that migrat-ion at the inter-regional scale is primarily determined by variations in economic opportunity and would suggest the existence of strong relationships between overall employment change and age structure change. However, a major exception should arise in the case of the above pensionable age groups whose retirement migration should be primarily determined by environmental consideration.

The percentage changes in the four age groups in MELAs summed to Economic Planning Region level generally support these expectations (see Table 2.23). It is partic- ularly instructive to consider the regional values for each age group in relation to the national average change for each group at the foot of the columns. The 0 to 14 and 15 to 29 age groups display general conformity to the overall pattern of population and employment change in the regions. The regions with generally above average increases in these groups - the South West, South East, East Anglia, West Midlands and East Midlands - all have what might be termed southern or 'central' locations, while those regions with generally below average increases - Wales, Yorkshire and Humberside, the North West, the North and Scotland - all have what might be termed northern or peripheral locations. Although the majority of regions had percentage declines in the 30 years to pensionable age groups, reflecting the national decline in this group between 1961 and 1971, the relative differences bet- ween these decreases once again reflect the north-south division. Regions with either increases, or decreases below the national average for this group are all located in the relatively prosperous southern half of the country; alternatively regions with decreases in this group greater than the national percentage decrease all occupy locations in areas traditionally characterised by chronic unemployment. As predicted, the above pensionable age group is remarkable for its lack of align- ment with the percentage changes revealed by the other groups. There is no clear north-south pattern but the regions with largest percentage increases are East Anglia and the South West. These are both substantially non-industrial regions with attractive environments and this would seem to reflect the impact of retire- ment migration.

TABLE 2.23   Age Group Change by Region, 1961-1971.   Absolute (000's), Percent and Extreme Percentage Increases by Urban Zone - Cores (C), Rings (R) and Outer Rings (OR)

	0 - 14			15 - 29			30 to pen- sionable age			Pensionable age and above		
	Abs	%		Abs	%		Abs	%		Abs	%	
South East	378	10.6	OR	527	16.6	OR	-292	-4.1	OR	374	14.8	OR
West Midlands	161	13.8	R	132	13.2	R	-34	-1.6	R	124	19.7	R
East Midlands	86	14.9	R	96	20.4	R	-13	-1.3	R	67	19.4	R
East Anglia	41	12.1	R	58	20.0	R	18	3.0	R	55	23.6	R
South West	82	12.7	R	100	18.5	R	4	0.3	R	105	22.2	OR
Yorkshire and Humberside	82	7.1	R	110	11.7	R	-128	-6.1	R	114	16.3	R
North West	121	7.4	R	161	12.5	R	-221	-7.5	R	137	13.4	R
Northern	-5	-0.6	R	48	8.4	R	-76	-6.1	R	64	16.4	R
Wales	15	3.4	R	35	9.8	R	-51	-6.4	R	42	16.5	R
Scotland	21	1.9	R	60	6.7	R	-130	-7.2	R	109	19.4	R
Britain*	981	8.6		1,327	13.9		-993	-4.4		1,192	16.7	

*includes unclassified areas

The absolute changes in the four age groups reveal a pattern broadly similar to that observed previously for total population. The 0 to 14, 15 to 29 and above pensionable age groups all have the largest absolute increases in the main indust- rial corridor of Britain extending from the South East, through the West and East Midlands, to the North West. The 30 years to pensionable age group is the major exception to this pattern for, apart from East Anglia and the South West, all reg- ions have decreases in this group. These decreases were largest in the South East, North West and to a lesser extent in Yorkshire and Humberside. The rows of this table are particularly interesting for they indicate the contribution made by the age groups to the overall population change in the regions. In the case of Scotland, the North, Yorkshire and Humberside, Wales and the South West, the above pensionable age group makes the largest contribution to the overall population increase. How- ever, the above pensionable age group makes a much smaller contribution to the over- all population increase in the South East, East Anglia, West Midlands, East Midlands and North West. Although the South West and East Anglia appear attractive to those of retirement age, the population growth of these regions results from increases in all age groups.

Although conceptually distinct, natural change and net migration are frequently related. Younger, child bearing age groups tend to be the most mobile, and areas with high rates of inmigration therefore often have younger age structures and high rates of natural increase. Alternatively areas with high rates of outmigration tend to have residual populations of older age groups. The major exceptions to this trend are the seaside resorts with high rates of retirement inmigration. However, at the regional scale no such relationships emerge with any consistency (see Table 2.24). Scotland and the Northern region have rather young age structures, but as noted previously, high rates of outmigration while the South East, East Anglia and the South West have extremely old age structures but high rates of inmigration.

TABLE 2.24   Age Group Structure by Region, 1971. Percent
and Extreme Proportions by Urban Zone - Cores (C), Rings (R)
and Outer Rings (OR)

	0 – 14		15 – 29		30 to pens- ionable age		Pensionable age and above.	
South East	22.7	R	21.4	C	39.1	R	16.7	OR
West Midlands	25.0	R	21.5	R	39.4	R	14.2	OR
East Midlands	24.7	R	21.4	C	38.6	R	15.4	OR
East Anglia	23.0	OR	21.2	C	38.2	R	17.6	OR
South West	23.1	R	20.5	C	37.9	R	18.5	OR
Yorkshire & Humberside	24.4	R	20.7	C	38.8	R	16.1	C
North West	24.7	R	20.5	C	38.3	R	16.4	OR
Northern	25.0	C	20.8	C	39.0	R	15.2	OR
Wales	24.0	R	20.6	C	39.5	OR	16.0	OR
Scotland	26.1	R	21.3	C	37.7	R	14.9	OR
Britain	24.0		21.1		38.8		16.1	

Range of Percentages		0 – 14	15 – 29	30 to pens-ionable age	Pensionable age and above
	)Cores	21.8 – 25.6	20.8 – 23.1	37.2 – 39.2	14.5 – 18.1
	)Rings	23.8 – 28.0	19.9 – 21.5	38.4 – 40.1	12.7 – 17.2
	)Outer Rings	22.9 – 26.0	19.4 – 21.7	37.1 – 39.9	15.6 – 20.2

These results largely reflect the scale of analysis for the Economic Planning Regi
conceals many intra regional variations. However, these patterns also reflect a
complex interplay between age structure, natural increase, employment fortunes, ne
migration and population change. An attempt is made to summarise these relationships in Table 2.25.

TABLE 2.25   Relationships Between Age Structure, Natural
Increase, Relative Employment Change, Net Migration and
Population Change by Region, 1961-1971.

	Age Structure	Natural Increase Rate	Percentage Employment Change	Net Migration Rate	Percentage Population Change
South East	'Old'	High	Increase	Large increase	Increase
West Midlands	'Young'	High	Increase	Increase	Increase
East Midlands	'Young'	High	Increase	Increase	Increase
East Anglia	'Old'	Low	Large increase	Large increase	Large increase
South West	'Old'	Low	Large increase	Large increase	Large increase
Yorkshire & Humberside	'Normal'	Average	Decrease	Small decrease	Increase
North West	'Normal'	Low	Decrease	Increase	Small increase
Northern	'Young'	Average	Small increase	Large decrease	Small increase
Wales	'Normal'	Low	Increase	Small decrease	Increase
Scotland	'Young'	High	Large decrease	Large decrease	Small increase

In Scotland a young regional age structure gives rise to a high rate of natural
increase but there is an overall decline in employment leading to large net outmigration and only a small increase in total population. The northern region is
somewhat similar, for although the young age structure gives rise to an average
rate of natural increase, and there is in this case a small increase in employment
this region shares with Scotland a large rate of outmigration and, consequently, a
small increase in total population. The fortunes of Scotland and the North contra
sharply with the East and West Midlands which also have young age structures and
high rates of natural increase, but also have large percentage increases in employ
ment, resulting in net inmigration and much larger overall increases in population
Wales has a 'normal' regional age structure and a low rate of natural increase
coupled to an increase in employment. Consequently, despite a small rate of net
outmigration there is a substantial rate of overall population increase in this
region. The behaviour of the North West is rather more complex. This region shar
with Wales a normal age structure and low rate of natural increase but, despite a
decrease in employment, maintains a high rate of net inmigration. Similarly Yorkshire and Humberside has a decrease in employment but only a small decrease in net
migration. This could reflect the presence of overseas immigrants in these region
and this issue is considered in the next section. The South West and East Anglia
both have 'old' age structures and low rates of natural increase but in both regions this is counter-balanced by large percentage increases in employment, large
rates of inmigration and consequently large percentage increases in total populati

The relationships between employment growth and net immigration in these regions serve to reinforce the view that their total population growth is not solely the result of retirement migration. Finally, despite an old age structure the South East has a high rate of natural increase, an increase in percentage employment, net migration and total population. The association between the old age structure and high natural increase rate in this region reflects considerable differences between urban areas within this region.

The aggregate regional changes displayed a broad conformity with the north-south division of Britain for all age groups except the eldest. The national intra-urban changes revealed absolute decentralisation of the 0-14 groups, relative decentralisation of the 15-29 and above pensionable age groups, and decentralisation 'in decline' in both cores and rings in the 30 to pensionable age group. Did the regional or the intra-urban changes dominate the regional intra-urban patterns?

In all regions, with few exceptions, the largest percentage increases or the smallest percentage decreases were in the metropolitan rings. (see Table 2.23). This is striking evidence of the all-pervasive nature of decentralisation for all age groups in all regions. The main exception to the pattern was the South East where for all groups, the increases in the outer rings was greatest. This accords with the largest percentage increase in total population in this region being in the outer rings.

In fact, there is even greater uniformity in the urban changes within regions. In all regions, there were increases in the rings in all age groups and decreases in the cores in the number of 30 to pensionable age. Also, there were increases in the cores in the 15-29 and above pensionable age groups in all regions except Scotland. Therefore, there was absolute decentralisation in the 30 to pensionable age group in all regions, and relative decentralisation of the 15-29 and above pensionable age groups in all regions except Scotland. There was a more diverse pattern for those aged 0-14.

Similar intra-urban changes can therefore be recognised in all regions, but does the strength of centralisation-decentralisation vary according to the north-south regional distinction? With few exceptions this is so, with the largest increases or smallest decreases being in the South East, East Anglia, South West, West Midlands and East Midlands. This is illustrated by considering the 15-29 and the 30 to pensionable age groups that is, the two groups with the largest increases and decreases, respectively. The increases in the rings are greater (or the decreases are less) than in the cores in all regions for both age groups. In fact, the smallest increase in the rings, in Yorkshire and Humberside, is greater than the largest increase (smallest decrease) in the cores, in East Anglia. The outer rings are less uniform; in some instances some of the changes in the outer rings are greater than in the rings but, in other cases, are less than in the cores. However, in individual regions the increases in the rings exceed those in the outer rings. The one exception, of course, is the South East where there were particularly large increases in both age groups, associated with the major decentralisation of population to this zone in the London MELA.

Both the intra-zonal and north-south regional distinction were evident in the changes. Is this also the case with age composition in 1971? Table 2.24 summarises the proportion of total population in each age group, by zone and region. The ranges of the percentages in each age group for the cores, rings and outer rings reveal little difference in the age composition of the zones, broken down by regions. The greatest differences appear in the rings where, in particular, there was a larger proportion aged 0-14 and a smaller proportion above pensionable age. Between 23.8 and 28.0% of the ring populations compared to 22.9 - 26.0% of the outer ring populations were aged 0-14. In contrast, only 12.7 and 17.2% of the populations in rings as against 15.6 to 20.2% of the outer ring populations were over pensionable age. Therefore, the age composition of the urban zones, broken down by regions, are remarkably uniform.

Considering the regions individually, in most cases the largest proportions in the 0-14 and 30 to pensionable age groups were in the rings, in the 15-29 group were in the cores and for those above pensionable age were in the outer rings. Therefore, in terms of the age composition of zones there is considerable uniformity between the regions. No simple interpretation of the patterns is possible; they reflect different rates of in and out-migration and of natural increase in each zone. Tentatively, it can be suggested that the large proportion above pensionable age in the outer rings may reflect the presence of many retirement centres in this zone. The large proportion of 15-29 year olds in the cores may be the result of the continued immigration of this group into the larger cities at a time of overall declin of population in these areas. Because of the dependence of young children on their parent's residential location it is not surprising that the largest proportions of the 0-14 and 30 to pensionable age groups are found together, that is, in the rings

Overall, there are simple patterns for these age groups with relatively little deviation from those of the population as a whole. The changes revealed decentralisation from the cores with the greatest percentage increases in the rings in all regions, except the South East, while the age composition of areas differed little between zones or regions. This is in marked contrast to the regional intra urban patterns of other socio economic characteristics.

Birthplace structure

The changing inter-regional distribution of overseas immigrants raises rather different considerations from those for age groups. These largely reflect the fact tha immigrants are an injection of persons into the system rather than merely the outcome of the rearrangement of the system's internal structure. Nevertheless, considerable pattern regularity is to be expected. It is commonly accepted that the post war immigration of West Indians, Indians and Pakistanis has served to fill spaces at the bottom of the occupational structure created by the growth of the British economy. Immigrants have thus concentrated in the areas of employment growth - the South East and West Midlands - and have avoided the peripheral regions of high unemployment such as Wales, Scotland, the North and North East. Immigrants have also tended to avoid the South West and East Anglia where a high rate of net immigration of British born persons, which appears to act as a barrier to overseas immigrants. Despite the restrictions imposed by the 1962 and 1965 Immigration Acts the spatial distribution of immigrants in Britain during the sixties is also likely to reflect the availability of employment opportunities. The existing pattern may also be reinforced by a tendency for later arrivals to locate in the same areas as initial migrants into a country. This would suggest that immigration into Britain in the sixties will have been concentrated in the areas in which there were already substantial numbers of immigrants at the beginning of the time period. A final consideration which may influence the aggregate distribution of immigrant groups is the length of residence in this country. Thus, longer established immigrant groups may be more likely to follow the patterns of population change of the indigenous population through their assimilation into the wider society. A word of caution is necessary, however, prior to the interpretation of the changing distribution of birthplace groups for it cannot directly be assumed that the regions of greatest increase have resulted from immigration during the sixties. It may be that later migrants are locating in the well established immigrant areas while olde migrants are moving to new regions. It is most probable that both types of process are in operation but where a large influx of immigrants in the sixties is associate with a relatively large increase in particular areas during the same time period this suggests strongly the impact of new groups. The following analysis concentrat es upon four of the important immigrant groups - the Irish, Indian sub-continent, African and West Indian migrants.

The percentage changes of these birthplace groups with MELAs aggregated to Economic Planning Region level (Table 2.26) provide strong support for the occupational replacement hypothesis but there are considerable differences between the immigrant groups. As expected, the patterns of change in the longer established Irish immigrant group follows closely the pattern of change for total population. There are percentage declines of Irish immigrants in the economically depressed regions of Scotland, Wales and the North, and while all other regions have percentage increases, these are especially large in the regions of high percentage employment growth – the South West and East Anglia.

The percentage changes of the Indian sub-continent immigrants are in general much greater, largely reflecting the small base numbers of these immigrants in some regions in 1961, but they also indicate a pattern of regional change somewhat different from the Irish. The regions of largest percentage growth include the West Midlands and East Midlands, with their percentage increases in employment, but also include two regions with percentage decreases in overall employment – the North West and Yorkshire and Humberside. These percentage increases in the last two regions provide strong support for the suggestion made in the discussion of age groups that the apparent discrepancy between employment decrease and net in-migration in the North West and Yorkshire and Humberside is largely accounted for by the influx of immigrants. In contrast, the South West and East Anglia have much smaller percentage increases in the Indian sub-continent group than would be expected by either their high percentage employment growth or net inmigration rate, suggesting that white immigration is forming a barrier to coloured immigrants in these regions. The percentage increases of the African immigrants are in general similar to the Indian sub-continent in their relative magnitude between the regions (apart from the East Midlands which has a smaller increase than might be expected) and in general provide additional support for the replacement and barrier hypotheses.

The percentage increases in West Indian immigrants are again relatively small in the economically depressed regions of Scotland, Wales and the North but, in contrast to the Indian sub-continent and African immigrants, the largest percentage increases of West Indians are in East Anglia and the South West.

In absolute change terms (Table 2.26) the general pattern for all immigrant groups is one of largest increases in the main urban and industrial regions of the South East, West Midlands, East Midlands, North West and Yorkshire and Humberside. The North West has a larger absolute increase in Irish immigrants than might be expected given the population size of the region and this no doubt reflects the large Irish communities in Liverpool and Manchester. The absolute increases of Indian sub-continent immigrants in Yorkshire and Humberside and the North West are 32,000 and 31,000 respectively, indicating that the large percentage increases in this group in these regions do reflect a considerable influx and are not merely the result of small numbers in 1961. The absolute increases in the African and West Indian groups are both heavily concentrated in the South East.

The contribution of all immigrant groups to the overall population increase in the ten Economic Planning regions is shown in Table 2.27. In the South East over half of the total population increase is composed of immigrants, a remarkable figure when it is considered that the absolute increase of all immigrants in this region far exceeds the absolute increase of immigrants in all other regions combined. Table 2.27 confirms that the absolute increases of population in Yorkshire and Humberside have been substantially increased by overseas immigrants, although in neither region is the proportion over half. The Northern region also has large percentage of its total population increase made up of immigrants but in this case the absolute number of immigrants is much smaller than either Yorkshire and Humberside or the North West. Smaller proportions of the total population increase are composed of immigrants in the West Midlands and East Midlands (29.9 and 22.0%

TABLE 2.26   Birthplace Group Change by Region, 1961-1971
Absolute (000's), Percent and Extreme Percentage Increase
by Urban Zone - Cores (C), Rings (R) and Outer Rings (OR)

	Irish		Indian sub-continent		African		West Indian	
	Abs	%	Abs	%	Abs	%	Abs	%
South East	22	5.3 OR	105	94.4 C	74	309.1 C	80	72.2 R
West Midlands	4	3.6 R	62	231.6 C	11	634.5 C	17	59.3 R
East Midlands	4	11.7 R	19	260.5 C	9	85.5 C	7	20.8 R
East Anglia	3	24.5 R	2	52.8 C	1	178.2 R	1	89.6 OR
South West	5	13.1 R	2	20.1 C	3	141.6 C	4	89.3 C
Yorkshire and Humberside	3	6.0 R	32	223.9 C	4	265.1 C	7	85.5 R
North West	7	5.7 R	31	235.4 C	8	253.0 C	6	68.7 R
Northern	-0	-1.5 R	2	44.2 C	1	138.6 R	0	31.7 OR
Wales	-1	-8.0 C	2	86.1 C	1	138.7 OR	1	41.2 OR
Scotland	-12	-17.1 OR	3	35.1 C	2	101.9 OR	0	19.2 OR
Britain*	35	3.8	260	125.3	116	296.4	123	71.3

	Other Commonwealth		Other Migrants		Great Britain		Total	
	Abs	%	Abs	%	Abs	%	Abs	%
South East	34	20.9 R	207	49.3 R	463	3.1 OR	987	6.1 OR
West Midlands	3	18.6 OR	18	35.5 R	267	5.7 R	384	7.8 R
East Midlands	2	22.9 OR	11	27.6 R	184	7.9 R	235	9.7 R
East Anglia	3	46.8 OR	6	13.8 C	156	11.1 R	172	11.7 R
South West	4	20.6 R	18	47.6 R	256	9.4 R	291	10.3 R
Yorkshire and Humberside	2	20.8 R	15	27.5 R	114	2.4 R	178	3.6 R
North West	4	25.8 R	26	39.5 R	116	1.7 R	198	2.9 R
Northern	2	25.3 R	9	57.1 R	18	0.6 R	32	1.1 R
Wales	1	15.4 R	8	50.6 R	30	1.7 R	41	2.2 OR
Scotland	3	16.1 R	10	26.9 OR	54	1.3 R	60	1.4 R
Britain*	58	21.5	340	42.1	1,759	3.6	2,691	5.3

*includes unclassified areas

TABLE 2.27   Contributions of All Overseas Birthplace Groups
to Total Population Change by Region. Absolute (000's) and
Percent

	Total population increase (a)	Total immigrant increase (b)	Proportion (b) of (a)
South East	987	523	53.0
West Midlands	384	115	29.9
East Midlands	235	52	22.0
East Anglia	172	17	9.4
South West	291	35	12.1
Yorkshire & Humberside	178	63	35.7
North West	198	81	41.5
Northern	32	14	44.6
Wales	41	9	26.7
Scotland	60	6	10.0

respectively) and despite the high rates of natural increase in these regions (see previous section on age groups) this suggests that these areas of employment growth have been attractive to both internal and overseas migrants. The South West and East Anglia are both areas with relatively high rates of net immigration and their proportions of population increase due to migrants is correspondingly small. Small proportions are also recorded in the less prosperous regions of Wales and Scotland.

The final issue for consideration in this section is the extent to which immigrants have grown in the areas in which they were already most numerous. Table 2.28 shows the proportions of the total population composed of the selected immigrant groups in 1971, and it is clear that in all cases the largest proportions are in the South East and West Midlands – the areas with the largest absolute growth between 1961 to 1971.

The national intra-urban trends revealed absolute decentralisation of the British and Irish born, in line with the changes for total population. In contrast, there was relative decentralisation of the West Indians and relative centralisation of those born in the Indian sub-continent and Africa. There were also differences between these groups in the aggregate regional patterns. For the British and Irish the largest increases were in the Midlands, East Anglia and the South West. In contrast, the largest percentage increases in the Indian sub-continent and Africa groups were in the Midlands, South East, North West and Yorkshire and Humberside, that is, in the main urban-industrial axis of Britain. The pattern for the West Indians resembled those for the other groups, the largest increases being in the North West, Yorkshire and Humberside, the Midlands, the South East, East Anglia and the South West. This section considers the intertwining of these themes at the regional intra-urban level.

Were the national centralisation-decentralisation changes repeated within the regions? Certainly there was decentralisation of the British-born in all regions; this was absolute rather than relative decentralisation in all regions except the South West and East Anglia – the two regions with the fastest growth rates. There was also decentralisation of the Irish-born in all regions except Wales; the

British Cities

TABLE 2.28   Birthplace Group Structure by Region, 1971.
Percent and Extreme Proportions by Urban Zone - Cores (C),
Rings (R) and Outer Rings (OR)

	Irish		Indian sub-continent		African		West Indian		Great Britain	
South East	2.6	C	1.2	C	0.6	C	1.1	C	89.7	R
West Midlands	2.3	C	1.7	C	0.2	C	0.8	C	93.3	OR
East Midlands	1.5	C	1.0	C	0.4	C	0.5	C	94.4	R
East Anglia	0.9	C	0.3	C	0.1	C	0.2	C	95.0	OR
South West	1.3	C	0.4	C	0.2	C	0.3	C	95.4	R
Yorkshire and Humberside	1.0	C	0.9	C	0.1	C	0.3	C	96.0	R
North West	2.0	C	0.6	C	0.2	C	0.2	C	95.5	OR
Northern	0.5	C	0.2	C	0.1	C	0.0	C	98.0	OR
Wales	0.7	C	0.2	C	0.1	C	0.1	C	97.3	OR
Scotland	1.3	C	0.3	C	0.1	C	0.0	C	96.8	R
Britain	1.8		0.9		0.3		0.6		93.6	

Range of percentages in		Irish	Indian sub-continent	African	West Indian	Great Britain
	Cores	0.6-3.4	0.4-2.8	0.1-0.8	0.0*-1.9	86.3-97.8
	Rings	0.5-1.8	0.1-0.8	0.1-0.3	0.0*-0.2	93.0-98.0
	Outer Rings	0.4-1.3	0.1-0.4	0.0*-0.2	0.0*-0.2	94.6-98.3

* Less than 0.05%

largest increases were in the rings in most regions (Table 2.26). There was also relative centralisation of the Indian sub-continent group in all regions. There-fore, for these three groups the national intra-urban patterns were repeated within the regions. For the African group, the largest percentage increases were in the rings or outer rings in Scotland, the North, Wales and East Anglia. Therefore, although centralisation of this group was observed in the regions in which it had the fastest growth rates, the expected centralisation pattern was not uniform for all regions. For the West Indians the largest percentage increases were in the rings or outer rings in all regions except the South West. However, when only the SMLAs are considered there is centralisation of the West Indians in Scotland, Wales and the South West - all regions where there were only small numbers in 1961. Therefore, the national centralisation - decentralisation patterns are repeated in the regions for all groups in most cases, but to a lesser extent for the African and West Indian groups. Finally, note that in the South East the largest increases in the British and Irish were in the outer rings, as with total population changes. This was not the case for the other immigrants. Therefore, decentralisation of the New Commonwealth immigrants to the outer rings in this region was not yet occurring, as was the case for all the age and socio-economic groups.

The two extreme cases, therefore, were the Indian sub-continent group, centralising in all regions, and the British born, decentralising in all regions. There were no areas, except the South West outer ring, in which there was a decrease in the Indian sub-continent group, but there were decreases in the British born in most cores and in some outer rings. The increases in the Indian sub-continent group exceeded those in the British born in most areas. The increases in the rings were greater than in the cores in all regions for the British born; and greater in the cores for the Indian sub-continent group. The position of the outer rings is not so simple and the decreases in this zone in some regions is greater than in the cores, for example, the North and Wales for those born in the Indian sub-continent. However, the increases in the outer rings are greater than in the cores and less than in the rings in most regions for the British born; and less than in the cores and greater than in the outer rings for the Indian sub-continent group.

Finally, some aspects of the impact of these changes on the birthplace group composition of zones are summarised in Table 2.28. The summary range statistics make two important points. Firstly, despite the very large percentage changes observed, most immigrant groups are still relatively small. The largest proportion of total population in any one immigrant group is only 3.4%, this being for the Irish in the South East cores. The largest proportions of all the other immigrant groups are also in the cores, mostly in the South East. These are 2.8% for the Indian sub-continent group, 0.8% for the African born and 1.9% for the West Indians. Given these relatively small numbers it is not surprising that in all zones and regions the British born form at least 90% of the population, with the exception of the South East cores where the proportion is 86.3%.

The second point is that despite the large increases recorded in the rings, 1961-1971, the ranges of percentages in 1971 show that all immigrant groups are still far more concentrated in the cores than in any other zone. The smallest proportion of the British born is only 92.3% in the rings (South East) and 94.6% (East Anglia) in the outer rings. With regard to the South East, this confirms the impression given by the percentage changes that the New Commonwealth immigrants had not yet decentralised to the outer rings to the same extent as the British born.

The strength of the concentration in cores is further verified by examining the individual regions. There is a remarkably consistent pattern. All the immigrant groups form the largest proportion of total population in the cores of all regions. With few exceptions, the second largest proportions are found in the rings and, therefore, the smallest proportions are found in the outer rings. The complement of this is, of course, that the smallest proportions of the British born are found in the cores in all regions. The largest proportions of the British born are found in the rings or outer rings.

These birthplace group profiles of the zones in 1971 do seem to conform to the idea of a diffusion model of immigrants in cities, with outmovement over time to first the rings and, then, the outer rings. However, the changes between 1961 and 1971 suggest that such a simple form of decentralisation did not exist. Rather, the regional intra-urban changes revealed that absolute decentralisation of the Irish, relative decentralisation of the West Indians, and relative centralisation of those born in the Indian sub-continent or Africa existed in most, but not all regions. Irrespective of the direction of these changes, all immigrant groups remained relatively concentrated in the cores.

2.2.3 Socio-economic trends: individual British Cities compared

In the preceding two sections contrasts in patterns of intra urban change between the largest cities and the rest of Britain and between urban areas in different regions of the country have been noted. At both the national and regional levels processes of intra and inter urban change are difficult to separate, although by adopting a functional definition of urban areas this study has attempted to minimise this particular problem. It is now widely appreciated that the process of decline in the inner areas of the largest cities is part of a broader process of

metropolitan decline whereby the entire city region is losing jobs and people to
adjacent and relatively free standing smaller towns. The fact that the larger
cities are concentrated in particular parts of the country has in turn implied net
shifts in the inter regional distribution of population and economic activity.

The aim of this section is to re-interpret these broad regional trends in urban
terms by examining patterns of change throughout the 126 MELAs. The analysis of
each of the variables concerned will seek to ask the simple question: which MELAs
have experienced the most rapid growth or decline in the period in question? For
practical purposes attention will be focussed on the extremes of the distribution
of cities although for certain variables national change maps at the MELA scale
and therefore covering virtually the whole of Britain will be presented. Some
brief attempt will be made to incorporate intra-urban dimensions of change at this
scale. The levels of information at this level are however rather high and select
ivity is mandatory. Some emphasis will be given to the picture in the Million
Cities and at other times the extremes of the full distribution of MELAs will be
examined.

Male and female employment trends

The growth of female employment has already been established as a highly dynamic
element in patterns of intra-urban change. In addition distinct regional variations in female employment trends have been observed. If intra urban contrasts are
ignored for the moment, then important changes amongst the leading cities in terms
of female employment opportunities between 1951 and 1971 become apparent (Table
2.29). In 1951 the MELAs with the highest proportions of female jobs were not
surprisingly the cotton and woollen textile towns of Lancashire and Yorkshire, together with two resorts (Southport and Worthing). The position had not changed
dramatically by 1961; however, in 1971 only one textile town (Wigan) ranked among
st the top ten of female employers. By this date the leading positions were held
by small MELAs in the South East, several with a resort element in their urban
character, but including also places like St. Albans, Hemel Hempstead and Woking
which have all benefitted from the decentralisation of routine office jobs from
London.

At the other extreme, the towns with the lowest proportions of female jobs have
remained more or less the same throughout the period. However, all have experienc
ed significant increases in the relative importance of female employment of the
order of ten percentage points in most cases, which contrasts with small increases
of around 4% at the top end of the range. The net effect has been a marked reduction in the inter-urban variation in the proportion of jobs held by women, most of
this reduction having occurred in the latter period (1961-71). Thus while the med
ian proportion of female jobs in each MELA increased from 28.5% in 1951 to 30.8%
in 1961 and 36.4% in 1971, the inter quartile range fell from 8.4% to 7.4% and
finally 3.6%.

While female employment increased relative to male employment chiefly in the later
period, Table 2.30 shows there were also important contrasts between the 1950s and
1960s in the towns experiencing the highest rates of female employment growth. In
the period 1951-61 the towns in which female employment increased its share of the
total most dramatically were virtually all in the southern half of the country.
In the 1960s the pattern had been dramatically reversed with the majority of leading towns in terms of increase in the relative share of female employment being
located in assisted areas. Thus in Rhondda, Hartlepool and Darlington, all places
with low levels of female employment in 1961 (Hartlepool ranked 124th), the share
of jobs held by women increased by over 9%. In contrast textile towns with the
highest female employment proportions in 1951 recorded some of the smallest increa
ses, and in some instances declines in female employment in the next twenty years.

TABLE 2.29   Rankings of Female Proportion of Total Employment
in MELAs, 1951, 1961 and 1971. (Percent)

(a) Highest Ten Rankings

1951		1961		1971	
Southport	43.5	Southport	43.5	Southport	47.9
Rochdale	40.7	Rochdale	40.9	Tunbridge Wells	43.0
Bolton	40.2	Bolton	40.1	Hastings	42.3
Burnley	37.9	Burnley	39.3	Southend	42.2
Blackburn	39.5	Blackburn	39.2	Worthing	41.7
Halifax	37.0	Dewsbury	38.8	Wigan	41.3
Wigan	37.0	Wigan	38.3	St. Albans	41.0
Dewsbury	36.3	Eastbourne	38.0	Eastbourne	40.9
Worthing	36.2	Halifax	38.0	Hemel Hempstead	40.7
Bury	36.1	Leigh	37.9	Woking	40.7

(b) Lowest Ten Rankings

Newport	21.7	Peterborough	26.0	Doncaster	32.3
Plymouth	21.6	Ipswich	25.7	Teeside	32.1
Darlington	21.5	Hartlepool	25.3	Plymouth	32.1
Kings Lynn	21.1	Kings Lynn	25.0	Newport	32.0
Doncaster	21.0	Newport	24.1	Warrington	32.0
Scunthorpe	21.0	Scunthorpe	24.1	Kings Lynn	31.7
Port Talbot	20.4	Doncaster	24.0	Scunthorpe	29.2
Thurrock	20.4	Thurrock	23.2	Port Talbot	28.3
Salisbury	19.7	Port Talbot	22.4	Thurrock	28.0
Ellesmere Port	15.8	Ellesmere Port	20.2	Ellesmere Port	17.6

TABLE 2.30   Rankings of Changing Female Proportion of Total
Employment in MELAs, 1951-1961 and 1961-1971 (Percent)

(a) Highest Ten Rankings

1951-61		1961-71	
Harlow	10.6	Rhondda	11.7
Crawley	9.5	Hartlepool	9.6
Aldershot	7.2	Darlington	9.1
Salisbury	7.0	Dunfermline	9.1
Aylesbury	6.9	Swindon	8.4
Stevenage	6.3	Doncaster	8.3
Plymouth	5.0	Burnley	8.2
Grimsby	4.7	Milton Keynes	8.2
Chatham	4.5	Exeter	8.1
York	4.4	Newport	7.9

(b) Lowest Ten Rankings

Ayr	-3.3	Ellesmere Port	-2.5
Luton	-1.0	Rochdale	-1.1
Preston	-0.9	Bolton	-0.7
Burnley	-0.4	Blackburn	-0.2
Blackburn	-0.3	Burnley	-0.5
Walton & Weybridge	-0.3	Halifax	0.6
Bolton	-0.1	Bury	0.8
Southport	-0.02	Huddersfield	1.2
Woking	-0.04	Dewsbury	1.3
Stoke	0.07	Leeds	1.8

It is tempting to associate this pattern of inter urban convergence in female employment opportunities, particularly the contrast between the 1950s and 1960s, with
the differential effects of urban and regional policies in the two decades. The
1950s were in the main characterised by relatively weak regional policy with a net
movement of industry from London to towns in the rest of the South East, encouraged
by new and expanded town policies and urban renewal in the capital. As a result
many previously dormitory towns experienced increases in employment opportunities
especially for women; indeed one of the reasons for industrial movement during
this period was labour shortages in London no doubt exacerbated by rapidly growing
office sector employment. Industrial movement was also associated with the introduction of new manufacturing processes often associated with the replacement of
skilled manual jobs for men by semi-skilled female jobs. However, by the 1960s
this essentially intra-regional process was transformed into an inter-regional one
as industrial development control was more strongly applied in the South East, regional incentives increased, and female activity rates began to hit a peak in South
East labour markets with increased competition from office jobs now also beginning
to decentralise from London.

Some further support for these notions, particularly the peaking thesis is given
by Table 2.31. The ten leading labour markets in terms of female activity rates
in 1961, with the exception of Stoke, were all textile towns. By 1971 all but
Rhondda and Burnley had been overtaken at the top of the list by South East labour
markets (together with Leicester). Two New Towns, Crawley and Harlow, had female
activity rates in 1971 in excess of 50%, chiefly a reflection of their young population. Their position was in marked contrast to other towns in the South East
like Worthing, Eastbourne, Hastings and Canterbury which Table 2.31 shows ranking
at the bottom of the list in terms of female activity rates - chiefly because of
their ageing population. It is also perhaps significant that these retirement
towns replaced some of the heavy industrial centres such as Rhondda and Swansea
which were at the bottom of this particular league table in 1961.

TABLE 2.31   Rankings of Female Activity Rates in MELAs, 1961 and 1971

(a) Highest Ten Rankings

1961		1971	
Rochdale	51.7	Crawley	56.2
Burnley	50.2	Harlow	52.2
Blackburn	48.4	Hemel Hempstead	49.0
Bury	47.0	Rochdale	48.4
Preston	46.7	Slough	48.3
Leigh	46.4	London	47.6
Halifax	45.7	Burnley	47.4
Manchester	45.0	Leicester	47.1
Dewsbury	44.7	Watford	46.6
Stoke	44.2	Stoke	46.4

(b) Lowest Ten Rankings

Worthing	25.0	Worthing	29.2
Port Talbot	25.1	Torbay	30.3
Swansea	26.7	Eastbourne	32.6
Hastings	27.1	Cambridge	32.7
Motherwell	27.6	Hastings	32.9
Canterbury	27.7	Canterbury	33.9
Rhondda	27.8	Exeter	34.1
Torbay	27.8	Plymouth	34.2
Hartlepool	28.1	Port Talbot	34.5
Ipswich	28.2	Ashford	34.6

Trends in the growing importance of female compared to male employment within individual British cities will of course largely represent the population decentralisation theme already outlined. Although there is not space to consider the full
distribution in detail some indication of the trends can be seen in Fig. 2.1, which
illustrates activity rate changes for the million cities.

Male activity rates are in decline over all urban zones in million cities. In general the rate of decline seems to be sharpest in the urban cores although there are
even more rapid rates of decline elsewhere due to special circumstances - the case
of the Newcastle outer metropolitan ring is an example. In 1961 then the highest
activity rates for males in million cities were to be found without exception in
the cores. By 1971 the highest activity rates were to be found again without exception in the metropolitan rings.

Female activity rates although all much lower than for males are increasing over
all urban zones in million cities. In general the rate of growth is sharpest in
the metropolitan rings and in some cases such as Birmingham in the outer metropolitan rings. The urban core zones however in all cases still record the highest
female activity rates although the rate of change in this zone is not so pronounced.
In fact in Manchester's urban core there was no change in activity rate and in Leeds
a slight decline was to be found. The highest female activity rates in 1971 were
located in London's urban core followed by Manchester's core zones so reversing
their positions in 1961. This feature for London is no doubt related to the continued growth of office occupations in the capital, a theme that will be taken up in
this section.

Occupational and industrial trends

Support for the notion that employment decline in large cities has resulted in important shifts in the economic activity at both the inter as well as the intra regional scales is given by Fig. 2.2 and Table 2.32. The map clearly suggests that
while employment was declining in London, the inner West Midlands and the highly
urbanised parts of Lancashire and Yorkshire during the period 1966-71, it was increasing in the outer South East and peripheral areas in the South West, East
Anglia, Wales, the eastern parts of Yorkshire and Humberside and the North East
(the A1 corridor), central Lancashire and the Lake District (the M6 corridor) and
eastern parts of the Highlands of Scotland.

The extremes of the distribution described in Fig. 2.2 are given in Table 2.32.
This shows Ellesmere Port and Crewe to be the only MELAs outside the South East to
record total employment increases over 10% during the period 1966-71. Significantly,
some of the towns with the highest relative employment increases also ranked amongst
the leading towns in terms of absolute employment gains (e.g. Basingstoke 11,450
and Colchester 10,250). Nevertheless, these increases are small compared with the
losses recorded by the largest cities which also rank with some of the smaller individual centres like Rhondda, Burnley and Bury as having the highest relative decline. Thus total employment in the entire city regions of Liverpool, Glasgow and
Manchester declined by in excess of 6% in these five years. The London MELA, because of its sheer size, had a lower percentage decrease, but nevertheless lost
something of the order of 20,000 jobs a year between 1966 and 1971.

It has frequently been suggested that the decline of employment in the larger cities
has chiefly been in manufacturing and lower level services like transport and communications while office employment opportunities have continued to grow. Table
2.33 lends some support to this suggestion: some of the largest cities, notably
London, Birmingham, Glasgow and Newcastle, ranked amongst the ten leading MELAs
in terms of absolute office employment increase between 1966 and 1971, in marked
contrast to their large declines in total employment. (See Table 2.35). However,

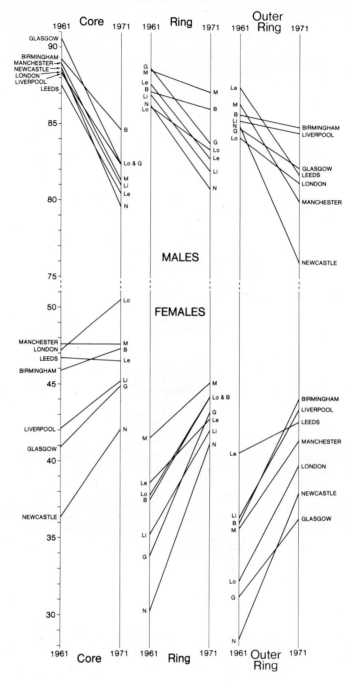

Fig. 2.1   Changes in male and female activity rates by urban
            zone for the million cities, 1961-1971.

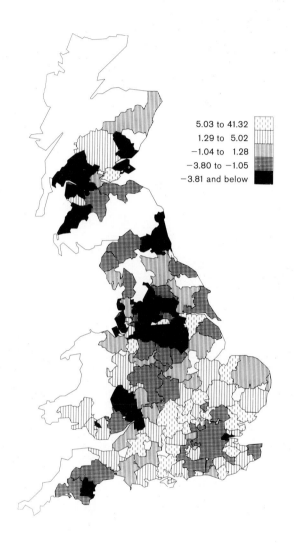

Fig. 2.2   Total employment change in MELAs,
           1966-1971 (Percent)

TABLE 2.32   Rankings of Total Employment Change in MELAs,
1966-1971.   (Absolute 000's and percent)

(a) Highest Ten Rankings

Absolute change		Relative change	
Ellesmere Port	13.95	Ellesmere Port	41.3
Oxford	12.12	Basingstoke	36.1
Southampton	11.71	Harlow	20.8
Basingstoke	11.45	Milton Keynes	25.9
Cardiff	10.52	Crewe	14.9
Bedford	10.39	Basildon	13.6
Colchester	10.25	Crawley	13.4
Crewe	9.57	High Wycombe	11.6
Milton Keynes	7.22	Colchester	10.8
Swansea	6.97	Worthing	10.7

(b) Lowest Ten Rankings

London	-191.39	Rhondda	-15.4
Leeds	-95.19	Leeds	-13.1
Manchester	-80.98	Halifax	-11.0
Glasgow	-53.54	Burnley	-8.2
Liverpool	-51.75	Liverpool	-7.5
Birmingham	-43.87	Manchester	-7.4
Sheffield	-26.04	Glasgow	-6.7
Newcastle	-24.44	Blackburn	-6.4
Halifax	-10.08	Bury	-6.4
Burnley	-8.29	Mansfield	-6.4

TABLE 2.33   Office Employment Change by Functional Class
of MELA, 1966-1971.   (Absolute 000's and percent)

	Office as % total employment		1966-71 Change	
	1966	1971	Abs.	%
Million Cities	27.3	30.0	116.09	4.1
Major Industrial	20.4	23.0	88.88	11.3
Secondary Industrial	16.3	18.4	52.37	12.5
Lancs/Yorks.	16.3	18.9	18.87	14.0
London Peripheral	23.5	26.8	42.61	16.8
New Towns	25.0	29.5	24.05	37.9
Resorts	19.8	22.8	38.16	15.4
Southern Freestanding	20.3	22.8	37.83	16.1
Peripheral Freestanding	16.5	18.4	36.90	18.4

several other large cities, notably Sheffield, Liverpool and Manchester, recorded some of the lowest relative increases in office employment while the highest relative increases occurred in smaller towns in the London periphery (e.g. Brighton, High Wycombe and Hemel Hempstead) with a number of medium sized towns such as Southampton, Bristol and Leicester ranking in the top ten in terms of absolute office employment change. In other words, there is not a clear relationship between city size and office employment change during this period. There is obviously a regional effect at work with some of the smallest absolute and relative increases in office employment and even declines occurring in peripheral labour market areas like Barrow and Rhondda.

It has frequently been hypothesised that office employment is essentially an urban phenomena, being able to derive maximum advantages of agglomeration in large urban centres. Central locations within large cities offer ease of personal communication between senior office staff both within the city and to places in its hinterland, and also ready access to a large potential supply of clerical labour. And, in so far as the office sector provides a service function, it would be reasonable to hypothesise that the size of the office workforce should increase in line with city size (i.e. in relation to increases in size of hinterland and the local population served). It is possible to test this hypothesis using data for the Metropolitan Economic Labour Areas (126) using a simple regression model. There is indeed a close positive relationship between city size (total employment) and total office employment in both 1966 and 1971. (R^2 of 0.95 for both dates).

Although total employment is an important factor in accounting for variations in the absolute amount of office employment within a town, the relative importance of office jobs in the overall employment structure is more strongly related to regional factors. Table 2.34 highlights the extremes of the distribution of towns in terms of the proportion of employment accounted for by office occupations. The towns with the highest proportions are all in the South East peripheral to London and do not include any of the largest cities. Towns at the bottom of the ranking are primarily centres of heavy industry. Amongst the different types of office employment, the greatest variation is for clerical jobs, from 21.1% of total employment in London to 7.9% in Rhondda. Again, because of definitional problems, the range for managerial employment is smaller - from 5.8% in Letchworth to 2.3% in Barrow. The ranking of towns according to each type of employment is similar with the notable exception of the large proportion of clerical jobs in places that have received government office dispersal, notably Blackpool (17.2% clerical, ranked fifth), and Liverpool, (16.7% clerical, ranked tenth).

TABLE 2.34   Rankings of Office Proportion of Total Employment in MELAs, 1971   (Percent)

(a) Highest Ten Rankings		(b) Lowest Ten Rankings	
London	36.3	Doncaster	16.4
Crawley	34.6	Port Talbot	16.2
Hemel Hempstead	32.3	Scunthorpe	15.9
Stevenage	32.2	Ayr	15.4
Watford	30.8	Workington	15.0
Walton & Weybridge	30.8	Kings Lynn	14.7
Letchworth	29.7	Barnsley	14.7
Harlow	29.6	Hartlepool	13.8
Worthing	29.0	Mansfield	13.2
Reading	28.5	Rhondda	12.9

Fig. 2.3 indicates that regional factors strongly influence the localisation of office employment. It shows that only five labour market areas outside the South East (Bristol, Bath, Cheltenham, Harrogate and Edinburgh) have location quotients for total office employment in excess of 1.0. Moreover, the six largest cities after London, all with populations in excess of a million (Birmingham, Glasgow, Manchester, Liverpool, Newcastle and Leeds) all have smaller shares of national office employment than of total employment. That regional factors are more important than city size in explaining the localisation of office employment can be clearly demonstrated. Using a multiple regression model an attempt can be made to

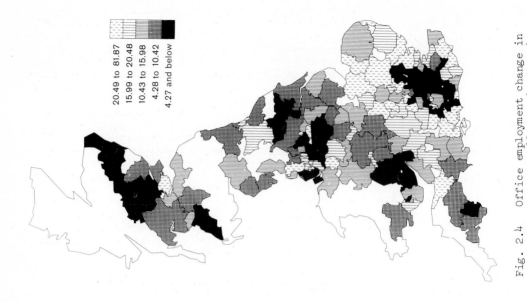

Fig. 2.4   Office employment change in
           MELAs, 1966-1971 (Percent)

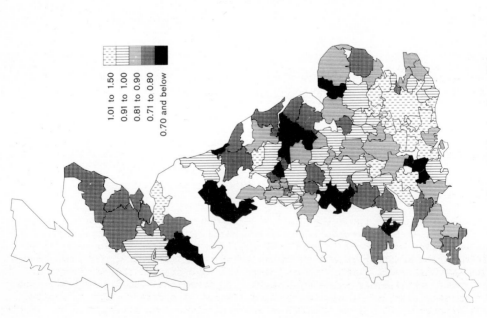

Fig. 2.3   Location quotients for office
           employment in MELAs, 1971.

explain the location quotient for total office employment in each MELA by the log-
arithm of its road distance from London and its total employment. The model reveals
that the localisation of office employment is not surprisingly inversely related to
distance from London; this factor is also a more powerful explanatory variable than
city size. The relatively poor performance of the model (R^2 0.46) suggests also
that a number of other factors are at work accounting for variations in the localisation of office employment.

Examination of office employment changes between 1966 and 1971 again reinforces the
importance of labour market areas in the South East, together with parts of East
Anglia and the South West. Fig. 2.4 shows that few towns North and West of a line
between the Severn and the Wash recorded significant increases in office employment,
while some of the largest cities, including London, had relative increases well below the national average. Although some of the largest absolute increases in office
employment were recorded by major cities, a number of medium-sized towns, such as
Portsmouth, Southampton, Edinburgh, Cardiff and Leicester, also figure prominently
in the list of leading towns in terms of absolute office employment increase (Table
2.35). Given that relatively slow growing clerical employment forms a larger component of the total office workforce in the largest cities, a decline here relative
to the rest of Britain might be expected.

TABLE 2.35   Rankings of Office Employment Change in MELAs, 1966-1971. (Absolute 000's and Percent)

(a) Highest Ten Rankings

Absolute Change		Relative Change	
London	68.52	Basingstoke	81.8
Birmingham	16.65	Milton Keynes	60.1
Portsmouth	13.35	High Wycombe	45.5
Southampton	10.55	Dunfermline	44.4
Bristol	10.23	Worthing	41.6
Edinburgh	9.37	Harlow	40.3
Newcastle	9.36	Hemel Hempstead	36.8
Glasgow	9.00	Dewsbury	33.1
Cardiff	8.59	Great Yarmouth	32.6
Leicester	8.12	Crewe	32.2

(b) Lowest Ten Rankings

Southport	.60	Newport	3.1
Barrow	.58	Sheffield	1.7
Torquay	.57	Liverpool	1.6
Harrogate	.44	Manchester	0.9
Perth	-0.15	Perth	-1.7
Rhondda	-0.15	Hereford	-2.3
Hereford	-0.22	Halifax	-2.5
Halifax	-0.38	Aberdeen	-3.9
Ayr	-0.60	Rhondda	-4.7
Aberdeen	-0.92	Ayr	-5.7

Such expectation is confirmed by the results of a shift/share analysis. This
analysis breaks down the difference between the actual growth of total office employment and that which might have been expected if employment had grown at the national rate into two components. First, the proportionality shift identifies the
amount by which employment has grown or declined as a result of specialisation in
nationally slow or fast growing components of the total office labour force (cler-

TABLE 2.36   Differential Shift Component of Office Employment
Change in MELAs, 1966-1971. Absolute 000s and Percent

(a) Highest Ten Rankings   (b) Lowest Ten Rankings

	Abs.	%		Abs.	%
Portsmouth	9.33	20.2	Halifax	-1.77	-11.7
Southampton	6.42	13.6	Coventry	-2.41	-3.2
Oxford	4.81	12.1	Aberdeen	-3.01	-13.0
Cambridge	4.62	16.7	Leeds	-4.15	-3.1
Dunfermline	4.23	36.1	Glasgow	-4.72	-2.8
High Wycombe	3.87	36.1	Sheffield	-7.12	-7.0
Northampton	3.83	19.7	Liverpool	-10.10	-6.4
Preston	3.66	12.9	Birmingham	-10.72	-3.5
Reading	3.65	10.3	Manchester	-19.74	-7.6
Worthing	3.48	33.0	London	-76.95	-4.6

ical, managerial or professional). Second, the differential shift reflects the
surplus or deficit of employment resulting from each category of office employment
growing at a faster or slower rate than nationally. Table 2.36 demonstrates that
some of the major cities experienced less office employment growth than might have
been expected, principally because of slower growth rates in each type of office
employment locally than nationally (negative differential shift). Owing to the
small variation between cities in the proportion of managerial and professional
workers the proportionality shift accounts for only a small part of the total shift
Again, substantial positive differential shifts are to be found in the South East,
notably in the larger centres, such as Portsmouth, Southampton, Cambridge, Oxford
and Reading.

The overriding conclusion of this inter-MELA analysis is that office employment is
not only moving away from London to smaller and particularly medium-sized towns in
the South East, but is also declining relatively in other major urban centres.
These inter-urban trends are undoubtedly an extension of a well-established tendenc
for office activity to decentralise from the inner to the outer parts of large cities. A brief consideration of this last theme might usefully conclude this analysi
of occupational change.

Table 2.37 shows that although office jobs are relatively more important in the occ
upational structure of employment in urban cores than in other zones, there has indeed been a significant net shift of office jobs to the metropolitan rings of all
the major cities. In urban cores of all of the seven million cities impressive
percentage growth rates were achieved in administrative employment - the lowest
being in Newcastle with 5.3% growth. However in absolute terms London's core still
managed to acquire some twenty thousand extra jobs in this category compared to a
total growth of around 13,000 in all of the other six core zones put together.
Even in London though, in common with all other million cities there was a reduction in the core share of this type of employment which has traditionally been heavily central city oriented.

In contrast to administrators and managers declines were recorded in six out of the
seven million city cores for clerical employment - the exception being Leeds with
a modest 2.3% growth. Although the highest percentage decline was in Manchester
(-7.1%) London's decline of -4.8% amounted to by far the highest absolute loss of
around forty thousand jobs. As expected core areas of all million cities suffered
a reduced share of clerical MELA employment. Decentralisation of these jobs was
of course directed towards the metropolitan rings and outer rings. Double figure

TABLE 2.37 Changes in the Distribution of Office Occupations Within Million City MELA's 1966-1971

	CORE			RING			OUTER RING		
	% MELA 71	% Change	% Change in MELA Share	% MELA 71	% Change	% Change in MELA Share	% MELA 71	% Change	% Change in MELA Share
LONDON									
Administrators & managers	77.1	10.4	-2.1	19.2	23.8	1.6	3.7	31.1	0.5
Clerical	78.7	-4.8	-3.0	18.1	14.3	2.4	3.2	19.4	0.6
Other office	78.4	10.6	-0.8	18.2	23.1	1.7	3.3	-12.9	-1.0
All other employment	67.6	-10.9	-2.3	25.9	-2.7	1.3	6.5	4.8	1.0
BIRMINGHAM									
Administrators & managers	71.2	12.7	-2.7	24.3	28.7	2.2	4.5	31.0	0.5
Clerical	75.5	-2.6	-3.2	20.9	16.3	2.6	3.6	22.2	0.6
Other office	74.3	1.1	-4.3	21.9	27.0	3.5	3.9	40.0	1.0
All other employment	70.3	-8.7	-2.6	24.5	2.9	2.0	5.2	8.5	0.7
MANCHESTER									
Administrators & managers	68.6	11.9	-2.6	27.5	27.0	2.3	3.9	23.6	0.3
Clerical	75.6	-7.1	-3.5	21.4	17.1	3.7	3.1	-6.8	-0.1
Other office	72.2	-2.2	-2.6	24.8	15.0	3.0	3.1	-7.7	-0.3
All other employment	65.2	-11.6	-1.2	30.6	-4.5	1.8	4.3	-7.9	-0.5
GLASGOW									
Administrators & managers	74.9	17.0	-1.3	20.9	34.7	2.4	4.2	-7.5	-1.2
Clerical	80.7	-4.1	-2.7	15.6	19.6	2.7	3.7	0.2	0.0
Other office	80.1	15.2	-1.1	15.8	19.8	0.4	4.1	41.9	0.7
All other employment	69.0	-13.1	-2.8	23.6	-0.8	2.1	7.3	3.3	0.7
LIVERPOOL									
Administrators & managers	71.7	6.2	-4.9	24.1	31.8	3.3	4.2	80.4	1.6
Clerical	78.4	-5.6	-3.5	18.1	14.3	2.5	3.6	40.9	1.1
Other office	75.7	1.0	-2.6	21.4	15.1	2.0	2.9	34.3	0.6
All other employment	68.3	-14.0	-3.0	27.8	-0.2	2.8	3.9	-4.5	0.2
LEEDS									
Administrators & managers	68.0	8.9	0.1	22.7	16.6	1.5	9.3	-6.9	-1.6
Clerical	75.6	2.3	-1.5	15.8	22.4	2.4	8.6	-5.4	-0.9
Other office	73.3	4.1	-2.1	17.6	21.4	2.1	9.1	7.4	0.0
All other employment	62.7	-24.2	-5.8	22.7	3.4	4.5	14.5	-10.0	1.4
NEWCASTLE									
Administrators & managers	58.7	5.3	-7.1	27.3	60.0	7.2	14.1	17.8	0.0
Clerical	60.5	-6.1	-7.9	22.7	41.5	5.7	16.8	22.2	2.2
Other office	64.8	-4.1	-7.9	21.0	60.8	7.0	14.3	15.7	1.0
All other employment	53.2	-10.3	-1.9	23.8	3.6	2.5	23.0	-9.3	-0.6

percentage growth rates were achieved in all metropolitan rings the highest being
in Newcastle with 41.5% and growth was achieved in five out of the possible seven
outer rings in this category. Change in other office employment was more varied
over the million city set. Only in the cores of London and Glasgow was there important relative growth with 10.6 and 15.2% respectively. However, in the rings of
all cities impressive relative growth rates of other office employment were clearly
to be seen.

The residual non office category in Table 2.37 is interesting in that it provides
a valuable comparison by which to assess the changing fortunes of office employment
over the five year period. Ubiquitous and substantial decline both in absolute as
well as relative terms was apparent in the cores of all million cities in non-office
occupations. London lost -10.9% of these occupations, over a quarter of a million
jobs.   In addition Leeds lost close on 100,000 jobs in non-office employment, a
massive -24.2% relative decline. Even in the metropolitan rings of these large
cities growth in this non-office employment category was modest and in some cases,
London, Manchester, Glasgow and Liverpool, declines were recorded even though in
net terms decentralisation of such activity was taking place.

So in the larger cities of the nation the decline in non-office employment in urban
cores has not been compensated for by an increase in office employment. Only higher
level managerial office jobs have been increasing while clerical jobs have been
declining. (In the smaller cities, office jobs of all types but especially managerial occupations, have been increasing more rapidly). Employment growth in the
outer urban zones has been spearheaded by growth in office jobs of all types but
again especially administrative occupations. Many of these are likely to have been
in population oriented service activities notably in the public sector.

In considering industrial change at this scale difficulties of selection and presentation of information are again apparent. As an expedient only some four industrial orders are considered. Table 2.38 lists the extremes in the absolute change
performance of the two manufacturing orders selected and Figs. 2.5 and 2.6 illustrates the full national distributions. Absolute change statistics, although of
course highly correlated with city size, have been chosen here because of the difficulties of interpreting large percentage changes on small initial bases. For engineering and electrical goods manufacture clearly the largest losses at the MELA
scale are in the largest cities. London, not noted as a centre of this sort of
activity, lost close on 60,000 jobs some 12.3% of its total engineering employment.
Double figure percentage losses are also to be found in Manchester, Glasgow and
Liverpool. Birmingham, which is a traditional engineering centre, suffered only a
6.9% loss, which totalled some 12,740 jobs. Coventry also suffered a similar percentage fate. The list of gaining MELAs in this category although spatially widespread does have an intermediate size characteristic and additionally several members do have some form of expanded town status or contain a new town within their
boundaries. This latter feature probably explains the large percentage gains in
Dunfermline and Basingstoke calculated on rather small original bases.

For textiles the list of gaining MELAs is again dispersed over the country save for
an absence of this type of activity in the South East. In the main these towns are
also of small to intermediate size. The exception here, and a surprising inclusion
in the list, is Liverpool. Interestingly, Darlington, which heads the list, also
figures prominently in the high gaining MELAs for engineering and electrical goods
manufacture. Not unexpectedly the list of MELAs losing heavily in textile employment is much more spatially focussed in the North West and Yorkshire and Humberside
Leeds suffers the highest decline with over 22,000 jobs, a loss of 27.6%. Declines
of 20% and 30% are not unusual in the list and in the case of Burnley the figure
is over 40% decline (over 9,000 jobs). Dundee and Glasgow, together with Leicester
make the other contributions to the highest ten losers not coming from the above two

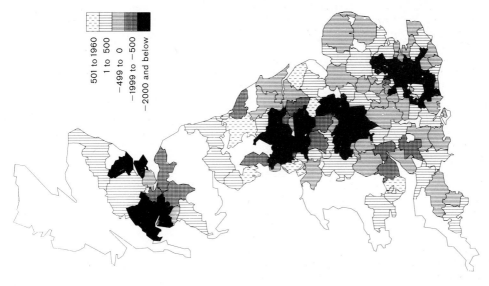

Fig. 2.6   Absolute employment change in
textile manufacture in MELAs
1966–1971

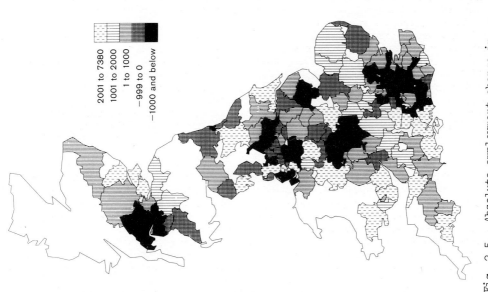

Fig. 2.5   Absolute employment change in
engineering and electrical
goods manufacture in MELAs,
1966–1971

TABLE 2.38 Rankings of Employment Change in Textiles, Engineering and Electrical Goods in MELAs, 1966-1971. (Absolute 000s
and Percent). Highest Ten Rankings and Lowest Ten Rankings.

Engineering and Electrical Goods			Textiles		
	Abs.	%		Abs.	%
Portsmouth	7.38	37.9	Darlington	1.96	41.8
Dunfermline	6.02	150.9	Cardiff	1.36	79.5
Stoke	5.60	29.7	Mansfield	0.85	7.5
Darlington	5.11	35.9	Liverpool	0.84	14.8
Basingstoke	4.32	125.9	Barrow	0.64	54.7
Dundee	4.05	25.8	Grimsby	0.62	30.4
Leicester	3.74	8.3	Swansea	0.44	84.6
Warrington	3.68	53.1	Cambridge	0.44	258.8
Reading	3.37	35.5	Crewe	0.43	138.7
Preston	3.17	57.6	Ayr	0.47	10.9
Blackburn	-2.01	-9.2	Blackburn	-4.68	-24.0
Sunderland	-2.12	-15.2	Rochdale	-5.17	-22.3
Lincoln	-3.14	-18.6	Huddersfield	-5.24	-18.7
Coventry	-3.83	-6.4	Glasgow	-5.31	-25.3
Leeds	-4.25	-6.8	Halifax	-5.41	-23.8
Liverpool	-9.77	-16.6	Leicester	-5.66	-13.7
Glasgow	-11.72	-13.5	Dundee	-6.77	-34.5
Birmingham	-12.74	-6.9	Burnley	-9.27	-41.5
Manchester	-20.20	-14.2	Manchester	-17.14	-24.9
London	-58.29	-12.3	Leeds	-22.79	-27.6

mentioned traditional regions of textile manufacture.

Table 2.39 and Figs. 2.7 and 2.8 illustrate the absolute change fortunes of the two
service orders selected. Insurance, banking and financial services are heavily
concentrated in the capital and so is their principal absolute growth. In all well
over 28,000 new jobs were created in London in this order over the five year period
reflecting some 10% growth. Birmingham too also had some important absolute gains
although it was outmatched by Glasgow, Liverpool and Newcastle, and especially so
in percentage terms. Other interesting gainers include Southend and Northampton
by now well known for their decentralised banking functions involving credit cards,
and Worthing and Blackpool wherein are located some decentralised insurance functions. Thus, mainly city size together with decentralised specialist financial functions tend to explain the extremes of high growth. In comparison the figures in
the list of declining MELAs are much less significant with mainly small towns and
cities losing out. The exception is of course Manchester but here only modest
losses are experienced.

The much less specialised professional and scientific services are in the main
growing in absolute terms in accordance with population size. As a result the list
of high growth values includes all the million cities plus Sheffield, Cardiff and
Edinburgh. Nonetheless these impressive absolute gains are also important in percentage terms, with double figure gains being recorded in all the top ten places
save for Glasgow's 9.3%. The list of declining places, or more accurately declining and slow growing, reflect much less dramatic change both in absolute and percentage terms. They include some new towns and some resorts and some smaller freestanding towns in rural areas.

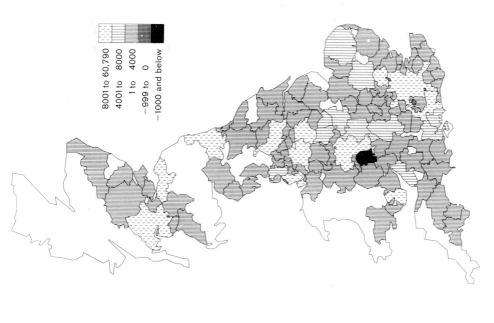

Fig. 2.8 Absolute employment change in professional and scientific services in MELAs, 1966-1971

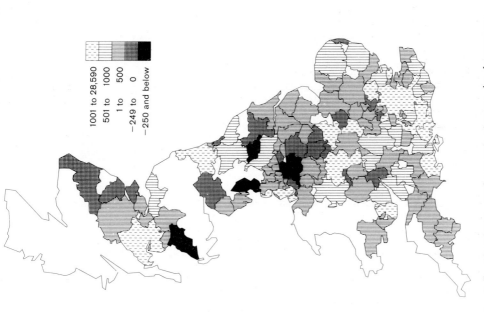

Fig. 2.7 Absolute employment change in insurance, banking and financial services in MELAs, 1966-1971

TABLE 2.39   Rankings of Employment Change in Insurance,
Banking and Finance, and Professional and Scientific Services
in MELAs, 1966-1971. (Absolute 000s and Percent). Highest
Ten Rankings and Lowest Ten Rankings.

Insurance, Banking and Finance			Professional and Scientific Services		
	Abs.	%		Abs.	%
London	28.59	10.5	London	60.79	10.8
Glasgow	4.37	24.8	Birmingham	23.47	19.9
Liverpool	3.97	23.1	Manchester	14.67	14.3
Newcastle	2.05	18.0	Newcastle	13.72	23.0
Birmingham	2.04	7.3	Leeds	13.57	22.6
Northampton	1.72	77.1	Sheffield	9.06	18.8
Worthing	1.63	87.6	Glasgow	8.64	9.3
Blackpool	1.56	30.4	Liverpool	8.57	11.8
Leicester	1.28	26.6	Cardiff	8.42	26.6
Southend	1.25	43.9	Edinburgh	8.02	17.0
Dundee	-0.06	-2.2	Warrington	0.15	1.3
Hemel Hempstead	-0.07	-7.7	Barrow	0.09	2.0
York	-0.09	-3.8	Hereford	0.06	1.0
Burton on Trent	-0.17	-23.9	Walton & Weybridge	0.04	0.7
Carlisle	-0.17	-11.3	Worthing	0.03	0.5
Stevenage	-0.22	-31.0	Harlow	-0.05	-1.1
Ayr	-0.29	-21.3	Woking	-0.09	-1.9
Manchester	-0.45	-1.6	Southport	-0.18	-4.4
Harrogate	-0.53	-18.5	Crawley	-0.41	-11.8
Lancaster	-0.55	-23.7	Worcester	-2.16	-16.2

Perhaps a more easily assimilated way of presenting some of these patterns, but wit
a core and metropolitan ring dimension, is to consider the changing fortunes of the
nine functional groups. Tables 2.40 and 2.41 list the absolute and percentage changes for the four selected industries for cores and metropolitan rings respectivel
For engineering and electrical goods manufacture the largest losses, both absolute
and percentage, occur in the million cities for urban cores. The southern freestanding and London peripheral groups do not perform too well either. The major
source of absolute growth in core areas is in the secondary industrial towns, although more impressive relative gains are to be found in the new towns, the resort/
retirement centres and the peripheral freestanding group. A similar, but perhaps
clearer, picture emerges for this type of employment at the metropolitan ring scale
Only the million cities record declines here and much more modest they are too when
compared to the performance in urban cores. Double figure relative growth rates
are achieved in all other groups and the southern freestanding class has the highest rate at 47.4% (recall that this group suffered declines in the core). So for
this type of economic activity, peripheralisation coupled with decentralisation,
seems to sum up the pattern of growth, declines being heavily focussed on the main
conurbation centres.

Textiles, being an industry in marked decline nationally, exhibits a much more
widespread pattern of decline in the urban cores of the functional groups. Again
the million cities take the brunt of the decline both in absolute and relative
terms. But heavy losses are also to be felt in the major and secondary industrial
towns and in the Lancashire/Yorkshire group. The pattern for the performance
across the nation's metropolitan rings is not much better, with eight out of the
nine categories again suffering decline. Perhaps if anything the magnitudes of

TABLE 2.40   Selected Employment Change by Functional Group
in Urban Cores, 1966-1971. (Absolute 000s and Percent)

	Engineering and Electrical Goods		Textiles	
	Abs.	%	Abs.	%
Million Cities	-112.30	-14.5	-37.22	-30.1
Major Industrial	0.79	0.4	-15.99	-19.6
Secondary Industrial	5.51	3.8	-10.55	-17.9
Lancashire/Yorkshire	1.23	3.0	-16.92	-26.8
London Peripheral	-0.46	-0.6	-0.75	-24.7
New Towns	4.73	9.6	0.09	34.6
Resorts	4.08	10.2	-0.65	-10.0
Southern Freestanding	-2.63	-4.6	-1.72	-12.8
Peripheral Freestanding	2.85	4.6	-5.04	-19.8

	Insurance, Banking and Finance.		Professional and Scientific Services	
	Abs.	%	Abs.	%
Million Cities	28.32	8.5	81.80	11.2
Major Industrial	4.22	7.5	46.92	19.0
Secondary Industrial	3.94	16.9	23.08	20.1
Lancashire/Yorkshire	1.57	19.9	9.21	21.0
London Peripheral	4.94	26.8	12.28	17.4
New Towns	1.10	27.8	6.52	30.9
Resorts	3.64	14.6	13.90	17.0
Southern Freestanding	1.73	13.9	13.76	18.6
Peripheral Freestanding	1.94	8.1	21.06	23.6

relative declines are not as marked, but certainly the same groups of areas, headed by the million cities, record the highest losses as did for urban cores. Widespread declines across the nation then typify the employment change pattern of textiles manufacture.

Textiles contrasts completely with the first of the service industries selected, the specialised financial services. In this category impressive growth was achieved in the urban cores nationwide. The largest absolute gains were in the main centres of population, dominated of course by the million cities, but more impressive relative growth was achieved elsewhere in the country. Interestingly, this was not primarily focussed on the major industrial group, although some growth was recorded here. Rather it was the London peripheral and new towns groups which headed the list, supported by the other groups containing small to medium sized towns. In the metropolitan rings considerable decentralisation of this type of employment is apparent. The million cities group again records the highest absolute gains but here the relative increase is far higher than in the urban cores. The same can be said, but perhaps to a greater degree, for the major industrial group. Elsewhere decentralisation is also clear, save for the new towns where the process just has not started. So for financial services, some peripheralisation of employment has taken place, especially at the urban core level, decentralisation trends becoming more important at the scale of metropolitan rings.

Professional and scientific services are much less spatially specialised than

TABLE 2.41   Selected Employment Change by Functional Group
in Metropolitan Rings, 1966-1971. (Absolute 000s and Percent)

	Engineering and Electrical Goods		Textiles	
	Abs.	%	Abs.	%
Million Cities	-9.46	-3.7	-9.40	-14.5
Major Industrial	15.80	21.8	-1.41	-4.7
Secondary Industrial	11.23	31.9	-4.47	-17.3
Lancashire/Yorkshire	4.14	17.3	-7.29	-17.6
London Peripheral	9.26	24.9	-0.10	-5.3
New Towns	0.40	17.2	0.06	42.8
Resorts	2.16	18.8	-0.20	-8.1
Southern Freestanding	7.18	47.4	-0.31	-4.9
Peripheral Freestanding	4.42	36.7	-0.92	-15.9

	Insurance, Banking and Finance.		Professional and Scientific Services	
	Abs.	%	Abs.	%
Million Cities	9.68	20.7	49.18	18.5
Major Industrial	2.41	24.8	21.34	24.9
Secondary Industrial	0.73	13.7	7.65	14.8
Lancashire/Yorkshire	0.32	17.8	2.05	8.7
London Peripheral	1.99	31.3	10.93	18.0
New Towns	-0.21	-30.4	2.11	40.0
Resorts	1.79	24.9	5.51	19.8
Southern Freestanding	0.49	23.3	7.00	27.6
Peripheral Freestanding	0.71	23.4	6.26	18.5

financial services. As a result the high absolute growth values for the urban core
of the functional groups are much more widespread. This is perhaps one of the few
industrial orders where percentage change measures assume full, real and comparative value. The new towns head the list of high gainers followed by the peripheral
freestanding group. Additionally important double figure percentage growth is
achieved everywhere else. The million cities record the lowest value of 11.2%.
In the metropolitan rings a slightly different pattern is revealed with the million
cities securing important absolute and relative gains showing the outcome of decentralisation processes. However the new towns still record the highest percentage
change value followed here by the southern freestanding and major industrial groups
Thus, a similar summary can be given as for the other service employment selected,
there is some deconcentration of employment occurring over the country but superimposed on this, and especially apparent at the scale of metropolitan rings, is the
familiar trend towards decentralisation.

Finally, themes of decentralisation of industry can be further elaborated upon with
respect to the seven million cities considered individually. Table 2.42 lists the
absolute and percentage employment changes for all urban zones of these cities for
the four selected industries. Ubiquitous decline characterises the urban cores of
the million cities for employment in engineering and electrical goods, and double
figure percentage decline, save for Leeds, at that. Declines are even to be found
in the metropolitan rings of London, Glasgow and Liverpool although they are much
reduced compared to the cores. Generally then this form of activity has fared
better in the metropolitan rings and especially noteworthy is the high growth

TABLE 2.42   Selected Employment Change in the Urban Zones of
the Million Cities, 1966-1971.   (Absolute 000s and Percent)

	CORE		RING		OUTER RING	
	Abs.	%	Abs.	%	Abs.	%
Engineering and Electrical Goods						
London	-48.86	-15.3	-14.02	-10.4	4.59	24.1
Birmingham	-16.69	-11.5	2.94	8.8	1.01	16.4
Manchester	-20.81	-18.5	0.02	0.1	0.59	44.4
Glasgow	-8.97	-15.4	-2.81	-12.5	0.06	0.2
Liverpool	-8.96	-19.8	-1.12	-8.6	0.31	58.5
Leeds	-2.03	-4.9	1.17	10.2	-3.39	-35.1
Newcastle	-5.98	-11.8	4.36	39.6	0.69	10.1
Textiles						
London	-3.14	-17.3	-0.39	-9.6	-0.04	-12.5
Birmingham	-2.71	-54.8	0.28	24.8	-0.08	-8.5
Manchester	-9.58	-29.9	-6.14	-20.3	-1.42	-21.4
Glasgow	-3.98	-25.7	-1.02	-27.1	-0.31	-18.0
Liverpool	-1.31	-31.1	2.04	142.6	0.11	550.0
Leeds	-15.43	-33.4	-4.69	-19.8	-2.67	-20.7
Newcastle	-1.07	-41.6	0.52	78.8	0.74	91.3
Insurance, Banking and Finance						
London	20.60	8.7	6.00	19.3	1.99	40.8
Birmingham	0.76	3.4	1.18	24.7	0.10	11.2
Manchester	-1.55	-6.3	1.10	28.8	0.00	0.0
Glasgow	4.09	26.4	0.37	25.7	-0.09	-13.6
Liverpool	3.70	25.6	0.17	6.6	0.10	66.6
Leeds	0.59	4.5	0.29	17.8	-0.02	-1.7
Newcastle	0.13	1.7	0.57	40.7	1.35	52.9
Professional and Scientific Services						
London	36.41	9.5	19.74	13.2	4.65	15.3
Birmingham	12.69	15.3	8.94	29.3	1.84	43.0
Manchester	7.26	9.8	6.82	27.5	0.59	13.9
Glasgow	5.56	8.0	3.14	17.8	-0.05	-1.0
Liverpool	4.87	9.8	3.07	14.5	0.63	40.6
Leeds	9.27	22.2	2.47	22.2	1.83	25.6
Newcastle	5.74	17.4	5.00	44.0	2.98	19.3

performance in this zone for Newcastle. In the outer rings London records by far
the largest absolute growth with around 5,000 jobs, an increase of just under 25%.
This goes some way to offset, in the London MELA, the marked loss of over 14,000
jobs of this type from the metropolitan ring. Clearly decentralisation tendencies
are apparent in the million cities and they seem once again to be at their most
advanced stage in London.

London does not of course dominate the picture for employment change in textiles
production. In this activity all cores of million cities again are in decline, the
list being headed by Leeds, with a massive one third decline in five years, losing
some 15,000 jobs. The losses in Manchester are only slightly less significant.
The metropolitan rings of the million cities do not seem to be suffering as much

as the cores, but it is only in Liverpool that any substantial growth is recorded.
This may reflect decentralisation from Manchester in addition to that from Liverpool of course. Similar tendencies are also apparent in the outer ring zones.
Overall though the pattern is one of decentralisation in decline for this type of
nationally declining economic activity.

In financial services the urban cores of all the cities except Manchester managed
to record growth. London was the most important in absolute terms with a gain of
over 20,000 jobs. Glasgow and Liverpool however had more impressive relative
growth with over 26% and 25% respectively.   Some decentralisation of this traditionally core centred activity is apparent in the figures for metropolitan rings
and in some cases OMRs. London for example records growth of 19.3% in the rings
and 40.8% in the OMRs compared to only 8.7% in its core zone. Similar patterns
are shown for Birmingham and Newcastle. The loss from Manchester's core also seems
to be made up for by roughly equivalent absolute growth in the ring. Decentralisation but with some bouyant core growth may perhaps best typify this type of
activity.

A similar summary can also be placed on the fortunes of professional and scientific
services in the million cities. This nationally very fast growing activity makes
impressive absolute gains in the cores of all million cities, with most cities
approaching double figure percentage gains and some, such as Leeds (22.2%) even
more. The percentage gains are even more impressive in all of the metropolitan
rings and in some OMRs. Noteworthy in this respect are the 44% growth in the
Newcastle ring, gaining 5,000 jobs, and the 43% growth in the Birmingham outer ring
gaining almost 2,000 jobs of this type. This sector is then a high growth, highly
decentralising, form of activity in the million cities, a feature which is not
really surprising when the range of high status, population oriented, servicing
activities which it includes are recalled. Such are the contrasts between the
sample manufacturing and servicing activities which have been selected to illustrate industrial change at this scale.

Socio-economic structure

Considerable variations in patterns of socio-economic group change have been shown
to exist at the regional scale. These changes followed the general pattern of employment change being strongly differentiated between southern and northern regions. This section first examines the consistency of these trends when cities are
considered individually.

The top ten rankings of SMLAs according to their percentage changes do also accord
with this broad trend (Table 2.43). New or expanding towns in the South East dominate the rankings of all the four socio-economic groups. In contrast, SMLAs in
the South East are almost totally absent from the bottom ten rankings of percentage
change. In this case Scotland, Wales, the Northern region, Yorkshire and Humberside and the North West are the most frequent locations for SMLAs with either the
smallest percentage increases or fastest rates of decline in the four socio-
economic groups. However, superimposed on this regional trend is another pattern,
for it is clear that amongst the low percentage rankings are many large SMLAs.
For example, London has large percentage of intermediate non-manual and skilled
manual workers and is the major exception to the general pattern of increase in the
South East. Most of the large SMLAs prominent in these low ranks of percentage
change are from less prosperous regions and include Manchester, Liverpool, Hull,
Glasgow and Sheffield.

The absolute changes of the professional and managerial group within SMLAs are
shown in Fig. 2.9, the most striking features of the distribution are the large
increases in the major SMLAs. (London, Birmingham, Manchester, Glasgow and Bristol

TABLE 2.43 Rankings of Socio-Economic Group Change in SMLAs, 1961-1971 (Percent)
Highest Ten Rankings and Lowest Ten Rankings

Professional and Managerial		Intermediate Non Manual		Skilled Manual		Semi and Unskilled Manual	
Basildon	104.4	Harlow	80.0	Basingstoke	54.2	Ellesmere Port	42.2
High Wycombe	98.6	Maidstone	57.1	Harlow	44.4	Crawley	31.2
Aldershot	84.1	Aylesbury	53.6	Basildon	38.5	Harlow	29.1
Crawley	81.3	High Wycombe	50.6	Ashford	28.4	Milton Keynes	23.0
Milton Keynes	80.6	Basingstoke	49.8	Thurrock	28.4	Stafford	15.1
Basingstoke	73.1	Basildon	49.5	Stevenage	28.3	Basildon	15.0
Chelmsford	72.5	Stevenage	45.7	Mansfield	27.4	Peterborough	11.4
Chatham	69.5	Milton Keynes	44.6	Eastbourne	23.4	Basingstoke	9.3
Luton	68.8	Thurrock	44.5	Kings Lynn	21.7	Letchworth	8.6
Reading	64.2	Chatham	42.9	Aylesbury	20.5	Gloucester	6.7
Liverpool	5.7	Blackburn	-4.5	Blackburn	-9.9	Sheffield	-22.3
Workington	5.5	Southport	-5.4	Huddersfield	-10.6	Burnley	-22.4
Hull	5.5	Greenock	-7.1	Liverpool	-10.8	Doncaster	-25.3
Aberdeen	5.3	Liverpool	-7.7	Rhondda	-11.0	Stoke	-25.6
Taunton	4.0	Rhondda	-8.4	Halifax	-11.9	Sunderland	-29.5
Carlisle	2.4	London	-8.4	Manchester	-12.1	Leigh	-30.0
Huddersfield	0.3	Falkirk	-9.4	Ayr	-12.4	Rhondda	-35.6
Hereford	-5.5	Manchester	-9.6	London	-15.9	Dunfermline	-38.0
Halifax	-8.5	Halifax	-10.2	Perth	-16.1	Mansfield	-43.9
Rhondda	-20.5	Glasgow	-12.8	Glasgow	-17.5	Barnsley	-44.4

all had increases of over 9,000 in this group). This no doubt reflects the need f
close contacts between the higher echelons of industrial management, the legal pro
fession and the civil service, which is aided by proximity in the major city centres. Fig. 2.9 indicates that the relatively large increase of this group within
Scotland is the result of a substantial increase in Glasgow's SMLA that is likely
to represent the growth of administrative functions in the Scottish region. Never
theless, surrounding these peaks of increase is the familiar regional pattern, for
most of the remaining large increases (between 6,000 and 9,000) are in the South
East or West Midlands while the majority of SMLAs in remaining regions have extremely small increases.

The distribution of changes in intermediate non-manual occupations presents a rath
different pattern (Fig. 2.10) but one that is by now familiar for it broadly resembles the patterns of change observed for total population, total employment, and
it is the same as that for the 0 to 14 years age group, 30 years to pensionable ag
group and the Irish immigrant community. The largest increases occurred in a belt
of SMLAs stretching from Birmingham to Portsmouth including Coventry, Oxford,
Reading, Basingstoke and Southampton. Large increases were to be found encircling
but excluding, London. This pattern would seem likely to reflect the efforts that
have been made to decentralise the more routine office functions away from the congestion of central London. It has been shown that intermediate non-manual occupations underwent expansion between 1961 and 1971, and whether by outmigration from
London, or newly generated growth within SMLAs, these occupations have served to
greatly influence total population and employment trends. Increases of those of
working age (and their children) have thus followed the pattern of change in this
social grouping.   The few areas which experienced a reduction in the number of
intermediate non-manual occupations were outside the South East; the decreases of
over 10,000 being in the large SMLAs of Glasgow, Manchester and London.

Apart from substantial declines in the West Midlands the pattern of changes in
skilled manual occupations (Fig. 2.11) broadly follows that observed for intermediate non-manual workers with both regional and city size factors in evidence. The
largest absolute increases were in a ring around London in the South East while
most of the decreases in this group were outside this region and especially concentrated in South Wales, Scotland,the North West, Yorkshire and Humberside and
the North. Again, however, the main feature of those SMLAs which experienced a
large reduction in skilled manual occupations (greater than 20,000) was their large
size (Glasgow, Newcastle, Leeds, Liverpool, Manchester, Sheffield, Birmingham and
London).

The main feature of the absolute changes in semi and unskilled manual occupations
(Fig. 2.12) is, again, the prevalence of the largest decreases in the largest SMLAs
for London, Birmingham, Glasgow, Newcastle, Liverpool, Manchester, Stoke, Sheffield
and Leeds all had decreases in excess of 10,000. However, the regional pattern was
less clustered for this social group and SMLAs in all regions experienced decreases
The small number of SMLAs with increases in this group were in the South East and
Midlands.

Taken as a whole, these changes of socio-economic groups within SMLAs confirm the
existence of the powerful regional pattern noted before, but they also indicate
that within regions urban change patterns are dominated by the behaviour of the
large SMLAs. More particularly however, these SMLAs have some of the largest relative declines in the middle status intermediate non-manual and skilled manual
occupations, the largest absolute increases of professional and managerial groups
and the largest absolute declines of all other socio-economic groups. In contrast
smaller SMLAs surrounding the major cities frequently have larger relative or absolute increases in these socio-economic groups. This indicates a process of intra-
regional decentralisation which is to be found in its most extreme form in the

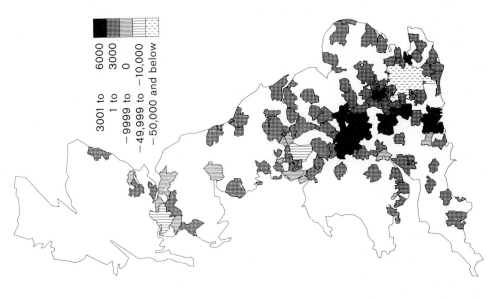

Fig. 2.10 Absolute change in intermediate
non-manual social groups in SMLAs,
1961–1971

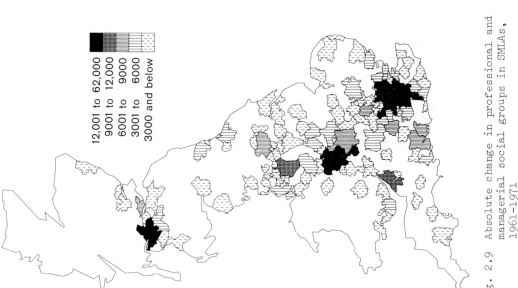

Fig. 2.9 Absolute change in professional and
managerial social groups in SMLAs,
1961–1971

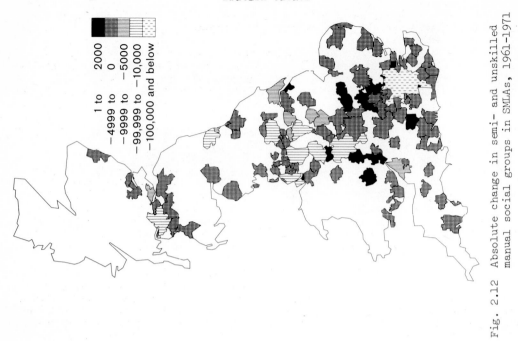

Fig. 2.12 Absolute change in semi- and unskilled
manual social groups in SMLAs, 1961–1971

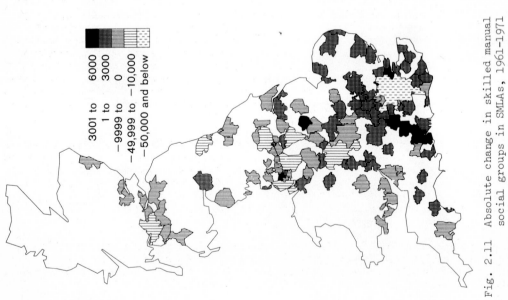

Fig. 2.11 Absolute change in skilled manual
social groups in SMLAs, 1961–1971

South East around London but also exists around other major centres including
Birmingham, Manchester, Leeds, Liverpool and Glasgow.

This raises the issue of what effect these population losses have had upon the
social composition of the major cities. Fears have frequently been expressed that
the social structure of the centres of the major urban areas is becoming polarised
in one of two possible ways; first by a tendency for higher rates of outmigration
by the comparatively affluent social groups leaving behind the relatively deprived
sections of society; or, second, by the tendency for higher rates of outmigration
by the middle status social groups, resulting in the juxtaposition of social extremes in the form of rich and poor.

National intra-urban changes indicated that there was relative decentralisation of
the professional and managerial (rings growing faster than cores), limited decentralisation in decline of the semi- and unskilled manual (cores declining faster
than rings), and absolute decentralisation of the other middle-status groups (core
decline - ring growth). This theme is considered in greater detail next concentrating on the distributions of the professional and managerial and the semi- and
unskilled manual within SMLAs.

The highest rankings for the percentage changes are broadly similar for the two
groups in the cores, being mainly new or expanded towns in the South East; many
are the same SMLAs in both instances, (see Table 2.44). Therefore, despite the
overall national decrease in the number in semi- and unskilled manual occupations,
there have been considerable increases in the number in this group in the zone of
most rapid urban growth in Britain, that is, in the belt surrounding London. There
are differences in the magnitude of these changes, however, the range for the top
rankings for the professional and managerial occupations is 57.8 to 104.4% as opposed to 15.8 and 91.2% for the semi- and unskilled manual. Note that the highest
ranked SMLAs for the middle-status groups were also located in this zone in the
South East, confirming the influence of the overall population redistribution on
the changes in the individual socio-economic groups.

The highest ranked rings are different. For the professional and managerial they
are, again, mainly new and expanded settlements in the South East. (Most of the
highest rankings for the middle-status groups are also in this region). However,
for the semi- and unskilled manual the highest ranks are a mixture of expanding
SMLAs in the South East, such as Thurrock and Letchworth, and industrial towns
elsewhere in Great Britain, including Preston, Teesside, Glasgow and Northampton.
This list can only be explained by resort to detailed analysis of the industrial
structure of these towns. Note that, in comparison to the cores, the increases
were relatively small, the range being only 2.8-27.4% in the highest ranked SMLAs.
Therefore, although there was little difference at the aggregate national level,
there were considerable differences in the individual city cores and rings in the
magnitude of the changes in the semi- and unskilled manual.

The bottom rankings in both cores and rings are similar for both groups, being
mainly SMLAs located outside the South East and the Midlands in the peripheral regions of Wales, Scotland, the North, North-West and Yorkshire/Humberside. The magnitude of the decreases in the semi- and unskilled manual are of the same order for
both cores and rings. In contrast, there are large decreases in the number of professional and managerial in the bottom ranked cores, ranging from -9.6 to -22.1%,
but only in four of the rings were there decreases.

These rankings suggest that different patterns of centralisation-decentralisation
are to be expected for the two groups. In fact, the patterns observed reflect
both the contrasting overall changes in the sizes of these groups and the overall
redistribution of population. (See Figs. 2.13 and 2.14).

TABLE 2.44 Rankings of Socio-Economic Group Change by Urban Zone, 1961-1971 (Percent)
Highest Ten Rankings and Lowest Ten Rankings.

Cores Professional and Managerial		Cores Semi and Unskilled Manual		Rings Professional and Managerial		Rings Semi and Unskilled Manual	
Basildon	104.4	Basingstoke	91.2	High Wycombe	123.1	Thurrock	27.4
Crawley	81.2	Milton Keynes	81.2	Harlow	117.9	Teesside	24.5
Milton Keynes	78.6	Ellesmere Port	42.2	Swindon	111.9	Grimsby	14.5
Basingstoke	70.6	Harlow	35.3	Thurrock	110.9	Preston	10.2
Aylesbury	69.6	Crawley	31.2	Chelmsford	105.6	Aldershot	8.2
Stevenage	67.8	Stevenage	29.0	Aldershot	101.8	Great Yarmouth	7.7
Hemel Hempstead	66.8	Stafford	27.6	Southend	99.3	Letchworth	5.7
Ashford	64.0	Aylesbury	24.2	St. Helens	98.7	Glasgow	5.5
Tunbridge Wells	59.4	Peterborough	18.3	Reading	97.9	Northampton	4.1
High Wycombe	57.7	Letchworth	15.8	Luton	96.6	Peterborough	2.8
Huddersfield	-9.6	Wigan	-24.0	Workington	16.2	Wakefield	-27.0
Workington	-10.7	Doncaster	-24.5	Ayr	14.1	York	-27.9
Newcastle	-11.1	Portsmouth	-25.8	Plymouth	13.5	Port Talbot	-28.0
Liverpool	-11.9	Burnley	-26.7	Dewsbury	6.8	Leigh	-28.9
Hull	-12.4	Stoke	-29.0	Kilmarnock	0.0	Sheffield	-31.8
Scunthorpe	-12.9	Warrington	-29.0	Halifax	0.0	Harlow	-37.5
Lincoln	-13.1	Leigh	-30.8	Carlisle	-0.5	Mansfield	-43.1
Halifax	-15.7	Rhondda	-35.6	Taunton	-2.1	Dunfermline	-45.3
Rhondda	-20.5	Barnsley	-39.0	Hereford	-12.7	Sunderland	-46.9
Preston	-22.1	Mansfield	-45.3	Perth	-18.0	Barnsley	-48.4

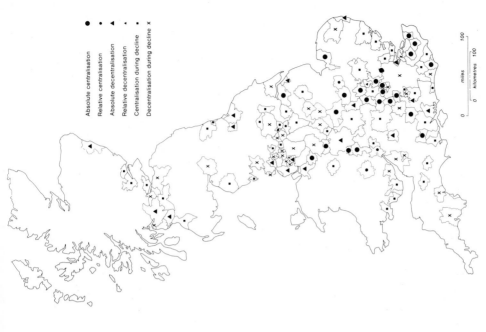

Fig. 2.14 Centralisation and decentralisation of
semi- and unskilled manual social
groups in SMLAs, 1961–1971

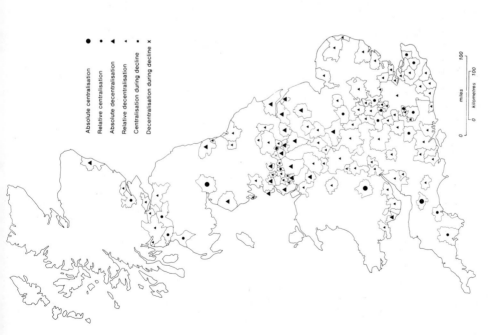

Fig. 2.13 Centralisation and decentralisation of
professional and managerial social
groups in SMLAs, 1961–1971

For the professional and managerial there is a predominance of decentralisation and
in particular, there was relative decentralisation in 78 SMLAs, which dominated mos
regions and most city-size groups. Absolute decentralisation occurred in 20 cases
and this included a number of SMLAs in Yorkshire/Humberside and the North West. It
also included three of the largest SMLAs (Liverpool, Manchester and Newcastle) whic
is in conformity with the absolute decentralisation of population. However, it excludes Birmingham, London and Glasgow which also experienced the absolute decentralisation of population; instead, there was relative decentralisation in these
SMLAs. In contrast, to the dominant decentralisation theme, there was centralisation in only 20 SMLAs, being relative centralisation in 17 of these. As expected,
relative centralisation was observed in a number of SMLAs in the South East, such
as Ashford, Aylesbury, Basingstoke and Hemel Hempstead, but was also present in 4
Scottish SMLAs, (Ayr, Kilmarnock, Motherwell and Perth).

In contrast, for the semi- and unskilled manual there is an almost equal division
between centralisation (63 SMLAs) and decentralisation (in 56 SMLAs). This reflect
a truly bipolar situation with few cases of relative centralisation or decentralisation, the largest numbers being centralisation or decentralisation in decline.
Of the 63 SMLAs which experienced centralisation, 36 were in decline, 23 were absolute and only 4 were relative. Centralisation in decline seems to occur in SMLAs
in most regions and the only strong regional clusterings occur in Scotland (5 out
of 11 SMLAs), Yorkshire and the North. Absolute centralisation typifies many of
the new and expanding towns of the South East.

Of the 56 SMLAs which experienced decentralisation of the semi- and unskilled manual, 17 were absolutely decentralising and 39 were decentralising in decline. Ther
were no instances of relative decentralisation. The distinctive locational characteristic of these SMLAs is that most are outside the South East, otherwise, they
are found in most regions. All the largest SMLAs, except Newcastle, experience
decentralisation, either absolutely (Birmingham, Liverpool and Glasgow) or in decline (London and Manchester).

The figures do not, by and large, indicate instances of clear polarisation in individual SMLAs. Certainly there are many SMLAs which experienced centralisation in
decline of the semi- and unskilled manual in the cores, and decentralisation to
the rings of the professional and managerial. However, disregarding these SMLAs
and considering only those which experienced absolute or relative centralisation
of the lowest status in the cores and absolute or relative decentralisation of the
highest status in the rings, there are only 17 SMLAs which experience this measure
of polarisation (Bedford, Crewe, Eastbourne, Harlow, High Wycombe, Kidderminster,
Kings Lynn, Leicester, Maidstone, Gloucester, Milton Keynes, St. Albans, Salisbury,
Scunthorpe, Slough, Stafford and Worcester). There is, therefore, no clear evidence for polarisation of the highest and lowest status occupational groups in the
large SMLAs. However, if centralisation in decline is taken as evidence of the
concentration of the semi- and unskilled manual in the cores, there was polarisation in many more SMLAs but still only including Newcastle of the largest metropolitan areas.

Age structure

Many intra-regional differences in age structure change could be concealed by the
previous analysis of MELAs aggregated to the regional scale. This section will
examine the extent to which regional patterns are manifest when cities are considered individually.

Table 2.45 presents the ten SMLAs with the highest percentage increases for each
of the four age groups. Not unexpectedly, the new or rapidly expanding towns such
as Basildon, Stevenage, Crawley, Harlow and Milton Keynes dominate the rankings for

TABLE 2.45   Rankings of Age Structure Change in SMLAs, 1961-1971 (Percent)
Highest Ten Rankings and Lowest Ten Rankings

0-14 Years		15-29 Years		30 to Pensionable Age		Pensionable Age and Above	
Basingstoke	72.8	Harlow	76.4	Basildon	42.4	Harlow	96.3
Milton Keynes	48.7	Basingstoke	75.2	Harlow	41.4	Crawley	65.3
Ellesmere Port	47.0	Milton Keynes	67.2	Basingstoke	36.1	Stevenage	50.0
Reading	46.8	Ashford	62.1	Stevenage	28.7	Eastbourne	40.4
Aldershot	46.1	Basildon	61.1	Ellesmere Port	26.7	Ellesmere Port	40.1
Basildon	45.9	Crawley	60.1	Aldershot	25.0	Edinburgh	38.5
Ashford	45.3	Stevenage	53.9	Crawley	22.1	Hemel Hempstead	34.4
High Wycombe	42.6	Canterbury	51.7	Chelmsford	21.6	Motherwell	33.5
Chelmsford	42.5	Thurrock	51.5	Aylesbury	20.2	Basildon	32.3
Wigan	40.1	Ellesmere Port	46.3	Milton Keynes	19.3	Torquay	32.2
Dundee	-1.0	London	4.6	Glasgow	-9.3	Bury	9.5
Kings Lynn	-2.8	Sunderland	4.6	Bolton	-9.5	Rochdale	8.7
Dunfermline	-3.2	Dunfermline	4.6	Liverpool	-9.8	Barrow in Furness	7.7
Watford	-3.4	Carlisle	4.1	Blackburn	-10.1	Rhondda	7.5
Aberdeen	-4.0	Ayr	4.0	Huddersfield	-10.9	Southport	7.3
Sunderland	-4.0	Workington	3.6	Edinburgh	-11.7	London	6.8
Workington	-4.1	Kings Lynn	2.1	Manchester	-11.8	Burnley	5.5
Newcastle	-4.2	Liverpool	1.1	Burnley	-12.6	Halifax	5.3
Liverpool	-4.5	Greenock	0.7	Halifax	-13.3	Falkirk	5.0
Greenock	-6.8	Glasgow	0.1	London	-13.7	Blackburn	4.3

all age groups. With a few exceptions (such as Ellesmere Port) these SMLAs are located mainly in the South East. These are towns with large proportions of child bearing adults and high rates of natural increase, supplemented, of course, with high rates of net inmigration, mostly from Greater London. The pattern is less consistent in the case of the above pensionable age group for the seaside resorts of Torquay and Eastbourne both figure in the ranks for large percentage increase. In contrast to the new towns these are SMLAs with already old age structures and net decreases in population due to natural change. The considerable percentage increases of the elderly in these resorts therefore reflects a substantial net inflow of retirement migration.

The ten bottom ranking SMLAs with either the largest percentage decreases or smallest percentage increases for each of the four age groups are also shown in Table 2.45. The vast majority of these SMLAs are located in the regions of Yorkshire and Humberside, the North West, the North, Wales and Scotland. Amongst these northern SMLAs are many of the largest large cities, despite the fact that the rankings refer to percentage changes. Liverpool, Glasgow, Newcastle, Edinburgh and Manchester all figure prominently in these low ranks and this serves to emphasise the enormous population loss that has occurred in these cities in the recent years. The major exception to the broad pattern is the London SMLA which recorded only small percentage increases in the 15 to 29 and above pensionable age groups and the largest percentage decline in the 30 years to pensionable age group. This last result is indicative of the substantial outmigration from London of those of working age to the new and expanding SMLAs surrounding London during the sixties.

The absolute changes in age groups reveal a more complex pattern than the percentage changes. The absolute changes in the population aged between 0 and 14 years in SMLAs between 1961 and 1971 are shown in Fig. 2.15. The most striking feature of the pattern is the large increase in the Midlands (Birmingham, Coventry and Leicester) together with the cities of Leeds, Manchester, Bristol, Reading, Oxford, Portsmouth and Luton. However, other large cities, notably London, Newcastle, Liverpool, Hull and Aberdeen also have declines in this age group. With the exception of London and Watford, the largest absolute decreases in the 0-14 age group are exhibited by SMLAs in the North, Scotland and Wales. Conversely apart from Wigan, Leeds and Manchester, the vast majority of SMLAs with increases in this age group are located either in the South West, the South East or the two Midlands regions. In the case of the South East, Fig. 2.15 illustrates that the absolute increase in the 0-14 years group observed for this region as a whole conceals considerable differences within the region. London's SMLA shows a decline in this age group while a belt of surrounding SMLAs have considerable increases.

Figure 2.16 shows the absolute increases in the 15-29 years age group within SMLAs between 1961 and 1971. The pattern indicates large increases in the major cities including London, Birmingham, Leeds, Manchester, Coventry, Bristol and Southampton. Large cities have traditionally been attractive to persons in the 15-29 years age groups because of their educational, employment and recreational facilities but it is noticeable that many of the other large cities have relatively small increases in this age group. These include Liverpool and Glasgow, and again cities in the northern regions tend to have smaller absolute increases than those in the south of the country.

The absolute changes in the 30 years to pensionable age group in SMLAs (Fig. 2.17) indicate a pattern different to those observed for the two previous age groups. In this case the largest absolute declines occur in the large cities including London, Manchester, Birmingham, Leeds, Sheffield, Newcastle, Liverpool, Glasgow and Edinburgh. The largest absolute increases exist in a belt of SMLAs surrounding London but there are clearly smaller belts of absolute increase surrounding the other major conurbations in the West Midlands, North West and Scotland. This

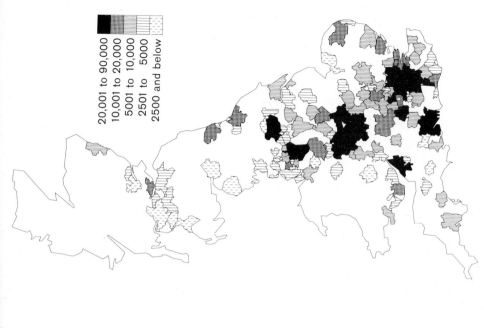

Fig. 2.16 Absolute change of population aged
between 15 to 29 years in SMLAs, 1961–1971

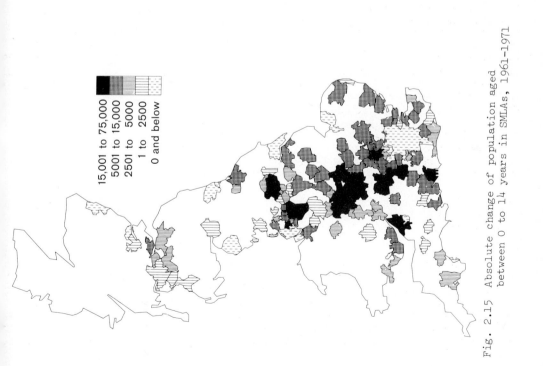

Fig. 2.15 Absolute change of population aged
between 0 to 14 years in SMLAs, 1961–1971

suggests a form of intra-regional decentralisation in which those in the 30 years to pensionable age groups are leaving the major conurbations for surrounding smaller urban areas. Again it is clear that superimposed upon this pattern is a powerful regional trend since there are decreases or only small absolute increases in many northern SMLAs.

The changes in the above pensionable age group (Fig. 2.18) are closely aligned with the 15-29 years age group for the largest absolute increases again occur in large cities such as London, Birmingham and Manchester. However, unlike the 15-29 years age group, the absolute changes in the above pensionable age group show little of the north-south distinction. Thus, Glasgow, Newcastle and Liverpool all have large absolute increases in pensioners while many southern SMLAs have relatively small increases.

Comparing these patterns of change for the four age groups some important relation- ships emerge. Both the 15-29 years and above pensionable age groups are clearly increasing in the major cities. In the case of the former group this is likely to reflect large rates of net inmigration while in the case of the old age group this is likely to reflect an unwillingness or inability to move out of the major cities. In contrast, the 30 years to pensionable age group shows declines in the major cities but increases in surrounding SMLAs. Given the importance of migration as a determinant of urban change, it may be inferred that many persons aged between 30 years to pensionable age (together with their children) have been leaving the major conurbations for smaller outlying areas and new towns. Superimposed on these intra regional processes is the powerful north-south pattern of change. Taken as a whole these disaggregated patterns for SMLAs therefore support the interpretation placed upon the aggregate regional patterns, for close or contiguous SMLAs frequently display remarkably consistent behaviour. The patterns observed within Economic Planning Regions thus encapsulate powerful processes of age specific population growth and decline which are not mere statistical artifacts.

The changes in the age groups in the urban zones of individual MELAs are similar to the changes observed in the distribution of total population. That is, the largest increases and decreases for all age groups are often in the same MELAs as experienced the greatest changes in total population. Therefore, to reduce the amount of data presented here and to avoid repetition, only the changes in the 15-29 age groups are presented in detail.

The highest and lowest rankings for the 15-29 group in the cores and rings are presented in Table 2.46. In both zones the highest ranking places are in similar areas, being new and expanded towns in the South East. For example in the cases of Harlow, Ashford and Canterbury, both the cores and rings of these SMLAs are in the highest rankings. All these SMLAs can be expected to have gained population from the decentralisation from London and this particularly would be the case in this age group, given the age specific nature of migration. However, this pattern is not peculiar to this age group for similar types of SMLAs also dominate the highest rankings in the other age groups. The increases in the other age groups, however, tend to be smaller and this applies particularly to those of 30 to pen- sionable age; the range of percentage changes in the top ten in the cores is only 12.40 to 72.20% for this group, compared to 49.0 to 139.8% for those aged 15-29.

The bottom rankings in the 15-29 group in the cores and rings are also similar in that most are located in the peripheral regions of Wales, Scotland, North, North West and Yorkshire/Humberside, that is, in the regions known to have experienced considerable population losses. However, there are differences between the cores and the rings. The losses in the cores are greater than in the rings and, in fact, there were decreases in only four of the latter. This is of course to be expected given the greater losses of population in the cores. Another difference is that

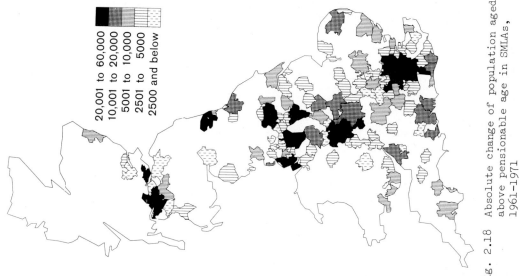

Fig. 2.18 Absolute change of population aged
above pensionable age in SMLAs,
1961–1971

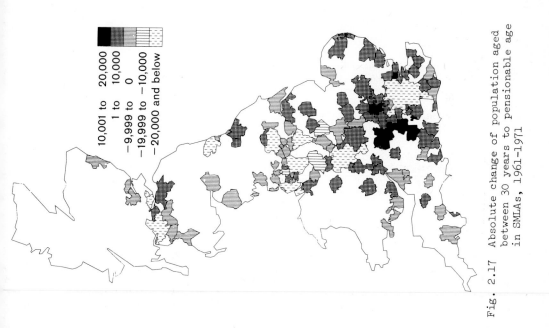

Fig. 2.17 Absolute change of population aged
between 30 years to pensionable age
in SMLAs, 1961–1971

TABLE 2.46   Rankings of Change in Population Aged 15-29 by
Urban Zone, 1961-1971 (Percent) Highest Ten Rankings and
Lowest Ten Rankings

CORES		RINGS	
Basingstoke	139.8	Thurrock	136.5
Milton Keynes	86.3	Harlow	93.2
Harlow	75.2	Ashford	71.8
Stevenage	74.8	Colchester	61.8
Basildon	61.1	Reading	59.4
Crawley	60.1	Swindon	57.4
Aylesbury	57.0	Chelmsford	57.1
Ashford	55.4	Maidstone	55.3
Hemel Hempstead	52.9	Southend	54.9
Canterbury	49.0	Canterbury	53.6
Portsmouth	-0.7	Sunderland	6.3
Greenock	-1.8	Barnsley	5.4
Manchester	-2.9	Workington	4.4
Newcastle	-3.5	Ayr	2.7
Birmingham	-3.7	Hereford	0.3
Liverpool	-7.6	Dunfermline	0.0
Warrington	-7.9	Harrogate	-1.5
Preston	-9.7	Swansea	-3.9
Glasgow	-10.1	Kings Lynn	-7.5
Rhondda	-11.1	Carlisle	-9.4

the bottom ranked cores include some of the largest cities, in particular, Manchester, Newcastle, Birmingham, Glasgow and Liverpool. Thus the very large population losses in the cores of these largest SMLAs receive notable contributions from
the 15-29 age group.

The bottom ranked areas for the other age groups are mostly from the same periphera
regions. The decreases, however, tend to be larger in the 0-14 and 30 to pensionable age groups; for example, the range for the bottom ten ranked cores is -17.4
to -24.4 for those of 30 to pensionable age. Surprisingly, however, no cores and
only two rings (Falkirk and Gloucester) experienced losses in the numbers above
pensionable age. The bottom rankings of the cores also reinforce the dominance of
the largest cities with London (30 to pensionable age, and above pensionable age)
added to the list of large cores with losses in particular age groups.

The rankings suggest that the centralisation-decentralisation patterns will resembl
those for total population. These are displayed for the 15-29 age group in Fig.
2.19. Given the overall increase in the size of this group, however, it is expecte
that there are far fewer instances of absolute centralisation or decentralisation,
but more examples of relative centralisation and decentralisation. This is so.
There are no SMLAs where there was a decline of population in both cores and rings,
therefore none are classified as centralising or decentralising in decline. There
are 3 SMLAs - Carlisle, Harrogate and King's Lynn - where there is absolute centralisation. Most of the small number of instances of centralisation, however, are
of relative centralisation; these 23 SMLAs, as expected, are dominated by a belt
of new and expanding towns surrounding London. Most SMLAs experienced decentralisation and this was mainly relative decentralisation (in 83 SMLAs). Only in 10
SMLAs was there absolute decentralisation and this included some of the largest
cities (Birmingham, Liverpool, London, Manchester, Newcastle and Glasgow). Therefore, outside of the South East and of the largest SMLAs relative decentralisation

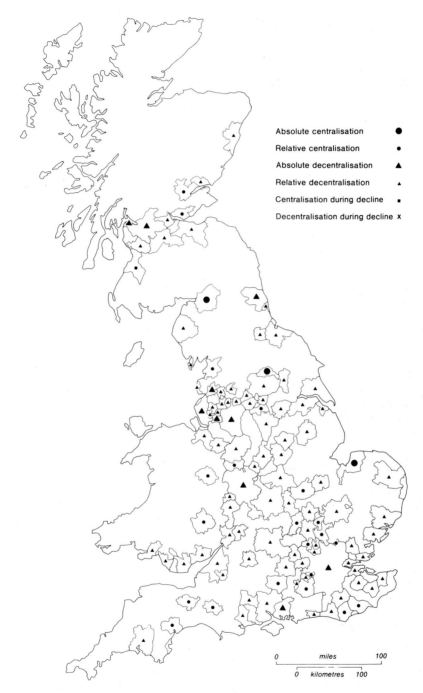

Fig. 2.19   Centralisation and decentralisation of population aged
between 15-29 years in SMLAs, 1961-1971

dominated the intra-urban changes in this group.

The pattern of centralisation-decentralisation in the other age groups bear some resemblance to the 15-29 group. For those above pensionable age the resemblance is very close, except that relative decentralisation is even more dominant, being recorded in 103 SMLAs. There was relative centralisation in 14 SMLAs, many of these being located in the South East. For the 0-14 group the majority of SMLAs were also classified as experiencing relative decentralisation, with absolute decentralisation in the largest SMLAs and relative centralisation in 14 SMLAs, mostly in the South East. The 30 to pensionable age group was somewhat different, however because of the large overall decrease in this group. Thus, most SMLAs experienced either decentralisation in decline or absolute decentralisation. But in the South East (excepting London) most of the SMLAs experienced relative decentralisation or centralisation, in line with the changes in total population in this region.

In summary, it has been observed that changes in the individual age groups were dominated by the overall redistribution of population which occurred, particularly in the South East and in the cores of the largest SMLAs. The combination of the high rates of growth in the rings and the national changes in the size of the age groups led to relative decentralisation in most areas for those above pensionable age, those aged 15-29 and, to a lesser extent, those aged under 14. The 30 to pensionable age groups experienced decentralisation, either absolutely or in decline, in most areas. However, in the South East the changes in this group resemble those for the population as a whole, that is, there was relative centralisation or decentralisation.

Birthplace structure

There is evidence to suggest that geographical concentration is a frequent characteristic of ethnic minorities in urban industrial societies. In consequence, although considerable regional variations were observed in the location of birthplace groups previously, these differences should be even more pronounced when SMLAs are treated individually. Table 2.47 shows the top ten ranking SMLAs in terms of their percentage increases in the Irish, Indian sub-continent, African and West Indies birthplace groups. As with the previous regional analysis, the percentage changes in these groups should be considered carefully because of the small numbers in many areas in 1961. For comparative purposes the absolute increases in each SMLA are also indicated in Table 2.47.

As expected, the percentage increases of the Irish birthplace group conform strongly to those for the total population, with new or expanding towns amongst the highest ranks. This would seem to indicate substantial immigration of Irish persons into these new communities although the presence of temporary Irish construction workers still engaged in activity of this sort at the time of the Census cannot be discounted.

Amongst the most remarkable features of the percentage increases for the Indian sub-continent group is their enormous size (ranging from approximately 1600 to 400%. However, the absolute increases put the results into some perspective, for they indicate relatively small numbers of this immigrant group in many of the SMLAs in 1961. Nevertheless, the increases, amounting in some cases to over ten times the original number of persons in these birthplace groups in 1961, do represent, in many cases, a considerable influx of Indian sub-continent immigrants into these areas during the sixties. Leicester should be noted for its particularly large increase of 10,467 upon a total of 2,350 persons in the Indian sub-continent group in 1961. No less remarkable than the size of the percentage increases is the spatial patterning of these high ranking SMLAs for, with the exception of Leicester, they are all located in a belt of towns stretching from Bolton to Wakefield which includes Rochdale, Blackburn, Burnley, Bury, Dewsbury, Huddersfield and Halifax.

TABLE 2.47 Rankings in Birthplace Structure Change in SMLAs, 1961-1971 (Percent and Absolute)
Highest Ten Rankings and Lowest Ten Rankings

Irish	%	Abs	Indian Sub-Continent	%	Abs	African	%	Abs	West Indies	%	Abs
Basingstoke	98.8	976	Rochdale	1,588.7	3,654	Bolton	2,986.3	1,523	Harlow	516.0	129
Milton Keynes	63.7	466	Blackburn	1,212.4	4,110	Leicester	2,184.5	7,034	Ashford	420.0	126
Ashford	57.1	269	Bolton	800.3	4,626	Coventry	1,140.3	2,634	Basingstoke	398.2	219
Basildon	53.3	665	Burnley	594.0	998	Rochdale	1,111.5	289	Barnsley	350.0	21
Stevenage	49.6	755	Bury	525.2	751	Crawley	1,092.6	295	Hartlepool	300.0	9
Harlow	45.2	575	Dewsbury	509.6	3,735	Preston	1,055.0	633	Bury	300.0	96
Darlington	38.2	219	Wakefield	470.3	602	Dewsbury	800.0	112	Corby	270.8	65
Bury	37.5	588	Leicester	445.4	10,467	Luton	757.4	977	Great Yarmouth	266.7	56
Norwich	36.3	472	Huddersfield	443.7	4,029	Birmingham	734.3	7,167	Luton	247.4	2,335
Great Yarmouth	36.1	217	Halifax	425.3	1,697	Bedford	732.2	432	Peterborough	235.7	370
Hereford	-10.9	-86	Salisbury	-2.4	-7	Ellesmere Port	75.0	12	Taunton	8.6	3
Kilmarnock	-12.3	-147	Plymouth	-4.6	-41	Liverpool	73.2	746	Port Talbot	7.1	8
Ayr	-13.0	-144	Workington	-5.8	-6	Greenock	72.2	13	Carlisle	6.7	1
Falkirk	-13.4	-204	Liverpool	-6.4	-178	St. Helens	66.7	14	Blackburn	3.1	2
Dunfermline	-14.6	-191	Bournemouth	-8.0	-122	Hull	66.0	130	Exeter	2.3	2
Rhondda	-18.9	-50	Hastings	-8.0	-49	Kilmarnock	63.3	19	Edinburgh	-0.8	-3
Glasgow	-21.2	-276	Hereford	-11.7	-18	Edinburgh	53.0	436	York	-9.8	-8
Newport	-21.9	-535	Torquay	-12.2	-38	Yeovil	42.0	21	Torquay	-22.2	-14
Motherwell	-24.9	-938	Carlisle	-17.4	-33	Torquay	33.7	31	Kilmarnock	-25.0	-3
Greenock	-29.7	-843	Perth	-20.0	-35	Corby	6.9	7	Sunderland	-37.9	-11

The employment opportunities offered by the textile industries of these areas together with a suitable residential environment not dominated by local authority
housing may be suggested as key factors leading to these locations. Previously it
was indicated that both the North West and Yorkshire and Humberside experienced
considerable percentage increases in the Indian sub-continent group and, clearly,
within these regions the large percentage increases have been highly concentrated.

Percentage increases of the African birthplace group are even larger than those
for the Indian sub-continent, but only in Bolton, Leicester, Coventry and Birmingh
do these represent increases above 2,000 persons. The location of these high rank
ing SMLAs is less consistent than the Indian group, for despite increases in the
North West and Yorkshire and Humberside, there are also large percentage increases
in the West Midlands and the South East.

Section 2.2.2 indicated less regional concentration in the distribution of percent
age increases from the West Indian birthplace group than for either the Indian sub
continent or African groups. Similarly, the top ten ranking SMLAs in terms of
percentage increase in the West Indian birthplace group reveal a less distinct
pattern than the two previous groups. Not only do new or expanding towns in the
South East figure prominently in the ranks but there are widely dispersed SMLAs
including Corby in the East Midlands, Great Yarmouth and Peterborough in East
Anglia, Barnsley in Yorkshire and Humberside, Bury in the North West and Hartlepoo
in the North. However, the absolute increases indicate that, with the exception o
Luton, these large percentage increases signify extremely small absolute increases
of the West Indian birthplace group.

The bottom ten ranking SMLAs in terms of their percentage change in the four birth
place groups are also shown in Table 2.47. The largest percentage decreases in th
Irish group occur in Scotland and Wales and suggest that poor employment opportunities have prompted considerable outmigration of the Irish from these regions. Th
largest percentage decreases of the Indian sub-continent group include a heterogeneous set of SMLAs from various regions. The most prominent type of SMLA are
south coast seaside towns including Bournemouth, Hastings, Torquay and Plymouth.
The absolute decreases are extremely small in all these low ranks of percentage
change in the Indian sub-continent group and this may indicate relatively small
fluctuations around what is essentially a stable population. The lowest ranking
SMLAs in terms of percentage change in the African immigrant group are all increas
and, apart from Yeovil, Torquay and Corby, are all located in Scotland, Yorkshire
and Humberside or the North West. A similar pattern is displayed by the West
Indies immigrant group with a combination of SMLAs either in the South West (Torqu
Exeter and Yeovil) or the northern regions. Again, however, the absolute changes
associated with these low ranks of percentage change are all extremely small.

Apart from the Irish birthplace group, the low ranks of percentage change amongst
SMLAs indicate a situation which is essentially static rather than one of decline.
Nevertheless, these SMLAs are important for prominent amongst them are southern
urban areas with high rates of net immigration of the indigenous population togeth
with northern urban areas with poor employment opportunities. As such they provid
additional evidence to support the 'barrier' and 'employment' hypotheses outlined
previously.

The absolute changes of Irish immigrants (Fig. 2.20) reveal a remarkable belt of
increases in large SMLAs stretching through the centre of the country from Leeds t
Southampton. The largest increases within this belt include Manchester, Birmingha
Coventry, Oxford, Bristol, Luton and Reading, while SMLAs with either decreases or
small absolute increases are predominantly in the peripheral regions and include
Glasgow, Cardiff and Newcastle. This pattern of change follows in broad outline
the pattern of population and employment change throughout the country during the

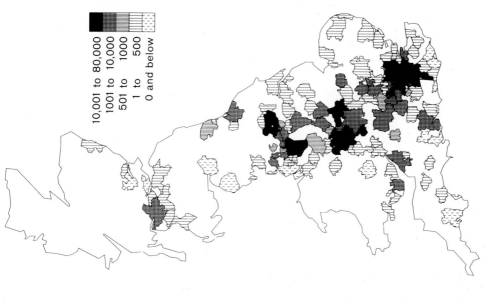

10,001 to 80,000
1001 to 10,000
501 to 1000
1 to 500
0 and below

Fig. 2.21 Absolute change of Indian sub-continent immigrants in SMLAs, 1961-1971

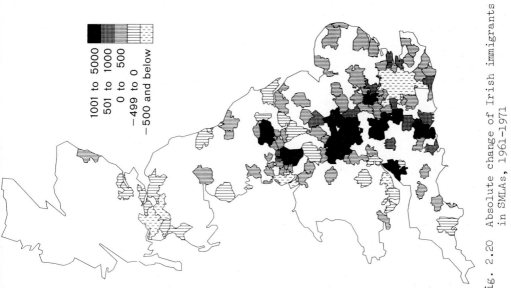

1001 to 5000
501 to 1000
0 to 500
-499 to 0
-500 and below

Fig. 2.20 Absolute change of Irish immigrants in SMLAs, 1961-1971

period 1961 to 1971 and indicates the importance of employment opportunities as a
determinant of Irish immigrant location. In this respect it is interesting to not
that both London and Liverpool have declines in their Irish immigrant communities
while some of the SMLAs with increases in this birthplace group are important moto
manufacturing centres. The considerable decline of employment in London coupled
with chronic unemployment on Merseyside have therefore led to increases in the siz
of the Irish communities in the SMLAs of the West Midlands with their expanding
employment structures. Manchester is the major exception to this pattern for despite a considerable population and employment decline during the sixties this SMLA
has the largest absolute increase of persons born in Ireland. This may reflect
Manchester's role as a reception area for Irish immigrants into this country.

The absolute changes in the Indian sub-continent birthplace group (Fig. 2.21) reve
a somewhat different pattern to the Irish, for the largest increases are concentra
ted to a much greater extent in the major cities. Thus, apart from Birmingham,
Manchester, Leeds and Coventry, there are also increases of this group in London
and Glasgow.   Substantial increases are also recorded in the much smaller SMLAs
in the North West and Yorkshire and Humberside, such as Bolton, Blackburn and
Huddersfield. Unlike the Irish immigrant group, then, changes in the Indian sub-
continent category display much less obvious correspondence with the general pattern of employment change. They have, nevertheless concentrated in the major SMLAs
many of which have experienced population and employment loss between 1961 and 197
and from this it might reasonably be inferred that they have taken up occupations
vacated by the outmigration of the indigenous population.

The absolute changes of the African birthplace group (Fig. 2.22) are similar to th
Indian sub-continent group in that the largest increases occur in the largest SMLA
but in this case London dominates the increases to a much greater extent. Once
again, outside of this major industrial corridor the absolute magnitude of the increases in this group are extremely small. The absolute changes in the West Indie
birthplace group (Fig. 2.23) also reveal a massive concentration of the increase
in the South East with extremely small increases in Scotland, the Northern region,
Wales, East Anglia and the South West.

It is clear from these maps of absolute changes that, within the regions of larges
increase, overseas immigrants have concentrated in particular SMLAs, these usually
being the largest. This process is most noticeable in the South East where London
has a massive increase in most of the immigrant groups but the surrounding areas
have extremely small increases. This phenomenon raises the issue of whether these
increases are a natural reflection of the large size of these SMLAs or if this represents a tendency for immigrants to be over represented in these large urban
areas. Table 2.48 is an attempt to answer this question by an examination of the
top ten proportions in the four immigrant groups in SMLAs in 1971. The SMLAs with
the largest percentages of the Irish immigrant group include the large centres of
London, Manchester and Birmingham but also include a set of smaller SMLAs (Luton,
Coventry, Watford, Slough, St. Albans, Corby and Rochdale). Significantly these
SMLAs are all located in the main industrial axis of the country. A somewhat diff
erent pattern is revealed by the SMLAs with the largest proportions in the Indian
sub-continent birthplace group for these are predominantly the North West and
Yorkshire and Humberside (Dewsbury, Blackburn, Rochdale, Bolton, Huddersfield and
Leeds) and the West Midlands (Birmingham, Leicester and Coventry).   The percentag
in the top ten ranking SMLAs for the African group are much smaller than those for
the two previous groups but again include London and the large urban areas of the
Midlands (Coventry and Leicester). In this case, however, there are also relatively large percentages in some of the SMLAs surrounding London, including Slough,
Crawley, Woking, Luton and Bedford. The rankings of the percentages in the final
group - the West Indies - also include London and some of its surrounding SMLAs
(High Wycombe, Bedford, Luton and Letchworth) together with Birmingham and a set

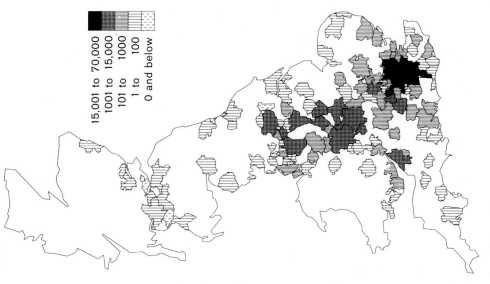

Fig. 2.23 Absolute change of West Indies
immigrants in SMLAs, 1961–1971

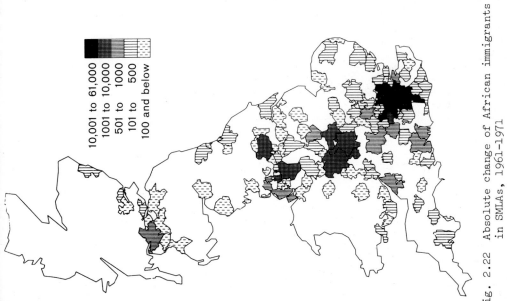

Fig. 2.22 Absolute change of African immigrants
in SMLAs, 1961–1971

TABLE 2.48 Rankings of Birthplace Structure in SMLAs, 1971 (Percent)
            Highest Ten Rankings and Lowest Ten Rankings

Irish		Indian Sub-continent		African		West Indies	
Luton	3.9	Dewsbury	4.1	Leicester	1.4	London	1.9
Coventry	3.8	Blackburn	3.1	London	0.9	Huddersfield	1.6
London	3.4	Rochdale	3.1	Bolton	0.6	Birmingham	1.4
Watford	3.0	Slough	2.9	Slough	0.5	High Wycombe	1.3
Manchester	2.9	Huddersfield	2.5	Crawley	0.5	Bedford	1.2
Slough	2.7	Birmingham	2.4	Blackburn	0.5	Gloucester	1.1
St. Albans	2.7	Leicester	2.4	Coventry	0.4	Luton	1.0
Birmingham	2.7	Leeds	2.0	Woking	0.4	Letchworth	1.0
Corby	2.6	Bolton	2.0	Luton	0.4	Nottingham	0.9
Rochdale	2.6	Coventry	1.9	Bedford	0.4	Reading	0.9
Grimsby	0.6	Leigh	0.10	Ellesmere Port	0.04	Carlisle	0.01
Stoke	0.6	Dunfermline	0.10	Motherwell	0.04	Workington	0.01
Barnsley	0.6	St. Helens	0.09	Scunthorpe	0.04	Hartlepool	0.01
Dundee	0.6	Greenock	0.09	Hartlepool	0.03	Leigh	0.01
Hartlepool	0.5	Motherwell	0.08	Wigan	0.03	Falkirk	0.01
Newcastle	0.5	Kilmarnock	0.08	Greenock	0.03	Greenock	0.01
Hull	0.5	Workington	0.07	St. Helens	0.02	Kilmarnock	0.01
Sunderland	0.3	Falkirk	0.07	Leigh	0.02	Motherwell	0.00
Aberdeen	0.3	Rhondda	0.05	Barnsley	0.01	Sunderland	0.00
Rhondda	0.2	Barnsley	0.05	Rhondda	0.01	Rhondda	0.00

of more widely dispersed SMLAs (Gloucester, Huddersfield, Nottingham and Reading).

The bottom ten rankings of SMLAs with the smallest proportions in the four birthplace groups in 1971 are all remarkably similar in their general pattern. The
vast majority of these SMLAs are located in the regions of Scotland, Wales, the
Northern region and to a lesser extent certain areas of the North West and Yorkshire
and Humberside.

Combining this information with that described previously it is apparent that the
large increases in the major SMLAs of the South East and Midlands have resulted in
relatively higher proportions of certain immigrant groups in these areas. However,
many smaller SMLAs, and particularly some in the belt from Bolton to Wakefield, also
frequently have relatively large proportions of certain groups. Despite the diversity of the ranks of percentages at either extreme, they suggest a pattern in which
the SMLAs with the largest proportions of the birthplace groups are found in the
main industrial zone from the South East, through the Midlands to the North West,
with much smaller proportions outside this belt. But even with the relatively large
influx of many of these birthplace groups into British SMLAs in the sixties it is
important to stress that in no case do these individual groups exceed 5% of the
total population.

The regional and national trends examined previously indicated considerable differences in the intra-urban changes of the British and New Commonwealth immigrant groups. Did these changes also exist at the level of most individual SMLAs, or was
the overall redistribution of population a more important influence at this scale?
This section considers the distributions of the West Indians and Indian sub-
continent group; for the former there was relative decentralisation in most regions, and for the latter there was relative centralisation in all regions.

The changes in the cores and rings, 1961-71, are displayed in Table 2.49. It is
once again not greatly helpful to consider percentage changes for the rankings in
individual SMLAs because these are distorted by the very small absolute numbers in
some areas in 1961. For example, a 300% increase in the number of West Indians in
the core of Hartlepool represents an absolute increase of only 9 as there were only
3 West Indians in this area in 1961. Therefore, the rankings of absolute changes
are considered here. For both immigrant groups the highest rankings in both cores
and rings were in the largest SMLAs (London, Birmingham, Leeds, Manchester and
Liverpool) and in the regions, already identified, of greatest overall increase for
these groups; that is, the South East and Midlands for the West Indians and Yorkshire and Humberside, the North West for those born in the Indian sub-continent.
The increases in the cores were, of course, far larger and, in fact, there were
only small increases of the West Indians in the rings, exceeding 400 only in London
and Birmingham. For both groups in both zones the increases are dominated by London
to the extent that the increase in this single SMLA exceeds the <u>combined</u> total of
the increases in the next nine highest ranked areas. (The rankings of percentage
changes incidentally include SMLAs from the same regions but exclude the largest
cities).

The bottom rankings are very small decreases and are characterised as being mainly,
but not entirely, located in the peripheral regions. However, a surprising number
of South East SMLAs did experience decreases. Of the largest SMLAs only Liverpool,
for the West Indians, and Newcastle, for the Indian sub-continent group, appear in
the bottom rankings. (The bottom rankings of the percentage changes include SMLAs
of similar size and location but are not actually the same as for absolute changes).

The rankings of absolute changes, therefore, included similar SMLAs in both cores
and rings, although the changes were of very different magnitude. The largest increases were in the largest SMLAs but, otherwise, the increases and decreases

TABLE 2.49   Ranking of Birthplace Structure Change by Urban Zone, 1961-1971 (Absolute)
Highest Ten Rankings and Lowest Ten Rankings

Cores	Cores	Rings	Rings
Indian Sub-Continent	West Indies	Indian Sub-Continent	West Indies
London 63,830	London 62,995	London 13,241	London 4,849
Birmingham 46,530	Birmingham 12,927	Birmingham 2,730	Birmingham 1,227
Leeds 16,579	Manchester 4,280	Dewsbury 1,650	Letchworth 378
Leicester 10,225	Leeds 3,284	Manchester 1,264	Nottingham 290
Coventry 9,300	Bristol 2,339	Slough 961	Manchester 261
Manchester 8,936	Luton 2,250	Letchworth 724	Oxford 173
Slough 5,054	Nottingham 2,142	Chatham 540	Leicester 156
Bolton 4,560	Coventry 1,663	Burnley 410	Slough 137
Blackburn 4,071	Reading 1,628	Leeds 404	Reading 131
Huddersfield 3,975	Huddersfield 1,522	Reading 348	Liverpool 127
Perth -9	Port Talbot -1	Harrogate -10	Milton Keynes -2
Carlisle -13	Carlisle -2	Hastings -11	Falkirk -2
Salisbury -19	Kilmarnock -2	Exeter -12	Aberdeen -3
Hastings -38	Yeovil -2	Dunfermline -12	Stafford -5
Torquay -38	Dewsbury -4	Gloucester -13	Aylesbury -8
Edinburgh -61	Taunton -5	Carlisle -20	Northampton -11
Plymouth -72	Sunderland -9	Hereford -22	Blackburn -26
Portsmouth -80	York -14	Ayr -23	Edinburgh -30
Bournemouth -123	Torquay -14	Perth -26	Newport -40
Liverpool -224	Newcastle -20	Guildford -31	Watford -48

conformed to the known regional patterns of change for these immigrant groups.

Did the two groups have different patterns of centralisation and decentralisation? These patterns are displayed in Figs. 2.24 and 2.25 which return to the use of percentage changes. It is clear that very different patterns did exist. The pattern for the West Indians bears the same resemblance to that for total population. There was decentralisation in 59 SMLAs and in 47 cases this was relative. There was absolute centralisation in 12 SMLAs and centralisation in decline in Sunderland. There was decentralisation in almost an equal number of SMLAs, 57; of these, 47 were relative decentralisation, 9 were absolute decentralisation and there was decentralisation in decline in Edinburgh.

As with total population, centralisation of the West Indians is observed in a number of new and expanding SMLAs in a ring surrounding London. However, unlike the total population, centralisation is also observed in East Anglia, Scotland, the North and in parts of Yorkshire and Humberside, and the North West. There is decentralisation in the Midlands, Yorkshire and Humberside, and south of London. In the largest SMLAs, there was centralisation in Leeds and Glasgow and decentralisation in London, Birmingham, Liverpool, Manchester and Newcastle. There is, therefore a tendency for decentralisation to occur in the areas where the largest numbers of West Indians are found with the exception of the centralisation in the new and expanding towns of the South East. However, this pattern is by no means clearly developed.

A different pattern is observed for those born in the Indian sub-continent. In contrast to all other immigrant groups, there was centralisation in a majority (85) of SMLAs. This centralisation, mostly relative (68 SMLAs), dominated in a braod area stretching from the South East through the Midlands to Yorkshire and Humberside, and the North West, that is, in the areas where the largest increases were observed in this group. This reinforces the suggestion that centralisation is occurring because the more recent Indian sub-continent immigrants are more likely to be non-white than those in this group who were resident in Britain in 1961. Note that centralisation occurred in all the largest SMLAs except Newcastle and Liverpool. Decentralisation occurs in 34 SMLAs located peripherally to the main urban-axis, that is, in East Anglia, the South West, Scotland and the North. These are areas which displayed relatively small increases in this group which again reinforces the belief that in such areas a larger proportion of the immigrants were likely to be white and, therefore, more likely to be subject to the same decentralisation tendency that characterises the British-born. Decentralisation was absolute in 12 SMLAs and relative in 21 SMLAs.

Therefore, although the largest absolute changes in the West Indians and the Indian sub-continent group were largely in the same areas, they display markedly different patterns of centralisation-decentralisation in these areas.

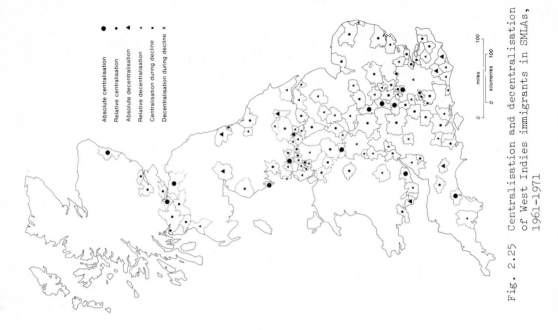

Fig. 2.25 Centralisation and decentralisation
of West Indies immigrants in SMLAs,
1961-1971

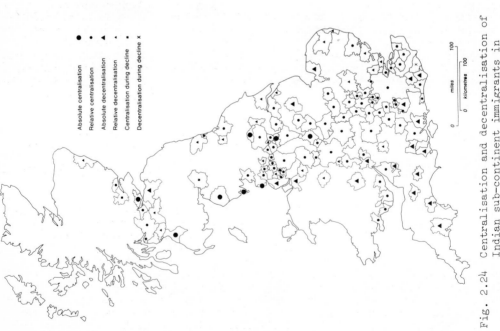

Fig. 2.24 Centralisation and decentralisation of
Indian sub-continent immigrants in
SMLAs, 1961-1971

PART THREE

Migration and British Cities

3.1 URBAN CHANGE AND MIGRATION

It has been demonstrated that in the study of population change several distinctive features could be delimited during the 1961-1971 decade. These included the inter-regional disparity in labour market growth performance; the regional variation of rapidly expanding small and medium size systems and the decline of associated large labour markets, usually centred on the conurbations, and the decentralisation of population out of urban cores. Clearly such aggregate shifts of population can be attributed only to variations in the natural change rates and net migration. The latter was shown to be the dominant influence.

A striking conformity was observed between net migration and population change for whole labour markets on the one hand, and their constituent urban zones on the other. Whilst the vast majority of areas showed natural change rates approximating the nation's 6% decennial increase, the exceptions could easily be categorised. Those areas with particularly low natural change rates (a few actually recorded a decrease) were principally identified as resort/retirement centres. Those with high natural increase rates were almost entirely new or expanded towns. Of course, these extreme levels of natural change can in themselves be viewed as being partially attributable to differential net migration.

So the vast proportion of the spatial variance of population change is due to the process of migration. Part one was briefly able to look at net migration shifts. This may now be enhanced with the analysis of detailed exchanges by origins and destinations. Thus it is possible to compare the redistribution of migrants within and between local labour market areas in detail.

The migration data source is the 1971 British Census which like its 1966 predecessor, contained questions concerning the residence of the respondent one and five years earlier. Such data are far from ideal for deriving an understanding of the migration process. Other studies (Gray and Gee, 1972; Willis, 1974; Rees, 1976; Kennett, 1978) have examined their statistical shortcomings, sampling bias and enumerator error being the most important. The nature of the question asked has lead to a major under-estimation of the number of moves. Persons moving more than once are attributed only one migration, migrants who return home again within the period are missed entirely as are those moving and dying and children aged under five or one year (depending on the question). Clearly each could be crucial to the understanding of the process.

A second limitation is that although data are available for migrants entering
Britain (a subject which is given brief attention later), there are no details
concerning those leaving the country. The analysis is then principally restricted
to moves within Great Britain, although the net figures for the decade used in the
earlier report do incorporate the effects of international migration.

A further difficulty relates to the periods under consideration. Results from the
1966-71 and 1970-71 migration tables have frequently to be placed within the context of the whole decade. Although there was a 1966 Census in Great Britain,
because it was entirely conducted on a 10% sample basis, the errors attributable
to under enumeration are much higher than either the 1961 or 1971 estimates.
Consequently it is difficult to obtain accurate details concerning the base data
population of the five year migration tables for the areas of interest. These
shortcomings are exacerbated by the fact that the 1966-71 quinquennium was one of
very low natural growth so that even small percentage point inaccuracies may become
important. Proportions of population migrating refer in the text to the 1971 total
rather than the base year, because of the underenumeration in 1966.

While the 1966 Census posited similar migration questions to that of 1971, comparison of the two data sets is complicated by more than the problems referred to
above. Substantial boundary changes within certain areas were undertaken for example. Compensation for such boundary changes is particularly difficult when using
interaction data. This is especially so for migration since the number of interactions involved is large although many will involve only small numbers. Unlike
other data sources, however, migration tables in themselves provide a window in
which to view the processes of urban change and do not require a secondary source
for comparison.

The inter-local authority migration flow matrix was first used to assess the relative importance of movements within and between a hierarchy of places. Table 3.1
shows that between 1966 and 1971 nearly 17.5 million people had moved within Britai
- some 36% of the population over five years of age. During the single year 1970-
71, just under 5.9 million (about 12%) of the population are recorded as changing
residence. This, of course, does not imply a rise in migration propensities during
the period. The one and five year periods are essentially discrete since different
aspects of migration will manifest themselves variably over time periods of different length. Thus comparison of one and five year figures to derive notions of
trends in the changing migration patterns is only exceptionally a valid approach.

Table 3.1 and Fig. 3.1 suggest that, as expected, there was a negative relationshiµ
between numbers migrating and the distance moved. It is useful to discriminate the
portion of moves falling within and between successive tiers of the urban system.
Despite the differing mobility rates in the one and five year periods, the structural hierarchy of migration remained virtually constant. About half of all moves
recorded were within the confines of the same local authority area. A further 10%
changed their local authority but remained in the same urban zone, leaving 40% to
traverse the zonal boundaries and remain of direct interest to the study. Inter-
zonal migration was represented by 6.8 million five year and 2.3 million one year
movers. Of all inter-zonal movers about 30% remained within the same MELA.

Migrants between labour markets may be subdivided into those moving within and
those moving between the ten economic planning regions. These two groups were almost identical numerically, representing about 12% of total migration. It is the
inter-regional scale that has most frequently been used to assess national migration patterns. Thus although this study still fails to review 60% of all movers (i
those who moved within the same urban zone) it does provide considerably more
detail than inter-regional studies. Short distance movers may still cross the
regional boundaries. To derive a subset of long-distance, inter-regional moves,
persons migrating between non-contiguous planning regions were adopted. This

TABLE 3.1 Movers by Origins and Destinations (a) Totals in Thousands (b) Percent of all Movers (c) Percent of Inter-zonal Movers

	(1966-71)			(1970-71)		
	(a)	(b)	(c)	(a)	(b)	(c)
Movers in Great Britain	17,444			5,869		
Movers within Local Authorities	9,075	52.0		3,010	51.2	
Movers between Local Authorities	8,368	47.9		2,859	48.7	
Movers within Urban Zone but between Local Authorities	1,549	8.8		561	9.5	
Movers between Urban Zone including Unclassified	6,818	39.0		2,297	39.1	
Movers within MELAs but between Urban Zones	2,092	11.9	30.6	689	11.7	29.9
Movers between MELAs	4,179	23.9	61.2	1,418	24.1	61.7
Movers between MELAs in same Planning Region	2,128	12.2	31.2	718	12.2	31.2
Movers between MELAs in different Planning Regions	2,050	11.7	30.0	700	11.9	30.4
Movers between MELAs in non-contiguous Planning Regions	866	4.9	12.7	298	5.0	12.9
Movers between MELAs (including Unclassified Areas)	4,726	27.0	69.3	1,608	27.4	70.0
Movers between MELAs (including unclassified Areas) in same Planning Region	2,365	13.5	34.6	798	13.6	34.7
Movers between MELAs (including unclassified Areas) in different Planning Regions	2,360	13.5	34.6	810	13.8	35.2
Movers between MELAs (including unclassified Areas) in Non-contiguous Planning Regions	996	5.7	14.6	346	5.9	15.0

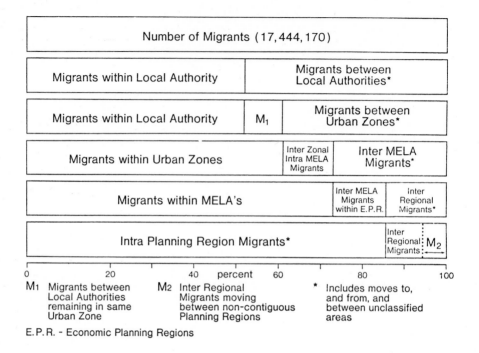

Fig. 3.1 Relative migration in Britain by type of movement, 1966-71

represented 5% of all migrants and 15% of inter-local authority exchanges.

Finally, because the definition of urban Britain does not exhaust the country, more
than 8% of inter-zonal migrants (about 500,000 in the five year interval) have yet
to be included. For convenience these unclassified areas may be allocated to their
respective planning regions.

This then is the urban change context, the data source and an outline of the migration magnitudes involved. This part of the study is subsequently divided into two
sections. First the basic patterns of migration will be analysed, and second the
characteristics of migrants themselves reviewed.

3.2 MIGRATION PATTERNS IN THE URBAN SYSTEM

3.2.1 Population Redistribution within British Cities

Net migration trends between 1961 and 1971 revealed a considerable redistribution
of population within the nation's cities. Patterns for 1966-71 and 1970-71 were
broadly similar. The average net migration growth for urban cores in the decade
was 0.6%. This figure hides a considerable dispersion, with the largest cities
suffering absolute levels of net out movement which far outweighed those with net
inflow, principally the new and expanded towns. Altogether, cores lost about
2.5 million people by net outmigration over the decade (including international
migration); 1.13 million to the rest of Great Britain during 1966-71 and 286,000

during 1970-71. In contrast metropolitan rings experienced a mean population growth of 14.7% attributable to net migration during 1961-71. Unlike the urban cores,
rings were much more uniform in their experience. Finally, the outer rings, while
having an average population increase of 5.1% due to net migration during the
decade, exhibited a slightly higher degree of variation in their rates of gain
compared with the rings.

The aim here is to determine the actual origins and destinations of specific migrations, commencing with an overview at the national level and proceeding down through
various tiers in the hierarchy to the individual labour market area. Using the more
detailed migration tables from the Census, several important questions will be an-
swered. These include an estimation of the relative significance of intra-MELA
and inter-MELA decentralisations; the ability to assess the strength of movements
into core areas and observe their origins; an investigation of relatively long
distance decentralisation and, finally, a view of the varying strengths, directions
and structure of migration streams for individual MELAs, as well as their functional groups.

Redistribution of population by national zonal aggregates.

Details of the origins and destinations for inter-zonal movements within the nation
are presented in Table 3.2. The net core-ring shift of 900,000 people (1966-71) was
achieved by an outflow of almost 1.9 millions outweighing the inflow of almost one
million. Thus moves centralising from rings to cores represented the second largest inter-zonal flow. Indeed the proportion of the metropolitan rings' population
that moved to cores (6%) was in fact only slightly less than the proportion of the
urban cores' population that moved to rings (7%). Results during 1970-71 were
similar, 571,000 core to ring moves contrasting with 352,000 ring to core migration.
The volume of exchanges within the SMLA tended to submerge some of the other interesting features. An evolving pattern of decentralisation is suggested as outer
rings made substantial net gains from each of the other three zones. Between 1966
and 1971 the outer rings grew through net migration by some 250,000 persons. Of
these almost 80,000 were directed from metropolitan rings. Similarly during 1970-71
some 30% of the net inflow of 85,000 migrants to the OMR were from metropolitan
rings. The unclassified areas, which have traditionally suffered population loss
were also growing by net migration, inflows stemming from both of the constituent
SMLA zones. Thus the notions that population was spreading into outer areas that
were expressed in the first report are verified, this decentralisation originating
not just from cores but from both zones within the SMLA.

How do patterns of population redistribution, caused by migration, vary when comparing movement within and between labour markets? The volume of inter-zonal migration within MELAs is about half that of the inter-MELA exchanges. Hall (1973)
using 1960-61 data for five study-areas suggested that there is a distinct difference in the zonal relocation of relatively short moves and those over longer distances. The central cities, it was shown, lost population to their rings, but the
balance was met in part (or full) by longer distance movers from other parts of the
country, or from overseas. The out migration totals for ring local authorities included some who moved back to the city, but by far the largest numbers decentralised
into the peripheries of the inner ring, nearby villages and small towns.

Concerning intra-MELA migrations, Table 3.3 reveals similar trends for the nation
a decade later, but the inter-MELA movements suggest some new developments
(Table 3.4). Both within and between labour markets, the most important re-
allocation of population was outward from cores to rings and thus, clearly, the
decentralisation processes were not just internalised within local systems. It is
true that counter-streams of migrants towards the centre remain substantial, and
illustrate increasing importance with exchanges over longer distances, yet net

TABLE 3.2 Inter-local Authority Migration by Urban Zone

(a) 1966-1971

DESTINATION   DESTINATION

Origin	C	R	O	U	T		C	R	O	U	T
C	1455	1865	530	115	3965	C	17.4	22.3	6.3	1.4	47.4
R	963	1128	494	90	2675	R	11.5	13.5	5.9	1.1	32.0
O	335	416	490	86	1328	O	4.0	5.0	5.9	1.0	15.9
U	82	76	87	156	401	U	1.0	0.9	1.0	1.9	4.8
T	2836	3485	1601	448	8369	T	33.9	41.6	19.1	5.3	100.0

(a) Absolute flows (000s)   (b) Percentage of total flows

(b) 1970-1971

DESTINATION   DESTINATION

Origin	C	R	O	U	T		C	R	O	U	T
C	527	571	176	37	1311	C	18.4	20.0	6.2	1.3	45.9
R	352	381	171	32	935	R	12.3	13.3	6.0	1.1	32.7
O	118	145	174	30	468	O	4.1	5.1	6.1	1.0	16.4
U	29	28	31	58	146	U	1.0	1.0	1.1	2.0	5.1
T	1025	1125	553	156	2859	T	35.9	39.4	19.3	5.5	100.0

(a) Absolute flows (000s)   (b) Percentage of total flows

C = Core
R = Ring
O = Outer Ring
U = Unclassified
T = Total

decentralisation persisted even over the greatest lengths. Within SMLAs (1966-71), centralisers equalled 42.4% of the number of decentralisers. This increased to 65% for inter-MELA exchanges within the same region, 69% for all inter-regional moves and 71% for those between non-contiguous planning regions.

Although the Hall study noted net outward shifts of population within the inner rings, the analysis did not encompass the outer zones. By 1966-71, both within and between labour markets the OMR gained by net migration from both cores and rings. The growth of the outer ring was greater by inter-MELA movement compared with rings where by far the larger proportion of gains came via intra-MELA shifts. In terms of inter-MELA gains, those going to the OMR in fact exceeded the increase accruing to rings despite the smaller population base. Within MELAs, the OMR's net growth by migration was only about 15% of the ring's, despite achieving net inflows from both the SMLA zones. The dominance of the local core-ring outflows is again confirmed.

TABLE 3.3   Inter-zonal Migration within Labour Markets

(a)   1966-1971

DESTINATION						DESTINATION			
	C	R	O	T			C	R	O	T

Origin:

	C	R	O	T			C	R	O	T
C	–	1136	136	1273		C	–	54.3	6.5	60.8
R	479	–	141	620		R	22.9	–	6.8	29.7
O	82	117	–	199		O	3.9	5.6	–	9.5
T	561	1254	277	2092		T	26.8	59.9	13.3	100.0

    (a) Absolute flows (000s)   (b) Percentage total flows

(b)   1970-1971

DESTINATION						DESTINATION			

Origin:

	C	R	O	R			C	R	O	T
C	–	342	46	388		C	–	49.7	6.7	65.4
R	179	–	50	229		R	26.0	–	7.3	33.3
O	30	41	–	71		O	4.4	6.0	–	10.3
T	209	383	96	688		T	30.4	55.6	14.0	100.0

    (a) Absolute flows (000s)   (b) Percentage total flows

C = Core
R = Ring
O = Outer Ring
T = Total

City-type variations in the redistribution of population

The dispersion around the decennial national average net migration rates for cores, rings and outer rings, make it important to investigate city-type variations. Previous ten year analysis suggested that population size, urban function, proximity to conurbations and proximity to Megalopolis Britain were four additional features which affected an area's migration performance. The classification of MELAs outlined in part one incorporated dimensions similar to these. Does this typology facilitate a clearer understanding of the migration trends amongst labour markets?

On the nine functional groups only the Million Cities incurred migration loss at the MELA level. Between 1966 and 1971, these seven areas lost 675,000 persons to the remainder of Britain, net out flows during the decade had consisted of 1.5 million people. Not surprisingly it was the New Towns which recorded the fastest growth rates, but additionally the Resort, London Peripheral and Southern Freestanding cities (MELAs principally located in the South East and South West regions) achieved growth rates of more than 3% between 1966 and 1971. With the exception of

TABLE 3.4   Inter-zonal Migration between Labour Markets

(a)   1966-1971

DESTINATION   DESTINATION

	C	R	O	U	T			C	R	O	U	T
C	794	729	393	115	2031		C	16.8	15.4	8.3	2.4	43.0
R	484	640	352	90	1567		R	10.2	13.6	7.5	1.9	33.2
O	253	298	235	87	873		O	5.4	6.3	5.0	1.8	18.5
U	82	76	87	10	255		U	1.7	1.6	1.8	0.2	5.3
T	1614	1744	1067	302	4726		T	34.1	36.9	22.6	6.4	100.0

Origin (left column label for both tables)

(a) Absolute flows (000s)   (b) Percentage of total flows

(b)   1970-1971

DESTINATION   DESTINATION

	C	R	O	U	T			C	R	O	U	T
C	275	229	130	37	671		C	17.1	14.2	8.1	2.3	41.7
R	172	215	121	32	540		R	10.7	13.3	7.5	2.0	33.6
O	88	103	84	30	306		O	5.5	6.5	5.2	1.9	19.0
U	29	29	31	4	92		U	1.8	1.8	1.9	0.3	5.7
T	564	576	366	102	1608		T	35.1	35.8	22.8	6.4	100.0

Origin (left column label for both tables)

(a) Absolute flows (000s)   (b) Percentage of total flows

C = Core
R = Ring
O = Outer Ring
U = Unclassified
T = Total

the Million Cities, the larger or industrial MELA groups revealed almost static populations in terms of migration and illustrate again the negative relationship between population size and population growth.

Do internal changes by functional group reveal more about migration characteristics? Fig. 3.2 shows patterns of change that are similar to the regional picture discussed in part one. With one exception, urban cores in each group had higher rates of out-migration (or lower rates of in-migration) when compared with the two commuting zones. Similarly the metropolitan ring usually achieved the fastest growth rates. Finally, there was clearer evidence to support the contention that groups faring relatively poorly in cores also performed weakly in the rings.

The results from the typology do however exhibit a slightly more complex pattern

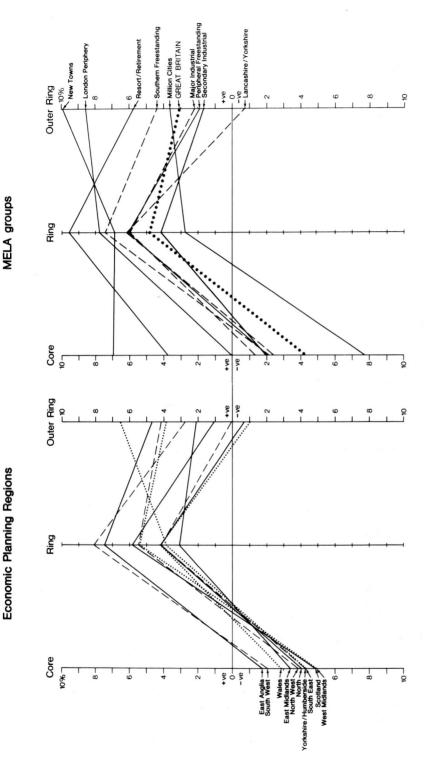

Fig. 3.2 Relative change in net migration by urban zone for Economic
Planning Regions and functional categories, 1966-1971

than those for the regions. Firstly, two functional categories, the New Towns and
Resorts, were still incurring net in-migration at their cores; the former by
over-spill, mainly from the capital, the latter principally due to retirement
migration. The London periphery towns received very small net inflows at their
cores during the 1966-71 period, but outflows during the final year, suggesting
that this group too will now be decentralising to its commuting hinterland.
Clearly the role of the capital is crucial and is examined later. Whilst the nation as a whole lost 4.36% of its core population to other parts of the British
Isles only the Million City group had faster decentralisation rates. For 1961-71
only Leeds of the seven metropolitan centres had net migration losses that were
lower than the national average. London, Newcastle and Manchester recorded losses
at about twice the rate of all cores and Liverpool and Glasgow declined at about
three times this average. Of the remaining five functional groups recording net
migration decline at the core, the Lancashire/Yorkshire group most closely approached the national out migration rate.

Turning to the commuting belts, highest in-migration rates were again usually port
rayed by the inner ring. However, Million City, London Peripheral and New Town
categories incurred their fastest growth rates in the OMR chiefly due to migration
out of the capital's SMLA. Note that the metropolitan rings grew slowest at the
'Million Cities' whilst their rate of growth at the OMR was above the national
average. By use of the typology it is possible to illustrate a small number of
systems which were important exceptions to a model which depicts core losses and
ring gains at faster rates than the OMRs, which fits nearly all systems so well.

The patterns discussed so far for these city groups refer to exchanges with all
areas and have thus failed to discriminate variations in redistribution within and
between categories of areas. The analysis of national zonal patterns (Table 3.3
and Table 3.4) suggests that slightly different processes might have been operatin
in the inter- and intra-labour marked migrations; the latter movements being
more strongly focussed on decentralisation, particularly to the metropolitan ring.
Was this the case for all functional aggregates? Highest rates of out migration
were found in the major centres: the Million Cities and Major Industrial towns
and, the New Towns. Lowest rates are clearly found for those groups fringing urba
Britain: the Resorts, Southern Freestanding and Peripheral Freestanding and additionally, the London Peripheral group. The association of New Towns with the
largest, most rapidly decentralising cities should not be considered surprising fo
a number of reasons. Firstly these areas may not have had sufficient time to develop their own local migration patterns in the 'town and country sense', their rin
population continuing to look to London as its centre. A large proportion of out
migrants from the New Towns might well be short distance relocations out of the co
after a brief acclimatisation period. Finally, these areas are particularly vulnerable to erratic rates due to their very small sized rings. Nevertheless, the
contrast in behaviour between the New Towns and the London Periphery group is interesting since these two categories are usually most similar in population redistribution characteristics. See Table 3.5.

Consider next the exchanges between SMLAs and their outer rings. Compared with
internal redistribution in the SMLA, a greater variation over space is clear.
Table 3.6 indicates that in both intervals the Million Cities decentralised most
rapidly into their outer rings, supporting the hypothesis suggesting a positive
relationship between city population size and out migration rates. More than 69%
of exchanges between SMLAs and OMRs in the seven largest systems were 'outward'
during 1966-71. Five other groups also revealed clear decentralisation; the Majo
Industrial, Secondary Industrial, Resort, London Peripheral and New Towns. On the
other hand three groups continued to centralise. Figures for New Towns should
however be treated with considerable caution here since only one of the group,
Stevenage, had an outer ring which consisted solely of Royston U.D. The Southern

Freestanding and Peripheral Freestanding groups are typified by large rural OMRs peripheral to Megalopolis Britain falling mainly in Scotland, East Anglia, and the South West. Finally, the Yorkshire-Lancashire group's OMR contains a number of depressed mining/cotton based communities which have long been suffering population decline. Notably, by 1970-71, this was the only group still centralising.

3.2.2 Population Redistribution and Individual British Cities

Internal decentralisation, 1966-71

So far inter- and intra-labour market population redistributions attributable to the migration process have been discussed in national or functional group terms. Although this provides a useful summary of the major trends within the urban system, a number of questions remain. These include the recognition of local labour markets where extreme or exceptional patterns prevail, and the identification of the most important inter-MELA migration streams. Internal exchanges within individual MELAs are examined first and then impacts of inter-MELA movements are reviewed. The patterns of interaction within individual MELAs are presented in Figs. 3.3 and 3.4. The proportions are, as before, based on the percentage of total moves between the core and ring (or SMLA and OMR) that decentralised. Within the SMLA, the picture of almost ubiquitous decentralisation that was suggested by the functional analysis is illustrated. Nevertheless, some of the systems at the periphery of the urban system continued to centralise, notably Hereford and Perth. The results at these areas reflect the final stages of the traditional flight to the cities that began with the industrial revolution. Although these local economies are experiencing population trends that were the reverse of those elsewhere, the problems of lack of opportunity and social/age balance in these ring areas should not be overlooked.

A more pronounced, but similar pattern, may be viewed in terms of the inter-action between the SMLA and its outer ring. The economies outside the main urban system, particularly in Scotland, the Welsh Marches, and, to a lesser extent in a belt of MELAs running along or near the east coast, continued to centralise.

Decentralisation within the SMLA was pervasive, but those with the most rapid rates of out movement were the largest cities and the industrial MELAs of Lancashire, Yorkshire and the Midlands. During the 1966-71 period strength of decentralisation appeared to have been related more to the location rather than the size of the local labour market. Decentralisation into the outer rings, like SMLAs, was more rapid within the confines of Megalopolis. However, it was particularly strong in the major focii, i.e. London, Birmingham, Coventry, Liverpool and Manchester (in each more than 70% of exchanges were 'outward' during the period). Thus the development of the 'life-cycle' model of population patterns that has been formulated (Department of the Environment, 1976) is recalled with, at the earliest stages, Perth and Hereford still centralising from both OMR and metropolitan ring, through to its most developed phases at London, Birmingham and other cities which are decentralising, not only to both of their commuting zones but also to neighbouring labour markets. Each MELA is then hypothesised to be at a point in a chain of events through which it will inevitably pass. A later section returns to the crucial role of inter-MELA decentralisation from the Million Cities.

Migration and population turnover

Recent research (Cordey-Hayes and Gleave, 1973) has suggested that not only are the total absolute in and out migration flows directly related, but for entire labour markets the relative inflows are also associated with outflows in the same way. It is hypothesised that population change is not simply a position of gainers and losers, or, drifts between regions (more formally that in and outmigration rates are inversely related) as is suggested by 'push-pull' economic models of migration;

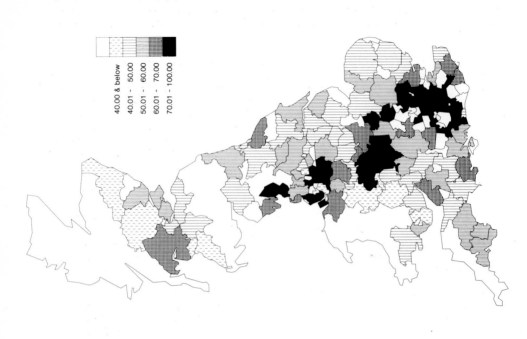

Fig. 3.4   Intra-MELA decentralisation, 1966-1971

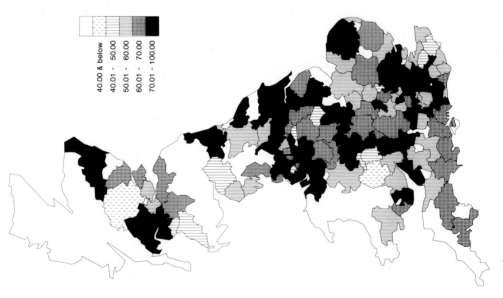

Fig. 3.3   Intra-SMLA decentralisation,
           1966-1971   (MELA base map)

or alternatively like the suggestions of Lowry (1966), that outmigration rates are consistent, and net migration rates vary solely according to strengths of in-migration streams. In reality the system resembles the notions of Ravenstein almost a century ago; that each migration stream has its own counter-stream and subsequently that there is a strong direct relationship between in and out migration per capita.

Cordey-Hayes and Gleave related firstly per capita gross in-migration and secondly per capita out migration to relative net migration change for twenty city regions in England and Wales. Whilst it was clear that gross out migration per capita was "more nearly constant" than in-migration, it was seen that areas with both high gross in-migration and out migration were associated with net in-migration. The relationship between gross in and out migration per capita is expressed for the 126 MELAs during the 1970-71 period in Fig. 3.5. This analysis shows that, even at the level of the local labour market, rather than the city region, the postulated relationship holds.

By using simple linear regression, for descriptive rather than causal purposes, out migration (Y) was regressed with in-migration (X). The resulting correlation co-efficient, 0.87, was very high for 126 observations and there was a low standard error. Each increase in out migration of 1% is likely to be accompanied by a slightly greater increase in inflow (1.54%) since the regression line takes the form $Y = 1.41 + 0.65X$ so the higher the rate of migration turnover the higher the net balance of in-migration.

These findings have important implications for the understanding of migration. Why do the most attractive areas lose most migrants? Why do those with highest rates of net out migration lose relatively few? In a more recent paper, Cordey-Hayes and Gleave (1974) argue that migration may well be stimulated in an economically healthy environment since risks will be relatively low for changing job or workplace. In environments under stress (such as those in development areas for example) the voluntary turnover of labour might be relatively low due to the uncertain economic climate and higher associated risk in change. Their argument might well be extended to incorporate a temporal dimension. If valid, this would imply that during the seventies voluntary quit rates and labour migrations would be lower compared with the sixties when there was a higher rate of growth. This contention is indirectly supported by the analysis which showed that during the 1971-74 period, according to Registrar General's estimates, population growth in rings and outer rings had indeed slowed down.

TABLE 3.5   The Proportion of Intra-SMLA, Inter-Zonal Moves
            Decentralising from Core to Ring Averaged for MELA
            Groups, 1966-71; 1970-71.

MELA Group	1966-71	1970-71
Million Cities	75.9	69.1
Major Industrial	70.6	66.0
Secondary Industrial	62.5	62.1
Lancashire/Yorkshire group	64.2	64.3
London Peripheral	58.0	56.8
New Towns	66.9	70.2
Resorts/Retirement Centres	58.6	57.2
Southern Freestanding	59.2	58.4
Peripheral Freestanding	59.0	61.3

British Cities

TABLE 3.6   The Proportion of Total Movement Between SMLAs
and the Outer Rings Decentralising, Averaged
for MELA Groups 1966-71; 1970-71

MELA Group	1966-71	1970-71
Million Cities	69.0	63.9
Major Industrial	57.9	60.0
Secondary Industrial	52.8	54.1
Lancashire/Yorkshire group	44.8	47.9
London Peripheral	62.7	54.2
New Towns	90.3	73.3
Resort/Retirement Centres	56.4	56.3
Southern Freestanding	49.9	54.7
Peripheral Freestanding	46.8	50.6

Cordey-Hayes and Gleave suggested that one result of some areas having rapid population turnover was that levels of information dissemination would be particularly
high. With an increased knowledge of the systems' opportunities, migrants were
thus more likely to move again. Evidence for this contention is, as yet, lacking.
Other studies (Plessis-Fraissard, 1975) in fact suggest that the duration of
residence (once age and other factors like social status have been partialled out)
is not in itself inversely related to migration propensities. This alone does not
invalidate the argument since, as later sections show, the majority of migrants are
young and mainly white collar workers. Thus the relatively footloose groups are
being exchanged between urban areas with high population turnover so that rapid
downturns in local economies could quickly lead to a marked change in both in and
out migration rates.

From the preceding discussion, the types of city systems suffering the lowest population turnover rates are likely to be in areas where economic problems are most
severe. Fig. 3.5 suggests that four areas within the Secondary Industrial group:
Rhondda, Greenock, Hartlepool and Sunderland had the system's lowest in and outflows.
Out-migration surveys of economically declining areas in the Rhondda Valley have
recently been conducted which support these suggestions. The out-migrants are
reluctant to leave their community but do so because of poor economic and housing
opportunities. The majority of movers are young. (Rees, 1978). This category did,
however, reveal considerably greater dispersion of values than the others and,
during the 1970-71 period, the MELAs in this group achieved an average inflow of
4.36% and an outflow of 4.11%. Sheffield, of the Major Industrial group, also
records inflows of less than 3%. The Million Cities were the only group to average
net deficits, although it can be seen that London had much higher rates of in and
out migration than others in the group. The London Periphery and New Towns groups,
as might be expected, had the highest turnover and associated net migration gains.
Among the former, Aldershot reported net out migration due presumably to armed
forces movements, and within the latter group, Basingstoke indicated very high
inflows that are not matched by corresponding outflows, due probably to the rapid
construction which occurred at this time. Higher than expected in-migration rate
for recorts occur particularly in those with cores actually lying on the coast
(Group 7A); these illustrate their rather specialised role in the migration
process with the inflow of retired population.

Finally, Fig. 3.5 shows the number of labour markets actually suffering net migration decline. In addition to the Million Cities, a number of labour markets in the
Major Industrial, Secondary Industrial, Lancashire-Yorkshire and Peripheral Freestanding groups were also in decline. In regional terms, Scotland, the North,
North West, Yorkshire-Humberside and Wales fared relatively poorly. Migration losses were, however, concentrated into relatively few labour areas, whilst (in absolute

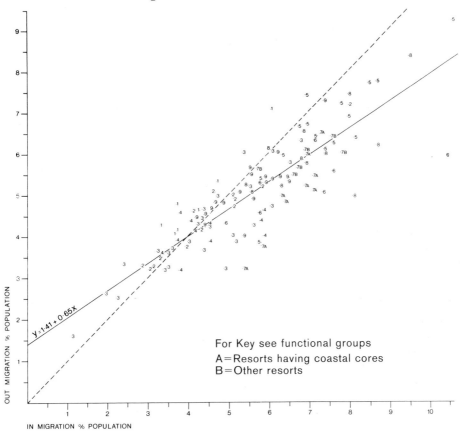

Fig. 3.5 Per capita in-migration (x) and per capita out
          migration (y) for MELA's 1970-71.

terms) lower, more widely scattered gains accrued to the majority of systems. The
largest of those were directed to medium growth centres (like Reading), the New
Town group (such as Basingstoke) and resorts (e.g. Bournemouth).

Zonal characteristics of inter-MELA moves

It has been suggested that moves between labour markets at the national scale
resulted in net decentralisation to both of the commuting zones. In absolute terms
it was the outer ring which gained the greater increase in the inter-MELA streams
indicating the importance of studying the whole MELA, although in terms of total
exchanges, the volume of interaction between core and ring remained dominant. The
previous subsection suggests an appreciable difference regarding per capita inflows
and outflows for economically stagnant and declining local labour areas, on the one
hand, and on the other, those rapidly growing systems adjacent to the conurbations.
Is there also an appreciable difference in the zonal character of inter-urban migration between these areas? Can further light be shed on the urbanisation-counter
urbanisation notions when comparing labour markets on the system's periphery with
the major centres that have been decentralising.

In terms of migration between the SMLAs, Table 3.4 shows that 3,598,000 (76.1%) of
the whole system's 1966-71 inter-MELA migrants left an SMLA and 3,358,000 (71.1%)

joined the SMLAs. 2,647,000 moved between SMLAs representing 56% of inter labour
market moves within Great Britain. Almost identical proportions are recorded for
the 1970-71 period. Fig. 3.6 suggests that the areas surrounding the conurbations
and largest cities received higher than average percentages from the core and ring
of their large neighbour, whereas those on the periphery (such as Aberdeen and
Hereford) received less than 60% of their in-migrants from other SMLAs. A similar
pattern is suggested in Fig. 3.7 - but the range in performance is lower. Few of
the SMLAs exported more than 80% of their out migrants to other SMLAs, although a
small number lying contiguous to the Million Cities of London, Leeds, Manchester ar
Liverpool often totally surrounded by other labour markets revealed such high level
The major centres, such as Birmingham, Teesside, Bristol, Manchester and Liverpool
revealed a clear tendency to import a lower proportion from SMLAs than they directe

Within the most urbanised sectors of Britain, net inter-MELA decentralisation into
the OMR and unclassified areas was occurring not just from the major centres but
from a majority of labour market areas. However, SMLA in-migrants were much more
likely to have originated in other SMLAs. At the periphery the reverse is true.
A number of SMLAs such as Hereford, Shrewsbury and Aberdeen actually exported
higher proportions of their out migrants to SMLAs compared with their inflows. Thi
implies a feeder role for these areas for migrants from unclassified areas and oute
rings centralising toward urban Britain. Six systems in Scotland, four in Wales,
three in the North and five in the Yorkshire-Humberside region indicated the main
concentrations of the twenty-six SMLAs in this group.

These notions are supported by studying the proportions of migrants moving between
individual urban zones. The small suburban systems contiguous with cities like
Liverpool, Manchester and London (particularly its eastern neighbours) imported hig
proportions from urban cores (the majority of course from their local conurbation);
relatively, they returned smaller proportions. London, Manchester, Newcastle and
Glasgow on the other hand continued to direct more than the national average of 39%
of their outflows to other core areas. This suggests that a disproportionately
large number of inter-MELA migrants from major cities retained their zonal status
in the smaller system destinations, whilst outmovers from their satellite cores wer
more likely to decentralise between zones when moving between MELAs. This suggests
a hierarchy of decentralisation moves. The urbanising trend at the periphery is
also supported. Many MELAs in the South West, East Anglia and Wales indicated that
higher proportions of their out migrants move to cores than their reciprocal inflow

Generally, the pattern of proportional exchanges between MELAs and unclassified are
approximated a close balance. For the nation, 93.6% of outmovers from MELAs were
directed to other MELAs compared with 94.6% of in-migrants. Nevertheless, there we
marked local variations. All MELAs in Scotland but Ayr and Falkirk, received and
directed more than 10% of their migrants to and from the unclassified zones (this
proportion rises to 38% of in-migrants and 28% of out migrants for Aberdeen).
Similarly, in England and Wales, Carlisle, Swansea, Chester, Shrewsbury, Hereford
and Lincoln also revealed important interactions. Regionally, there are important
deviations in trends. Whilst MELAs in Scotland, the North, Wales and the Marches h
higher proportions of their in-migrants arriving from unclassified areas, the opposite trend is denoted in the South West (Exeter and Taunton for example), together
with many labour markets along the east coast (including Ipswich and Peterborough).
The former probably represents continued rural out migration whilst the latter is
likely to be due to retirement moves. This is supported by the much larger proportional inflows from unclassified areas to Scottish cores compared with their outflow

Study of streams of migrants between individual MELAs (or cores) and the regional
unclassified area aggregates suggests the importance of Million Cities and local
centres in terms of both inflows and outflows. The exchanges between London and
unclassified areas as a whole are larger than that between the capital and any

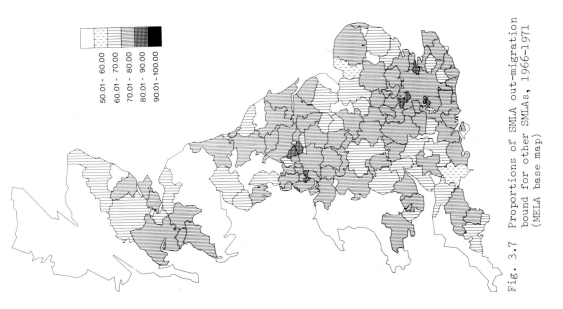

Fig. 3.7 Proportions of SMLA out-migration
bound for other SMLAs, 1966-1971
(MELA base map)

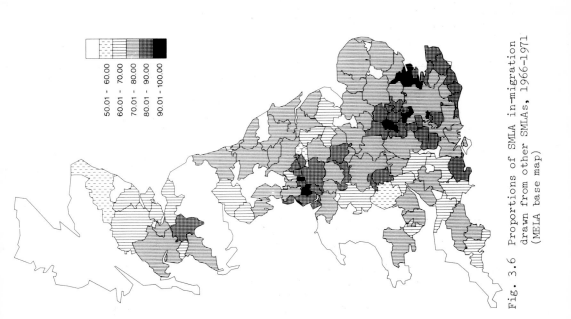

Fig. 3.6 Proportions of SMLA in-migration
drawn from other SMLAs, 1966-1971
(MELA base map)

individual MELA.

Major migration flows between urban areas

The analysis so far has concentrated on total inflows and outflows, net changes
and the major population shifts between urban zones. The last section suggested
evidence for a hierarchy both decentralising and centralising migrations between
urban zones and labour markets. A study of individual migration flows should en-.
able judgment on whether small or peripheral labour markets direct relatively larg¢
proportions of out migrants to increasingly larger centres, and if major cities'
movement patterns are dominated by decentralisation into their neighbouring areas
together with exchanges among themselves.

A number of simple complementary measures are used to study migration flows. Thes¢
are surprisingly successful even when compared with results from the more complicated techniques of factor and transaction flow analysis. The simplest measure of
all is connectivity. Over the five year period, London is shown to be the only
labour market with links to and from each of the other MELAs. However all the
Million Cities have virtually complete sets of exchanges with the rest of Great
Britain. Complete sets of outflows are recorded by each Million City except for
Leeds (to Greenock) and Newcastle (to Rhondda). In terms of inflows each drew
migrants from 120 MELAs or more during the 1966-71 period. Systems with relatively
small number of links form two types. Firstly, a number of small systems contiguou
to the conurbations such as St. Helens (Liverpool), Leigh (Manchester) and Thurroc}
(London) where the interaction with the dominant partner is overriding. Second is
a group of MELAs on the edge of the urban system such as Hereford, Carlisle, Barrov
and all in Scotland except Glasgow and Edinburgh. Within Scotland, Greenock,
Kilmarnock and Perth provide the most extreme examples with respectively only 45,6¢
and 66 inflows from other MELAs. Here again the majority of migrants are exchange¢
with contiguous systems and one or two major cities. The case of Rhondda incorporates both these elements since Cardiff acts as a regional focus in Wales. Thus
Rhondda has the smallest number of inflows and outflows, respectively 33 and 54,
between 1966-71, complementing the results concerning turnover presented earlier.
Of course connectively does not incorporate estimates of volume. Two methods are
adopted here. The first investigates streams exceeding flows of 1,500 migrants in
the 1966-71 interval, the second using a graph theory approach attempts to look at
each MELA's dominant inflow and outflow with the aim of deriving migration networks

Only 479 (or 3%) of the possible 15,750 inter-MELA migrations attained the 1,500
person threshold. Nevertheless in volume these streams represented 2,232,690 (or
47.5%) of all inter-MELA moves. This study like many others has noted the impact
of distance and city size. Hence the sample of streams have been categorised into
those between contiguous and non-contiguous MELAs and those exchanges with Million
Cities and those between the remaining 119 areas. Almost 1.4 million migrants move
in 274 streams between contiguous systems leaving a further 830,000 moving in 205
flows between the non-contiguous MELAs. However, the paramount importance of the
Million Cities is clear, since 81% of migrants in flows exceeding 1,500 interacted
with these areas (Table 3.7). Of the four groups, the largest mean size of flow
was between Million Cities and contiguous labour markets (7,685 persons). Flows
between Million Cities and non-contiguous MELAs averaged the second largest size
(4,265 persons) whilst the mean size of flows between contiguous areas reached only
2,759. Only 17 streams between non-contiguous MELAs excluding Million Cities
exceeded the threshold and the mean size of these streams was 2,105.

The effect of distance is clearly demonstrated with, in addition, the importance of
migration networks that hinge on the seven main areas. But what of the major flows
elsewhere? Figs. 3.8 and 3.9 indicate streams of 1,500 or more migrants between
contiguous and non-contiguous areas excluding the Million Cities. Flows are often

TABLE 3.7 Categorisation of Inter-MELA Migration Streams of 1,500 People or More Between 1966 and 1971

	Number of flows	Proportion of streams of more than 1,500	Number of migrants	Proportion of migrants in streams greater than 1,500	Proportion of total inter-MELA streams
(a) Flows between Million Cities and contiguous MELAs	130	27.1	999,090 ($\bar{x}$=7685)	44.75	23.91
(b) Flows between other contiguous MELAs	145	30.1	400,150 ($\bar{x}$=2759)	17.92	9.57
(c) Flows between Million Cities and other non-contiguous MELAs	187	39.0	797,610 ($\bar{x}$=4265)	35.72	19.08
(d) Flows between non-contiguous other MELAs	17	3.8	35,840 ($\bar{x}$=2108)	1.61	0.86
(e) Total	479	100.0	2,232,670 ($\bar{x}$=4661)	100.00	53.42

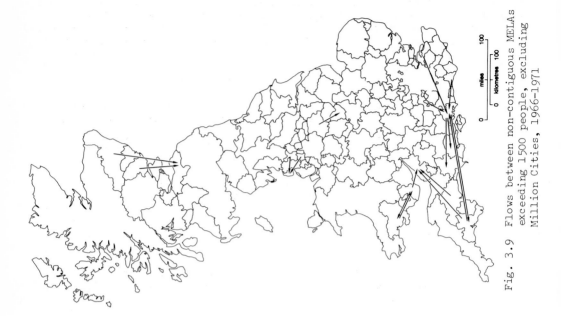

Fig. 3.9 Flows between non-contiguous MELAs
          exceeding 1500 people, excluding
          Million Cities, 1966-1971

Fig. 3.8 Flows between contiguous MELAs
          exceeding 1500 people, excluding
          Million Cities, 1966-1971

paired and local networks such as those in Wales, the South West, Kent, East Anglia, East Midlands, North West, North East and Scotland can clearly be delimited. The most coherent of these networks are also represented in flows between non-contiguous systems (Fig. 3.9). The impact of regional centres such as Edinburgh, Cardiff, Sheffield and Bristol are shown. The remainder of such moves can be explained in terms of retirement migrations to Blackpool and the movements of armed forces between Chatham, Aldershot, Portsmouth, Plymouth, Yeovil and Bournemouth.

Movements between Million Cities and contiguous labour areas control about 45% of the volume of migrant streams of more than 1,500 persons but only 27% of the number of flows. The role of decentralisation is emphasised since 696,520 move out of Million Cities in 69 streams, whilst only 302,750 move to them in 61 significant streams. An important component of the movement between the Million Cities and those areas not contiguous to them are the 33 streams containing 192,330 persons moved between the Million Cities themselves. London and Manchester alone have a full complement of significant inter-metropolitan streams whilst Glasgow has five significant out-flows (the exception being Glasgow to Liverpool) and three significant inflows (only London, Manchester and Newcastle). Although 86 streams (257,260 persons) are directed toward these seven cities from non-contiguous MELAs whilst 68 streams (comprising 348,020 persons) decentralise out to non-contiguous areas.

Of the 126 labour markets only four MELAs, Barrow, Carlisle, Lancaster and Workington, fail to direct a stream exceeding 1,500 persons to another labour market, and four: Barrow, Hereford, Rhondda and Workington do not receive an equivalent sized inflow. Thus only Barrow and Workington remain completely outside the influence of such streams. The use of graph theory permits the major flows accruing even to these areas to be seen. Graph theory has previously been utilised in a study of Hadjifotiou (1972) of inter-SMLA migration during the 1965-6 period for 100 1961 based SMLAs. Here the analysis is updated for 1966-71 flows over 126 areas extending the scope of the analysis to include MELAs, SMLAs and cores. For each unit the largest inflow and outflow was determined. The stream was recorded only if the inflow originated from, or outflow was directed to, an area with a larger population in 1971. Thus a hierarchy of flows can be established and independent networks delimited. An individual network is completed when the largest outflow or inflow, as appropriate, was exchanged with a smaller area.

Use of the method successfully delimited 12.7% of all inter-MELA outward streams to larger areas and incorporated 25.4% of inward flows from bigger systems. The resulting graphs are illustrated by Figs. 3.10 and 3.11. Although second and third order flows are visible, it can be seen that virtually all MELAs are within the London network. When the technique is applied to the SMLAs, 13.3% of all migration from SMLAs and 29.4% of all in-migration to SMLAs are included. The higher proportions of included migrants by SMLAs suggest a more complex pattern of local migration with the inclusion of outer rings in the MELA results. Altogether 65 prime outflows from SMLAs and 55 from MELAs were directed to London whilst 71 SMLA and 67 MELA inflows originated in the capital.

In terms of prime outward movements, 10 MELA and 8 SMLA networks independent of London could be identified. For MELAs, local centres at Cardiff, Birmingham, Nottingham, Liverpool, Preston, Teesside and Dundee complete networks, whilst Sunderland, Grimsby and Hereford direct their largest outflow to a smaller MELA. SMLA networks are completed by Birmingham, Grimsby, Liverpool, Preston, Glasgow and Ayr with Gloucester sending its largest outflow to a smaller SMLA. There are fewer networks of prime inward movements from larger systems, again illustrating the relative strength of decentralisation from the major areas. Apart from London, networks are completed at the MELA level by Nottingham, Grimsby and Blackburn, whilst only the Grimsby SMLA completes a network with Gloucester again receiving its dominant inflow from the smaller Cheltenham. The largest number of areas excluded from the London

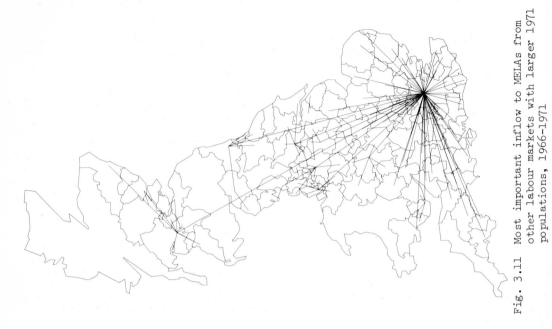

Fig. 3.11 Most important inflow to MELAs from
other labour markets with larger 1971
populations, 1966-1971

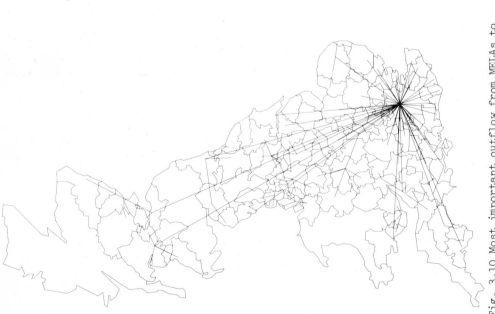

Fig. 3.10 Most important outflow from MELAs to
other labour markets with larger 1971
populations, 1966-1971

network in any of the four graphs is 37, this for the prime outward move to larger
MELAs.

Thus, as suggested earlier, moves between progressively more tightly bounded urban
units seem to have a higher propensity for remaining in the same zone. Hence 97 of
the prime destinations of inter-core movement are directed to London (with a further
20 outflows to other million cities), whilst 76 of the most important prime inflows
are directed from the capital (with an additional 36 from other million cities).
Other major centres, like Sheffield (3), Teeside (2) and Dundee provide their smaller
neighbours' biggest inflows.   Use of graph theory has further demonstrated the
importance of the capital and other major centres as well as the role of decentralisation.   These largest areas play an increasingly more important role with successively more tightly bounded urban regions. How much does the importance of the prime
inflow or outflow vary between the separate inter-zonal flow types? Does the nature
of major flows between the outer zone indicate more local interaction as hypothesised
above? Table 3.8 illustrates the continuing importance of the prime flow throughout
the sixteen possible combinations. Here, as the objective is no longer to define
hierarchical networks, the constraint that flows should be directed to, or received
from, larger centres is dropped. The table reveals that consistently higher levels
of movement are encapsulated by inflows than by outflows for the two SMLA zones:
thus the effect of the big cities controlling migration patterns is confirmed and
the ubiquitous role played by decentralisation is again suggested. However, with
the exception of core to OMR migrations, the interaction concerning prime inward
and outward flows for the outer ring is nearer balance. The idea that these streams
are not dominated by a few centres also suggested by comparison of SMLA and MELA
graphs is also investigated.

TABLE 3.8 Proportion of Inter-MELA Moves by Zone Encapsulated
by First Order Flows, 1966-71.

		Prime flow total	%			Prime flow total	%
Inter-MELA	outward	624,970	14.96	Inter-MELA	inward	1,089,880	26.08
Inter-SMLA	outward	426,730	16.12	Inter-SMLA	inward	781,480	29.52
Inter-core	outward	138,630	17.46	Inter-core	inward	241,670	30.44
Inter-ring	outward	110,660	17.29	Inter-ring	inward	188,780	29.50
Core-ring	outward	139,350	19.12	Core-ring	inward	223,400	30.60
Ring-core	outward	80,870	16.71	Ring-core	inward	145,520	30.10
Inter-OMR	outward	62,620	26.62	Inter-OMR	inward	66,150	28.14
Core-OMR	outward	68,500	17.43	Core-OMR	inward	131,080	33.35
OMR-core	outward	49,770	21.18	OMR-core	inward	49,080	20.89
Ring-OMR	outward	100,490	28.59	Ring-OMR	inward	97,830	27.79
OMR-ring	outward	57,130	19.23	OMR-ring	inward	71,010	23.23

Note: Core-ring outward refers to the largest outflows from urban cores to
metropolitan rings whilst core-ring inward refers to the largest inflows to metropolitan rings from urban cores. Thus 19.12% of total
interaction between cores and rings is encompassed by first order
outflows from cores, whilst 30.6% of the same interzonal movement
is depicted by first order inflows from rings.

Fig. 3.12 indicates the first of these notions to be valid. Despite the net outwa
movement between labour markets from cores to rings and despite the huge migration
loss from the capital, London's core is still the receiver of the vast bulk of the
119 prime centralising flows from rings. This is true of both short and long dist
ance moves, the latter including Edinburgh, Newcastle, Carlisle, Workington, Swans
and Plymouth, and the former including all but five local flows in the South East.
Those flows not centreing on London are principally directed to other major system
Edinburgh, Glasgow, Birmingham, Manchester, Sheffield, Leeds and Liverpool. The
largest flow from London's ring, which ranked only tenth in terms of outflows from
the entire MELA, is directed to Basildon. Each of the remaining prime ring – core
outflows are exchanges between contiguous systems. The second hypothesis also
seems valid although it is not elaborated on here. The vast majority of outer rin
direct their largest inflow to OMRs in adjacent labour areas and 18 separate networks can be defined. Very few non-contiguous flows are apparent; only seven sou
eastern OMRs direct their largest outflow to the capital's OMR.

The study of major flows using very simple techniques has emphasised the role of
distance and major centres on migration streams. Further, longer moves are predom
inantly associated with the two SMLA zones whilst major exchanges encountered by
the OMR are shorter. Using the 3% of the total possible streams (those with great
than 1,500 migrants), 48% of inter-MELA migration was described. Using 126 domina
inflows or outflows between 15 and 30% of inter labour market migration is encountered.

Other analyses have used more complex techniques for either the 1965-6 data sets o
the 100 original SMLAs, or the present study's 1970-71 data. A number of operatio
and interpretational difficulties limit the value of these approaches. Some of th
shortcomings are summarised by Willis (1974). The aims of factor analysis are similar to the work above; to reduce the number of flows to a set of coherent subset
or networks. The flows between the 100 1961 SMLAs were summarised independently b
Goddard (1973) using principal components analysis and Hadjifotiou using factor
analysis. Despite these technical differences there are broad similarities betwee
the results of these two studies and the present analysis. From the point of view
of receiving areas, the dominant pattern of inter-urban migration flows is represe
ted by relatively short distance movements outwards from the largest SMLAs. Outfl
from the London SMLA represented the leading pattern of decentralisation. Amongst
these movements, the most significant are those to a ring of SMLAs up to 100 kilo-
metres away from the capital, together with some long distance moves to the South
West. The same pattern of metropolitan decentralisation from each major SMLA to
surrounding smaller SMLA systems could be seen for Birmingham, Nottingham, Cardiff
Liverpool, Manchester, Leeds and Newcastle, just as they could in the dominant outflows discussed above.

Considering migration origins,as also noted above, virtually the converse applied.
Major provincial centres like Manchester and Birmingham attracted immigrants from
surrounding labour market areas, while on an inter-regional scale these centres in
turn also direct migrants toward London. London itself acted as an inter-regional
focus for surrounding SMLAs. The similarity between the component and factor
analyses using 1965-66 data with those for the graph and principal flow analyses
outlined above are thus drawn, yet the latter avoids the problems of interpretatio
of loadings and scores as well as the problems of transformation in order to asses
the importance of small flows. Using the more complicated techniques significant
in-migration patterns accounted for approximately 33% of inter-SMLA migration, and
out migration patterns accounted for about 25% of inter-SMLA migration, again thes
are not dissimilar to the present graph analysis.

More recently, Flowerdew and Salt (1979) have subjected the 1970-71 inter-SMLA
migration flow matrix to transaction flow analysis. This method attempts to

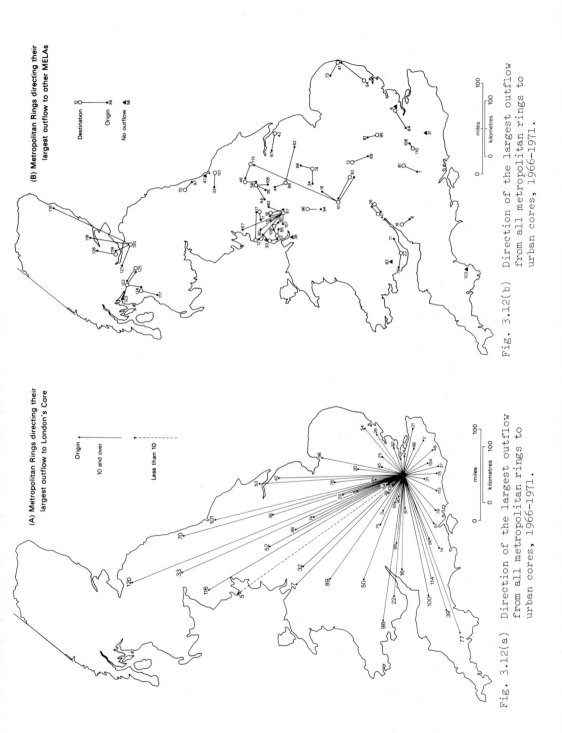

(A) Metropolitan Rings directing their
largest outflow to London's Core

Origin

10 and over

Less than 10

Fig. 3.12(a)   Direction of the largest outflow
from all metropolitan rings to
urban cores, 1966-1971.

(B) Metropolitan Rings directing their
largest outflow to other MELAs

Destination   12

Origin   34

No outflow   56

Fig. 3.12(b)   Direction of the largest outflow
from all metropolitan rings to
urban cores, 1966-1971.

standardise for the population size of both origin and destination simultaneously
and thus to delimit flows between places that are larger (or smaller) than expected
Once again the conclusions from this work complement those here, despite the recur-
ring problem of some very small inter-SMLA flows. Flows that are larger than
expected accrue mainly to contiguous areas emphasising the importance of distance
once size has been allowed for.

Having noted the crucial role of distance, Flowerdew and Salt went on to investigat
the main migration distances between the labour markets. Not surprisingly for the
labour areas on the periphery of urban Britain, both in and out migrants were characterised by longer distances, whilst shortest average lengths were located around
London and the other major centres. However, London had a relatively long mean
distance for the South East (especially regarding in-migrants) reflecting the
perpetuation of the drift to the South. When comparing in and out mean migration
lengths the southward shift of population was again emphasised since many northern
SMLAs had longer out migration distances.

Finally, Flowerdew and Salt incorporated both the effects of distance and origin/
destination size into an unconstrained gravity model. Just under 53% of the
migration in the 15,750 possible flows was explained. By use of population size at
the origin and destination of each flow as independent variables, it would be
suggested that people are less likely to move to another SMLA from a larger centre
than a smaller centre.

Clearly, however, the variation in areal size of the labour market will have critical influence since the majority of migrations are of such short distance. An
examination of the major residuals shows the importance of movement between naval
bases (these were illustrated in Fig. 3.9) and interaction between Scottish SMLAs
and Corby, as a result of active recruitment for the steelworks. Negative residual
representing flows that are lower than expected, are scarce amongst all residuals
when ignoring sign. One regional grouping appears, however, in the Lancashire-
Yorkshire group of labour markets. A number of complementary techniques and sources have been adopted to analyse the complex exchanges. In many ways the most
simple are the most successful. The use of a cut off point of 1,500 persons determined 479 flows of representing nearly half inter-MELA migration. Labour markets
are, however, linked by a complex pattern of hierarchically ordered and usually reciprocal flows. Decentralisation from the national centres is more important
than the return flows. Other elements in the flow matrix, be they unidentified
migration networks or simply small scale random transactions remain unknown.
Clearly migration hinges on a few major centres and their contribution is reviewed
next.

Migration and the 'million cities'

For Britain as a whole, 688,000 one year and 2.1 million five year migrants moved
between zones whilst remaining in the same MELA. Of these, 47.4% and 50% in these
periods respectively moved within each of the largest seven systems alone.
Decentralisation rates were considerably faster than in the rest of Britain both
within the SMLA and out of this area into the OMR. A much greater proportion of
intra-Million City movers left their core areas than would be expected from their
population share. In terms of in-migration the cores also received lower shares of
intra MELA migrants than their population share would suggest. The rings received
considerably larger proportions than expected. Thus decentralisation within Millio
City SMLAs was gradually being superseded by out movement into their OMRs and neigh
bouring labour markets. In each period, just one of the seven, Leeds (1970-71) and
Newcastle (1966-71) had a lower rate of out movement to the OMR compared with the
national average (which incorporates these areas). Additionally, each Million City
ring (except Liverpool, 1970-71) incurs net loss by migration to its outer ring.

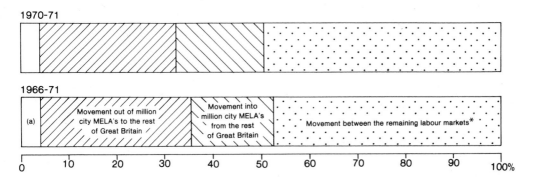

* Total includes migration into, out of and between unclassified areas

(a) Movement between 'Million Cities'

Fig. 3.13 Million city component of national inter-MELA
migration, 1966-1971 and 1970-1971.

Three types of migration flows involve Million Cities: (a) Migration into Million
Cities from other MELAs; (B) Migration from Million Cities to other MELAs and (C)
Migration between Million Cities. The first two categories have been subdivided
into those between contiguous and non-contiguous areas. Whilst the contiguous
exchanges were numerically the more important, net decentralisation was evident in
both cases. Fig. 3.13 indicates that only 4% of inter-MELA migrations are in fact
between the seven cities (in absolute terms 191,570 five year and 64,160 one year
migrants). Type B moves accounted for approximately 18% of all inter-MELA moves,
or almost 300,000 one year and 800,000 five year migrants. Those leaving the largest
systems, of course, are the most important group representing 28.3% of all total
inter-labour area migration during 1970-71 and 31.3% between 1966 and 1971. Table
3.9 reveals the inflows and outflows for the largest areas. In total their combined
losses to the rest of Great Britain reached 675,000 (1966-71) and 162,000 (1970-71).
The table shows that in both periods whilst total out migration decreases regularly
with rank size, the columns concerning total in-migration show Liverpool less attractive to in-migrants than Leeds.

The principal flows and how they are dominated by major cities have already been
discussed, but there is some scope for more selected detailed analysis. For the
1966-71 streams Figs. 3.14 and 3.15 report the size of exchanges between London and
elsewhere. Two labour markets contributed inflows of more than 15,000 to the capital,
Birmingham and Portsmouth. Ten labour markets, all within the South East region,
received outflows exceeding 20,000 migrants from London. Thus the other Million
Cities, all of which receive their largest inflow from the capital, fail to appear
among London's highest outflows. Examples of this inter-MELA decentralisation include Colchester, Chatham, Chelmsford, Reading and the New Towns. Almost without
exception, labour markets in the South East region receive more than 15,000 migrants
from the capital. Of the 400,000 that London lost to the rest of Britain 320,000
were lost to the South East region alone.

The hierarchy of flows through which decentralising streams are passed have been
discussed. It was postulated that relatively high proportions of the capital's
outflows were distributed to local SMLAs and, moreover, a greater proportion of
such migrants moved to (suburban) cores than was usual for decentralising streams).

TABLE 3.9 Absolute Migration Inflows, Outflows and Net Flows for 'Million Cities'

	1966-71 Total In	Total Out	Net Change	1970-71 Total In	Total Out	Net Change
London	490,800	898,980	-408,180	180,050	272,930	-92,880
Birmingham	120,440	180,040	-59,600	43,520	54,260	-10,740
Manchester	107,820	156,080	-48,260	36,830	50,560	-13,730
Glasgow	71,910	119,590	-47,680	24,860	41,810	-16,950
Liverpool	58,570	130,960	-72,390	22,200	40,240	-18,040
Leeds	85,950	96,760	-10,810	27,840	33,180	-5,340
Newcastle	58,380	86,400	-28,820	21,940	26,480	-4,540
Total for Million Cities	993,870	1,668,810	-674,940	357,240	519,460	-162,220
Total Movement between Million Cities	191,570	191,570	—	64,160	64,160	—
Total Inter-MELA Migration	4,726,000	4,726,000	—	1,608,420	1,608,420	—
Proportion all Inter-MELA Migrants in Exchanges with Million Cities	16.98	31.26		18.22	22.31	

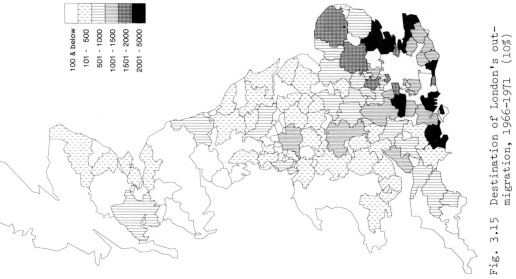

Fig. 3.15 Destination of London's outmigration, 1966-1971 (10%)

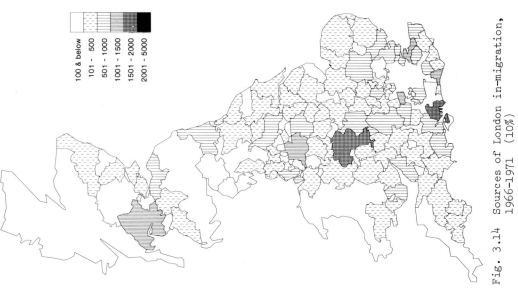

Fig. 3.14 Sources of London in-migration,
1966-1971 (10%)

From the metropolitan rings of towns around London still further decentralisation can be noted, though intra-MELA migration was much more likely to decentralise across urban zones. How critical is the role of the capital's population change to these areas? Fig. 3.16 shows that of 37 other labour areas in the South East, 35 grew by overall net in-migration in both the 1966-71 and 1970-71 periods. This total is reduced to only 13 of the region's peripheral MELAs if the net gain from London is excluded. Thus the notion that population is moving away from the capital through the urban hierarchy in the form of a ripple is supported. This view is further enhanced when the net losses of even the South East's peripheral MELAs to their contiguous neighbours outside the region is recorded. This process appears to affect the New Town labour markets as much as the other 'established' centres. It suggests that the New Towns may be vulnerable to a shift in the direction of net migration should the supply of migrants from London in any way diminish (for example, through changes of policy of population redistribution). It also supports the ideas expressed in the sections concerning population turnover. It is worth recalling that the New Towns have the highest in and out migration rates per capita in Britain.

The importance of the 42 flows between the Million Cities themselves is the final topic for review. The role of these streams as dominant inflows among these areas in particular has already been emphasised. In total, however, they represented only 4% of all inter-MELA migration. What are the redistribution characteristics of these flows? In net terms London is the only city to reveal migration gains in both intervals. Birmingham reports net inflows in 1970-71 whilst Manchester and Leeds have inflows over the five year spell. The absolute flows are depicted in Fig. 3.17.

Analysis of the net direction of individual exchanges between the seven areas indicates a remarkably distinct southerly shift of Million City population. London reported net in-migration in both periods from all other Million Cities, and Birmingham had net in-migration from each of its northern counterparts. Compare this with Glasgow where there were net outflows of population to each of the six other areas, and Newcastle which revealed net losses to each Million City except Glasgow.

3.3 CHARACTERISTICS OF MIGRANTS IN THE URBAN SYSTEM

3.3.1 Age Specific Migration

This section introduces the review of the differential impact of the migration process. Like the preceding section, each element begins with a national overview, and progressively narrows its scope to the individual labour market level. All data in this section refer to the 1966-71 interval. Census migration information for the 1970-71 period was not available by either the socio-economic status or for immigrants. For simplicity, the age structure of one year migrants, which principally replicates the patterns produced by the five year figures, have also been omitted. Unfortunately, there is no information available at the local authority level (and hence for MELAs) concerning the composition of migrant streams between areas. Additionally, the use of data illustrating characteristics of total migrants moving into, and out of, a MELA retain the problem that more than 10% of all migrations are made between local authorities within the same labour market. Use of net total (in-migrants minus out migrants) is the only way in which this difficulty may be overcome.

Differential mobility by age has commonly been alluded to within migration studies. Fig. 3.18 portrays national migration propensities between 1966 and 1971. This as with all tables within this section refers to the age of a person up to five years

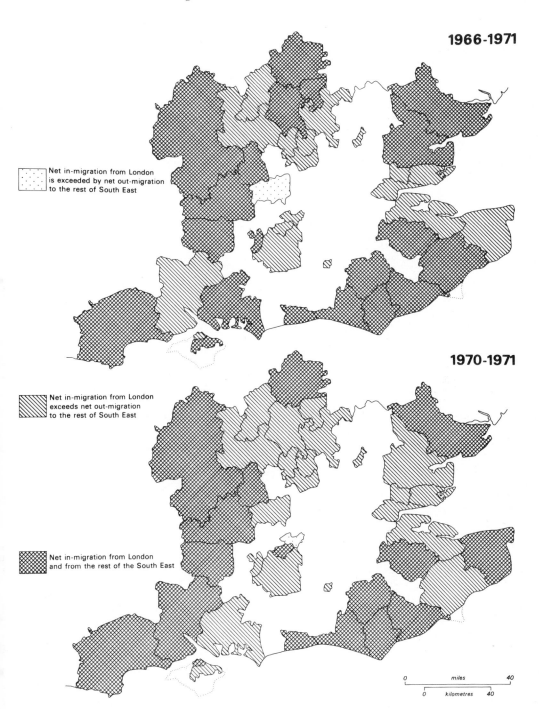

Fig. 3.16   London and net migration flows within the
             South East Region, 1966-1971 and 1970-1971

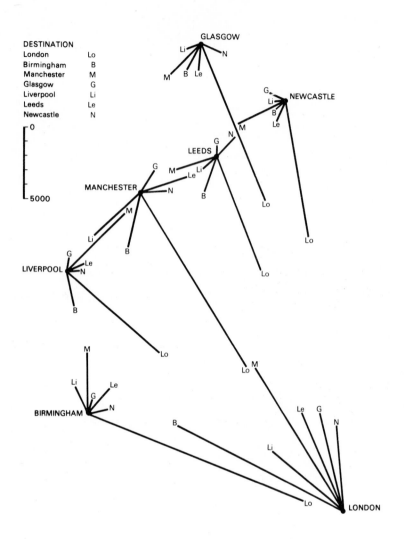

DESTINATION
London   Lo
Birmingham B
Manchester M
Glasgow   G
Liverpool   Li
Leeds   Le
Newcastle   N

Fig. 3.17 Migration flows between million city MELAs, 1966-1971

after migrating. Despite this limitation a clear pattern emerges. Highest mobili
rates accrue to populations aged in 1971 between 20 and 29 years. This period of
the life-cycle will usually include leaving home, marriage, and, entering the labou
market. The migration rates steadily decline with increasing age. At its peak, i
excess of 60% in the 25-29 year old group move, slowing down to about 20% in the
55-59 year group after which mobility levels remain virtually constant. A small
peak is, however, discernable within those of age 65-69 years, representing moves
on retirement.

Mostly, migrations of the three young people's groups reflect the mobility of thei
parents. It has been argued that family mobility is not necessarily restricted by
the number of children. However, it is perhaps possible that a move may be delaye

Fig. 3.18 Propensity to migrate by age of all movers within
           Britain, five year age groups, 1966-1971.

(or brought forward) when one child (or more) has left school, has attained secondary school age, or has completed a particular section of education.

The national mobility tabulations permit estimation of migration within and between
local authorities and within and between planning regions. Fig. 3.18 suggested,
that with the exception of the 30-44 year group (which is particularly poorly represented in terms of inter-regional migration), the ratios between the three types
of movement remain virtually consistent.

Here the analysis of changing age structures in the urban system, subdivides the
population into those aged under 15 (the minimum school leaving age in 1971), between 15 and 29, between 30 and pensionable age (60 for women, 65 for men) and those
of pensionable age. Fig. 3.18 demonstrates a considerable variation within the pen-
ultimate group. Hence to increase the understanding of the patterns, this cohort
has been subdivided into those between 30 and 44, and those of between 45 and pensionable age.

Age specific migration and population redistribution by aggregate urban zone

Changes in the age characteristics of areas are the outcome of births and deaths

within the area, and, of net migration in each age group. Because migrants tend to
be of younger child bearing age there is a relationship between migration change
and age characteristics. Areas with high rates of in-migration are also likely to
have disproportionately large numbers of young adults and, consequently large numbers of children. Areas with rapid rates of population decline by migration are
likely to have relatively older populations. The main exceptions will be coastal
resorts which receive inflows of predominantly older persons.

How does differential migration vary between the urban zones? Urban cores suffered
net migration losses in each age group. However, the central cities appear to be
becoming areas consisting of higher proportions of both the elderly and children
due to particularly severe outflows within the 15-44 age bands. Table 3.10 and
Fig. 3.19 reveal that outmigration within the 15-29 year olds' cohort amounted to
28% of the total outmovement and that only slightly lower levels were recorded for
those aged between 30 and 44 (i.e. a quarter of tht total of 1.1 million net decentralisers).

TABLE 3.10   Net Gains and Losses of Migrants by Age and
Urban Zones, 1966-71.

| | | | Age | | |
	5-14	15-29	30-44	45-pen	pen
Cores absolute	-192,080	-316,350	-280,460	-197,120	-143,300
per cent	(-17.01)	(-28.01)	(-24.33)	(-17.45)	(-12.69)
Rings absolute	146,280	276,260	214,450	119,000	53,250
per cent	(18.08)	(34.14)	(26.50)	(14.70)	(6.58)
OMR absolute	42,440	47,910	57,890	57,490	67,590
per cent	(15.53)	(17.53)	(21.18)	(21.03)	(24.73)
MELA* absolute	-3,360	7,820	-8,120	-20,630	-22,460

* net exchanges between MELAs and unclassified areas.

(Figures in brackets denote the proportion that each age
group's gain or loss represents of the total).

The situation for rings, mirrors that of the cores. Net in migration was recorded
by each age group, though the influx was particularly marked within the 15-29 year
group. (Tables 3.10 and 3.11). Together the net in-movement of the 15-29 and 30-
44 cohorts represented more than 60% of the rings gain. Proportional inflows of
the pensionable aged and under 15 cohorts were lower than those for total in-
migration to this zone (Table 3.12). Thus the rings were becoming younger by differential net migration.

Outer rings revealed a different composition among their net inflows. The two
oldest groups, consisting of those aged over 45, moved most rapidly into these
areas. Fig. 3.19 shows that gains in these groups were some 68,000 of pensionable
age and 57,500 for both those within the 30-44 and 45-pensionable age groups.
These net gains, although large, were considerably smaller than those incurred by
rings (except among the elderly). Thus, it is clear that the population of the
OMR was ageing by differential net migration.

In summary, economically active aged populations were leaving the core areas at a

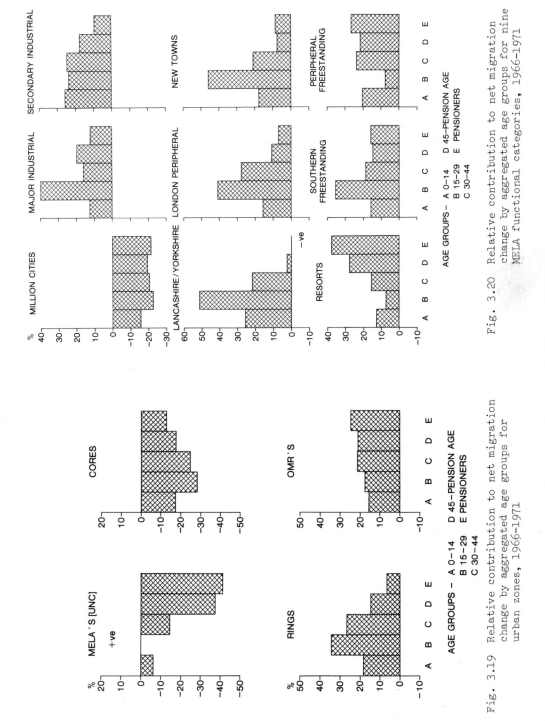

Fig. 3.20   Relative contribution to net migration
change by aggregated age groups for nine
MELA functional categories, 1966-1971

Fig. 3.19   Relative contribution to net migration
change by aggregated age groups for
urban zones, 1966-1971

British Cities

TABLE 3.11   Age Specific Migration Change per Thousand Population

			Age			
	5-14	15-29	30-44	45-pen	pen	Total
Cores	-5.55	-14.92	-10.06	-9.21	-0.88	-9.01
Rings	45.38	93.62	85.13	51.84	38.83	64.44
OMR	20.67	19.71	37.81	33.29	26.18	30.64

TABLE 3.12   Relative Age Specific Migration Change Compared with
             Zone Population Totals. (rate of change)

			Age			
	5-14	15-29	30-44	45-pen	pen	Total
Cores	0.62	1.66	1.17	1.02	0.10	---
Rings	0.70	1.45	1.32	0.80	0.60	---
OMR	0.68	0.64	1.23	1.09	1.18	---

rapid rate, with the effect of polarising the age of their remaining populations. Considerable implications are likely to result for social service provision within those areas. At metropolitan rings the inflow of migrants are chiefly among those within the younger economically active groups and thus likely to give rise to disproportionate numbers of children.   On the other hand decentralisation into the OMR is most marked by those in the older age groups - especially pensionable age. This, as is demonstrated later, reflects decentralisation of the relatively wealthy, as well as the retired, who can afford longer journeys to work.

This is a 'snap-shot' view of the migration process. Using a 'life-line' concept for individual migrants a generalised schema of the process begins with a number of young economically active entering the labour force or further education centralising to the core (or at least SMLA) when first leaving home, in search of accessible and cheaper, rented accommodation. On, or about, the age of marriage this group may decentralise to the rings and in later life decentralise further to the OMR. The cross-sectional data cannot support this contention directly. In addition it is likely that the entire sequence will be undertaken by only a minority of those in the system. However, in terms of net interaction between national constituent zones described above, the ideas postulated would appear to account for many of these patterns.

The notions are further confirmed by the comparison of results with other studies. The Redcliffe-Maud report (1969) shows that differential age specific migration was on-going in the early sixties. Using 1966-66 data for a representative sample of County Boroughs, the 25-44 male working age group was found to be more likely to decentralise to local areas than all males over 15. Results from Greater London (Gilje, 1975) reveal that in-migration to the capital in 1970-71 was heavily dominated by a peak in the early twenties whilst the peak associated with out migration flows was not so concentrated. There was, however, an additional peak coinciding with retirement.   It should be underlined that the capital, as shown see later, was nevertheless losing population in all groups and in the 15-29 cohort especially.   Thus the peak of in-migrants within their early twenties is more than compensated by outflows within later years of this cohort.

Finally, the exchanges between MELA units and unclassified areas produce four net
outflows from urban Britain and one net inflow. The age group still centralising
was predictably those in the 15-29 cohort (7,820 were drawn from unclassified
areas to MELAs in the period). Small outflows were recorded in the 5-14 and 30-44
age groups, but relatively large numbers left urban Britain in the two oldest categories. Thus these findings support the contentions that unclassified areas were
increasingly becoming the destinations of retirement areas (particularly the South
West, Wales and East Anglia) whilst they continued as a whole to loose their
younger populations. Clearly the differential effect of migration is likely to
have an important impact on the demand for services in small communities where only
a relatively small number of people need to be involved to cause a significant
change in demand for facility provision.

Age specific migration by functional MELA groupings

How does differential migration affect the composition of populations in each MELA
category? As demonstrated earlier, it is only the Million Cities which as a group
suffered population decline in the period. Table 3.13 indicates that these lost
population in each age cohort ranging from just over 100,000 of those aged between
5 and 14 to more than 150,000 of those between 15 and 29. Out migration from
Million Cities fuels net in-migration within each age cohort of the other 8 groups,
with one exception, a small net outflow of those in pensionable age in the
Lancashire/Yorkshire category.

TABLE 3.13   Age Specific Net Migration by Functional Group
and Urban Zone: MELAs: 1966-71

MELA group	5-14	15-29	Age 30-44	45-pen	pen
Million Cities	-106,010	-151,290	-136,930	-132,860	-145,480
Major Industrial	3,240	10,440	4,200	5,200	3,150
Secondary Industrial	12,120	11,200	11,680	8,280	4,600
Lancashire/Yorkshire	7,730	15,650	6,520	640	-1,670
London Peripheral	13,170	48,170	32,350	12,280	6,860
New Town	8,490	22,170	10,010	3,570	3,950
Resorts	24,150	14,060	30,130	53,280	72,460
Southern Freestanding	14,110	31,780	16,670	13,390	14,140
Peripheral Freestanding	14,640	5,640	17,250	15,570	19,530

Although there is a virtual ubiquitous net in-migration by all ages in eight of
the nine groups, there is a considerable difference in the proportional composition of these streams. These are summarised in figure 3.20. The Major Industrial,
Lancashire-Yorkshire, London Periphery, New Town and (to a lesser extent) Southern
Freestanding MELAs shows the highest proportion of their in-migrants within the
15-29 age cohort. This represents the continued relative attraction of both the
second tier cities and the South East to those entering the labour force. In each
example (except the Southern Freestanders) the lowest inflow accrued to the pensionable age group.

The resort category of course revealed particularly high inflows among those of

retirement age, and also of those between 45 and pensionable age, whilst less than
10% of net in-migration to these towns was aged between 15 and 29.   Similarly,
only small net inflows among the young economically active were drawn to the Peripheral Freestanding MELAs, but whilst this category did record its greatest inflow
in the pensionable age, Fig. 3.20 demonstrates a much more even attraction between
groups over 30 entering these areas. Finally, the Secondary Industrial MELAs reveal
roughly numerically equal inflows for the three groups less than 45 and only relatively small attraction to those over this age.

The analysis of composition of migrant streams fails to take account of either the
absolute or relative size of these net changes. Table 3.14 suggests that population
structure makes only a limited impact on the pattern of gains and losses presented
above. Although Million Cities averaged a 4% outflow of those aged between 15 and
29, outflows of 2.9% (30-44 cohort), 2.1% (45-pensionable age) and 2.8% (pensionable age) are also found. The relatively important differential gains of the young
economically active may be depicted for the New Towns (14.3%) and London Periphery
systems (8%) and Southern Freestanders (5.39%). Proportional increases in the
Resort and Peripheral Freestanding groups were also most pronounced among the two
eldest cohorts, despite already having population biased towards these ages in 1966.
The net inflow of elderly into the Peripheral Freestanding MELAs was, however, less
than 3% of its total population.

TABLE 3.14   MELA Proportional Gains and Losses by Age Groups:
Averaged by MELA group (1966-71)

			Age		
	5-14	15-29	30-44	45-pen	pen
Million Cities	-1.74	-4.07	-2.87	-2.05	-2.75
Major Industrial	0.27	0.56	0.44	0.43	0.31
Secondary Industrial	1.01	0.55	1.27	0.63	0.38
Lancashire/Yorkshire	1.40	3.92	1.86	0.00	0.53
London Peripheral	2.83	8.02	6.51	2.38	1.41
New Towns	3.96	14.25	7.00	2.81	6.25
Resorts	3.77	2.19	5.91	7.73	8.44
Southern Freestanding	2.03	5.39	3.42	2.46	3.08
Peripheral Freestanding	1.12	0.02	1.88	1.44	2.32

(Figures: percentages of 1971 population)

Comparison of the impacts of differential net migration between age cohorts in the
city groups is particularly revealing. Note that the New Towns incurred the
second largest rate of increase in the pensionable age group, albeit from a small
base. There is thus a marked contrast here with the London Peripheral Group, which
revealed only low proportional increases (also suggested by the small absolute
numbers drawn to these systems). Note the very small impact of differential age
migration on the Major Industrial and Secondary Industrial MELAs' populations.
Neither category increased its population in any cohort by more than 1.5% due to
differential migration. The Peripheral Freestanding Cities and Lancashire/
Yorkshire systems also reveal relatively small increases by net in-migration within
each cohort.

Figs. 3.21-3.23 display per capita net migration change rates for individual labour markets. Fig. 3.21 shows the trends for total populations. Very few labour markets grew in excess of 10% by net in-migration and those that did almost exclusively surround the capital. The rapid growth areas of 5% or more accrue to those areas fringing conurbations again especially around London. Although a similar pattern persists in Fig. 3.22 the greater mobility of those in the 15-29 year group is illustrated by the larger number of areas which recorded migration decline (often at more rapid rates) and, conversely, the equally sizeable net inflows experienced around the capital. Only five MELAs outside the South Eastern group recorded inflows in excess of 10%; all were adjacent to Million Cities. Fig. 3.23 indicates the distribution of per capita gains and losses for those of pensionable age. Whilst areas of decline were broadly similar to the total population, the pattern of the fastest growth rates was concentrated around the South East coast, the South West and a few MELAs in the North West. The majority of labour markets clearly fell within the confines of the 5% gain or loss reflecting the lower mobility rates of the pensionable age. London was the only system where total out migration exceeded 5% (a rate which, in fact, exceeded the decline of its 15-29 year population). For MELAs within Wales and the Marches, the 15-29 age group continued to move out, whilst a net inflow of pensionable aged are recorded thus supporting in detail some of the points made above concerning these areas' changing composition of population.

How do migration trends vary between the MELA groups at the zonal level? Table 3.15 outlines the position for urban cores: six of nine categories suffered net migration decline in each cohort; Million Cities, Major Industrial, Secondary Industrial, Lancashire/Yorkshire, Southern Freestanding and Peripheral Freestanding. Additionally the London Peripheral towns incurred deficits in four of five age groups. The 15-29 age group continued to be drawn to the London Peripheral cores. Net inflows of this group alone exceeded the combined deficits of the other cohorts. Thus only New Towns and Resorts experienced inflows of migrants in each of the five age groups. Table 3.15 re-emphasises the relative importance of the Million Cities when compared with other groups in absolute terms.

TABLE 3.15 Age Specific Net Migration by Functional Group and Urban Zone: Cores: 1966-71.

	Age				
	5-14	15-29	30-44	45-pen	pen
Million Cities	-162,510	-243,360	-219,630	-163,090	-142,000
Major Industrial	-25,150	-55,840	-40,230	-27,090	-15,520
Secondary Industrial	-8,140	-18,740	-14,670	-7,630	-3,980
Lancashire/Yorkshire	-1,410	-7,390	-3,840	-5,510	-3,910
London Peripheral	-180	7,410	-730	-4,920	-450
New Towns	5,250	18,480	5,690	2,030	3,930
Resorts	8,240	530	8,380	15,520	21,980
Southern Freestanding	-2,680	-5,530	-6,600	-2,740	-700
Peripheral Freestanding	-5,500	-11,410	-8,830	-3,690	-2,650

As suggested in the national zonal summary, most urban cores were getting older by selective migration. However, two processes were at work and manifested themselves differently (see Table 3.16). Firstly, in some areas the relatively rapid decline

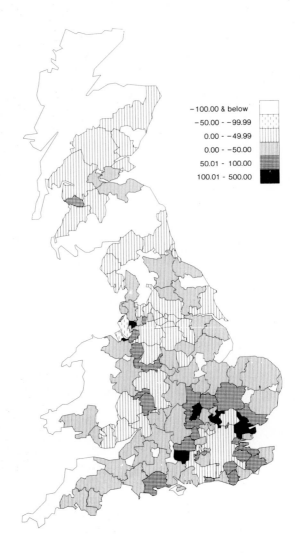

Fig. 3.21 Net migration per thousand population in MELAs, 1966-1971

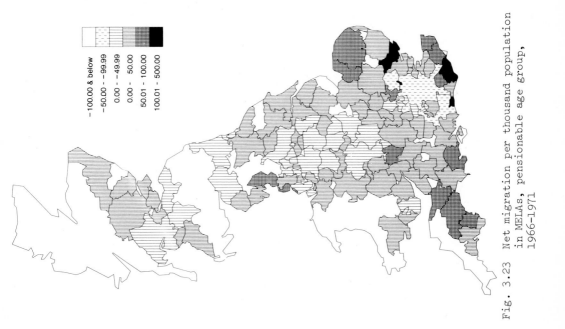

Fig. 3.23 Net migration per thousand population
           in MELAs, pensionable age group,
           1966-1971

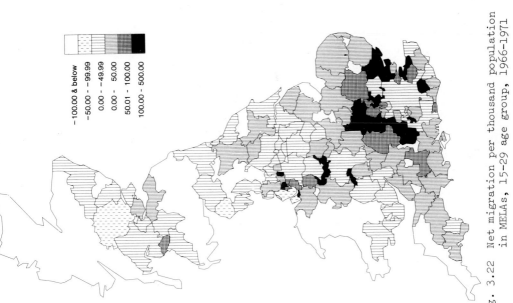

Fig. 3.22 Net migration per thousand population
           in MELAs, 15-29 age group, 1966-1971

of those between 15-44 (for example, in Million Cities, where the loss exceeded 10
Major Industrial, Secondary Industrial, Southern Freestanding, Peripheral Freestanding and Lancashire/Yorkshire cores) left an older residual population. Secon
in the Resorts especially rapid in-movement of the oldest groups to the resorts ag
the populations. Only the New Towns' and London Periphery Centres' were getting
younger by migration, although ironically the latter was one of only two core grou
to report net migration gains of those of retirement age.

TABLE 3.16 Mean Relative Net Migration at Urban Cores by Functional Group and Age Cohorts 1966-71

			Age		
	5-14	15-29	30-44	45-pen	pen
Million Cities	-5.57	-11.29	-10.31	-5.36	-5.44
Major Industrial	-2.32	-5.69	-5.47	-2.82	-2.07
Secondary Industrial	-1.10	-3.74	-3.07	-1.38	-1.10
Lancashire/Yorkshire	-0.29	-3.77	-2.40	-2.64	-2.31
London Peripheral	0.41	3.75	0.64	-1.76	-0.84
New Towns	3.34	16.96	6.00	2.87	9.93
Resorts	2.37	0.15	2.77	3.91	4.53
Southern Freestanding	-1.29	-2.05	-4.10	-1.37	-0.38
Peripheral Freestanding	-1.00	-2.77	-2.52	-0.59	-0.60

(Figures are averages of proportions of 1971 populations entering or leaving
MELAs by their functional group. Figures exceeding 5% emphasised.)

Table 3.16 also suggests the relative rates at which these processes were operating
Each cohort within the Million Cities' cores averaged a decline in excess of 5%,
however as noted above the rates of out migration are twice this level in the two
age groups 15-29 and 30-44. The losses for Major Industrial cities also measured
in excess of 2% of their population in each group, although again the two cohorts
between 15 and 45 revealed decline at twice this level.   Lower net out migration
per capita was recorded for each cohort in the Secondary Industrial, Lancashire/
Yorkshire towns and Peripheral Freestanding group. The Lancashire/Yorkshire eleme
did, however, show considerably less peaking in the loss of young economically
active than the other combinations.

Of those MELA groups reporting net in-migration at the core, the New Towns averaged
an increase approximating 17% in the 15-29 year group and 10% (due to very small
bases) of the pensionable aged. In-migration of the 45-pensionable age group was
relatively low at less than 3% revealing the extraordinary concentration of young
migrants and the importance of the impact of differential migration. Cores in the
resort group attained increases of more than 4% of their population over 45 in the
1966-71 period despite their high proportions of the elderly in 1961. For the
London Periphery cores, differential migration was much less important, averaging
above 1% in only two groups, a decline of -1.75% in the 45-pensionable age cohort
and an increase of 3.75% within the 15-29 group. Note the small positive values
for the 5-14 and 30-44 groups which resulted from the use of MELA average rates of
change rather than the absolute totals which were used to derive Table 3.14. Small
absolute values are likely to change sign when relative or average methods are compared.   Rings received the majority of outflows from the urban cores and subse-

quently by selective migration were getting younger. With the exception of the pensionable age cohort in the New Towns and Million Cities net inflows were evident for each of the other categories (Table 3.17). As expected, the highest inflows in terms of total population pertained to the 15-29 years group in 5 out of the 9 classes. Highest increase rates were illustrated by the 30-44 years group at the Million Cities, New Towns and Peripheral Freestanding areas reflecting in the former two cases the relative affluence of these areas and commensurate inaccessibility to those just joining the labour market and, in the latter example, the relatively lower opportunities of these areas to those just joining the labour force.

TABLE 3.17 Age Specific Net Migration by Functional Group and
Urban Zone: Rings: 1966-71

	Age				
	5-14	15-29	30-44	45-pen	pen
Million Cities	46,890	73,290	67,570	19,990	-12,180
Major Industrial	24,670	65,760	39,950	25,060	11,540
Secondary Industrial	13,300	24,360	17,320	10,220	5,130
Lancashire/Yorkshire	9,350	23,350	10,920	6,030	2,520
London Peripheral	16,300	34,510	29,930	14,960	6,470
New Towns	3,030	3,370	4,060	1,610	-80
Resorts	9,270	11,800	12,560	20,160	23,810
Southern Freestanding	9,880	23,400	13,270	7,860	5,710
Peripheral Freestanding	13,590	16,420	13,870	13,110	10,330

The rates of in-migration into Resort MELA's metropolitan rings did not reveal the same dominance by the pensionable age group. Most rapid increases accrued to the 45-pensionable age cohort (12%), but even those between 15-29 increased in excess of 8%. The relatively rapid gain in the 45-pensionable age band was possibly the result of two complementary forces: the higher base level of population over retirement age already present; and a relatively lower need to be near central functions on the part of the 45 to retirement age group compared with those experiencing increasing difficulty of mobility in later life.

Due to its smaller base, the influx of decentralisers from cores had a greater proportional impact on the growth of the ring population. Each city grouping recorded on average at least a 5% increase in one of its ring cohorts and the majority show at least one which had 10% gains. (Table 3.18). This reveals the importance of five year inflows into these areas.. Only Million Cities, Secondary Industrial, Resort and Peripheral Freestanding rings failed to grow on average by more than 10% in the 15-29 cohort. The Resort group was the only instance of similar growth rates in the pensionable age category. Finally, in terms of rates of increases, the lowest levels may be seen for the rings of Million Cities and Peripheral Freestanding towns. The former represented the continued decentralisation into their OMRs and neighbouring MELAs. This is supported by the fact that the two young economically active groups (those aged between 15 and 44) continued to move into the seven major systems' metropolitan rings at four times the rate of the elderly. The lower inflows to Peripheral Freestanding rings represented their relative lag in the centralization/decentralization cycle probably due to continued lower opportunities for the young economically active in their cores.

British Cities

TABLE 3.18   Mean Relative Net Migration at Rings by
Functional Group and Age Cohorts, 1966-71

	Age				
	5-14	15-29	30-44	45-pen	pen
Million Cities	3.39	7.13	6.36	2.74	1.27
Major Industrial	3.79	10.92	7.85	4.69	3.02
Secondary Industrial	3.67	7.14	6.44	3.09	2.16
Lancashire/Yorkshire	3.86	12.94	6.80	3.33	2.32
London Peripheral	5.22	13.38	11.73	6.29	3.57
New Towns	9.08	12.36	16.42	6.70	-0.02
Resorts	5.76	8.31	9.83	11.82	10.53
Southern Freestanding	5.37	10.79	8.68	5.09	5.22
Peripheral Freestanding	3.79	5.39	7.48	4.23	4.57

(Figures exceeding 10% emphasised)

Finally, some comment should be made of the out migration of retired from Million
Cities and New Towns. Comparison of Tables 3.17 and 3.18 reveal that although
Million Cities lost 12,180 migrants in the pensionable age group they averaged a
proportional inflow of 1.3%. This is entirely due to the effect of the capital.
London's ring declined by 23,440 of pensionable age, outweighing inflows to the
other six areas' rings. The London ring is also unusual in that it was also suffering out migration within the 45-pensionable cohort (-4,970), but this loss was
offset by gains by the other Million City rings. The combined losses from these
two cohorts ensured a total population decline in London's ring, although net inflows were recorded by other ages. Decline or very slow growth in the whole London
region of those aged over 45 supports the contention that the decentralisers to the
outer rings and beyond the London MELA tend to be older and are likely to have come
from the inner rings. (This may also indicate why the out migrants from rings in
this area also show a disproportionate tendency to migrate to other rings in smaller systems.) Persons concerned in this discussion were also likely to be in the
non-manual socio-economic groups. This point is verified later. It has been demonstrated that, as a whole, the outer rings were getting older by differential net
migration. Was this due to the relatively large impact of decentralisation from
Million Cities, or, is the trend ubiquitous to all systems? Tables 3.19 and 3.20
suggest that the relative ageing of these areas is due mainly to disproportionately
rapid growth in the Major Industrial, Peripheral and Resort systems. The Million
Cities' OMRs are drawing disproportionate numbers of young, aged between 15 and 45,
and this possibly indicates that the older ring decentralisers are leaving the
system altogether. The neighbouring groups' OMRs around London provided no further
insight to such a hypothesis since these areas are very small (only 3 MELAs in the
London Periphery group and Stevenage alone amongst the New Towns have an OMR).
(The total migration flows from London's OMR were in fact principally composed of
streams to systems just outside the region in the South West, although substantial
numbers are directed to the Freestanding MELAs.)

Of the other age groups, the mobile 15-29 year olds fared poorly within the outer
rings. Net deficits persisted within this age group at the Peripheral Freestanding
OMR, whilst they were clearly not so attracted to the Major or Secondary Industrial
OMRs either. Outflows were also indicated amongst some cohorts in the Lancashire/

TABLE 3.19   Age Specific Net Migrations by Functional
             Group and Urban Zone: OMR: 1966-71

	Age				
	5-14	15-29	30-44	45-pen	pen
Million Cities	9,610	19,280	15,130	10,240	8,700
Major Industrial	3,720	5,200	4,480	7,250	7,130
Secondary Industrial	6,960	5,580	9,030	5,690	3,450
Lancashire/Yorkshire*	-210	-310	-560	120	-280
London Peripheral*	2,050	6,250	3,150	2,240	840
New Towns*	210	320	260	-70	100
Resorts	6,640	1,730	9,190	17,600	26,070
Southern Freestanding	6,910	13,910	10,000	8,270	9,130
Peripheral Freestanding	6,550	630	7,210	6,150	11,850

* Relatively few labour markets in these categories have OMRs.

Yorkshire outer rings. (The three youngest cohorts in this city group's OMR revealed absolute total declines but averaged relative inflows). Care should be taken
not to attach too much significance to these results since many MELAs in the
Lancashire/Yorkshire category, like those in the London Peripheral and New Towns
systems, do not possess an OMR.

Broadly, when studying individual labour markets for those aged 15-29 the OMRs with
highest growth rates accrued to Million Cities and other areas within the axial
belt, whilst the pensionable aged group increased most rapidly at coastal resort
OMRs.

TABLE 3.20   Mean Relative Net Migration at OMRs by Functional
             Group and Age Cohorts, 1966-71

	Age				
	5-14	15-29	30-44	45-pen	pen
Million Cities	2.67	4.61	5.01	2.71	1.79
Major Industrial	2.98	1.96	3.71	4.52	3.98
Secondary Industrial	2.52	1.34	4.31	2.14	1.55
Lancashire/Yorkshire*	0.42	1.68	0.72	1.23	-1.63
London Peripheral*	2.77	9.83	7.83	5.77	0.77
New Towns*	9.30	17.10	15.30	-4.60	10.40
Resorts	2.55	1.70	5.23	8.76	10.71
Southern Freestanding	1.68	3.81	4.28	3.53	4.43
Peripheral Freestanding	0.61	-1.41	1.14	1.08	3.07

* These groups - especially New Towns - have small population bases, as many in
  these groups do not possess outer rings and those that do often consist of one
  local authority.

3.3.2 Net Migration and Socio-Economic Group

Income or occupation, like age, has been shown to affect the propensity to migrate.
The closest approximation to either, allowed by the Census, is the economically
active population categorised by socio-economic status. In part two the definition
of these groups was explained with the rationale for reducing 17 economically active
male categories to four orders. The present part subdivides two of these groups
further because a number of migration studies have suggested that the professional
workers (SEG 3 and 4) are considerably more mobile than managers (SEG 1 and 2).
Differences in mobility patterns between the unskilled (SEG 11) and semi-skilled
(SEG 7, 10 and 15) are also likely to manifest themselves, particularly due to
variation in their housing tenure characteristics. Thus the final classes adopted
are:

                A - Managerial (SEGs 1, 2 and 13)
                B - Professional (SEGs 3 and 4)
                C - Intermediate Non Manual (SEGs 5 and 6)
                D - Skilled Manual (SEGs 8, 9, 12 and 14)
                E - Semi-skilled Manual and Service Workers (SEG 7, 10 and 15)
                F - Unskilled Manual (SEG 11)
                G - Armed Forces and Inadequately Described (SEG 16 and 17)

There is a considerable size range between the groups. Whilst the skilled manual
class enumerated almost 7 million (Table 3.21), the professional group comprised
only 900,000 workers. Nevertheless the breakdown is considered valuable as distinct variations in migration patterns may be demonstrated.

Socio-economic characteristics of migrants are available in data sets which are
inferior even to those of age selective migration. At the local authority level,
data are available by the socio-economic group of the family head. Census definitions of family heads differ markedly from head of households (or economically
active males) yet total populations are only available for the last two. It is
thus impossible to derive rates of socio-economic migration change for labour markets like the age structure migration data. Migration data for MELAs and their
constituent zones may be presented only in absolute terms by net flows. Other
migrants within the family are allocated to the family head's socio-economic group.
Clearly there is a variation between the groups in the numbers of migrants that
will be married (and have children), but no account can be made of this. Nevertheless, in spite of such grave limitations, some indication of the patterns of selective migration operating at this scale may be derived.

Conurbations and regional remainders are the lowest spatial order for which published material tabulates both total and migrant populations according to their own
SEG. These data have been used to derive an additional perspective on the differential decentralisation from conurbations by socio-economic group and sex. Age
specific migration has the most profound effect on population age structure.
However in situ social mobility has been estimated as equally or more important in
the changing structure of the population compared with differential net migration.
(Dugmore, 1975). Due to absence of compatible population structure data, no estimation can be made of social mobility in the areas.

Finally, no account can be made of a migrant who simultaneously changes socio-
economic group and moves, or indeed, moves and later changes socio-economic status.
Migrants are only defined by their 1971 socio-economic status.

Of the 17.4 million migrants between 1966-71, only 9.25 million were made by those
within economically active groups. The remainder comprised students and children
under 15 (3.76 million), those retired (1.25 million) and others outside the labour
force (3.21 million) principally housewives.

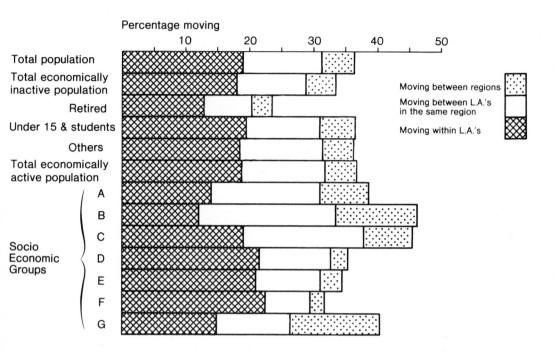

Fig. 3.24   Propensity to migrate within Britain by economic
classification of individual movers, 1966-71

Examining the six socio-economic aggregates and these inactive groups in a national
context, Table 3.21 and Fig. 3.24 indicate that the most mobile category were the
professional workers (group B) of whom more than 46% moved between 1966 and 1971.
The second highest propensities are recorded by the intermediate non-manual workers
(group C) of whom 45.4% moved in the five years. (Both classes contain relatively
high proportions in the 15-29 age group which were illustrated as being most mobile
in the previous section.) The remaining white collar category, the managerial workers (class A) also recorded a high migration propensity compared with all those
economically active (38.5% of group A changing residence against 36.9% for the
totals). The 8% differential between groups A and B (which in fact is as great as
that between the managerial and unskilled groups) supports the decision not to combine those two groups.

As expected, the manual workers, particularly the unskilled, reveal lower migration
propensities. Only 31.6% of the unskilled in 1971 had moved in the study period.
The skilled and semi-skilled workers reflect intermediate levels of mobility with
rates of 35 and 34% respectively. Finally, of the armed forces and inadequately
described, the smallest of the combinations, just over 40% migrated in the period
due to particularly high mobility rates amongst the armed forces.

The Census allows assessment of varying national migration rates within and between
local authority areas and planning regions. Whilst the majority of moves are made
within local authority areas in the manual groups, the opposite is true for white
collar workers. This may reflect a number of complementary factors: on the one

TABLE 3.21 Propensity to Migrate Within and Between Local Authority Areas and the Ten Economic Planning Regions by Mover's Own SEG, 1966-71 (males and females)

| | Socio Economic Groups | | | | | | | Total economically active | Total Population over five years |
	A	B	C	D	E	F	G		
Total 1971 Population									
Thousands	2,435	886	6,290	6,979	4,680	1,888	903	25,021	49,629
Movement within GB									
Thousands	937	409	2,855	2,464	1,603	597	363	9,226	17,444
% of total GB	38.5	46.2	45.4	35.3	34.2	31.6	40.2	36.8	35.1
Movement within regions									
Thousands	761	296	2,389	2,272	1,452	555	238	7,966	15,019
% of total GB	31.2	33.4	37.9	32.5	31.0	29.4	26.3	31.8	30.2
Movement within local authority areas									
Thousands	345	108	1,207	1,497	982	426	135	4,703	9,075
% of total GB	14.1	12.2	19.1	21.4	20.9	22.5	14.9	18.8	18.2

hand the constraints on residential mobility due to the former groups' high dependence on Council housing sector, coupled with the relative ease with which manual workers may change job or occupation, and on the other a relatively high perception of opportunities in other regions (together with a generally higher income with which access to these opportunities may be gained) on behalf of the white collar workers. The higher specialisation of these last groups results in lower job substitutability. Thus, for example, more professional workers move between the ten economic planning regions than move within the same local authority and, additionally, inter-regional movements represent 25% of group B's migrations compared with less than 10% in the unskilled group (a total of 15,000 of 160,000 in absolute terms).

Two of the three economically inactive subgroups, the retired and students together with children under 15, are closely influenced by migration propensities according to age. Accordingly, the retired illustrate relatively low migration rates, just under 1 in 4 moved against 36% of the whole population, and the students and young people were relatively mobile. The remaining category, consisting principally of housewives, revealed mobility rates only marginally below the average for the whole population and illustrates the universal coverage of family income bands within this group.

In aggregate, almost identical proportions of male and female migrants moved within and between the 18 conurbations and regions (Table 3.22). Between the groups the range is, however, considerably lower for females, possibly indicating their domestic role and the greater importance attached to their husbands' careers (and subsequent movements). Both male and females show particularly high proportions of their retired migrants leaving conurbations. Of the two groups the females are, however, more likely to move in the same region possibly as a result of their longer life-span and subsequent short distance moves after being widowed.

Flows of socio-economic groups between conurbations and regions

The principal patterns of differential migration attributable to socio-economic group between conurbations and planning regions have been described by Kennett and Randolph (1978). This study indicated that in terms of movement between those 18 areas alone the manual groups, especially the unskilled, revealed greater proportions of their migrants being exchanged between, and decentralising out of, the conurbations. However in terms of total migration propensities, such movement is considerably less important than that within white collar groups. This suggested the greater significance of counter flows for the more mobile groups, an assessment supported by correlations between absolute inflows and outflows. The highest associations were found for the white collar groups (and the professional workers in particular). Correlations were weakest for the unskilled and retired. These trends are revealed for both the sexes although higher correlations are usually recorded for females indicating a closer approximation of their inflows and outflows. Independently, these measures may be considered to be inconclusive because of statistical difficulties. Collectively, however, there is little doubt that although the professional and other white collar groups were decentralising from the conurbations the most rapidly in terms of all migrations, when the interaction between conurbations is taken alone, the proportion of counter stream movement was often higher among the white collar groups.

The analysis of net flows suggested that the tendency for counter streams is mainly due to the influence of London and the rest of the South East continuing to act as a magnet for those among white collar groups. Each conurbation suffered net out migration in each socio-economic group aggregate with the exception of unskilled males to the West Yorkshire conurbation, unskilled females to the South East Lancashire conurbation and, more significantly, female professional workers to

TABLE 3.22   Proportion of Total Male and Female Migrants
              Moving Between 18 Conurbations, Regions and
              Regional Remainders, 1966-71

	Males	Females
Total	23.68	23.29
Retired	25.81	22.99
SEG A	32.77	27.89
B	46.12	45.92
C	30.89	26.03
D	15.07	15.88
E	16.21	16.50
F	12.52	11.15
G	52.55	27.87

/ See text for details of SEG aggregates/

Greater London (Tables 3.23 a and b). As expected Wales, Scotland, and the North
recorded inter-regional deficits in the intermediate non-manual group (containing
particularly high proportions of those aged between 15 and 29). In this group the
main destinations were the Outer Metropolitan Area and the Outer South East.

At this scale differential rates of relative migration could only be obtained for
males. However, very high associations between migration changes per capita and
migration efficiencies (which examine net migration in terms of all exchanges
accruing to the region) suggests a considerable degree of similarity for female
migration patterns. Tyneside and Merseyside were conurbations with highest overall
rates of out movement of economically active males. In relation to these two
flows Tyneside, West Midlands and West Yorkshire conurbations suffered greater proportional outflows of males in white collar occupations (in terms of rank, Table
3.24) than did Greater London, Merseyside and Clydeside. In terms of destinations,
the North West regional remainder and East Anglia revealed a tendency to attract
manual workers (again in terms of rank) compared with the Outer South East and
South West.

Socio economic characteristics of net migration by urban zone

At the MELA level data available allow only an indication of net flows by persons
in families, according to the head of family's socio-economic group. Consequently,
analysis must be restricted to absolute net flows in these areas.

Like age specific net migration, urban cores suffered decline in each socio-
economic aggregate. The largest proportion of out migrants accrued to those with
family heads in the skilled manual group, representing one third of the total (in
absolute terms 430,000) (Table 3.25, Fig. 3.25). Those allocated to intermediate
Non-manual and Managerial groups combined, represent a further 40% of the total,
each recording a loss of about 250,000. The remaining groups made up less than
10% of the outflow. Metropolitan rings mirror this position. Inflows are recorded by each socio-economic aggregate and their relative importance in terms of
inflows were closely akin to the outflows from cores. In migration of more than
315,000 persons allocated to the skilled group represented more than 35% of the
total; slightly greater than their corresponding proportional core decline.
Similarly, the Intermediate Non-manual group, also contained a slightly greater
proportion of the ring zone's entrants compared with urban core's decline. Other
socio-economic aggregates contributed lower proportions.

TABLE 3.23a.   Absolute Net Migration (males) by Socio-economic Aggregate Ranked, 1966-71 (Thousands)

For each column the first value refers to the region (1–18), the second to absolute net change.

Total Change		Economically Active Change		Socio-Economic Groups													
reg	val	reg	val	A reg	A val	B reg	B val	C reg	C val	D reg	D val	E reg	E val	F reg	F val	G reg	G val
12	-227.8	12	-144.6	12	-28.1	12	-11.7	12	-30.0	12	-52.7	12	-15.1	12	-5.1	6	-2.6
9	-58.9	9	-42.0	9	-7.3	9	-3.4	9	-6.9	9	-15.9	9	-5.5	15	-2.1	17	-2.2
5	-43.0	5	-30.4	6	-4.3	17	-2.2	5	-4.9	5	-7.8	5	-4.6	5	-1.7	9	-2.1
17	-35.8	17	-24.2	3	-3.6	6	-2.2	3	-3.9	17	-7.8	17	-3.0	9	-0.7	3	-2.0
6	-29.9	6	-20.4	5	-2.7	16	-1.7	6	-2.9	6	-6.0	3	-1.8	3	-0.3	5	-1.9
1	-17.5	1	-13.4	4	-2.4	4	-1.7	1	-2.7	1	-4.4	1	-1.2	1	-0.2	7	-1.8
3	-15.9	3	-12.4	17	-2.2	3	-1.6	3	-2.5	3	-2.2	18	-0.8	18	0.1	8	-1.7
4	-6.1	4	-6.0	1	-1.0	1	-1.4	1	-2.5	4	0.9	16	-0.5	16	0.1	16	-1.6
16	3.3	16	-0.6	16	0.6	18	-0.7	18	-0.2	2	1.4	4	0.5	4	0.2	12	-1.6
2	5.9	2	3.4	8	1.2	2	0.0	2	-0.1	18	2.1	2	0.5	2	0.3	11	-1.6
18	15.0	18	6.1	18	1.4	11	1.0	4	0.9	10	3.1	18	0.7	8	0.4	4	-1.6
8	16.3	8	12.5	2	1.8	8	1.1	11	2.7	8	7.2	8	1.2	6	0.6	1	-1.1
11	34.4	11	21.4	11	3.8	8	1.7	8	3.0	11	7.8	6	2.0	10	0.7	2	-0.9
10	39.0	10	28.2	10	4.6	10	1.7	15	3.4	15	9.1	10	3.4	11	0.7	11	0.8
15	52.9	15	31.5	15	5.3	15	1.9	10	4.8	10	14.2	11	4.4	13	1.2	18	1.3
7	59.0	7	41.2	7	5.9	7	2.8	7	6.1	14	16.6	13	6.2	15	1.2	13	3.2
13	96.8	14	67.2	14	11.4	14	5.8	14	15.9	7	18.2	15	6.5	14	1.6	15	5.0
14	112.3	13	82.5	13	15.4	13	11.1	15	25.8	13	19.4	7	6.9	14	3.0	14	9.2

Key: 1. Tyneside Conurbation   10. Remainder of West Midlands Region
       2. Remainder of North Region   11. East Anglia
       3. West Yorkshire Conurbation   12. Greater London
       4. Remainder of Yorkshire & Humberside Region   13. Outer Metropolitan Area
       5. Merseyside Conurbation   14. Outer South East
       6. South East Lancashire Conurbation   15. South West Region
       7. Remainder of North West Region   16. Wales
       8. East Midlands Region   17. Central Clydeside Conurbation
       9. West Midlands Conurbation   18. Remainder of Scotland

For details of socio-economic aggregates, see text.

TABLE 3.23b Absolute Net Migration (females) by Socio-economic Aggregate Ranked, 1966-71 (Thousands)

Total Change	Economically Active Change	A	B	C	D	E	F	G
12 −246.6	12 −37.7	12 −2.7	6 −0.2	12 −13.8	12 −5.3	12 −10.1	12 −3.5	12 −2.4
9 −59.1	9 −20.0	9 −1.1	5 −0.2	9 −10.7	9 −1.3	9 −4.4	5 −0.8	9 −1.2
5 −46.4	5 −15.8	6 −0.9	3 −0.2	5 −8.4	5 −1.1	7 −3.5	9 −0.8	6 −1.0
17 −36.9	17 −12.3	3 −0.7	4 −0.2	17 −6.0	6 −1.0	17 −3.0	17 −0.5	17 −0.9
6 −36.7	6 −11.3	5 −0.6	9 −0.2	16 −5.2	17 −0.8	6 −2.5	1 −0.2	5 −0.8
1 −20.2	1 −7.5	17 −0.6	17 −0.2	6 −5.2	1 −0.3	1 −1.1	4 −0.1	2 −0.5
3 −15.7	4 −6.8	1 −0.4	16 −0.1	4 −4.9	3 −0.1	3 −1.0	16 −0.0	1 −0.5
4 −4.4	3 −6.1	8 −0.2	15 −0.0	1 −4.7	4 −0.1	4 −0.9	3 0.0	3 −0.5
16 3.0	16 −5.3	4 −0.0	1 −0.0	3 −2.9	2 −0.0	18 −0.3	18 0.2	4 −0.4
2 6.0	2 −2.0	2 0.1	18 −0.0	2 −1.5	18 0.0	16 −0.3	8 0.3	16 −0.3
18 15.4	18 −1.1	10 0.3	7 0.0	18 −1.4	10 0.2	2 0.0	15 0.3	18 0.0
8 18.5	8 8.9	16 0.3	8 0.0	8 2.4	16 0.4	8 1.5	11 0.3	8 0.5
11 39.2	11 10.3	11 0.4	11 0.0	15 3.5	8 0.9	11 2.4	10 0.6	7 0.6
10 40.2	15 11.5	18 0.5	2 0.1	11 5.1	11 0.9	15 2.7	7 1.0	10 0.9
7 61.6	10 12.3	13 0.7	10 0.1	10 6.5	13 0.9	10 3.6	14 1.6	11 0.9
15 63.4	7 24.2	7 0.7	12 0.3	7 7.2	15 0.9	13 4.8	13 1.9	15 1.5
13 95.6	13 33.8	15 1.3	14 0.4	14 17.6	7 2.2	17 5.4		13 2.0
14 123.0	14 34.6	14 2.8	13 0.8	13 22.5	14 2.7	14 6.9		14 2.3

For each column the first value refers to the region (1–18), the second to absolute net change

Key:
1. Tyneside Conurbation
2. Remainder of North Region
3. West Yorkshire Conurbation
4. Remainder of Yorkshire & Humberside Region
5. Merseyside Conurbation
6. South East Lancashire Conurbation
7. Remainder of North West Region
8. East Midlands Region
9. West Midlands Conurbation
10. Remainder of West Midlands Region
11. East Anglia
12. Greater London
13. Outer Metropolitan Area
14. Outer South East
15. South West Region
16. Wales
17. Central Clydeside Conurbation
18. Remainder of Scotland.

For details of socio-economic aggregates, see text.

TABLE 3.24   Relative Net Migration by Socio-Economic Aggregates Ranked, 1966-71 (males) (Percent of 1971 Base Populations)

Total Change		Economically Active Change		Socio-Economic Groups															
				A		B		C		D		E		F		G			
5	-7.1	5	-8.5	1	-11.6	1	-15.3	5	-7.9	5	-8.7	5	-7.2	5	-4.9	3	-22.8		
12	-6.4	12	-6.3	5	-10.8	5	-12.6	9	-6.3	12	-6.9	12	-4.9	12	-3.1	1	-20.3		
9	-5.0	1	-5.7	9	-9.8	9	-11.4	1	-6.2	9	-4.8	17	-4.4	17	-3.0	17	-20.0		
1	-4.5	9	-5.6	12	-8.8	3	-11.4	17	-5.7	1	-4.4	9	-4.3	9	-1.3	5	-18.8		
17	-4.3	17	-4.9	17	-6.2	12	-8.4	12	-5.5	17	-3.9	1	-3.7	1	-1.0	6	-18.5		
6	-2.5	6	-2.9	6	-5.3	17	-7.6	6	-3.2	6	-2.1	6	-1.7	3	-0.9	9	-13.7		
3	-1.9	3	-2.4	3	-4.0	6	-6.8	3	-3.1	3	-1.0	3	-1.0	18	0.1	7	-11.7		
4	-0.4	4	-0.6	4	-1.0	4	-5.4	16	-2.5	4	0.2	4	-0.3	16	0.2	16	-7.1		
16	0.2	18	-0.3	16	0.8	16	-2.3	4	-2.1	18	0.3	18	0.3	4	0.3	8	-6.9		
2	0.4	16	-0.0	8	1.1	2	0.3	2	-0.1	2	0.6	2	0.4	2	0.5	4	-4.9		
18	0.9	2	0.4	18	1.6	18	2.4	18	-0.1	16	0.9	16	0.5	8	0.7	2	-4.4		
8	0.9	8	1.2	2	2.0	8	2.4	15	1.9	8	1.5	8	0.8	6	0.9	12	-2.3		
10	2.8	15	2.6	15	3.7	15	3.8	8	1.9	15	2.2	15	1.2	10	1.3	10	3.9		
15	2.9	10	3.7	10	4.5	10	4.5	11	3.7	13	3.6	13	3.0	13	1.3	18	4.1		
13	3.7	11	4.3	7	5.6	11	4.8	10	3.9	14	3.7	10	3.1	15	1.6	11	5.4		
7	3.9	7	4.6	13	5.8	7	6.6	7	4.2	10	4.0	14	3.5	14	2.2	13	6.4		
11	4.2	13	5.1	11	6.1	13	8.4	14	6.9	11	4.3	11	3.7	11	2.3	15	8.4		
14	5.3	14	5.4	14	6.7	14	8.4	13	7.7	7	5.0	7	5.0	7	3.8	14	13.0		

For each column the first value refers to the region (1-18), the second to percentage change

Key: 1. Tyneside Conurbation
      2. Remainder of North Region
      3. West Yorkshire Conurbation
      4. Remainder of Yorkshire & Humberside Region
      5. Merseyside Conurbation
      6. South East Lancashire Conurbation
      7. Remainder of North West Region
      8. East Midlands Region
      9. West Midlands Conurbation
     10. Remainder of West Midlands Region
     11. East Anglia
     12. Greater London
     13. Outer Metropolitan Area
     14. Outer South East
     15. South West Region
     16. Wales
     17. Central Clydeside Conurbation
     18. Remainder of Scotland.

For details of socio-economic aggregates, see text.

TABLE 3.25   Net Gains and Losses of Migrants by Socio-
Economic Group and Urban Zone, 1966-71

		Socio-Economic Groups						
		A	B	C	D	E	F	G
Cores	absolute	-247890	-114920	-263490	-429930	-120600	-32380	-66900
	percent	(-19.43)	(-9.01)	(-20.65)	(-33.69)	(-9.45)	(-2.54)	(-5.24)
Rings	absolute	155200	80470	200480	314640	83990	21750	40870
	percent	(17.29)	(8.97)	(22.34)	(35.06)	(9.36)	(2.42)	(4.55)
OMR	absolute	64020	23860	51640	91040	30250	7610	16050
	percent	(22.50)	(8.39)	(18.15)	(32.00)	(10.63)	(2.68)	(5.64)
MELA*	absolute	-28670	-10590	-11370	-24250	-6360	-3020	9980
	percent	(-30.42)	(-11.24)	(-12.06)	(-25.73)	(-6.75)	(-3.20)	(-10.59)

* Net exchanges between MELAs and unclassified areas

(Figures denote numbers of migrants allocated to SEG of family head. Figures in
brackets denote the proportion that each group's gain or loss represents of the
total.)

For details of socio-economic aggregates - see text.

Somewhat different emphases are experienced in the patterns of net in-migration to
the OMRs. Whilst in absolute terms no group approached the inflow experienced by
the rings, a slightly higher preponderance of in-migrants was recorded amongst the
managers (although lower proportions are evident for the Professional, Intermediate
Non-Manual and Skilled families).

The tables suggest that the inflow to ring areas contained slightly greater proportions of migrants among the middle income range (i.e. the skilled and intermediate non-manual) when compared with the OMRs. The latter receive slightly higher
proportions in managerial families. This provides more indirect evidence for the
notion of gradual decentralisation: first of the relatively young (intermediate
non-manual and professional) to rings and, late in the life cycle of older (managerial workers) to the OMR. This idea is supported by the type of exchanges between
MELAs and unclassified areas. Each aggregate suffered net declines to the expanding rural areas, but the managerial groups, along with professional elements, form
relatively large proportions of the remote areas' total inflow. The former in fact
exceeded even those of the skilled workers (with 30% of the total compared with
26%).

Net flows by socio-economic groups between MELA functional groups

How do differential patterns of net migration vary between the MELA functional
groups? Table 3.26 suggests that Million City MELAs are losing relatively low
proportions of their total migration deficit within the managerial and professional
groups when compared with the national profile. This city grouping reveals particularly prominent losses in the intermediate non-manual, skilled and semi-skilled
families. These figures would suggest that the polarisation in decline of Million
Cities by differential age migration may also be occurring with regard to socio-
economic groups, although the unknown importance of social mobility must be borne
in mind.

Each of the other eight MELA groups revealed net overall migration gain. However,

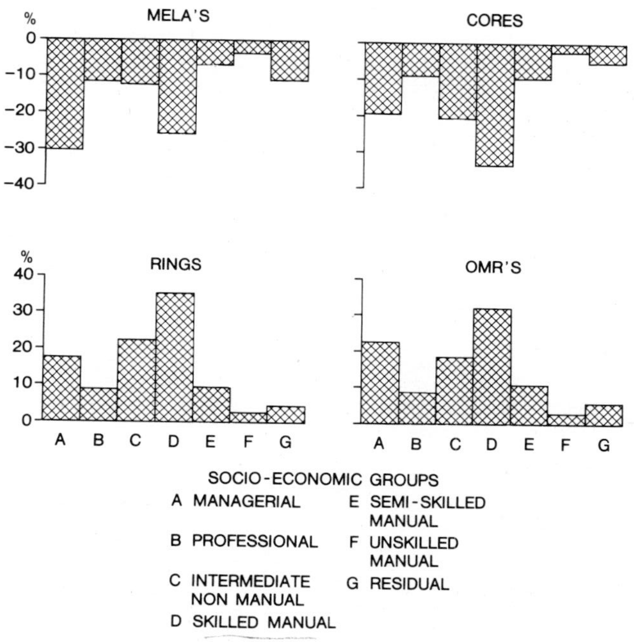

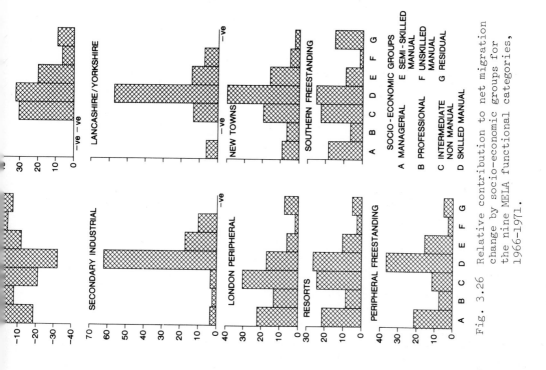

Fig. 3.26 Relative contribution to net migration change by socio-economic groups for the nine MELA functional categories, 1966–1971.

Fig. 3.25 Relative contribution to net migration change by socio-economic groups for urban zones, 1966–1971.

TABLE 3.26   Net Migration by Socio-Economic Group*, Labour
Area Functional Type and Urban Zone, 1966-71.   MELA

Socio-Economic Group

MELA Group	A	B	C	D	E	F	G
Million Cities	-133400	-56550	-149510	-232500	-82990	-27720	-44690
	(-18.34)	(-7.77)	(-20.56)	(-31.96)	(-11.41)	(-3.81)	(-6.14)
Major Industrial	-4150	-3260	9120	9820	6070	2080	2810
	+	+	(30.50	(32.84)	(20.30)	(6.96)	(9.40)
Secondary Industrial	2200	1270	2160	36690	10280	5940	-3220
	(3.76)	(2.17)	(3.69)	(62.68)	(17.56)	(10.15)	+
Lancs/Yorks	2540	-43	5080	21920	5500	2990	-2070
	(6.68)	+	(13.36)	(57.64)	(14.46)	(7.86)	+
London Peripheral	28530	17610	38950	21890	7810	2450	9510
	(22.51)	(13.89)	(30.73)	(17.27)	(6.16)	(1.93)	(7.50)
New Towns	4980	3610	10830	21800	8770	2910	1350
	(9.18)	(6.65)	(19.96)	(40.18)	(16.16)	(5.36)	(2.49)
Resorts	39190	16070	43730	47830	18930	4920	9320
	(21.77)	(8.93)	(24.30)	(26.57)	(10.52)	(2.73)	(5.18)
Southern Freestanding	16440	5770	20080	22200	8250	1690	13460
	(18.71)	(6.56)	(22.85)	(25.26)	(9.39)	(1.92)	(15.31)
Peripheral Freestanding	15000	5320	8190	26100	11020	1720	3550
	(21.16)	(7.50)	(11.55)	(36.81)	(15.54)	(2.42)	(5.01)

* Socio-Economic group determined by that of the migrants' family head
  Socio-Economic groups explained in text.
  Figures in brackets denote proportions of total gains (or losses)

a number of individual social groups indicated decline in particular elements.
The decline of managerial and professional families from the Major Industrial areas
by net migration is particularly interesting, although only very small net inflows
are derived for the other groups (Fig. 3.26). The professional group were also
moving out of the Lancashire-Yorkshire towns reflecting the relatively low levels
of opportunity in these smaller MELAs. This is further underlined by the out
migration of the armed forces and inadequately described groups from both these
and the Secondary industrial systems.   Migration streams within this aggregate are
dominated by the movements of the armed forces, and the number of young people
leaving to join the forces from these areas indicates lack of jobs for young people
in these areas. This is supported by the very low proportional in-migration of the
Intermediate Non-manual group (which consist of high proportions of young workers)
to both Secondary Industrial and Lancashire-Yorkshire towns, together with the low
rates of in-migration within the 15-29 cohort.

The remaining five functional groups of MELAs grew by net migration with some variation in profile within each socio-economic aggregate. Greatest differentials
probably occur between the London Peripheral and New Town groups which have consistently shown high rates of in-migration from the rest of Britain as in similar

profiles of age structure. Whilst the London Peripheral labour markets draw in
considerable proportions of families in the managerial, professional and intermediate non-manual (but low proportions in the three manual groups), the New Towns
show particular attraction for the manual groups. Inflows of persons in managerial
families exceed those of the skilled manual in the London Peripheral towns whilst
the latter represent 40% of inflows in New Towns. The fundamental difference between planned and unplanned decentralisation would seem to be exemplified here and
supports the results of recent survey studies. (Deakin and Ungerson, 1977).

The Resort, Southern Freestanding and Peripheral Freestanding MELAs also attract
relatively large proportions of managerial and professional group in-migrants (and
additionally the Intermediate Non-Manual families). Again the relatively low levels of attraction of the young economically active groups to peripheral systems is
illustrated. Subsequently the influx of manual workers (especially the skilled
group) reflects more closely the profiles illustrated by the Major and Secondary
Industrial MELAs, whilst the Resort and Southern Freestanding categories resemble
the London Peripheral distribution.

Consider next differential migration attributable to socio-economic status in terms
of urban zones of the MELA categories. Table 3.27 shows that the profile of migrant
losses from their cores much more closely approximated the national out migration

TABLE 3.27 Net Migration by Socio-Economic Group*, Labour
Area Functional Type and Urban Zone, 1966-71. Cores

MELA Group	Socio-Economic Group						
	A	B	C	D	E	F	G
Million Cities	−169490	−72000	−203030	−370070	−122300	−39990	−53040
	(−16.46)	(−6.99)	(−19.71)	(−35.93)	(−11.87)	(−3.88)	(−5.15)
Major Industrial	−43650	−22970	−38730	−59770	−11590	−920	−9770
	(−23.29)	(−12.26)	(−20.67)	(−31.89)	(−6.18)	(−0.49)	(−5.21)
Secondary Industrial	−17160	−9440	−19850	−7520	−180	−2700	−5590
	(−28.72)	(−15.80)	(−33.23)	(−12.59)	(−0.30)	+	(−9.36)
Lancs/Yorks	−3270	−3080	−6270	−5000	−1960	−680	−1920
	(−14.74)	(−13.89)	(−28.27)	(−22.54)	(−8.84)	(−3.06)	(−8.66)
London Peripheral	−2220	−380	670	−233	−280	940	2940
	+	+	+	+	+	+	+
New Towns	−1080	650	7500	19730	9130	2810	1200
	+	(1.58)	(18.28)	(48.10)	(22.26)	(6.85)	(2.92)
Resorts	7670	3200	10030	12900	6170	2170	4500
	(16.44)	(6.86)	(21.50	(27.66)	(13.23)	(4.65)	(9.65)
Southern Freestanding	−6480	−4720	−5860	−6390	−620	−130	−1680
	(−25.04)	(−18.24)	(−22.64)	(−24.69)	(−2.40)	(−0.50)	(−6.49)
Peripheral Freestanding	−12210	−6180	−7950	−11480	1030	720	−3540
	(−29.52)	(−14.94)	(−19.22)	(−27.76)	+	+	(−8.56)

*Socio-Economic group determined by that of the migrants' family head
 Definitions of SEGs explained in text
 Figures in brackets denote proportions of total gains (or losses)

profile than their MELAs' losses. The out migration of the skilled manual population is still more concentrated and losses among the professional groups are relatively low. Million City cores then are able to retain their white collar workers
(in terms of all out migrants) more readily than Major Industrial, Southern Freestanding and especially Peripheral Freestanding and Secondary Industrial categorie
These last two groups also have small net inflows of the unskilled and in the case
of the Peripheral Freestanding group additionally net increases of the semi-skille

Again the London Periphery, New Town and Resort cores come out most favourably in
terms of net migration exchanges. However, only the resorts record inflows in all
groups, the New Towns incur deficits in managers and London Periphery cores show
surpluses in only the Intermediate Non-manual, Unskilled and the Inadequately described sectors. As with the whole MELAs, the New Towns' cores reported their dominant inflow to be among the skilled groups (48% of all in-migrants). This peakir
is less evident at the Resorts. The outflows of managerial and professional migrants from the London Periphery group were particularly interesting in the light c
their MELA's large proportional influx. This is, however, partially compensated f
by important inflows among this group at their rings (Table 3.28). The New Town
rings also indicated a large proportional influx of Managerial and Professional
families, but due to their small size this subsequently makes little impact upon
the structure of their whole MELA group inflows. Previously it was suggested that

TABLE 3.28   Net Migration by Socio-Economic Group*, Labour
Area Functional Type and Urban Zone, 1966-71. Rings

MELA group	\multicolumn{7}{c}{Socio-Economic Group}
	A	B	C	D	E	F	G
Million Cities	25360 (10.90)	8910 (3.83)	37890 (16.28)	114890 (49.37)	31130 (13.38)	10780 (4.63)	3750 (1.61)
Major Industrial	28880 (15.49)	19190 (10.29)	45300 (24.29)	64210 (34.43)	15620 (8.38)	1920 (1.03)	11360 (6.09)
Secondary Industrial	15130 (19.21)	8320 (10.56)	17160 (21.79)	28640 (36.36)	5600 (7.11)	930 (1.18)	2980 (3.78)
Lancs/Yorks	6040 (10.46)	3010 (5.21)	12010 (20.80)	25606 (44.34)	7880 (13.65)	2940 (5.09)	260 (0.45)
London Peripheral	27700 (24.75)	16570 (14.81)	33520 (29.96)	19820 (17.71)	6490 (5.80)	1040 (0.93)	6760 (6.04)
New Towns	5820 (42.33)	2850 (20.73)	2750 (20.00)	2020 (14.69)	-260 +	130 (0.94)	180 (1.31)
Resorts	16280 (21.31)	8230 (10.77)	20210 (26.45)	20510 (26.84)	6290 (8.23)	1260 (1.65)	3620 (4.74)
Southern Freestanding	14260 (22.22)	5870 (9.14)	15840 (24.68)	14520 (22.62)	5160 (8.04)	1130 (1.76)	7410 (11.54)
Peripheral Freestanding	15730 (20.77)	7520 (9.93)	15800 (20.86)	24430 (32.26)	6080 (8.03)	1620 (2.14)	4550 (6.01)

*   Socio-economic group determined by that of the migrants' family head
    SEGs definitions explained in text
    Figures in brackets denote proportions of total gains (or losses)

inflows to the cores of London Peripheral and, more particularly, the New Town
groups stemmed disproportionately from London's core while those moving to their
rings came predominantly from the capital's inner commuting belt. Clearly, the
socio-economic structure of the relevant areas are crucial in determining suitable
destinations for out migrants, whilst the structure of the origins is likely to
determine who is more likely to leave.

Comparison of Tables 3.28 and 3.29 reveal that five labour market types: Million
Cities, Major Industrial, London Peripheral, Resorts and the Peripheral Freestanding have higher proportions of their in-migrants within the managerial group in
their OMR compared with rings. (In absolute terms the volume only approaches that
for the rings at the Resorts). Of these groups, only Million Cities and Peripheral
Freestanding systems report this relationship for the Professional families possibly suggesting that this group is not decentralising so markedly to the OMR. This
would also indirectly support notions concerning age structure, since professional
workers tend to be relatively younger than managerial groups. The proportion of
OMR managerial in-migrants is most pronounced in the Major Industrial cities.
This ties in with the notions that most affluent groups are always the pioneers of
decentralisation into new areas. In this light, the dominance of the skilled in-
migrants among the inflows to the Million City rings further indicates that a much
later stage in decentralisation has been attained by these areas.

TABLE 3.29   Net Migration by Socio-Economic Group*, Labour
Area Functional Type and Urban Zone, 1966-71. OMR.

Socio-Economic Group

MELA Group	A	B	C	D	E	F	G
Million Cities	10730 (15.36)	6540 (9.36)	15630 (22.38)	22680 (32.47)	8180 (11.71)	1490 (2.13)	4600 (6.58)
Major Industrial	10620 (45.36)	520 (2.22)	2550 (10.89)	5380 (22.98)	2040 (8.71)	1080 (4.61)	1220 (5.21)
Secondary Industrial	4230 (12.36)	2390 (6.99)	4850 (14.18)	15570 (45.51)	4860 (14.21)	2310 (6.75)	-610 +
Lancs/Yorks	-230 (-11.06)	-360 (-17.31)	-660 (-31.73)	1320 +	-420 (-20.19)	730 +	-410 (-19.71)
London Peripheral	3050 (19.43)	1420 (9.04)	4760 (30.32)	4400 (28.02)	1600 (10.19)	470 (2.99)	-190 +
New Towns	240 +	110 +	580 +	50 +	-100 +	-30 +	-30 +
Resorts	15240 (26.76)	4640 (8.15)	13490 (23.69)	14420 (25.32)	6470 (11.36)	1490 (2.62)	1200 (2.11)
Southern Freestanding	8660 (17.47)	4620 (9.32)	10100 (20.37)	14070 (28.38)	3710 (7.48)	690 (1.39)	7730 (15.59)
Peripheral Freestanding	11480 (32.43)	3980 (11.24)	340 (0.96)	13150 (37.15)	3910 (11.04)	-62 +	2540 (7.18)

* Socio-economic group determined by that of the migrants' family head.
  Definitions of SEGs explained in text
  Figures in brackets denote proportions of total gains (or losses)

Concentrate lastly on the poor performance of the outer rings in the Lancashire-
Yorkshire group (especially among white collar workers), in comparison with the
relatively rapid growth at their rings (particularly among the skilled). Again the
very small size of the New Towns' OMRs prohibit valid comparisons with this group's
metropolitan ring.

3.3.3 Immigration

Lastly this section deals with the distribution of immigrants within urban Britain.
As mentioned earlier no data exist on the origins of emigrants from Britain and thus
it is impossible to derive a complete net population balance for MELAs. Even relevant national data are difficult to find. However, some indication of origins and
destinations may be derived from the results of the International Passenger Survey.
Details here are derived principally from Davis and Walker (1975) and Walker (1977).
These papers published results for the whole of the United Kingdom and are worth
outlining in detail to set the data for immigration by previous residence in a
better context.

Table 3.30 indicates the pattern of net international migration for Britain using
Registrar General's returns. Since 1962, each year (with the exception of 1972-73)
has resulted in a decline of population totalling over 500,000 up to 1976. The
levels of this net decline have varied from -20,000 (1975-76) to -66,000 (1973-74).
The small net inflow during 1972-73 was just above 8,000. This year also recorded
net deficits if the loss from N. Ireland is included. Davis and Walker's analysis
of country of birth data suggests considerable return and repeat migration. Table
3.31 shows that by country of birth, 34% of immigrants had actually been born in
Britain, whilst 33% of emigrants had been born in the rest of the world.

TABLE 3.30   Net Migration Between Great Britain and the Rest
of the World. Registrar General's Annual Midyear Estimates (000s)

1961-2	118	1966-7	- 82	1971-2	- 32.4
1962-3	- 24	1967-8	- 33	1972-3	8.2
1963-4	- 24	1968-9	- 49	1973-4	- 66.5
1964-5	- 24	1969-70	- 54	1974-5	- 63.2
1965-6	- 50	1970-71	- 32	1975-6	- 19.8

Table 3.32 indicates the origins and destinations of migrants. Approximately 60%
of both inflows and outflows are exchanges with Commonwealth countries. Within
this broad group there is a difference in emphasis. The most important destination was Australia (29% of the total). Among the Commonwealth countries, inflows
were very much more balanced, however, 23% of all immigrants stemmed from European
nations. In terms of interactions with Commonwealth countries alone, 73% of emigrants were to the Old Commonwealth (Australia, Canada and New Zealand) and 27% to
the New Commonwealth. The proportions for immigrants are respectively 42 and 58%.
Although immigration from Old Commonwealth countries is thus relatively large, a
considerable number were UK citizens (as much as 68% of immigrants from Australia).
Of course not all British citizen immigrants were return immigrants, some having
been born abroad.

Like migration within Great Britain, there is considerable differentiation between
the age structure of inflows and outflows. Table 3.33 reveals that immigrants are
generally younger since they have greater emphasis upon the 15-24 age group, whilst
a much larger proportion of emigrants are aged between 25 and 44. Even so, about
half the population leaving the UK was under 25. Only 10% of inflows and outflows
were of persons over 45. In addition, there is considerable evidence to suggest

TABLE 3.31   Country of Birth of Immigrants and Emigrants to
              United Kingdom for Period 1971-73

	Immigrants (%)	Emigrants (%)
United Kingdom	34	67
Old Commonwealth	10	6
New Commonwealth	27	10
Other	29	17
Total	617000	719000

Source: Davis, N. and Walker, C. (1975) Migrants entering
         and leaving the UK 1964-74 Population Trends 1, HMSO.

TABLE 3.32   Where Immigrants Came From and Went To 1964-1973

	Immigrants (%)	Emigrants (%)
Australia	13	29
Canada	5	13
New Zealand	3	5
African Commonwealth	11	6
Indian Subcontinent	14	3
West Indies	5	3
Other Commonwealth	6	3
South Africa	3	6
U.S.A.	10	10
Europe	23	17
Other Foreign	7	5

(Citizenship is defined as the nationality of passport which
 the traveller is carrying)

Source: Davis, N. and Walker, C. (1975) Migrants entering
         and leaving the UK 1964-74 Population Trends 1, HMSO.

TABLE 3.33   Age of Migrants Moving Into and Out of Great
              Britain, 1974 and 1975

	Immigrants (%)		Emigrants (%)	
	1974	1975	1974	1975
0-14	19	16	21	22
15-24	34	36	24	25
25-44	37	39	45	44
45 and over	10	9	10	9
Total	184	197	269	238

(Figures in thousands)

Source: Walker, C. (1977) Demographic Characteristics of
         Migrants, 1964-75 Population Trends 8, HMSO.

that among immigrants men were more concentrated in the 25-44 year range compared
with women who figured more strongly among the 15-24 year olds. Differential migration in fact lead to a net inflow for both sexes in this age cohort.

Economically active migrants are only divided into 'professional and managerial'
and 'manual and clerical', because of the small size of the sample concerned.
Occupations refer to those before moving. The 'professional and managerial' group
accounts for about 35% of economically active emigrants and over 40% of immigrants,
illustrating this group's high mobility levels. In the estimated net loss of
45,000 workers per annum between 1964 and 1975, only 9,000 were in professional and
managerial occupations.

Immigration by urban zone

In total, just over one million migrants are recorded by the Census as having lived
outside Britain five years earlier (Table 3.34). Of these, 57% moved into urban
cores (2.3% of the 1971 total core population) and 26% moved to metropolitan rings
(1.6% of the ring population). The balance is comprised of 143,000 immigrants to
the OMR and 35,000 to the unclassified areas. Cores are therefore the only zone
to incur disproportionate immigration relative to their share of total 1971 population. Using location quotients a relative concentration (1.19) is obtained for
cores, whilst the other zones have lower than expected immigration levels (0.84 for
both rings and OMRs and 0.74 for unclassified areas).

TABLE 3.34   Immigrants by Urban Zone

	Total no. of immigrants	Immigrant prop- ortion of total immigrants (a)	Immigrant prop- ortion of total population	(a)/Prop- ortion of population
Cores	588680	56.81	2.28	1.19
Rings	269630	26.01	1.61	0.84
OMR	142990	13.80	1.61	0.84
MELA	1001330	96.63	2.01	1.01
UNC	34970	3.37	1.42	0.74
Total	1036270	-	2.01	-

How are immigrants distributed between MELA groups?   Table 3.35 indicates that
inflows to the seven Million City labour markets represented almost half of the
total. Clearly there is the expected relationship between total population size
and absolute strength of immigration. Thus the use of location quotients reveals
that disproportionate inflows accrued to the Southern Freestanding, London Periphery and Million City labour markets. The other groups received lower than expected levels of immigration. This distribution, as expected, is dominated by the
inflows to cores. Table 3.36 shows that 60% of immigration to urban cores accrued
to Million Cities, providing this group with a high location quotient (1.28).
Nevertheless, immigration in the period represented less than 3% of the total population. The London Periphery and Southern Freestanding groups are again the
groups that had cores with location quotients exceeding 1.0.

A different pattern is revealed for rings and outer rings (Tables 3.37 and 3.38).
Million Cities had marginally lower proportions of the nation's immigrants relative
to expected population distribution. Indeed at the OMR the Million Cities absolute inflows were outstripped by the Southern and Peripheral Freestanding groups.
Clearly it was the rings and outer rings in the southern and peripheral areas of
the country which incurred disproportionate immigration. The Southern Freestanding

TABLE 3.35   MELAs: Immigrants by Functional Typology

	Total no. of imm-igrants	Immigrant proportion of total immigrants (a)	Immigrant proportion of total population	(a)/Prop-ortion of population
Million Cities	488610	48.79	2.34	1.21
Major Industrial	122080	12.19	1.41	0.72
Secondary Industrial	73940	7.38	1.20	0.62
Lancs/Yorks	22650	2.26	1.17	0.60
London Peripheral	70780	7.07	2.62	1.35
New Towns	10990	1.10	1.60	0.83
Resorts	55920	5.58	1.08	0.86
Southern Freestanding	82670	8.26	3.01	1.55
Peripheral Freestanding	73660	7.36	1.65	0.85

TABLE 3.36   Cores: Immigrants by Functional Typology

	Total no. of imm-igrants	Immigrant proportion of total immigrants (a)	Immigrant proportion of total population	(a)/Prop-ortion of population
Million Cities	350570	59.55	2.91	1.28
Major Industrial	73980	12.57	1.59	0.70
Secondary Industrial	37690	6.40	1.41	0.62
Lancs/Yorks	15000	2.55	1.63	0.72
London Peripheral	32890	5.59	2.74	1.20
New Towns	7550	1.28	1.48	0.65
Resorts	26380	4.48	1.82	0.80
Southern Freestanding	22060	3.75	2.54	1.12
Peripheral Freestanding	22560	3.83	1.46	0.66

systems especially drew high levels of immigrants, though London Periphery, New Town, Resort and Peripheral Freestanding areas also revealed higher than expected concentration of immigrants.

Remember that without details of emigration it is impossible to assess the contribution of international movements to population change. Nevertheless, there appeared to be a dichotomy in performance between urban cores and the rest of the system. Urban cores, particularly Million Cities, drew in disproportionately large numbers of immigrants, whilst the moves to rings and outer rings favoured the broad population growth areas; those adjacent to the capital and peripheral groups. Could a similar dichotomy be detected for the characteristics of movers using the distinction between Million Cities and the rest of Britain?

TABLE 3.37   Rings: Immigrants by Functional Typology

	Total no. of imm-igrants	Immigrant proportion of total immigrants (a)	Immigrant porportion of total population	(a)/Prop-ortion of population
Million Cities	112500	41.72	1.57	0.98
Major Industrial	36100	13.34	1.28	0.80
Secondary Industrial	18710	6.94	1.10	0.69
Lancs/Yorks	6630	2.46	0.78	0.49
London Peripheral	34690	12.87	2.60	1.62
New Towns	3230	1.20	1.90	1.19
Resorts	12130	4.45	1.49	0.92
Southern Freestanding	25100	9.31	3.17	1.98
Peripheral Freestanding	20540	7.62	1.73	1.08

TABLE 3.38   OMR: Immigrants by Functional Typology

	Total no. of imm-igrants	Immigrant proportion of total immigrants (a)	Immigrant proportion of total population	(a)/Prop-ortion of population
Million Cities	25540	17.86	1.53	0.95
Major Industrial	12000	8.39	0.98	0.61
Secondary Industrial	17540	13.98	1.00	0.70
Lancs/Yorks	1020	0.81	0.59	0.41
London Peripheral	3200	2.55	1.88	1.33
New Towns	210	0.17	2.54	1.89
Resorts	17410	13.91	1.63	1.15
Southern Freestanding	35510	28.35	3.27	2.32
Peripheral Freestanding	30560	24.40	1.78	1.26

Again, it is possible to view the migrants in terms of their age and their family socio-economic group. Table 3.39 reveals that at cores much greater proportions of immigrants belonged to the 15-29 year age group (48.6%) compared with the 36% at the rings and outer rings and 31% at the unclassified areas. In fact, slightly more than 60% of all those between 15 and 29 moved to urban cores (due in part to movements of students). Although still dominated by the younger age groups, the outer areas attracted higher proportions among the older age groups. It must re-main conjecture whether the core areas were, in fact, revealing net gains in the young economically active cohort. However, since net surpluses of migrants were derived by the nation, it would seem likely that this is the case. It would also seem possible that the older migrants consisted mainly of those returning from

TABLE 3.39   Immigrants: Age Groups by Urban Zone

		5-14	15-29	30-44	45-pen	pen
GB	abs	218760	447800	252000	90240	27470
national	percent	21.11	43.21	24.32	8.71	2.65
age	percent	(100.0)	(100.0)	(100.0)	(100.0)	(100.0)
CORE	abs	112130	228600	129530	46410	14610
national	percent	19.05	48.58	22.00	. 7.88	2.48
age	percent	(56.26)	(63.87)	(51.40)	(51.43)	(53.18)
RING	abs	62160	99240	74550	26810	6870
national	percent	23.05	36.80)	27.65)	9.94)	2.55
age	percent	(28.41)	(22.16)	(29.58)	(29.71)	(25.01)
OMR	abs	35830	51560	38220	12910	4470
national	percent	25.06	36.06	26.73	9.03	3.13
age	percent	(16.38)	(11.51)	(15.16)	(14.31)	(16.27)
UNC	abs	8640	11000	9700	4110	1520
national	percent	24.71	31.46	27.74	11.75	4.35
age	percent	(3.95)	(2.46)	(3.85)	(4.55)	(5.53)

(Figures in brackets denote proportion of total immigrants by age
group. Other proportions refer to immigrant totals by zone.)

abroad.

The disaggregation of migrants into age cohorts comparing trends in Million Cities
and the rest of the nation would seem to support these notions. Table 3.40 shows
that the young economically active were drawn disproportionately to Million City
cores and rings. More than half of in-migrants to the Million Cities' cores were
within the young economically active group compared with 43% to cores in the rest
of Britain. The respective figures for rings were 40.6 and 34.0%. Each of the
other age groups for the rest of Britain's core immigrants attained a greater share
of the total compared with Million Cities. However, at their rings Million Cities
retained greater proportions of total immigrants within the two elder groups. The
two categories' outer rings indicated virtually identical distributions in terms
of age profiles.

As before immigrants may also be subdivided in terms of the socio-economic status
of the family head. The zonal distributions are provided by Table 3.41. The cores
were dominated by the intermediate non-manual group (25%) which is comprised mainly
of the younger cohorts and the skilled and semi-skilled. The picture for the rings
and outer rings was dominated by the immigration of the armed forces and inadequately described group. This principally reflected, of course, the return of troops
that had been serving abroad. However, in spite of this distorting influence, it
is still possible to see differential migration into rings by the white collar
socio-economic groups, principally the managers and professional groups.

TABLE 3.40   Immigrants: Age Groups by Urban Zone in
Million Cities

		5-14	15-29	30-44	45-pen	Pen
CORES						
Million Cities	abs	59120	184520	73160	26020	7750
	percent	(16.86)	(52.63)	(20.87)	(7.42)	(2.21)
Rest of Britain	abs	53010	101480	56370	20390	6860
	percent	(22.26)	(42.62)	(23.67)	(8.56)	(2.88)
RINGS						
Million Cities	abs	22900	45700	29620	11310	2970
	percent	(20.36)	(40.62)	(26.33)	(1C.05)	(2.64)
Rest of Britain	abs	39260	53400	44930	15500	3900
	percent	(25.01)	(34.01)	(28.62)	(9.87)	(2.48)
OMR						
Million Cities	abs	6230	8960	7050	2540	760
	percent	(24.39)	(35.08)	(27.60)	(9.94)	(2.98)
Rest of Britain	abs	29600	42600	31170	10370	3710
	percent	(25.20)	(36.27)	(26.53)	(8.83)	(3.16)

TABLE 3.41   Immigrants: Socio-Economic Groups by Urban Zone

SEG	A	B	C	D	E	F	G
Cores	40140	40110	114060	89720	89390	33910	53140
percent	(8.72)	(8.71)	(24.77)	(19.48)	(19.41)	(7.36)	(11.54)
Rings	35740	30280	56120	33910	24180	5690	68840
percent	(14.03)	(11.88)	(22.03)	(13.31)	(9.49)	(2.23)	(27.04)
OMRs	11130	7910	19090	19570	12330	3160	63470
percent	(8.14)	(5.79)	(13.97)	(14.32)	(9.02)	(2.31)	(46.44)
MELAs	87010	7830	189270	143200	125900	42760	185450
percent	(10.21)	(9.19)	(22.22)	(16.81)	(14.78)	(5.02)	(21.77)

(Socio-economic aggregates explained in text)

The OMR attached relatively larger proportions among the manual groups, although in absolute terms only the inflow of the unskilled attained even half the number moving into metropolitan rings. With the exception of the managers and troops and inadequately described categories, the inflow of each group to urban cores contributed more than 50% of the total's moving in within each socio-economic group.

Finally, Table 3.42 illustrates the differences in the profile of immigrants to Million City areas and the rest of Britain. Once again, the most important variation was due to the substantial number of troops being drawn to areas outside Million City cores. Nevertheless, it would appear that white collar workers were more likely to move to the seven major areas compared with cores in the rest of Britain. The intermediate non-manual group in particular was drawn to Million Cities

TABLE 3.42   Immigrants: Socio-Economic Groups by Urban Zone
in Million Cities

SEG	A	B	C	D	E	F	G
CORES							
Million Cities abs	24990	21290	75000	46350	54520	20670	19800
percent	(9.52)	(8.11)	(28.56)	(17.65)	(20.76)	(7.87)	(7.54)
Rest of Britain abs	15150	18820	39060	43370	34870	13240	33400
percent	(7.66)	(9.51)	(19.74)	(21.92)	(17.62)	(6.69)	(16.88)
RINGS							
Million Cities abs	18020	13970	27330	14260	11750	2930	13440
percent	(17.72)	(13.74)	(26.87)	(14.02)	(11.55)	(2.88)	(13.22)
Rest of Britain abs	17720	16310	28790	19650	12430	2760	55400
percent	(11.56)	(10.66)	(18.81)	(12.84)	(8.10)	(1.80)	(36.19)
OMR							
Million Cities abs	3250	2340	4220	3940	2860	610	6960
percent	(13.44)	(9.68)	(17.45)	(16.29)	(11.83)	(2.52)	(28.78)
Rest of Britain abs	7880	5570	14870	15630	9470	2550	56510
percent	(7.01)	(4.95)	(13.22)	(13.90)	(8.42)	(2.27)	(50.24)

(SEGs explained in text).

illustrating attraction of younger workers to the capital. Broadly equal numbers
of movers were attracted to rings in Million Cities and the Rest of Great Britain.
Thus when ignoring influences of the troops and inadequately described profiles
were virtually identical. Like their cores, the Million City OMRs appeared to
attract much greater proportions of immigrants in the white collar groups, even
allowing for differential troop movements. The absolute inflows were, however,
smaller reflecting the population size of this area.

Thus immigrants to cores tended to be younger and more likely to be among the intermediate non-manual and manual groups. They were principally drawn to Million Cities,
but here the proportions among white collar groups appeared to be higher. Their age
and socio-economic structure suggested that immigrants to rings and outer rings tended to be older and also dominated by those within the troops and inadequately described aggregate, both suggesting the relative importance of return migrants.

That the proportion of foreign born persons is greater in terms of core immigration
is suggested by earlier discussion. The absolute changes for the British born revealed decreases in the cores and increases in the rings and outer rings. The same
pattern was observed for the Irish born. For all the New Commonwealth immigrants,
however, there were increases in all zones and the largest, in fact, were in the
cores. This increase of New Commonwealth immigrants in British urban cores was
sufficient to offset the large reduction in the British born from -1,335,000 to
produce a net population loss of -719,000 in this zone between 1961 and 1971. Not
all New Commonwealth groups, however, behaved alike. In percentage terms it was
only for the Indian Sub Continent and the Africa born groups that the largest increases were in the cores. For the West Indians the largest increase was in the
rings.

PART FOUR

Worktravel and British Cities

4.1 URBAN CHANGE AND WORKTRAVEL

The daily journey to work is an integral part of the lives of more than twenty million Britons. Vast amounts of time and money are consumed in overcoming the distance separating places of residence from places of work. This role, in linking together the two main spheres of human activity (home-based and work-based), has meant that many important social and economic changes of recent years have been reflected in journeys to work. The development of suburban housing and of increasing car ownership has had important effects upon work-travel patterns and characteristics. The growing tendency for manufacturing industry to seek locations in suburban areas and in towns and cities other than the major conurbations has had equally important ramifications.

But this massive intra-labour market decentralization of population and employment does not occur at the same time. The implications are clear: since employment has decentralized less than population, the cores, which still contain the main mass of employment, have become more dependent upon the supply of labour commuting from the outer zones. The immediate inference is an increase in the separation of homes and workplaces in urban Britain, with a consequent increase in the length of the journey to work. However this changing pattern of trip origins and destinations does not only increase journey lengths, it will inevitably produce a more complex pattern of crossing journeys, particularly in suburban areas, as work trips become less city-centre oriented. This shift from radial to non-radial journeys has important implications for both urban and suburban transport services, particularly in suburban areas where public transport routes and frequencies may not meet the changing pattern of demand.

An analysis of journey to work changes will thus help to make explicit the inter-relationships, and possible conflicts, between trends such as those outlined above. Such an understanding is vital in a policy context, for in an era when public expenditure is being closely scrutinized, the efficient use of scarce resources is given renewed emphasis.

This part of the study will examine journey to work changes between 1966 and 1971 and the first task is to review shifts in the zonal locations of employed population and employment between these dates, relating them to changes within the 1961-1971 period as a whole. Employed population refers to the employed workforce by place of residence, while employment refers to the workforce by place of work.

In journey to work terms, these correspond to journey origins and destinations respectively. It should be stressed that the resident employed population is not the same as the resident economically active population, for the latter includes the unemployed. Lastly the 1971 figures for employment used in this section do not correspond exactly to those presented in Part 2 because the worktravel tables use slightly differing definitions to the economic activity tables especially involving workplace or residence abroad.

The total number of employed persons in Great Britain declined by more than 400 thousand between 1966 and 1971, due to a substantial increase in the number of un-employed exceeding a much smaller increase in the size of the economically active population. In the 1966 Census, 0.7 million persons were recorded as being 'out of employment'. By 1971 this had almost doubled to 1.3 million and thus a marked rise in the rate of unemployment (from 2.8% to 5.2%) was recorded. In the preced-ing five year period, however, the number out of employment had increased only marginally and subsequently the rate of unemployment remained unchanged. The changes in the economy which these trends reflect have important locational implic-ations, particularly in the way they affect changes in the zonal distribution of employment.

There are substantial differences between the 1961-66 and 1966-71 periods with respect to changes in the locations of homes and workplaces within labour market areas (Table 4.1). In the earlier period, the urban cores recorded little net change in either employed population or employment (-0.6% and 1.0% respectively), for the nation's economic dynamism was channelled predominantly into the rings, which experienced 10% growth rates in both employed population and employment. (In 1961, only 20% of national employment was located in the rings, but these areas nevertheless captured 64% of the nation's job growth over the following five years.) In the 1966-71 period, the worsening economic background was reflected in substan-tial absolute declines in core employed population and employment, while the rate of ring growth in both elements was much reduced. In general terms, then, the two halves of the 1961-71 decade were characterised by a shift from relative to absol-ute decentralisation.

Of greater importance for journey to work patterns, however, is that in the second five-year period the shifts in employed population and employment between zones began to display a marked divergence. Whereas in the 1961-66 period both compon-ents had remained static in cores and had grown at the same rate in rings, between 1966 and 1971 employed population declined in cores at a faster rate than jobs (-7.0% and -4.1% respectively), and grew at a faster rate in rings (5.4% and 3.8% respectively). In absolute terms this resulted in an increasing net surplus of jobs in core areas, and an increasing net deficit in rings.

This trend towards a growing interdependency between urban cores and their surr-ounding commuting rings is further demonstrated by calculating the net commuting ratios of each zone type (Table 4.2). The net commuting ratio is simply the number of employed residents in a zone divided by the number of jobs. A ratio of less than 1.0 means an excess of jobs over employed residents resulting in net in-commuting to the zone, and a ratio greater than 1.0 indicates a deficiency of jobs and hence net out-commuting from the zone. If a ratio is moving further away from 1.0 the zone is becoming more imbalanced in net commuting terms. Between 1961 and 1966 the ratio for core areas decreased from 0.876 to 0.862, due to a small increase in employment and a smaller decline in employed residents. The ratio for ring areas remained virtually unchanged over the same period (1.349 in 1961; 1.347 in 1966), as both the number of jobs and of employed residents grew at the same rate. In the second half of the decade, however, the disparity between the shifts in these two components were reflected in more imbalanced ratios. The core ratio dropped from 0.862 to 0.836, and the ring ratio rose from 1.347 to 1.368.

TABLE 4.1   Resident Employed Population and Employment by
Urban Zone in Britain.

(a)

	1961		1966		1971	
	Employed Population	Employment	Employed Population	Employment	Employed Population	Employment
Core	12,558	14,337	12,488	14,482	11,619	13,891
Ring	6,364	4,719	7,044	5,231	7,424	5,428
SMLA	18,922	19,055	19,532	19,713	19,043	19,319
Outer Ring	3,445	3,313	3,653	3,488	3,701	3,449
MELA	22,367	22,368	23,185	23,200	22,744	22,768

(b)

	1961-66		1966-71		1961-71	
	Employed Population	Employment	Employed Population	Employment	Employed Population	Employment
Core	-70 (-0.6%)	145 (1.0%)	-869 (-7.0%)	-591 (-4.1%)	-939 (-7.5%)	-446 (-3.1%)
Ring	680 (10.7%)	512 (10.8%)	380 (5.4%)	197 (3.8%)	1060 (16.7%)	709 (15.0%)
SMLA	610 (3.2%)	658 (3.5%)	-489 (-2.5%)	-394 (-2.0%)	121 (0.6%)	264 (1.4%)
Outer Ring	208 (6.0%)	175 (5.3%)	48 (1.3%)	-39 (-1.1%)	256 (7.4%)	136 (4.1%)
MELA	818 (3.7%)	832 (3.7%)	-441 (-1.9%)	-432 (-1.9%)	377 (1.7%)	400 (1.8%)

(a) Absolute totals, 1961, 1966, 1971 (thousands)
(b) Absolute changes (thousands) and rates of change
     1961-66, 1966-71, 1961-71

Even in the more 'self-contained' outer rings a similar trend was apparent, with
the ratio remaining almost constant between 1961 and 1966, but then increasing from
1.047 to 1.073 in 1971.

So the second half of the decade was characterised by a development of trends which
were only barely distinguishable earlier. The economic downturn appears to have
accentuated the variations between residential and workplace shifts, in that a considerable brake was put upon the growth of employment in ring areas, while the outward movement of population was less strongly curtailed. The implications for
journey to work manifest themselves by a growing functional interdependency between
the urban core areas and their surrounding commuting rings.

Before considering in detail the worktravel implications of these changing zonal
locations of homes and jobs, brief attention should be given to changes in the

TABLE 4.2   Net Commuting Ratios by Urban Zones in Britain,
1961-1966-1971

	1961	1966	1971	1961-66	1966-71	1961-71
Core	0.876	0.862	0.836	−0.014	−0.026	−0.040
Ring	1.349	1.347	1.368	−0.002	0.021	0.019
SMLA	0.995	0.991	0.986	−0.004	−0.005	−0.009
Outer Ring	1.040	1.047	1.073	0.007	0.026	0.033
MELA	1.002	0.999	0.999	−0.003	0.000	−0.003

proportion of journeys made within and between a hierarchy of areal units which form the building blocks of this analysis - namely the local authority, the constituent zone, and the whole labour market area.

The data sets upon which all subsequent analysis is based are the 1966 and 1971 Census journey to work files. These define the worktrips from each local authority to all other local authorities, and were obtained on a 10% sample (the published tables specify only those destinations receiving 5 or more persons from a particular origin authority, but no such cut-off exists in the files analysed here). Each transaction within or between local authorities can be disaggregated by nine modes of transport, eight socio-economic groups, three categories of household car ownership, and a male/female subdivision.

In order to make the areal bases of the 1966 and 1971 data sets compatible, it was necessary to take into account local authority boundary changes which involved transfers between urban zones or labour market areas. The project had previously used a simple pro-rata transfer method, and this was extended to enable the much more complex problem of origin-destination interaction data to be treated in a consistent manner.

Although with employment decline the total number of worktrips fell 1.8% between 1966 and 1971, certain categories of work trip recorded substantial absolute increases. There is a remarkably consistent trend in the changes; at all three spatial scales of analysis, journeys between areas grew at the expense of intra-area journeys, suggesting an increase in average journey lengths.

Journeys between local authorities (the smallest areal units under consideration) increased in total by 0.38 million (4.3%), whereas journeys contained within these areas declined by 0.8 million. Consequently, inter-authority movements increased their share of total work travel from 36.0% to 38.2% (Table 4.3 and Fig. 4.1).

The trend towards the growth of inter-area movement at the expense of intra-area movement becomes more prominent in relative terms at successive levels in the spatial hierarchy. Thus journeys between urban zones, for example, grew in total by 0.5 million (9.5%) during a period in which journeys within zones declined by 0.9 million. As a result this increased their share of total work travel from 22.4% in 1966 to 25.0% in 1971. Finally, at the aggregate labour market area level, journeys between MELA's grew by 0.3 million (19.2%), while journeys within MELA's declined by 0.8 million. Inter-MELA worktravel thus increased its share of the total by 1.4% from a small 1966 base of 6.6%. Despite the substantial decline in the number of intra-MELA work journeys, trips between zones within labour markets recorded a growth of 0.2 million; the overall decline is thus due solely to the within-zone component, which decreased by 0.9 million.

TABLE 4.3 Absolute and Relative Changes in Worktravel Within and Between Local Authorities, Urban Zones and Metropolitan Labour Areas in Britain, 1966-71 (thousands).

	Absolute			Percentage					
	1966	1971	Change	1966 (Percentage of total)	1971	Change	1966 (Percentage of subtotal)	1971	Change
Total	24,143	23,711	-432	100	100	-			
Within Local Authorities	15,453	14,645	-808	64.0	61.7	-2.2			
Between Local Authorities	8,691	9,066	375	36.0	38.2	2.2			
Intra-MELA	21,527	20,751	-776	89.1	87.6	-1.5			
Inter-MELA	1,604	1,912	308	6.6	8.0	1.4			
To and/or from Unclassified	1,012	1,028	16	4.1	4.3	0.1			
Intra-zonal	18,740	17,794	-946	77.6	75.0	-2.5			
Inter-zonal	5,403	5,917	514	22.3	24.9	2.5	100	100	-
i) intra MELA	3,675	3,857	182	15.2	16.2	1.0	68.0	65.2	-2.8
ii) inter MELA	1,604	1,912	308	6.6	8.0	1.4	29.6	32.3	2.6
iii) Unclassified	124	148	24	0.5	0.6	0.1	2.3	2.5	0.2
Intra MELA	21,527	20,771	-756	89.1	87.6	-1.5	100	100	-
i) intra zonal	17,852	16,914	-938	73.9	71.3	-2.6	82.9	81.4	-1.5
ii) inter zonal	3,675	3,857	182	15.2	16.2	1.0	17.0	18.5	1.5
Inter Local Authority	8,691	9,066	375	36.0	38.2	2.2	100	100	-
i) intra MELA	6,794	6,815	21	28.1	28.7	0.6	78.1	75.1	-3.0
intra zonal	3,119	2,957	-162	12.9	12.4	-0.4	35.8	32.6	-3.2
inter zonal	3,675	3,857	182	15.2	16.2	1.0	42.2	42.5	0.2
ii) inter MELA	1,604	1,912	308	6.6	8.0	1.4	18.4	21.0	2.6
iii) Unclassified	293	339	46	1.2	1.4	0.2	3.3	3.7	0.3

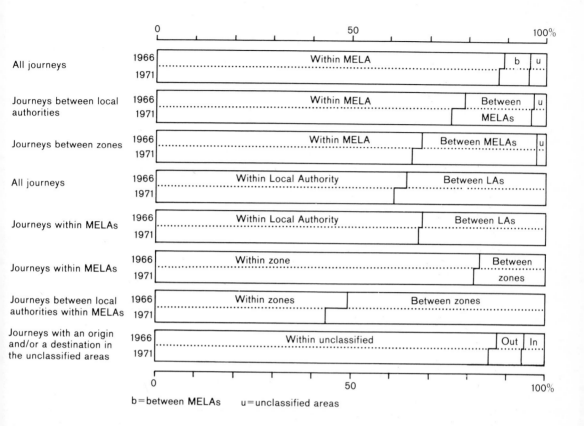

Fig. 4.1   Relative changes in worktravel within and between
           local authorities, urban zones and Metropolitan
           Economic Labour Areas in Britain, 1966-1971.

Although there is no explicit measure of journey distance in this type of analysis,
the uniformity of the trends displayed at different areal scales must lead to the
conclusion that home-workplace separation has increased in aggregate terms over
the 5-year period. Nevertheless, the strength of this trend should not be allowed
to obscure the fact that even in 1971, more than 60% of the nation's employed population both resided and worked in the same local authority area. This study will
then use changes in commuting within and between areal units as an implied surro-
gate for changes in worktravel length. It must be stressed that this can only be
justified on a generalised, aggregate level, for it is quite possible to envisage
plausible situations in which an increase in inter-area _vis a vis_ intra-area commuting results in an actual shortening of trip lengths. Nonetheless increases in
commuting between areas and the complexity of work travel pattern have important
implications for the planning of transport networks and city planning generally.
This is true regardless of the actual extent to which journey lengths are increasing.

4.2 WORKTRAVEL PATTERNS IN THE URBAN SYSTEM

4.2.1 Changes in Worktravel Patterns within British Cities

Although the share of total journeys in the nation within labour markets declined
by 1.6% between 1966 and 1971, the vast majority of work trips (87.6%) are still
of this type (Table 4.3). However, there have been significant changes in the
zonal location of intra-MELA trip origins and destinations (Table 4.4) which closely reflect the shifts in total employed population and employment described earlier
Journeys that originate within cores declined by a larger absolute amount than did
journey destinations (-0.95 million and -0.77 million respectively), and grew by a
larger amount in rings (0.22 million against 0.11 million). These changes have
accentuated the net surplus of jobs in core areas and the net deficiency in rings.
The net inflow of journeys to work to core areas increased from 1.73 million in
1966 to 1.91 million in 1971 while the net inflow from ring areas increased from
1.59 million to 1.70 million. The difference between the core and the ring figures
is made up by a much smaller net outflow from the outer rings, which also increased
between the two dates (from 0.14 to 0.20 million).

How have such changes affected the pattern of flows within and between the three
urban zone types? The analysis of such flows is often made in this study and is
based on the notion of a 3 x 3 origin and destination matrix.

The absolute and relative changes in each of the nine components of intra-MELA
travel are given in Table 4.5. These are:

(i) journeys originating within cores:

The flow type recording the largest change is the within-core component, which
declined by 0.9 million (-8.3%). As a result, the share of total intra-MELA work
travel accounted for by journeys within core areas fell from 51.6% in 1966 to 49.1%
in 1971. 'Reverse commuting' from cores to rings also declined, but at a slower
rate (-3.4%), with the consequence that the relative importance of total core
origins which were destined for rings increased from 6.4% to 6.7% (Table 4.6a).

(ii) journeys originating within rings:

The greater decentralization of employed population compared with employment in the
1966-71 period is clearly reflected in the ring to core work-trip flow. Such journeys increased by 111,000 (4.7%), and by 1971 accounted for 11.9% (2.5 million)
of total intra-MELA work travel (compared with 10.9% in 1966). Although within-
ring journeys also increased substantially by 94 thousand, this produces a lower
growth rate (2.5%) because total ring to ring trips are substantially greater than
total ring to core trips. As a consequence, the percentage of total ring origins
which are destined for cores increased from 37.2 to 37.6 (Table 4.6c). Thus in
spite of the fact that there was an increase of over 100,000 jobs within ring areas
between 1966 and 1971, this was not enough to prevent the rings from becoming more
dependent upon the job surplus of the core areas.

(iii) journeys originating within outer rings:

The total number of journeys originating in outer ring areas declined by 49,000,
but this was due to the contraction of journeys within the outer rings by 121,000
outweighing increases in commuting to core and rings. Indeed, the flows from
outer rings to cores and rings recorded higher rates of growth than any of the
other flow types (20.4% and 25.9% respectively). Consequently, journeys within
outer rings declined as a percentage of total outer ring origins from 89.3 in 1966
to 86.7 in 1971 (Table 4.6d). The outer rings are still much more 'self-contained'
than the ring areas, in which the corresponding intra-zone share of total origins
is only 60.0%. Despite the high growth rates mentioned above, it should be stresse

TABLE 4.4   Origins and Destinations by Urban Zone for
Journeys within MELAs, 1966-71

(a) Absolute totals and changes (thousands)

	Core		Ring		Outer Ring		
	Origins	Destinat-ions	Origins	Destinat-ions	Origins	Destinat-ions	Total
1966	11,938	13,664	6,333	4,743	3,256	3,120	21,527
1971	10,989	12,895	6,551	4,848	3,207	3,007	20,750
Absolute change	-949	-769	221	105	-49	-113	-777
Rate of change (percent)	-7.9	-5.6	3.5	2.2	-1.5	-3.6	-3.6

(b) Percentage shares and changes

	Core		Ring		Outer Ring	
	Origins	Destinations	Origins	Destinations	Origins	Destinations
1966	55.5	63.5	29.4	22.0	15.1	14.5
1971	53.0	62.1	31.6	23.4	15.5	14.5
Change in share	-2.5	-1.4	2.2	1.4	0.4	0

(c) Net commuting ratios

	Core $\frac{\text{Origins}}{\text{Destinations}}$	Ring $\frac{\text{Origins}}{\text{Destinations}}$	Outer Ring $\frac{\text{Origins}}{\text{Destinations}}$
1966	0.874	1.335	1.044
1971	0.852	1.352	1.066
Change	-0.022	0.017	0.022

that such journeys make only a small contribution to total work travel. Even if inter-zonal flows alone are considered, journeys originating in outer rings are insignificant compared with the two-way exchange between core and rings areas (journeys from outer rings to cores and to rings together account for 11.1% of the inter-zonal total, while the ring to core component alone accounts for 63.9%).

Two principal themes then have characterised this description of changes in intra-MELA worktravel patterns at the national aggregate scale. First, the overall pattern of worktrip origins and destinations is becoming less dominated by core areas, as witnessed by the massive decline in the within-core component. Second, there is a growing functional interdependency between urban cores and their

TABLE 4.5   Flows Within and Between Urban Zones for Journeys Within MELAs, 1966-71

(a) Absolute (thousands)

	C – C	C – R	C – OR	R – C	R – R	R – OR	OR – C	OR – R	OR – OR	Total
1966	11,105	760	73	2,354	3,840	140	206	143	2,908	21,527
1971	10,182	734	73	2,465	3,934	155	248	180	2,780	20,750
Absolute change	-923	-26	0	111	94	15	42	37	-128	-777
Rate of change (percent)	-8.3	-3.4	0	4.7	2.5	10.7	20.4	25.9	-4.4	-3.6

(b) Percentage shares

	C – C	C – R	C – OR	R – C	R – R	R – OR	OR – C	OR – R	OR – OR	Total
1966	51.6	3.5	0.3	10.9	17.8	0.6	1.0	0.7	13.5	100.0
1971	49.1	3.5	0.4	11.9	19.0	0.7	1.2	0.9	13.4	100.0
Change in share	-2.5	0	0.1	1.0	1.2	0.1	0.2	0.2	-0.1	–

TABLE 4.6   Relative Changes in the Pattern of Selected Inflows
and Outflows for Journeys within MELAs, 1966-71

(a) Core Origins

Destinations	Urban Zone \ Year	1966	1971	Change 1966-71
	Core	93.0	92.7	-0.3
	Ring	6.4	6.7	0.3
	Outer Ring	0.6	0.7	0.1
	Total	100.0	100.0	-

(b) Core Destinations

Origins	Urban Zone \ Year	1966	1971	Change 1966-71
	Core	81.3	79.0	-2.3
	Ring	17.2	19.1	1.9
	Outer Ring	1.5	1.9	0.4

(c) Ring Origins

Destinations	Urban Zone \ Year	1966	1971	Change 1966-71
	Core	37.2	37.6	0.4
	Ring	60.6	60.0	-0.6
	Outer Ring	2.2	2.4	0.2

(d) Outer Ring Origins

Destinations	Urban Zone \ Year	1966	1971	Change 1966-71
	Core	6.3	7.7	1.3
	Ring	4.4	5.6	1.2
	Outer Ring	89.3	86.7	-2.6

surrounding metropolitan rings (and, to a lesser extent, their outer rings), due to
the differential rates of population and employment decentralisation. The importance of this differential should not be underestimated, for it can explain the
paradox of a substantial increase in commuting from rings to cores while at the
same time the number of jobs within cores is contracting. The overriding impression, then, is one of increasing complexity in the pattern of journey to work movements.

Worktravel patterns by functional MELA groupings

This summary of trends at the national aggregate level disguises of course a wide
range of variations in labour market behaviour, many of which produce conflicting
influences upon the 'national average'. Many of the variations in labour market
area behaviour can be identified by examining groups of cities which have similar
characteristics in terms of relative location and/or size. The nine group classification which was devised is the same as that used in the migration analysis
and is fully detailed in part one.

The first point to establish is that the 3.6% (0.78 million) decline in the total
number of intra-MELA work journeys in the nation is not a trend experienced by all
types of labour market. Six of the nine groups have indeed declined absolutely,
but the national figure is to a large extent produced by the 'Million City' labour
markets, which contracted by 0.63 million and at a rate much faster (-6.4%) than
any of the other declining groups (Tables 4.7 and 4.8). Nevertheless, the Million
Cities still contained 44.1% of the nation's total intra-MELA work journeys in
1971, which puts into context the extent of the group's influence on national trends.
The complex interrelationships between different types of labour market is clear
since an increase in intra-MELA worktravel is revealed by the London Peripheral
and New Town systems (the major recipients of decentralization from London),

TABLE 4.7   Absolute Changes in Origins and Destination by Urban Zone for Journeys within MELAs; Labour Market Groups, 1966-71 (thousands)

	Core		Ring		Outer ring		Total	Change in share of national total
	Origins	Destinations	Origins	Destinations	Origins	Destinations		
New Towns	25.9	28.1	1.6	-0.5	0.1	0.1	27.6	0.17
Secondary Industrial	-53.6	-36.7	6.2	-0.9	-28.1	-31.9	-75.5	0.04
Resorts/Retirement centres	-13.1	3.9	8.9	0.7	-2.4	-11.3	-6.7	0.17
Peripheral Freestanding	-31.3	0.1	34.0	21.1	-24.9	-43.5	-22.2	0.20
Southern Freestanding	-7.0	4.1	27.8	22.1	2.3	-3.0	23.1	0.29
Lancashire/Yorkshire group	-30.6	-19.3	2.3	-8.9	-2.4	-2.4	-30.7	-0.02
London Peripheral	-10.8	-4.3	19.1	14.4	3.1	1.2	11.4	0.21
Major Industrial	-134.5	-111.2	55.8	38.1	0.9	-4.6	-77.6	-0.25
Million Cities	-693.0	-633.7	64.1	24.8	2.7	-17.3	-626.1	-1.32
Total	-948.3	-768.9	220.8	105.4	-48.7	-112.8	-776.3	

TABLE 4.8 Percentage Change in Origins and Destination by Urban Zone for Journeys within MELAs; Labour Market Groups, 1966-71 (*indicates a small base)

	Core		Ring		Outer ring		Total
	Origins	Destinations	Origins	Destinations	Origins	Destinations	
New Towns	16.5	17.2	3.8	-1.4	4.6*	4.1*	13.6
Secondary Industrial	-4.9	-3.0	1.0	-1.4	-4.3	-5.1	-3.2
Resorts/Retirement centres	-2.4	0.7	3.3	0.3	-0.7	-3.1	-0.6
Peripheral Freestanding	-4.7	0.0	8.1	6.6	-3.7	-6.7	-1.3
Southern Freestanding	-1.9	0.9	9.6	10.2	0.6	-0.8	2.2
Lancashire/Yorkshire group	-8.2	-4.6	0.9	-4.2	-4.4	-4.5	-4.5
London Peripheral	-2.5	-0.8	4.9	4.7	5.3	2.3	1.3
Major Industrial	-6.3	-4.7	5.2	4.7	0.2	-1.1	-2.1
Million Cities	-11.2	-8.9	2.1	1.2	0.4	-3.1	-6.4
Total	-7.9	-5.6	3.5	2.2	-1.5	-3.6	-3.6

together with the third group, the Southern Freestanding cities.

Turning to the changes affecting urban zones of the groups, a number of similaritie between the groups can be identified. Firstly, note the uniform developments among journey origins (i.e. employed residents). These declined absolutely in core areas within all groups (except the New Towns) and increased in each type's rings. No such uniformity extends to journey destinations (jobs) however, because employment decentralization was not as strongly established. Nevertheless, at the urban core the relationship between zonal population and employment shifts is, in one import- ant respect, similar for all of the MELA groups; this is that journey origins fared poorly compared with journey destinations. Three main city types may be dis- tinguished: firstly, those cities where journey origins were declining in cores at a faster rate than destinations (6 groups), secondly, where origins were declining while destinations continued to increase (2 groups), and thirdly, where origins were increasing at a slower rate than destinations (1 group). The reverse relation ship held for each group's rings and outer rings (with the exception of the Souther Freestanding rings). The result of these changes is an increase in the net surplus of jobs in core areas, and the net deficit in ring and outer ring areas. This is reflected in changes in the zonal net commuting ratios (Table 4.9). In all of the nine groups, core ratios have moved further <u>below</u> 1.0 while corresponding ring and outer ring ratios have moved further <u>above</u> 1.0 (again, the only exception being a small decline in the ring ratio of the Southern Freestanding labour markets, indic- ating that its ring areas became slightly more balanced in net commuting terms). Interestingly, this group had an unbalanced ring ratio in 1966 (only the Million Cities' was more so), and between 1966 and 1971 recorded the highest rate of ring employment growth.

Thus in labour market groups ranging in size from the Million Cities to the New Towns, and in locations ranging from the Lancashire/Yorkshire group to the south coast Resort-retirement centres, there has been a uniform trend of increasing net commuting interdependencies between cores, and rings and outer rings. The strength of the trend, however, and the stage it has reached, does vary markedly between the labour market groups. The Million cities have reached the furthest stage, in that their ring and outer ring net commuting ratios are more imbalanced than in any of the other groups. At the other extreme, the New Town group displays a considerable degree of balance in the number of journey origins and destinations within each of its zones.

This suggests the efficacy of a simple typology of labour market groups according to the nature of the zonal shifts in employed population and employment which are producing changes in their net commuting structures. It will be easier for compar- ative purposes to consider these shifts using percentage share data, rather than absolute, for it will permit effects of changes in the total number of intra-MELA journeys within each of the groups to be isolated.

Table 4.10 thus sets out changes in each zone's share of intra-MELA journey origins and destinations. Considering firstly only the direction of change regardless of magnitude, in other words growth or decline, some five basic types can be identif- ied and described as follows. These types have been ordered in a sequence ranging from centralisation to decentralisation (at both SMLA and MELA levels) which perhaps correspond to stages in the evolution of metropolitan areas. Shifts in employed population and employment are related to changes in the patterns of worktravel within the groups at each stage in the sequence.

<u>Type 1 - The New Towns</u>. In this group, the core areas are increasing their share of total origins (employed residents) and destinations (jobs) at the expense of both rings and outer rings. Such towns are clearly at an early stage of develop- ment, for their commuting rings are small in relation to their cores and have not yet begun to share in the towns' rapid growth.

TABLE 4.9   Net Commuting Ratios by Urban Zone for Journeys
Within MELAs; Labour Market Groups, 1966-71

		Core	Ring	Outer ring
New Towns	1966	0.956	1.198	0.976
	1971	0.951	1.261	0.980
Secondary Industrial	1966	0.878	1.252	1.048
	1971	0.860	1.283	1.056
Resorts/Retirement centres	1966	0.923	1.185	1.010
	1971	0.895	1.221	1.035
Peripheral Freestanding	1966	0.847	1.314	1.032
	1971	0.807	1.333	1.065
Southern Freestanding	1966	0.813	1.344	1.028
	1971	0.791	1.336	1.043
Lancashire/Yorkshire group	1966	0.888	1.208	1.037
	1971	0.855	1.271	1.039
London Peripheral	1966	0.840	1.252	1.085
	1971	0.826	1.255	1.116
Major Industrial	1966	0.889	1.302	1.046
	1971	0.873	1.309	1.060
Million Cities	1966	0.870	1.413	1.081
	1971	0.848	1.427	1.120
Total	1966	0.874	1.335	1.044
	1971	0.852	1.352	1.067

As expected therefore, within-core journeys dominate the overall pattern of movement (with 77.0% of the total), and increased their share of this total between
1966 and 1971 by 1.9% (Table 4.11), an absolute increase of 25,000 journeys.
Although the ring areas have not yet begun to experience relative population increases, there is nevertheless a re-orientation of work travel originating within these
areas due to the growth of employment opportunities in the cores. The commuting
hinterlands are rapidly strengthening their links with the central areas while
local travel within the rings is contracting both absolutely and relatively. The
percentage of total ring origins which are destined for the cores increased from
25.3% in 1966 to 30.6% in 1971, still well below the national level (37.6%) but
closing the gap considerably (Table 4.13).

Type 2 - The Secondary Industrial, Resorts/Retirement Centres, and Peripheral
Freestanding Groups. The next stage is heralded by population out-movement. As
the core areas reach a certain density of development, further expansion of population must inevitably begin to spillover into the surrounding areas. In addition,
as value systems change and mobility levels increase with car ownership, many people are able to exercise a greater degree of choice in their residential location
and opt to live at lower densities of development at the edges of the built-up area
or beyond it, while still retaining jobs in the central city. Thus the number of
workers living in the core may begin to decline absolutely and this is the stage
reached by the Type 2 cities.

The number of journey origins within their cores are declining both absolutely and

TABLE 4.10 Changes in the Percentage Share of Total Origins and Destinations by Urban Zone for Journeys within MELAs; Labour Market Groups, 1966-71

	Core		Ring		Outer ring	
	Origins	Destinations	Origins	Destinations	Origins	Destinations
New Towns	1.98	2.51	-1.89	-2.40	-0.09	-0.10
Secondary Industrial	-0.82	0.14	1.14	0.38	-0.32	-0.53
Resorts/Retirement centres	-0.85	0.62	0.89	0.16	-0.03	-0.79
Peripheral Freestanding	-1.31	0.58	2.26	1.44	-0.95	-2.03
Southern Freestanding	-1.40	-0.54	1.99	1.61	-0.58	-1.06
Lancashire/Yorkshire group	-2.13	-0.10	2.12	0.09	0.00	0.00
London Peripheral	-1.84	-1.23	1.57	1.17	0.27	0.06
Major Industrial	-2.51	-1.69	2.21	1.57	0.29	0.12
Million Cities	-3.25	-1.96	2.80	1.75	0.45	0.21
Total	-2.50	-1.33	2.15	1.33	0.33	0.00

TABLE 4.11 Changes in the Percentage Share of Total Flows Within and Between Urban Zones for Journeys Within MELAs; Labour Market Groups, 1966-71

	Core to			Ring to			Outer ring to		
	Core	Ring	Outer ring	Core	Ring	Outer ring	Core	Ring	Outer ring
New Towns	1.88	0.10	–	0.58	-2.50	0.03	0.05	-0.01	-0.14
Secondary Industrial	-0.90	0.04	0.03	0.68	0.31	0.15	0.35	0.03	-0.71
Resorts/Retirement centres	-0.78	0.01	-0.09	0.86	0.04	-0.01	0.53	0.12	-0.68
Peripheral Freestanding	-1.11	-0.11	-0.09	1.26	0.67	0.33	0.43	0.89	-2.99
Southern Freestanding	-1.49	0.05	0.03	0.62	1.29	0.08	0.33	0.26	-1.17
Lancashire/Yorkshire group	-1.67	-0.47	0.01	1.47	0.56	0.09	0.10	0.02	-0.10
London Peripheral	-2.09	0.24	0.01	0.67	0.89	0.02	0.19	0.05	0.03
Major Industrial	-2.31	-0.20	–	0.47	1.62	0.13	0.19	0.15	–
Million Cities	-3.40	0.13	0.02	1.29	1.47	0.04	0.16	0.16	0.13
Total	-2.52	0.01	0.01	0.93	1.12	0.10	0.24	0.21	-0.11

relatively, while in contrast the rings are experiencing growth. The cores are still increasing their shares of total destinations, though at a much reduced rate, and ring areas too record small increases in their share of this total. It is comparatively unusual for cores and rings to exhibit similar trends, but here it is the outer rings which provide the missing element in the pattern. At this unadvanced stage of intra-urban development, the outer rings have not yet begun to share with the ring areas the effects of out-movement from the cities, and are still suffering from rural population decline and the contraction of local employment bases. This feature is most apparent in the Peripheral Freestanding labour markets (which generally have large outer rings extending long distances away from the central cities), in which the outer rings' share of total destinations fell by 2.0% (Table 4.10) an absolute decline of 43,000 jobs (Table 4.7).

How do changes in patterns of work travel reflect the restructuring of home and workplace locations within these labour markets? Firstly, the decline in within-core journeys has become established, with the fall in this component's share of the total ranging from -0.78% in the Resort/Retirement centres to -1.11% in the Peripheral Freestanding towns (Table 4.11). However, these declines are still lower than in any of the other labour market groups. Because the core's share of total destinations has not declined, the contraction in the within-core component is matched by the increase in commuting from rings to cores. In other words, it is the residences which have been decentralising, not the jobs, and consequently the proportion of ring residents engaged in commuting to the cores increased in each of the groups, though by 1971 these levels were still below the national aggregate level (Table 4.13). Whereas in the New Towns the rings displayed strengthening work travel links with the cores even though they were not growing in terms of the number of origins, in the Type 2 cities it is the outer rings which display this feature; thus the outer ring to core flow increased its share of the total in each group, while local journeys within outer rings became less important (Table 4.14). Although outer rings are beginning to display the same trends as rings, their level of self-containment is as expected considerably higher.

Type 3 - The Southern Freestanding Group. In this stage, employment begins to exhibit the same trend of relative decentralisation from cores to rings that previously has only been exhibited by the workforce. Relative growth in both employment and employed population is thus confined to the ring areas.

Consequently, the decline of the within-core share of total work travel is larger than in the Type 2 cities, but it is not matched by a commensurate increase in the ring to core flow's share. The expansion of jobs in the ring areas is reflected in the growing importance of within-ring journeys, which increases their share of the total by 1.3% compared with only 0.6% for the ring to core component (Table 4.11). Thus, whereas the rings of the Type 1 and 2 labour markets displayed rapid increases in the level of dependency upon the job supply of their core areas, in the Southern Freestanding group the percentage of ring residents destined for cores actually declined slightly (from 36.6% to 36.2%).

The outer rings have not progressed meanwhile beyond the previous stage; their share of total MELA employment and employed population continues to decline, while at the same time their level of self-containment falls as interaction with the core and ring zones increases.

Type 4 - The Lancashire/Yorkshire Group. At this stage of the sequence, the relative decline of the outer ring zones in terms of both origins and destinations has ceased, but they have not yet begun to experience growth, their share of the total remaining unchanged between 1966 and 1971.

A number of factors serve to make these labour markets rather a special case.

TABLE 4.12 Changes in the Pattern of Intra-MELA Journeys which Originate within Cores; Labour Market Groups, 1966-71

Destinations (%) Core Origins	1966			1971			Change 1966-71		
	Core	Ring	Outer ring	Core	Ring	Outer ring	Core	Ring	Outer ring
New Towns	97.42	2.56	0.00	97.36	2.62	0.01	-0.06	0.06	0.01
Secondary Industrial	92.14	6.17	1.68	91.82	6.37	1.79	-0.32	0.20	0.11
Resorts/Retirement centres	92.15	5.26	2.58	92.16	5.38	2.44	0.01	0.12	-0.14
Peripheral Freestanding	91.12	7.39	1.47	91.33	7.36	1.29	0.21	-0.03	-0.18
Southern Freestanding	88.78	9.17	2.03	88.05	9.72	2.21	-0.73	0.55	0.18
Lancashire/Yorkshire group	89.10	10.40	0.48	89.55	9.91	0.53	0.45	-0.49	0.05
London Peripheral	91.82	8.04	0.12	90.98	8.86	0.15	-0.84	0.82	0.03
Major Industrial	92.52	6.96	0.50	92.55	6.92	0.52	0.03	-0.04	0.02
Million Cities	94.09	5.74	0.16	93.51	6.26	0.21	-0.58	0.52	0.05
Total	93.02	6.37	0.61	92.66	6.88	0.66	-0.36	0.31	0.05

TABLE 4.13 Changes in the Pattern of Intra-MELA Journeys which Originate within Rings; Labour Market Groups, 1966-71

Destinations (%) Ring Origins	1966			1971			Change 1966-71		
	Core	Ring	Outer ring	Core	Ring	Outer ring	Core	Ring	Outer ring
New Towns	25.33	74.30	0.36	30.64	68.81	0.54	5.31	-5.49	0.18
Secondary Industrial	31.88	62.78	5.32	33.07	61.28	5.63	1.19	-1.50	0.31
Resorts/Retirement centres	26.06	69.34	4.58	28.76	66.88	4.35	2.70	-2.46	-0.23
Peripheral Freestanding	35.06	60.86	4.07	36.86	58.15	4.78	1.80	-2.71	0.91
Southern Freestanding	36.61	58.74	4.63	36.23	59.16	4.59	-0.38	0.42	-0.04
Lancashire/Yorkshire group	31.89	66.53	1.57	33.89	64.39	1.71	2.00	-2.14	0.14
London Peripheral	29.47	70.19	0.33	29.92	69.71	0.36	0.45	-0.48	0.03
Major Industrial	36.99	60.24	2.75	35.89	61.13	2.97	-1.10	0.89	0.22
Million Cities	41.28	57.73	0.98	41.66	57.30	1.03	0.38	-0.43	0.05
Total	37.17	60.63	2.21	37.63	60.05	2.37	0.46	-0.58	0.16

TABLE 4.14   Changes in the Pattern of Intra-MELA Journeys which Originate within Outer Rings; Labour Market Groups, 1966-71

Destinations (%) Outer ring origins	1966		1971			Change 1966-71		
	Core	Ring	Outer ring	Core	Ring	Outer ring	Core	Ring	Outer ring
New Towns	2.92	1.67	95.39	8.00	0.80	91.20	5.08	-0.87	-4.19
Secondary Industrial	6.71	5.61	87.67	8.08	5.79	86.11	1.37	0.18	-1.56
Resort/Retirement centres	4.93	3.09	91.96	6.65	3.48	89.86	1.72	0.39	-2.10
Peripheral Freestanding	5.03	2.15	92.81	6.34	4.60	89.05	1.31	2.45	-3.76
Southern Freestanding	5.16	2.90	91.93	6.14	3.64	90.21	0.98	0.74	-1.72
Lancashire/Yorkshire group	7.57	6.37	86.04	8.78	6.57	84.64	1.21	0.20	-1.40
London Peripheral	6.81	4.08	89.10	9.21	4.61	86.16	2.40	0.53	-2.94
Major Industrial	7.00	6.44	86.55	8.00	7.51	84.48	1.00	1.07	-2.07
Million Cities	8.22	5.70	86.06	10.13	7.65	82.20	1.91	1.95	-3.86
Total	6.33	4.39	89.31	7.73	5.61	86.69	1.40	1.22	-2.62

Firstly, although the change in the performance of the outer rings would suggest that they are evolutionary more advanced than the previous groups, at the SMLA level they are clearly less advanced than the Type 3 (Southern Freestanding) labour markets. Thus, although the employed population is undergoing strong relative decentralisation, employment shifts are much less marked. Consequently, the ring to core component increased its share of the intra-MELA total by a larger percentage than did the within-ring component, and the share of total ring residents who commute to the cores increased by 2.0% to 33.9% (Table 4.13). A second unusual feature is that these relative changes are almost completely due to varying rates of absolute decline, rather than decline in one zone being compensated for by growth in another. Employment, for example, declined absolutely in all three zone types, but at a slightly faster rate in the cores than in the rings, producing relative decentralisation (Table 4.8). Nevertheless even in labour markets in such marked decline the pattern of internal redistribution is closely akin to other types of labour market in which overall growth provides the impetus for this redistribution.

Type 5 - The Million Cities,Major Industrial and London Peripheral labour markets. At this, the most advanced stage in the sequence, outer ring areas have begun to share in the relative growth of jobs and employed persons previously confined only to the rings, while the relative decline of the core areas has become more pronounced, with the three Type 5 groups exhibiting the largest negative shifts in the core shares of both journey origins and destinations. The strength of these trends does vary between the three groups, however, with the Million Cities exhibiting the strongest shifts and the London Peripheral group the weakest.

The redistribution of homes and jobs within the Type 5 labour markets has of course led to a marked restructuring of work travel patterns within them. On the one hand the within-core components' shares of the respective totals have declined in each case by more than 2.0%, reaching a maximum of -3.4% in the Million City group (the scale of which can best be comprehended when translated into absolute terms - a decline of 0.7 million journeys in just five years). This alone has major implications for the provision of public transport in the conurbations.

Because jobs as well as homes have been decentralising from core to ring areas, the increases in the within-ring components' shares of the intra-MELA totals have exceeded the increases in the respective ring to core components. This does not necessarily indicate that levels of interdependency are falling, however, for the within-ring flows were larger in number to begin with. In the Million City group, for example, the rings became relatively more dependent on the cores (the proportion of their residents working in cores increased by 0.4% to 41.7% in 1971, a level much higher than those displayed by the other labour market groups). Nevertheless, in the Major Industrial group the core-destined share of ring origins did indeed decline (by 1.1% to 35.9%).

Finally, journeys to work originating in the outer rings of the Type 5 cities are beginning to display trends which are characteristic of only the ring areas of the less advanced labour market groups. Thus the Million City and London Peripheral groups recorded small increases in the share of total intra-MELA worktravel accounted for by journeys within outer rings, reflecting the onset of relative job decentralisation into these areas. As a result of residential decentralisation being further established, however, dependencies with the more central urban zones are continuing to increase, indicative of the outward spread of commuting fields. Thus the outer rings of the Type 5 labour markets have above-average outflow levels, led by the Million Cities in which 10.1% of outer ring residents work in cores and a further 7.7% work in rings (compared with the national aggregate levels of 7.7% and 5.6% respectively).

What are the characteristics of the different labour market groups which may help to explain their relative position in the evolutionary sequence? The size of labour market areas is obviously an important factor associated with the most advanced stage in the sequence, for the Million Cities and the Major Industrial groups together comprise the twenty largest MELAs (by population) in the British urban system.   The London Peripheral group is less easy to account for, its labour markets ranging in size quite considerably (from Reading, ranked 40, to Woking, ranked 118).

Part of the explanation may lie in the fact that the London Peripheral labour markets have high levels of external interaction; almost 30% of their total workforce commute to other labour markets, with London the major destination. Intra-MELA worktravel is thus only one component of their aggregate journey to work structures, and, as will be seen later, the least dynamic component at that. In this particular case, then, a biased impression of aggregate labour market restructuring may be gained by concentrating at this stage on the origins and destinations of journeys within labour markets.

Size, being a function of their unique development, would also seem to be a major factor in explaining the New Town labour markets' position at the least advanced stage in the sequence. The intervening stages between the extremes of least and most advanced, however, cannot be simply explained by labour market size variations, and factors such as relative location become more important. The Peripheral Freestanding towns (Type 2), for example, tend to be large, predominantly rural, labour markets peripheral to the main axis of urban Britain. As a consequence, their growth performance in the past has tended to be sluggish, and both cores and rings have increased their shares of total employment at the expense of the large, but declining, outer ring hinterlands. The Southern Freestanding labour markets (Type 3), on the other hand, have been more dynamic in growth terms, and their core areas have recorded a drop in the share of total employment due to particularly high rates of ring growth (and outer ring stability instead of marked contraction), rather than in situ employment decline.

Thus labour market size, relative location, and growth experience are important interrelated factors which contribute to explaining a particular group's position in the evolutionary sequence. Having considered each stage of the sequence in turn, a summary of the points of similarity and difference between the labour market groups in the way in which their internal patterns of work travel are evolving can be given.

i) Core origins – the extent to which the decentralisation trend has come to pervade all levels of the urban hierarchy was illustrated by the decline of the within-core share of total journeys in all groups except for the New Towns. The strength of the trend varied considerably, however, with the most marked declines in this component occurring in the groups at the most advanced stage in the evolutionary sequence, led by the Million Cities (Table 4.11).

The pattern of change in the considerably less important reverse flow from cores to rings is not as clear, and this applies even to the Type 5 labour markets in which job decentralisation is firmly established. On the one hand, in the Million City cores the outward flow declined at a slower rate than did the within-zone component, and consequently slightly increased its share of total core origins (from 5.7% to 6.3%; Table 4.12). In the Major Industrial group, however, the reverse situation was true. There is certainly no evidence to suggest that 'inside-out' commuting is becoming a more important feature of work travel behaviour; even in the Million Cities, the positive shift in this component is based on an absolute decline of 11,000 such journeys.

A comparable analysis of intra-MELA journey to work changes in the 1961-1971 decade as a whole, however, suggested that reverse commuting did increase, especially in the largest labour markets (Gillespie, 1977). It was seen earlier that employment increased in ring areas at a fast rate in the 1961-66 period, and at a much slower rate in the second half of the decade. It may well be, then, that reverse commuting increased substantially in the first period due to the rapid decentralisation of jobs, but levelled out in the 1966-71 period as a consequence of the slower ring job growth.

ii) Ring origins - the almost universal trend of employed population decentralisation is reflected in the ring to core and within-ring flows capturing a larger share of intra-MELA work travel in all of the labour market groups with the predictable exception of the New Towns (Table 4.11). The time-lag between residence and workplace decentralisation resulted in increases in the proportion of ring residents who commute to the cores. This trend towards increasing relative dependency is strongest in labour market groups at the earlier stages of the evolutionary sequence where such interdependencies between zones are initially much lower than average. Thus there is a clear tendency for the levels displayed by the different groups to converge between 1966 and 1971. It can be hypothesised that this convergence indicates that the next stage is one in which ring-core dependencies actually begin to decline in relative terms in the most advanced areas, due to the continued (relative) decentralisation of employment. While it is true that the Major Industrial group did indeed record such a decline (the share of ring origins destined for cores fell from 37.0% in 1966 to 35.9% in 1971), it would be unwise to suggest that this constitutes a general trend. The fact remains, nevertheless, that the ring area's dependence on core areas is increasing slowly or not at all in the largest cities, while more rapid increases characterise the cities at lower levels in the hierarchy.

iii) Outer ring origins - two related trends characterise the changes in work travel originating in outer ring areas. Firstly, the widespread relative contraction in outer ring employment is reflected in the within-outer ring share of total inter-MELA journeys declining in all groups except for the Million Cities and London Peripheral towns. Secondly, and superimposed over the within-zone decline, journeys from outer rings to cores and to rings without exception increased their shares of the total. Although these shifts are small (all are below 1.0%) compared with the changes in some of the other flow components, this is due to small initial bases rather than sluggish growth. For example, the absolute rate of increase in the outer ring to core component ranged from 10.9% in the Lancashire/Yorkshire group to 42.5% in the London Peripheral towns.

These two trends, one reflecting employment decline and the other employed population growth, have together produced substantially stronger commuting interdependencies between outer rings and their respective cores and rings. The Million Cities once again represent the most advanced stage, having the lowest level of outer ring self-containment in 1971 and the largest negative shift in this level during the preceeding five-year period.

There can be little doubt from the above description of work travel changes that the level of commuting interdependency between urban zones increased between 1966 and 1971, and that this increase was not confined to a particular type of labour market area but was discernable in groups with widely varying size and locational characteristics. Although it is not possible to prove that commuting hinterlands have expanded in area (when using labour-market area definitions which are fixed, not floating), the intensity of commuting from these hinterlands certainly has increased. In the largest cities the ring areas have experienced only a marginal increase in their already strong dependency on the urban cores, but the outer rings have taken up the slack and exhibit rapid increases in their level of integration with the metropolitan centres. In the smaller and/or less advanced cities, it is the rings which dominate the pattern of change in work travel structure.

Either way, it is obvious that in a no-growth period such as the one under examination, an increase in one type of flow must be counter-balanced by a decline in another type. It is the within-core component that has borne the brunt of these changes, declining absolutely in all labour market groups except the New Towns. Yet it is in these core areas that the bulk of public transport infrastructure is located. Changes in the mode of work travel are obviously inter-related with the growth of this home – workplace separation but modal changes cannot be understood solely in terms of this spatial restructuring. A number of other factors are relevant, factors such as sex, socio-economic group and car ownership, which relate to the characteristics of the person making a journey, rather than the nature of the journey itself. These themes will be returned to later.

4.2.2 Changes in Worktravel Patterns Between British Cities

It has been established that journeys to work between labour markets were growing in numbers more rapidly than any other type of work travel. During the 1966-71 period in which the total number of work trips declined, inter-MELA journeys increased by 328,000 (20.5%). By 1971, almost two million people were making daily journeys of this type, and inter-MELA journeys to work increased their share of the national total from 6.6% to 8.1% by 1971.

Although such journeys remain numerically far less important than intra-MELA journeys, a number of features make them worthy of special attention. First, they have an extremely rapid growth rate. Second, they include few purely local journeys. Finally, the relative importance of inter-MELA journeys varies greatly in different parts of the country; around the major conurbations, for example, commuting across labour market boundaries accounts for a substantial share of total work travel movement.

The zonal origin and destination structure of inter-MELA work journeys (Table 4.15) is different in a number of respects from the intra-MELA structure. Core areas account for a lower percentage of both origins and destinations (in 1971, for example, only 32.2% of inter-MELA journeys originated in cores, compared with 53.0% of intra-MELA journeys). At the same time, the ratios of origins to destinations within each zone type are more imbalanced than in the intra-MELA case; i.e. cores have a larger relative net inflow, and rings and outer rings a larger relative net outflow (the core net commuting ratios for inter- and intra-MELA journeys are 0.64 and 0.85 respectively).

Turning to changes in this structure, Table 4.15 shows that for cores, rings and outer rings, the number of inter-MELA origins and destinations increased between 1966 and 1971. The largest increases were recorded by core destinations and ring origins (173,000 and 156,000 respectively), which both grew by over 20%. In 1966, the core was already the principal destination zone and the ring the principal origin zone, and thus the high growth rates were not built upon small initial bases. The fastest growth rate, however, was recorded by outer ring origins (26.7%), though the absolute increase was not large (95,000). Consequently, the core is the only zone to have increased its share of total journey destinations (from 50.1% to 50.6%), while the ring and outer rings both increased their share of journey origins (43.9% to 44.5%, and 22.2% to 23.3%).

The result of these net changes in the zonal origins and destinations of inter-MELA work travel can be seen in Table 4.16. Although all nine flow types grew absolutely, ring to core journeys increased by the largest amount (84,000) and outer ring to core journeys grew at the fastest rate (37.7%). Consequently, these two flow types increased their share of total inter-MELA work travel (by 0.4% and 1.0% respectively).

The rapid overall increase in inter-MELA commuting has not been based upon only one

British Cities

TABLE 4.15 Origins and Destinations by Urban Zone for Journeys
Between MELAs, 1966-71

(a) Absolute totals and changes (thousands)

	Core		Ring		Outer Ring		Total
	Origins	Destinations	Origins	Destinations	Origins	Destinations	
1966	545	804	703	481	356	320	1,604
1971	622	977	859	573	451	382	1,932
Absolute change	77	173	156	92	95	62	328
Rate of change (%)	14.1	21.5	22.2	19.1	26.7	19.4	20.5

(b) Percentage shares and changes

	Core		Ring		Outer Ring	
	Origins	Destinations	Origins	Destinations	Origins	Destinations
1966	34.0	50.1	43.9	30.0	22.2	19.9
1971	32.2	50.6	44.5	29.7	23.3	19.7
Change in share	-1.8	0.5	0.6	-0.3	1.1	-0.2

(c) Net commuting ratios

	Core $\frac{\text{Origins}}{\text{Destinations}}$	Ring $\frac{\text{Origins}}{\text{Destinations}}$	Outer Ring $\frac{\text{Origins}}{\text{Destinations}}$
1966	0.68	1.46	1.11
1971	0.64	1.50	1.18
Change	-0.04	0.04	0.07

or two types of movement, as all flow types increased in total by at least 13% over
the five year period. Nevertheless, there is evidence to suggest that in relative
terms commuting between labour markets is tending to become longer distance in
nature, as witnessed by the increasing importance of core areas as a destination
for inter-MELA journeys (journey to cores are less likely to be local movements
which happen to cross a labour market boundary). This feature, together with the
relative increase in inter- vis a vis intra-MELA commuting, are yet further indications of the growing spatial separation between homes and work places.

Variations between functional MELA groupings

The magnitude of inter-MELA commuting and the balance between in- and out-movement
varies considerably between different types of labour market. Table 4.17 shows the
average absolute inflows and outflows and the net balance for labour markets within

TABLE 4.16 Flows Within and Between Urban Zones for Journeys Between MELAs, 1966-71

(a) Absolute (thousands)

	C – C	C – R	C – OR	R – C	R – R	R – OR	OR – C	OR – R	OR – OR	Total
1966	314	164	67	376	219	108	114	98	144	1,604
1971	359	188	75	460	268	131	157	118	175	1,932
Absolute change	45	24	8	84	49	23	43	20	31	328
Rate of change (percent)	14.3	14.6	13.6	22.3	22.4	21.3	37.7	20.4	21.5	20.5

(b) Percentage shares

	C – C	C – R	C – OR	R – C	R – R	R – OR	OR – C	OR – R	OR – OR	Total
1966	19.6	10.2	4.2	23.4	13.7	6.7	7.1	6.1	9.0	100.0
1971	18.6	9.7	3.9	23.8	13.9	6.8	8.1	6.1	9.1	100.0
Change in share	-1.0	-0.5	-0.3	0.4	0.2	0.1	1.0	0	0.1	–

TABLE 4.17 Average Inter-MELA Inflows, Outflows and Net Balances: Labour Market Groups, 1966 and 1971 (thousands)

Labour Market Groups	Outflow			Inflow			Net balance Inflows(+) Outflows(−)	
	1966	1971	Changes 1961-71	1966	1971	Changes 1966-71	1966	1971
New Towns	10.03	12.38	2.35	7.17	9.17	2.00	−2.86	−3.20
Secondary Industrial	10.52	12.30	1.78	9.41	10.40	0.99	−1.10	−1.89
Resort/Retirement centres	6.84	8.45	1.61	4.20	5.10	0.90	−2.64	−3.35
Peripheral Freestanding	4.70	6.36	1.66	4.51	5.50	0.99	−0.19	−0.85
Southern Freestanding	6.91	9.19	2.28	7.39	8.25	0.86	0.48	−0.93
Lancashire/Yorkshire group	16.59	17.78	1.19	12.30	13.73	1.43	−4.29	−4.05
London Peripheral	17.33	21.24	3.91	11.97	13.49	1.52	−5.35	−7.74
Major Industrial	15.59	17.91	2.32	16.50	19.19	2.69	0.90	1.27
Million Cities	48.39	54.08	5.69	78.02	97.17	19.15	29.62	43.09

each of the nine classification groups. The first point to stress is that the Million Cities group provides the only 'sink' for inter-MELA journeys in net terms, with the total inflow in 1971 exceeding the total outflow by an average of 43,000 journeys. The Major Industrial group records a small average net inflow, while in all of the other groups the outflow exceeds the inflow (reaching a maximum in the London Peripheral labour markets, in which the average net loss is almost 8,000). Although in net terms the pattern of 'sources and sinks' is clear, in real terms of course the pattern is far more complex. Despite the substantial net inflow to the Million Cities labour markets, for example, they have an average daily outflow of 54,000 journeys, substantially higher than any other labour market group.

This discussion of absolute flows does not of course provide an indication of the relative importance of in and out commuting in comparison with journeys which remain within labour markets. Figure 4.2 thus shows for each labour market group the relationship between the inflow (expressed as a percentage of the labour market's total jobs) and the outflow (expressed as a percentage of the labour market's total workforce) for both 1966 and 1971.

There are substantial differences between the groups in the importance of inter-MELA commuting relative to total work travel structures. At one end of the 1971 spectrum, the average outflow percentage from the Million Cities was only 4.7% and the average inflow 6.1%. At the opposite extreme, three groups (the Lancashire/Yorkshire group, New Towns and London Peripheral) have such high levels of inter-MELA commuting that they constitute a cluster quite separate from the remaining six groups (only in the inflow to the first of these groups of towns does the level fall below 20%, with a maximum of 29.1% for the London Peripheral's outflow). It should be remembered that to a certain extent such variations are the product of labour market size and the degree to which the areal extent of certain types of labour market are constrained by their proximity to other labour markets. Around the major conurbations, for example, the density of urban development frequently results in a large number of small labour markets situated in close proximity to each other. The structure of the urban system in such areas is likely to accentuate the importance of commuting between labour markets vis a vis intra-labour market work travel.

Although the relationship between the level of outflow in a group and the level of inflow is clearly positive, in detail there are substantial differences between the groups. Only in the Million Cities and the Major Industrial group does the inflow as a percentage of total jobs exceed the outflow as a percentage of the total workforce (i.e. they are above the 45 degree line in Figure 4.2). Of the remaining groups, the Peripheral and Southern Freestanding not unexpectedly displayed the strongest balance between the inflow and outflow percentages, for as their names suggest labour markets in these groups are relatively closed commuting systems. Although low levels of inter-MELA commuting are then generally associated with a close degree of balance between inflows and outflows, a notable exception is provided by the Resorts/Retirement centres. In functional terms this group is less homogenous than any of the others, for it includes small free-standing resort towns such as Torbay as well as a number of large coastal towns in the South-East, such as Brighton, which have substantial one-way commuting interactions with London. The net effect of these different elements is to produce a group displaying a relatively low overall level of inter-MELA commuting but one in which the outflow percentage is much higher than the inflow (11.0% and 6.7% respectively).

A much clearer pattern characterises the Lancashire/Yorkshire group, New Town and London Peripheral groups, which have high levels of inter-MELA commuting and structures in which the outflow components substantially exceed the inflows, reflecting the importance of the major conurbations in attracting commuters from the smaller labour markets around their peripheries. The London Peripheral group has the most unbalanced structure of the three, with 1971 inflow and outflow percentages of

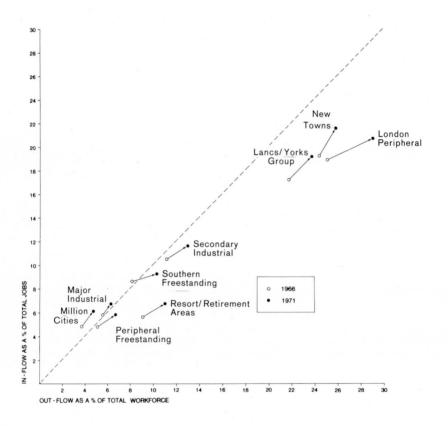

Fig. 4.2   Relationship between inter-MELA inflows and
           outflows. Labour market groups, 1966 and 1971.

20.7% and 29.1% respectively.

As with the absolute changes, in every group the relative importance of inter-MELA
inflows and outflows increased, but at differential rates which led to increasing
imbalances between the two components (i.e. the change arrows in Fig. 4.2 are diver-
ging from the 45 degree line). The only exception is the New Town group, in which
the gap between the inflow and outflow percentages narrowed from 5.3% in 1966 to
4.4% in 1971. This contrasts markedly with the London Peripheral group, in which
the gap widened from 6.3% to 8.4% due to a particularly rapid increase in the

outflow component. The differing experiences of these two groups is interesting in view of the criticism that has frequently been levelled at the New Towns concerning their degree of self-containment (meaning in this case the extent to which they have developed their own employment bases rather than merely acting as dormitory towns dependent upon London). While it is true that on average a quarter of their work-forces do indeed commute to other labour markets, the London Peripheral towns, which to a certain extent provide a control group, have an even higher outflow percentage. In addition, it would appear that the employment generated within New Towns has had a significant effect upon neighbouring labour markets, for in 1971 an average 21.5% of New Town jobs are filled by residents who commute in from elsewhere (a higher level than in any other group). Thus not only is the relationship between inflows and outflows more balanced in the New Towns than in the London Peripheral group, but the New Town group is alone in experiencing a convergence of these values bet-ween 1966 and 1971.

Variations between individual labour market areas

The importance of London's contribution on the national inter-MELA commuting totals is amply demonstrated by Table 4.18, which shows London to have the largest absolute outflow, inflow and gain (147,000, 402,000 and 255,000 journeys respectively). Other Million Cities (with the exception of Newcastle) also figure prominently in the top ten rankings, but a number of labour markets also feature whose importance in inter-MELA commuting terms far outweighs their general position in the urban hi-erarchy. Southend, for example, has a total outflow of almost 40,000 commuters (which ranks fifth, above Glasgow), and Chatham, Watford and Reading have outflows in excess of 30,000 journeys. With the exception of Watford (whose inflow ranks tenth in size), these levels of movement are due to non-reciprocal commuting links with London, and consequently their net outflows are also the highest in the country (Southend having a net loss of 33,000 journeys). Of the labour markets with the highest net inflows, Ellesmere Port and Port Talbot (ranked second and fourth res-pectively) are the most interesting inclusions. Ellesmere Port is the smallest labour market in the country in population terms, sandwiched as it is between the Liverpool and Chester MELAs, but its major role in providing employment must of course be viewed within the context of Merseyside as a whole.

The concentration of high levels of inter-MELA commuting in certain parts of the country is illustrated by Fig. 4.3, which shows the outflows as percentages of each MELAs workforce. The influence of London on its adjoining labour markets is clearly portrayed, for an almost unbroken chain of MELAs with outflow percentages in excess of 20% encircles the capital, reaching a maximum of 44.1% in Woking (Table 4.19). The only other concentrations of high levels occur in the small labour markets bet-ween Liverpool and Manchester and between Leeds and Sheffield. The lowest out-commuting percentages characterise the most peripheral parts of the urban system, as suggested by the presence of Aberdeen, Hull and Plymouth in the bottom three rankings, although the Million Cities also display low levels of out-commuting.

In many respects, the pattern of inflows as percentages of total jobs in each MELA (Fig. 4.4) is similar to the outflow pattern, with the small labour markets around London and in Lancashire featuring prominently among the highest values (six of the top ten are located in the South-East, and a further three are in Lancashire). The correlation coefficient between each MELA's inflow and outflow percentages is 0.725. The highest value of all is found in Ellesmere Port, the uniqueness of which in commuting terms has already been established; 54.2% of the jobs in this labour market are filled by residents of other MELAs, far in excess of the level in the area ranked second, Walton and Weybridge (37.6%).

Changes in these outflow and inflow patterns are less clearly differentiated on an areal basis (Fig. 4.5a and 4.5b respectively), although once again the South-East

TABLE 4.18   Inter-MELA Inflows, Outflows and Net Balances.   Top and Bottom Ten MELA Rankings, 1971
(thousands)

	Total employed population working in other MELA's		Total jobs filled by workers from other MELA's		Total net gain or loss	
1	London	147.4	London	401.9	London	254.5
2	Liverpool	48.7	Manchester	65.1	Ellesmere Pt	21.5
3	Manchester	46.6	Birmingham	56.0	Manchester	18.5
4	Birmingham	43.0	Liverpool	46.1	Port Talbot	15.2
5	Southend	39.5	Glasgow	43.4	Birmingham	12.9
6	Glasgow	37.5	Leeds	42.9	Sheffield	10.0
7	Chatham	33.7	Sheffield	30.7	Leeds	9.4
8	Leeds	33.5	Corby	29.8	Southampton	7.2
9	Watford	31.7	Slough	28.7	Glasgow	5.8
10	Reading	30.4	Watford	28.6	Warrington	5.3
117	Dundee	3.9	Torbay	2.6	Barnsley	-9.9
118	Exeter	3.6	King's Lynn	2.5	Stevenage	-9.9
119	Perth	3.5	Workington	2.5	Rhondda	-10.5
120	Salisbury	3.3	Rhondda	2.2	Woking	-10.9
121	Lancaster	3.0	Perth	1.9	Chelmsford	-11.5
122	Gt. Yarmouth	2.5	Hereford	1.8	Guildford	-11.6
123	Barrow	2.3	Carlisle	1.7	Reading	-14.9
124	Carlisle	2.1	Hastings	1.6	Wigan	-17.8
125	Workington	1.7	Barrow	0.9	Chatham	-22.8
126	Aberdeen	1.3	Aberdeen	0.8	Southend	-32.7

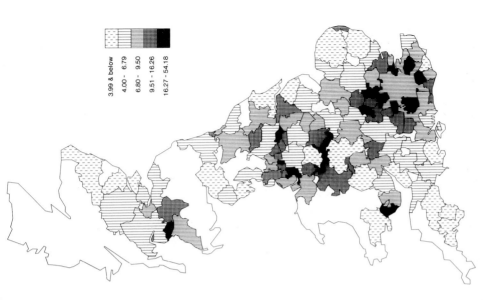

Fig. 4.4 Percentage of each MELA's total jobs filled by commuters from other MELA's 1971.

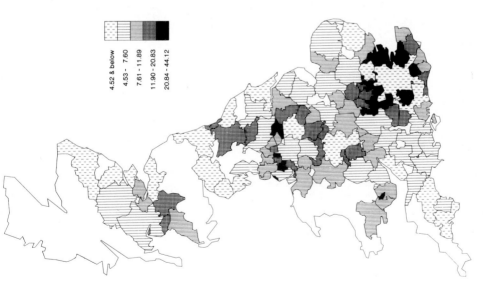

Fig. 4.3 Percentage of each MELA's resident employed population commuting to other MELAs, 1971.

TABLE 4.19   Inter-MELA Percentage Outflows and Inflows. Top and Bottom Ten MELA Rankings, 1971

	Percentage of employed population working in other MELA's		Percentage of jobs filled by workers from other MELA's		Ratio % outflow to other MELA's / % inflow from other MELA's	
1	Woking	44.1	Ellesmere Port	54.2	Southend	5.79
2	Walton & Weybridge	42.2	Walton & Weybridge	37.6	Rhondda	5.70
3	St. Albans	39.9	Watford	32.3	Hastings	3.65
4	Basildon	39.5	Basildon	31.1	Chatham	3.11
5	Rhondda	37.4	St. Helens	28.3	Swansea	2.71
6	Stevenage	34.7	Leigh	27.6	Wigan	2.52
7	Watford	34.7	Crawley	27.4	Norwich	2.41
8	Leigh	34.5	Woking	25.7	Barrow	2.35
9	Thurrock	32.9	Letchworth	25.7	Southport	2.33
10	Southend	32.7	Warrington	24.8	Blackpool	2.30
117	Exeter	3.3	Dundee	3.3	Letchworth	0.69
118	Workington	3.3	Exeter	3.3	Sheffield	0.67
119	Edinburgh	3.2	Swansea	3.3	Crawley	0.66
120	London	3.2	Ipswich	3.2	Peterborough	0.65
121	Carlisle	3.2	Plymouth	2.7	Southampton	0.63
122	Birmingham	3.1	Carlisle	2.5	Teesside	0.59
123	Dundee	2.9	Norwich	2.4	Gt. Yarmouth	0.43
124	Plymouth	2.8	Barrow	2.0	Port Talbot	0.39
125	Hull	2.4	Hull	1.6	London	0.37
126	Aberdeen	1.0	Aberdeen	0.6	Ellesmere Pt.	0.17

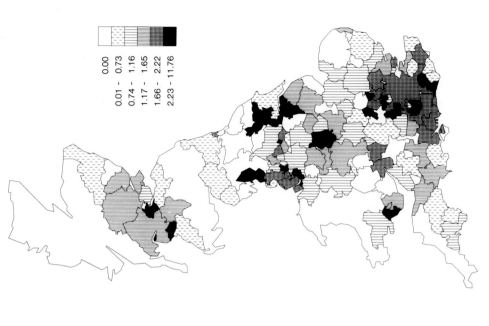

Fig. 4.5b   Changes in the percentage of each
           MELA's total jobs filled by commuters
           from other MELAs, 1966-1971.

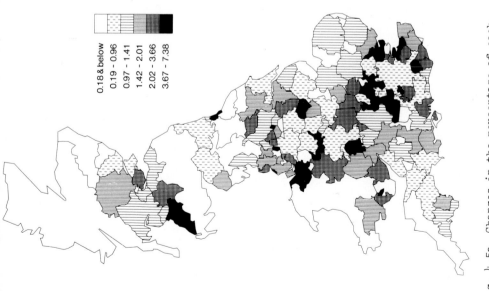

Fig. 4.5a   Changes in the percentage of each
           MELA's resident commuting to other
           MELAs, 1966-1971.

region accounts for many of the largest increases in both components. In London itself, the inflow as a percentage of total jobs increased by 2.1%, a change the scale of which can best be appreciated in absolute terms; the total number of journeys into the London MELA increased by 89,000 between 1966 and 1971, a 28% rate of growth.

One further interesting feature is the increasing influence exerted by Birmingham on its surrounding labour markets. In these terms, even by 1971 Birmingham did not have the same effect on its region as did Manchester, for example, but is is apparent from Fig. 4.5a that the situation is changing, with a general increase in percentage outflows from the labour markets adjoining the city (particularly so in Stafford and Worcester).

In summary then, it would appear that the overall importance of inter-MELA commuting varies substantially between different parts of the country. In the majority of labour markets, inter-MELA journeys are a minor component of total work travel, but in the areas around the major conurbations it is not uncommon for more than 25% of a labour market's workforce to commute elsewhere. Clearly in the case of London it is unrealistic to think in terms of discrete labour markets at all, for the capital attracts major flows of labour from areas well beyond its own boundary. The phenomenon will be considered further in the following section which deals with specific interactions rather than with total in- and outflows.

Major flows between individual labour market areas including the Million Cities

An overview of the major commuting linkages between the country's labour markets in 1971 is portrayed in Fig. 4.6. The flows shown are those where the principal destination MELA is larger in population size than the origin MELA. These are flows up the urban hierarchy, and by this method sub-systems based on dominant centres can be identified. This constraint is adopted in order to simplify the figure. The majority of flows to smaller MELAs are reciprocals of plotted flows. There are seven labour markets without any linkages shown (i.e. those from which the principal flow is to a smaller centre, and to which no other labour market sends its principal flow). These areas can for these purposes be considered as self-contained work travel systems (the areas being Ayr, Chester, Hull, Swansea, Plymouth, Taunton and Ipswich).

The largest system is of course based on London, which is the principal journey to work destination of 28 labour markets, almost a quarter of the country's total number. Although the previous section established that labour markets in the South-East had high levels of total outflow, total inflows were also high and hence it might have been expected that in many of the smaller labour markets the principal commuting links would be with their immediate neighbours. This is not the case, however, for only 9 labour markets in the South-East (from a total of 37) have principal destinations other than London. These are Portsmouth, Southampton, and Bournemouth (forming a linked sub-system), Basingstoke and Oxford (with Reading their principal destination), Milton Keynes and Bedford (to Luton), Letchworth (to Stevenage), and Worthing (to Brighton). The extent of London's dominance over the region is illustrated further by the fact that seven of the labour markets sending more commuters to the capital than to anywhere else are not even contiguous with the London MELA. Canterbury, for example, is thirty miles from the boundary of the London MELA, and yet sends almost 6,000 commuters to London, a larger flow than those to its contiguous neighbours (Ashford and Chatham) added together.

The uniqueness of the London based commuting system compared to the other Million Cities is reflected in the large gap between the number of labour markets incorporated into the respective sub-systems. Thus after London's 28 MELAs, the next largest are based on Glasgow, Liverpool, Birmingham and Leeds, each of which are the

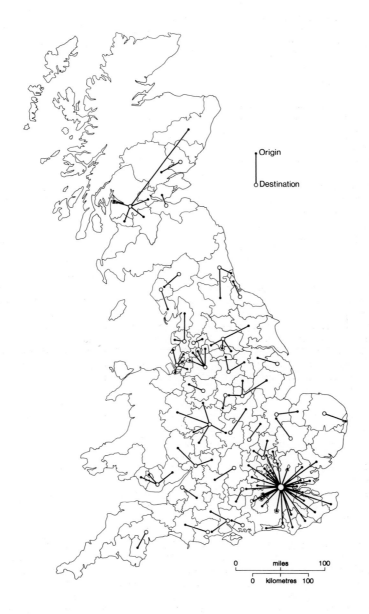

Fig. 4.6   Principal destination of inter-MELA journeys, 1971

principal destinations for five labour markets. Manchester has four dependent
MELAs in its sub-system and Newcastle only two. The position of Newcastle within
its region is different from the other conurbations, since much of its boundary is
with the unclassified areas of Northumberland. Only three MELAs (Sunderland,
Darlington and Carlisle) are contiguous with the Newcastle MELA, and only the first
two of these are incorporated into its commuting sub-system on the basis of their
principal destination.

Apart from the Million Cities, the only other major regional sub-systems are based
on Cardiff and Nottingham (the first incorporating Port Talbot, Rhondda and Newport
and the second Derby, Mansfield and Lincoln). With respect to the Nottingham sub-
system, it is interesting to note the exclusion of Leicester, the other large city
in the East Midlands region, which has Coventry as its principal destination (which
is in turn part of the Birmingham sub-system).

Although the principal destinations of inter-MELA journeys can help to identify the
major commuting systems, they provide no indication of the importance of these flow
The following discussion thus examines work travel interactions between specific
labour markets which exceed certain absolute or relative size thresholds.

Of the national total of 119 non-Million City labour markets, 48 send 5% or more of
their total workforces to the Million Cities. Fig. 4.7 shows the spatial distribution of these labour markets, together with the relative importance of the flows
in terms of successively higher 5% bands. It is at once apparent that London is
unique not only in the number of MELAs which surpass the 5% threshold, but even
more so in the intensity of commuting from these labour markets. Thus London is
the destination for slightly over one-half of the flows above 5%, two-thirds of the
flows above 10%, four-fifths of the flows above 15%, and accounts for all of the
flows above the 20% level (of which there are nine - St. Albans, Watford, Slough,
Woking, Walton and Weybridge, Tunbridge Wells, Basildon, Thurrock and Southend).
These levels reinforce the assertion made earlier that around the periphery of
London the reality of discrete labour markets breaks down.

Of the other Million Cities, Newcastle is alone in having no MELAs sending more tha
10% of their workforces, while Birmingham has none above the 15% threshold. Glasgo
Manchester, Liverpool and Leeds are each the destination for one labour market abov
the 15% outflow level (these being Motherwell, Bury, Southport and Dewsbury respectively). The pattern of inter-MELA commuting to the conurbations of Lancashire
and West Yorkshire deserves special mention due to its complexity. Because
Liverpool, Manchester and Leeds are in such close proximity to each other, it is
not always apparent from Fig. 4.7 to which Million City each flow is destined. In
all of these areas except Warrington, however, the direction of flow can be determined by the single Million City which is contiguous with the origin MELA.
Warrington is contiguous with both Liverpool and Manchester and sends more than 5%
of its workforce to each of these cities (8.1% and 5.1% respectively).

Turning to the changes in these patterns between 1966 and 1971, Fig. 4.8 shows the
shifts in levels of commuting to the Million Cities for those labour markets which
exceeded the 5% threshold in 1971. The dominant trend is one of increasing levels
of interaction with the conurbations.

Commuting to London increased particularly strongly during this period with the
majority of labour markets experiencing positive shifts in excess of 1.5% of their
total workforces. It should be pointed out that this relative measure, based on
the total MELA workforce, understates the true extent of increases in commuting to
London, for population decentralisation from the London MELA has led to substantial
increases in the total workforces of many of the labour markets in the South-East.
Consequently the share of the workforces which travel to London have increased at a

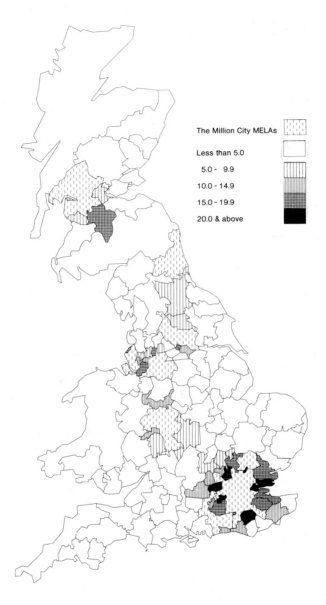

Fig. 4.7   Percentage of each MELA's resident employed population
commuting to the Million City MELAs, 1971.

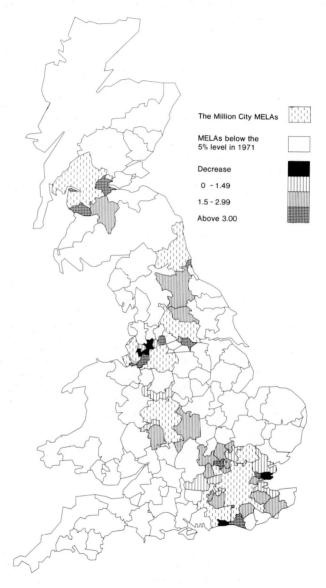

The Million City MELAs

MELAs below the
5% level in 1971

Decrease

0 - 1.49

1.5 - 2.99

Above 3.00

Fig. 4.8 Changes in the percentage of each MELAs resident
          employed population commuting to the Million City
          MELAs, 1966-1971.

time when the bases upon which these shares are calculated have themselves been expanding.   Tunbridge Wells recorded the largest shift (5.3%), with the share of its total workforce which worked in London increasing from 19.3% to 24.6% in 1971. At the other extreme, Southend and Worthing both recorded small negative shifts, although it should be stressed that these were relative changes and were not due to absolute contractions in the number of commuters.

Inter-MELA work travel to the Birmingham MELA increased on a similar scale to London, while the labour markets linked to Glasgow, Newcastle and Leeds recorded generally smaller increases (none of the shifts were above 3.0%).   In Lancashire, however, a clearly different pattern of change prevails.   There is no 'general trend' in the changes in commuting to the Liverpool and Manchester conurbations, for neighbouring labour markets had widely differing experiences.   In St. Helens, for example, the share of workforce which work in Liverpool declined from 14.4% to 13.6% (in this instance the decline was also absolute), while in neighbouring Wigan the share increased from 4.3% to 7.8%.   Similarly in the Manchester-linked labour markets, the flows from Leigh and Bolton declined relatively while Bury recorded a substantial increase.   The explanation for these variations may lie in the fact that the populations of Wigan and Bury grew rapidly between 1966 and 1971 due to net immigration from Liverpool and Manchester respectively, whereas St.Helens, Leigh and Bolton experienced much more sluggish growth.   The population growth in Wigan and Bury was not matched by employment growth, and consequently these labour markets became relatively more dependent upon the job concentrations in the adjoining conurbations.

This section has so far concerned itself only with flows between MELAs.   The importance of the Million Cities as destinations for inter-MELA journeys has been demonstrated, but the question of whether this is due simply to their overall size or whether they are qualitatively different from other labour markets (in terms of their range of job opportunities) has not yet been raised.   The Million Cities of course contain the major concentrations of the fastest growing occupational sector in the economy, offices.   To what extent then, is the scale of commuting to the Million Cities a reflection of long distance journeys to the central areas of the conurbations, where most of the office employment is located?   Although the Central Business Districts cannot be examined in this study (since the basic building block is the local authority), the importance of the Million City core areas in terms of the destinations of inter-MELA journeys can be analysed.

If the number of MELAs sending more than 5% of their workforces to each of the Million City cores in 1971 are considered the numbers involved and the levels of interaction are substantially lower than for the Million City MELAs as a whole. Only 28 labour markets have flows to the Million City cores in excess of 5% of their total workforces, whereas 48 surpassed this threshold when the destination was extended to encompass the whole of the Million City MELAs.

Core-destined commuting is very much a London phenomenon, for the capital has 20 labour markets above the 5% threshold and 9 above the 10% level (these being Chelmsford, Southend, Basildon, Thurrock, Tunbridge Wells, Guildford, Walton and Weybridge, Woking and Watford). Of the other Million City cores, only Manchester and Liverpool have more than one labour market above the 5% threshold.   With the exception of London then, it appears that much of the commuting to the Million Cities is relatively short distance interaction with their rings and outer rings, rather than with their central concentrations of employment.   In the country as a whole, 50.6% of all inter-MELA journeys are destined for core areas (Table 4.15); for journeys to London this rises to 62.1%, but for journeys to the rest of the Million Cities combined the proportion, 49.3%, is actually below the national average.

Even in the case of London, there are wide variations in the importance of its core

as a destination for journeys from the surrounding labour markets. Generally speaking, the labour markets to the east of London are more core-oriented than those to
the west. Southend and Slough, for example, both display strong commuting links
with the London MELA as a whole (accounting for 22.4% and 20.3% of their respective
workforces), but 90% of the flow from the former is destined for London's core compared with only 48% of the flow from the latter.

Flows to the Million Cities have been singled out for special attention because of
the concentration of high levels of commuting around their peripheries. It would
be quite wrong, however, to give the impression that inter-MELA work travel is destined only for these largest cities; indeed, 64.8% of total inter-MELA work travel
is destined for other MELAs.

Although 41 labour markets send 5,000 or more workers into the Million Cities, the
interaction is frequently reciprocal, with 27 labour markets receiving flows above
5,000 in return. When the threshold is raised to 10,000 journeys, however, the
pattern of exchange is more clearly in favour of the conurbations; 24 flows above
this level are destined for the Million Cities, while only 5 originate within them.
In addition to these return movements, there are 28 flows above 5,000 journeys which
are between non-Million City labour markets, though once again few of these exceed
the higher threshold. In total, then, there are more flows above the minimum threshold out of the Million Cities and between other labour markets than there are
into the Million Cities (55 and 41 respectively), but above the 10,000 journey level this pattern is reversed (12 and 24).

The movement streams which are not destined for the Million Cities are shown in
Fig. 4.9. Eleven labour markets receive more than 5,000 commuters from the London
MELA, while two of these (Watford and Slough) clearly provide major employment opportunities for the residents of north-west and west London in that they receive
inflows in excess of 15,000 journeys. A notable feature of commuting out of London
is the absence of return flows to the labour markets to the east of London, which
have been shown to be major origin areas for work trips into London's core.

Each of the other Million Cities also have return flows to labour markets around
their peripheries, and again these are almost invariably lower than the outflows.
The only exceptions are in Lancashire, where the outflows from Manchester to
Warrington and from Liverpool to St. Helens and Ellesmere Port are larger than the
respective inflows. Because of its tightly constrained labour market area (it
has no ring or outer ring), Ellesmere Port is a particularly pronounced case; the
journey into the Liverpool MELA is made by only 2,000 commuters, whereas 13,000
make the reverse trip; effectively, Ellesmere Port's labour market is the whole
of South Merseyside.

Of the work travel interactions which neither originate in nor are destined for the
Million Cities, the systems in South Wales and the East Midlands are the most important. Flows in excess of 10,000 journeys are received by Cardiff from Rhondda
and by Port Talbot from both Cardiff and Swansea; while in the second area the
interaction between Nottingham and Derby exceeds 10,000 trips in both directions.

The numbers of people involved in these movements generally increased between 1966
and 1971, though there are exceptions. The flows from London to Watford and Slough
both declined, for example, reflecting the fall in London's resident labour force.
The largest absolute increases were in the number of journeys to Ellesmere Port
from Chester and Liverpool, both of which expanded by more than 4,000 between 1966
and 1971.

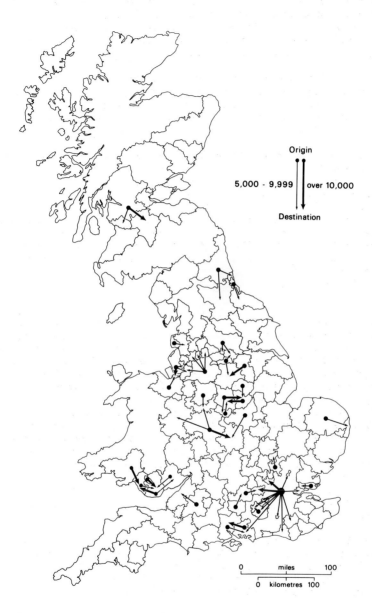

Fig. 4.9   Worktravel flows in excess of 5,000 journeys which are
destined for MELAs other than the Million Cities, 1971

4.3 CHARACTERISTICS OF WORKTRAVEL IN THE URBAN SYSTEM

4.3.1 Worktravel Patterns of Males and Females

The overall decline by 0.78 million in the total number of intra-MELA journeys
masks an important difference in the changing male and female labour market. The
loss is entirely due (Table 4.20a) to a decline in the male component (-794,000);
the number of females marginally increasing (18,000) during the same period.

At first sight, there also appears to be few similarities in the male and female
patterns of zonal change. Although both male and female employed population and
employment declined absolutely in core areas, the male rates of decline are double
the female rates. In the ring and outer ring areas, the differences are even more
pronounced. The growth in the total numbers of employed residents and jobs in ring
areas which was identified in section 4.1, is almost entirely a function of rapid
growth in the female component. Thus female employment increased by 133,000 (8.0%)
outweighing a decline by 28,000 (0.9%) in the number of male jobs within ring areas
A broadly similar pattern of change characterised the outer ring areas, although
here the decline in male employed population and employment were sufficiently large to exceed the female increases.

In spite of these differences, there are some similarities in the male and female
zonal changes. The nature of the relationship between employed population change
and employment change is constant for both males and females across all urban zones
For both sexes in core areas, the number of employed residents declined at a faster
rate than the number of jobs, while in the commuting hinterland zones the reverse
is found, with employed population faring better in relative terms than employment.
In the case of females in rings and outer rings, the rate of growth in employed
population exceeded that of employment; for males, employed population grew while
employment declined (ring areas), or declined at a slower rate than employment
(outer ring areas). The nature of this relationship is such that the job surpluses
of core areas, and the job deficits of ring and outer ring areas, increased for
both males and females. This is illustrated with a net-commuting ratio in Table
4.20b, all of the elements in the table diverged from 1.0 between 1966 and 1971,
indicating increasing net commuting imbalances. This table immediately suggests
another strong point of similarity; not only has the direction of change in zonal
interdependencies been the same for males and females, but the actual structure of
the interdependencies at a particular point in time is likewise very closely akin.
It is true that males display a stronger degree of relative zonal imbalance, but
the difference is slight although it has marginally increased in all zones. The
general similarity is perhaps surprising, for it is generally assumed that the trip
characteristics of men and women are substantially different, with women tending
(on average) to live much closer to their place of work. Women's employment is
generally poorly paid compared with male employment; consequently there is less
incentive to seek distant work, with the high travel costs which would be incurred.
Another factor is the much greater reliance on public transport which characterises
the female component of the labour force, for such a reliance obviously imposes
constraints upon the size of an individuals effective labour-market area.

This seems to be borne out by the pattern of commuting flows (Table 4.21), where
there is certainly some indirect evidence to suggest that journeys to work by females are shorter on average. Journeys within zones account for 85.2% of the female
intra-MELA total, but for only 79.1% of the male intra-MELA total. The bulk of
this difference in the intra-zonal proportion for males and females is due to the
within-core component, which in 1971 accounted for 52.5% of total female work travel, but for only 47.0% of the male total (Table 4.22). As a consequence 40.9% of
all within-core journeys are made by females, a higher proportion than any of the
other flow components (the second and third highest being the within-ring and

TABLE 4.20 Male and Female Origins and Destinations by Urban Zone for Journeys within MELAs, 1966-71

(a) Absolute totals and changes (thousands)

Urban Zone	1971 Males Origins	1971 Males Destinations	1971 Females Origins	1971 Females Destinations	Change 1966-1971 Males Origins	Change 1966-1971 Males Destinations	Change 1966-1971 Females Origins	Change 1966-1971 Females Destinations	Change 1966-1971 Totals Origins	Change 1966-1971 Totals Destinations
Core	6,626	7,858	4,363	5,037	-721 (-9.8%)	-615 (-7.8%)	-228 (-5.0%)	-154 (-3.0%)	-949 (7.9%)	-769 (-5.6%)
Ring	4,131	3,043	2,423	1,805	27 (0.7%)	-28 (-0.9%)	194 (8.7%)	133 (8.0%)	221 (3.5%)	105 (2.2%)
Outer Ring	2,064	1,920	1,143	1,087	-100 (-4.6%)	-151 (-7.3%)	50 (4.6%)	38 (3.6%)	-49 (-1.5%)	-113 (-3.6%)
Total	12,821	12,821	7,930	7,930	-794 (-5.8%)		18 (0.2%)		-777 (-3.6%)	

(b) Net commuting ratios and changes

Urban Zone	1971 Males $\frac{O}{D}$	1971 Females $\frac{O}{D}$	Change 1966-71 Males	Change 1966-71 Females
Core	0.843	0.866	-0.024	-0.018
Ring	1.358	1.342	0.022	0.009
Outer Ring	1.075	1.052	0.030	0.000

TABLE 4.21   Male and Female Absolute Flows Within and Between Urban Zones for Journeys Within MELAs, 1966-71 (thousands)

(a) Males

	C - C	C - R	C - OR	R - C	R - R	R - OR	OR - C	OR - R	OR - OR	Total
1966	6720	568	60	1607	2398	100	146	105	1912	13615
1971	6023	544	59	1656	2365	109	179	134	1752	12821
Absolute change	-697	-24	-1	49	-33	9	33	29	-160	-794
Percent change	-10.4	-4.2	-1.7	3.0	1.4	9.0	22.6	27.6	-8.4	-5.8

(b) Females

	C - C	C - R	C - OR	R - C	R - R	R - OR	OR - C	OR - R	OR - OR	Total
1966	4385	192	13	747	1442	40	59	38	996	7912
1971	4159	190	14	809	1569	46	70	46	1028	7930
Absolute change	-226	-2	1	62	127	6	11	8	32	18
Percent change	-5.2	-1.0	7.7	8.3	8.8	15.0	18.6	21.1	3.2	0.2

TABLE 4.22 Male and Female Percentage Flows Within and Between Urban Zones for Journeys Within MELAs, 1966-71

(a) Males

	C - C	C - R	C - OR	R - C	R - R	R - OR	OR - C	OR - R	OR - OR	Total
1966	49.35	4.16	0.43	11.80	17.61	0.73	1.07	0.77	14.04	100.0
1971	46.97	4.24	0.46	12.91	18.44	0.85	1.39	1.04	13.66	100.0
Change in share	-2.38	0.08	0.03	1.11	0.83	0.12	0.32	0.27	-0.38	-

(b) Females

	C - C	C - R	C - OR	R - C	R - R	R - OR	OR - C	OR - R	OR - OR	Total
1966	55.42	2.43	0.16	9.44	18.22	0.50	0.74	0.47	12.58	100.0
1971	42.45	2.40	0.17	10.19	19.78	0.58	0.87	0.57	12.96	100.0
Change in share	-2.97	-0.03	0.01	0.75	1.56	0.08	0.13	0.10	0.38	-

within-outer ring components respectively). Female work travel thus tends to be more strongly centralized in terms of both journey origins and destination than does the male pattern. In 1971, 55.0% of female trips originated in cores, and 63.5% were core-destined; the equivalent male figures were 51.7% and 61.3%. Nevertheless, these structures are clearly changing in the same way, with within-core journeys exhibiting rapid decline. The number of male journeys in this cat-egory fell by 697,000 (10.4%) between 1966 and 1971, and the number of female jou-rneys by 226,000 (5.2%).

The counterpart of the difference in degree of core centralization is that females exhibit weaker commuting dependencies between zones. For ring areas in 1971 for example, 40.1% of male residents commuted daily to the urban cores, compared with only 33.4% of female residents whereas the male ring/core dependency increased between 1966 and 1971, the female dependency fell back slightly. It should be st-ressed that these dependency measures are relative to the total number of ring residents, which in the case of females increased substantially. In absolute terms then, ring to core journeys by females increased by 62,000 (8.3%), while the male increase was only 49,000 (3.0%). The number of within-ring journeys made by fema-les increased by 127,000 (8.8%), and hence the ring to core share of total ring origins decreased slightly despite the impressive absolute increase.

The dependency of outer ring residents on the employment opportunities of the inner zones is also differentiated by sex, with males again showing the greater level of dependency. In 1971, 15.1% of male outer ring residents worked in their respective core or ring, with the equivalent female proportion being 10.1%. This dependency had become stronger between 1966 and 1971 for both sexes; the share of outer ring origins destined for cores and rings increased by 3.5% for male journeys and by 1.2% for females. The particularly marked change in the structure of male origins is due to an absolute decline by 160,000 (8.4%) in the number of within-outer ring journeys, coinciding with increases of 33,000 (22.6%) and 29,000 (27.6%) in outer ring to core and to ring journeys respectively. These latter rates of change are higher than the equivalent female rates, and are the only flow components in which this is the case. Consequently, these two components are alone in experiencing an increase in the male proportion of the total flow. By 1971, the male proportion of total journeys from outer rings to cores and to rings were 71.2% and 73.7% res-pectively, compared with the intra-MELA average of 61.8%.

To conclude then, a number of differences between male and female work travel pat-terns within the nation's MELAs have been identified. The main elements of this comparison are that the female pattern

   i)   is more dominated by the within-zone flow components, particularly
        the within-core; and

   ii) displays lower levels of dependency between the cores and their
        commuting hinterlands.

These features both suggest that journeys to work by females are on average shorter than those undertaken by males, but it is perhaps surprising that the differences are not more marked. The directions of changes between 1966 and 1971 have in many respects been similar, and the work travel structures are themselves closely akin.

Sex characteristics of inter-MELA worktravel.

At the inter-MELA scale in 1971, 78.0% of all journeys were made by males, compar-ed with only 61.8% of the intra-MELA total. Whereas the number of journeys by males within labour markets declined substantially between 1966 and 1971, male inter-MELA journeys increased by 237,000 (18.6%). Although the female increase was much smaller in absolute terms (75,000), this represents a 21.5% rate of change and consequently the female share of the total increased slightly.

The limiting effect of distance on female journeys to work is further reflected in the pattern of zonal origins and destinations. Journeys from the core of one MELA to the core of another, which can be categorised as relatively long-distance, have a high male proportion (82.1%), while journeys between outer rings, which are far more likely to be local trips, have the lowest (71.4%).

In section 4.2.2 it was suggested that the bulk of commuting into the Million City MELAs, London excepted, was of a relatively local nature in that it was mostly destined for their rings and outer rings rather than their cores. This is reflected in the male/female split of journeys into each of the Million Cities being generally close to the national inter-MELA average. Indeed, the female share of the total inflow to these cities is increasing in all cases with the exception of Glasgow. What is perhaps more surprising is that journeys into the Million City cores are not more strongly male-dominated, given the greater distances involved. Nationally, 79.2% of core-destined inter-MELA journeys are made by males, and only in London, Birmingham and Newcastle is this proportion exceeded. In London it is only slightly higher, (80.2%), and unlike the other Million Cities actually declined between 1966 and 1971 due to the particularly rapid growth in female journeys to the core. The explanation for this rapid growth, and indeed for the surprisingly high level of long-distance commuting by females into London, lies in a number of factors unique to the London region. Firstly, the capital has a large number of intermediate non-manual jobs which are predominantly filled by women; consequently the usual constraints upon women's labour market areas imposed by their generally low pay does not apply to the same extent. Secondly, London is served by an extensive commuter rail network which affords opportunities for overcoming another common constraint upon women's activity patterns, namely their generally low degree of car availability.

4.3.2 Worktravel Patterns by Socio-Economic Group

The trends in the socio-economic composition of total intra-MELA work travel are presented in Table 4.23 (see Appendix for details of SEGs used). A clear positive relationship exists between the characteristics of an SEG and its change performance; both of the non-manual groups grew absolutely and both of the manual groups declined. The rate of change in the professional and managerial group was particularly buoyant (increasing by 0.28 million, 12.3%), while at the other extreme the semi- and unskilled manual group shrank rapidly (by 0.74 million, 14.3%). As a result of these absolute changes, the share of total intra-MELA work journeys accounted for by manual workers fell by 3.8% to 49.5% in 1971. The non-manual groups expanded their share of the total to 41.8%, while the residual SEG remained with an unchanged share.

The strength of these trends is reflected in Table 4.24 which shows changes in the zonal location of origins and destinations for each of the five socio-economic groupings. The contrasts between the groups are remarkable. Professional and managerial group origins and destinations have grown substantially in all zones, whereas the semi- and unskilled manual group has universally declined. For all of the SEGs, ring areas have fared better than both cores and outer rings in terms of the rate of change in the number of journey origins and destinations. Non-manual journey destinations in ring areas increased by 247,000 (15.3%), with the professional and managerial group growing at the faster rate but the intermediate non-manual group growing by the larger amount. The total number of manual journey destinations fell by 148,000 (5.6%) in ring areas, but this was virtually all due to the semi- and unskilled manual group decline. In the previous section it was observed that the overall growth in employment in ring areas was in net terms very much confined to female jobs; results above indicate that it was even more

TABLE 4.23   The Socio-Economic Group Composition of Journeys
Within MELAs 1966-71 (thousands)

Socio-Economic Group	1971 Absolute	1971 Percentage	Change 1966-71 Absolute	Change 1966-71 Percentage	Rate of change 1966-71
Professional & Managerial	2569.3	12.38	281.5	1.75	12.31
Intermediate Non-Manual	6106.6	29.43	194.8	1.97	3.29
(Non Manual)	(8675.9)	(41.81)	(476.4)	(3.72)	(5.81)
Skilled Manual	5791.7	27.91	-455.3	-1.11	-7.29
Semi/Unskilled Manual	4480.2	21.59	-744.5	-2.68	-14.25
(Manual)	(10271.9)	(49.50)	(-1119.8)	(-3.79)	(-10.46)
Residual	1802.9	8.69	-52.4	0.07	-2.83
Total	20750.8	100.00	-776.3	-	-3.61

strongly confined to non-manual jobs (though the two are of course not unrelated).
In 1971, almost 50% of non-manual journeys to work within labour market areas were
by females, compared with only 38.2% of the intra-MELA total. The composition of
the two non-manual categories varies enormously however. Only 16.6% of professional and managerial group journeys are made by females, compared with 63.2% of
journeys by the intermediate non-manual group. Thus the positive association between females and non-manual jobs is largely due to the preponderance of females in
the intermediate non-manual SEG.

The changing nature of the home-workplace relationship with job surpluses growing
in core areas and deficits growing in rings and outer rings has been established
for an aggregate workforce. To what extent have differences existed between the
SEGs? In all cases (Table 4.25) the absolute job surpluses of core areas have increased and the SEG-specific net commuting ratios have dropped further below 1.0.
In ring areas though, the change is different: for both of the non-manual groups,
the rate of increase in ring employment is greater than the increase in employed
population; consequently, the net commuting ratios have moved closer to 1.0.
Thus in relative terms, the non-manual groups in ring areas had more balanced net
commuting structures at the end of the period than at the beginning (e.g. the ring
ratios of the professional and managerial group declined from 1.720 to 1.690).
In absolute terms, however, the net job deficit (and hence commuting outflows) of
ring areas increased substantially for both of the non-manual groups (e.g. the
professional and managerial group net deficit rose from 367,000 in 1966 to 423,000
in 1971). The apparent paradox is explained by the unbalanced structure of journey
origins and destinations; even though employment grew at a faster rate than the
resident employed population, it was from a much smaller base, and hence the number of journey origins increased by a larger absolute amount than did journey destinations. For the manual SEGs, the opposite trend is revealed. The skilled manual group remains virtually unchanged, but the number of semi- and unskilled manual
group origins and destinations declined markedly. Because the rate of decline of
destinations was greater than that of origins (-12.0% and -11.2%) the net commuting ratio increased slightly (from 1.119 to 1.129), indicating a small increase in
the relative dependency of semi- and unskilled manual ring residents on the other
zones. However, in absolute terms the decline in number of destinations was less
than in the number of origins, and consequently the net job deficit of this group
declined slightly (from 143,000 to 136,000).

TABLE 4.24   Changes in Socio-Economic Group Origins and Destinations by Urban Zone for Journeys Within MELAs, 1966-71

(a) Absolute (thousands)

Origins and Destinations by Urban Zone	Socio-Economic Groups	Professional & Managerial	Intermediate Non-Manual	Skilled Manual	Semi- and Unskilled	Residual	Total
Core	Origins	61.9	-68.4	-440.4	-457.9	-43.1	-948.3
	Destinations	129.8	19.5	-424.4	-454.1	-39.7	-768.9
Ring	Origins	161.3	207.7	-5.8	-150.5	8.2	220.8
	Destinations	105.7	141.5	-4.2	-144.0	6.5	105.4
Outer Ring	Origins	58.3	55.5	-8.7	-136.0	-17.9	-48.7
	Destinations	46.0	33.7	-26.6	-146.3	-19.6	-112.8
Total		281.5	194.8	-455.3	-744.5	-52.9	-776.3

(b) Percentage change

		Professional & Managerial	Intermediate Non-Manual	Skilled Manual	Semi- and Unskilled	Residual	Total
Core	Origins	5.8	-2.0	-12.6	-15.3	-4.4	-7.9
	Destinations	8.9	0.5	-11.0	-14.4	-3.9	-5.6
Ring	Origins	18.5	11.5	-0.3	-11.2	1.5	3.5
	Destinations	20.9	12.8	-0.3	-12.0	1.3	2.2
Outer Ring	Origins	17.3	8.0	-0.9	-15.3	-5.2	-1.5
	Destinations	14.6	5.3	-2.8	-17.0	-5.8	-3.6
Total		12.3	3.3	-7.3	-14.2	-2.9	-3.6

TABLE 4.25 Socio-Economic Group Net Commuting Balances by Urban Zone for Journeys Within MELAs, 1966 and 1971

(a) Absolute surplus or deficit (D-O) thousands.

Socio-Economic Groups		Professional & Managerial (D - O)	Intermediate Non-Manual (D - O)	Skilled Manual (D - O)	Semi- and Unskilled (D - O)	Residual (D - O)	Total (D - O)
Urban Zone							
Core	1966	388.8	753.6	368.3	167.8	47.7	1726.4
	1971	456.7	841.6	384.6	171.7	51.1	1905.9
Ring	1966	-367.3	-698.9	-337.4	-142.7	-44.0	-1590.4
	1971	-422.8	-765.1	-335.8	-136.2	-45.7	-1705.8
Outer Ring	1966	-21.5	-54.6	-30.9	-25.1	-3.7	-136.0
	1971	-33.8	-76.4	-48.8	-35.4	-5.4	-200.0

(b) Net commuting ratios (O/D)

Socio-Economic Groups		Professional & Managerial (O/D)	Intermediate Non-Manual (O/D)	Skilled Manual (O/D)	Semi- and Unskilled (O/D)	Residual (O/D)	Total (O/D)
Urban Zone							
Core	1966	0.735	0.819	0.904	0.947	0.953	0.874
	1971	0.714	0.799	0.888	0.937	0.948	0.852
Ring	1966	1.720	1.630	1.236	1.119	1.089	1.335
	1971	1.690	1.612	1.236	1.129	1.091	1.352
Outer Ring	1966	1.068	1.086	1.032	1.029	1.011	1.044
	1971	1.094	1.114	1.052	1.049	1.017	1.067

These differences between the various socio-economic groups nevertheless are insignificant compared to the differences in net commuting structures at a particular
point in time. It was mentioned above that the non-manual groups had unbalanced
commuting structures. The professional and managerial group in particular displays
zonal net commuting ratios indicative of extreme imbalance in the relationship between number of journey origins and destinations. In 1971, the core ratio for this
group was 0.714 and the ring ratio 1.690 (compared with the respective total intra-
MELA ratios of 0.852 and 1.352). In contrast, the semi- and unskilled manual group
displays a considerably more balanced commuting structure - its core and ring ratio
being 0.937 and 1.129 respectively. The two middle groups, the intermediate non-
manual and skilled manual, do not fall evenly along the continuum between these two
extremes. Thus the intermediate non-manual group has a structure less balanced,
but closely akin to, the professional and managerial group. Just as with changes,
therefore, it is clear that the net work travel structures of the non-manual and
manual SEGs are markedly different from one another, and the intra-MELA average is
quite misleading.

Clearly, the differences in net commuting structures and in the way these are changing over time are reflected in the gross patterns of commuting interaction. In
absolute terms, the differences between the non-manual and manual groups are pronounced. Each of the possible nine flow types have increased absolutely in both
of the non-manual groups, the one exception being the within-core flow of the intermediate non-manual group. The manual groups on the other hand are marked by
almost universal decline.

A summary of the flow patterns may be considered from each urban zone origin:-

i)   Journeys originating within cores - the within-core component has declined
absolutely for all SEGs except the professional and managerial group, in which it
increased by 50,000 journeys (5.0%). For all of the groups except the residual,
the within-core share of total core origins has declined (Table 4.26a). Reverse
commuting from cores to rings has thus increased relative to the total number of
core origins, though only in the two non-manual groups is this increase also an
absolute one. The structure of core origins in 1971 varies little between the
groups; the skilled manual group displays the strongest relative level of reverse
commuting (8.4% of core residents), while the lowest level is in the intermediate
non-manual group (5.5%).

ii)   Journeys originating within rings - in each of the SEGs, all three flow types
originating in ring areas increased their shares of the group intra-MELA total.
Predictably though, only in the non-manual groups are absolute increases recorded.
In both groups, the rate of increase in the within-ring component is larger than
in the ring to core component. Consequently the share of total ring origins destined for cores declined in the non-manual groups, even though the actual number
of ring to core journeys increased during the period by 145,000. Ring origins of
the skilled manual group remained virtually static in absolute terms, but the semi-
and unskilled manual group ring origins contracted substantially. Ring to core
journeys declined by 30,000 (8.4%) and the within-ring component declined by
116,000 (12.2%). Because of this pattern of decline, the proportion of semi- and
unskilled manual ring residents destined for cores actually increased (from 26.6%
in 1966 to 27.4% in 1971). There is evidence then to suggest that the differences
in ring-core dependency between non-manual and manual groups narrowed slightly
during the period. Nevertheless, the basic differences in patterns of commuting
remain substantial. In 1971, the proportion of ring residents commuting to cores
was 48.3% for the professional and managerial group and 47.1 for the intermediate
non-manual group. For the skilled manual and semi- and unskilled manual groups,
the respective dependency levels were 34.1% and 27.4% (Table 4.26b). Another way
of describing these differences is by the socio-economic composition of a particular

TABLE 4.26   Variations Between the Socio-Economic Groups in the Pattern of Outflows from each Urban Zone;   Intra-MELA Journeys, 1966-71

(a) Core Origins

| SEG | Urban Zone | | 1971 | | | Change 1966-71 | |
---	Core	Ring	Outer Ring	Core	Ring	Outer Ring
1	92.01	6.96	1.02	-0.70	+0.58	+0.12
2	93.99	5.48	0.51	-0.41	+0.36	+0.04
3	90.75	8.38	0.85	-0.88	+0.78	+0.10
4	92.50	6.97	0.52	-0.03	+0.05	-0.01
5	95.19	4.31	0.48	+0.19	-0.20	-
1 + 2	93.49	5.85	0.64	-0.51	+0.42	+0.07
3 + 4	91.55	7.74	0.70	-0.50	+0.45	+0.04

(b) Ring Origins

| SEG | Urban Zone | | 1971 | | | Change 1966-71 | |
---	Core	Ring	Outer Ring	Core	Ring	Outer Ring
1	48.32	49.57	2.10	-1.15	+0.84	+0.32
2	47.13	50.93	1.93	-1.09	+0.95	+0.14
3	34.12	62.93	2.94	-0.05	-0.22	+0.28
4	27.36	69.91	2.72	+0.81	-0.83	+0.02
5	15.82	82.34	1.82	-0.57	+0.21	+0.36
1 + 2	47.53	50.47	1.99	-1.10	+0.90	+0.19
3 + 4	31.39	65.75	2.85	+0.51	-0.68	+0.17

(c) Outer Ring Origins

| SEG | Urban Zone | | 1971 | | | Change 1966-71 | |
---	Core	Ring	Outer Ring	Core	Ring	Outer Ring
1	11.94	5.07	82.97	+1.67	+1.45	-3.12
2	12.26	5.46	82.26	+1.82	+1.02	-2.84
3	6.61	6.24	87.14	+0.98	+1.38	-2.35
4	4.63	6.16	89.19	+0.76	+1.29	-2.05
5	2.81	3.28	93.89	+0.49	+0.86	-1.36
1 + 2	12.15	5.33	82.51	+1.76	+1.15	-2.92
3 + 4	5.75	6.20	88.03	+0.94	+1.33	-2.29

flow type. Thus 58.8% of all ring to core journeys are made by non-manual workers, compared with only 41.8% of the intra-MELA total.

iii)   Journeys originating within outer rings – all outer ring origins increased absolutely except for the within-zone components of the manual groups (which together declined by 171,000). In the non-manual groups, the within-zone components increased more slowly than the flows destined for cores and rings, and consequently in each of the SEGs the within-zone share of total outer ring origins declined, with a range from -3.1% in the professional and managerial group to -2.1% in the semi- and unskilled manual (Table 4.26c).   Just as with ring origins, the non-manual groups display far greater relative levels of interaction with core areas than do the manual groups. The proportion of intermediate non-manual outer ring residents commuting to core areas is even higher than in the professional and managerial group (12.3% and 11.9% respectively), though both of these levels contrast markedly with the manual group dependencies (6.6% for the skilled manual and 4.6% for the semi- and unskilled manual). Notice though that this difference does not extend to journeys from outer rings to rings, for a higher proportion of manual residents commute to the rings than do non-manual workers.

So in summary the differences which were observed in male and female commuting patterns are not as pronounced as the differences between the various socio-economic groups. This is largely because the zonal locations of homes and work places vary quite markedly in the latter case. The professional and managerial group commuting pattern for example, is distinctive because its jobs are distributed between zones in similar proportions to employment as a whole, but its labour force is strongly decentralised. Consequently, within core journeys are relatively low is this group, and ring to core journeys are relatively high. The intermediate non-manual group is characterised by having the highest degree of job centralisation (68.5% of the groups' jobs are in core areas, compared with 62.1% of total jobs). Employed population is slightly more concentrated in core areas than average, and consequently both within-core and ring to core journeys are over-represented. The non-manual groups thus tend to have imbalanced zonal origin-destination structures in which employment is far more centralised than the employed population, resulting in substantial centripetal commuting flows (involving almost half of the total number of employed ring residents in these groups).

The manual SEGs have more balanced zonal commuting structures; 83.5% of journeys by manual workers are intra-zonal, compared to the respective non-manual figure of 76.9%. The semi- and unskilled manual group is characterised by having a high proportion of its total employed population located in cores, while the core proportion of its total employment is slightly lower than average. The low level of residential decentralisation which characterises the semi- and unskilled workers corresponds to that expected on the basis of the locational structure of the housing market. The owner-occupied sector, which is particularly dominant in ring areas, will have low levels of entry from this socio-economic group. One consequence of this structure is that inter-zonal commuting in general, and ring to core commuting in particular, is relatively unimportant for semi- and unskilled manual workers.

A sensible conclusion is that labour market areas defined for the population as a whole are unlikely to correspond closely to the labour market areas of individuals, or even of groups of individuals. These labour market areas vary in size, for different groups of people have differing abilities to overcome the effects of distance. These individuals have different mobility levels, which are related in turn to levels of car ownership and hence to social class.

Socio-economic group characteristics of inter-MELA worktravel.

At the inter-MELA scale the SEG composition of commuting flows is certainly

different. In 1971 50.2% of inter-MELA journeys were made by non-manual workers,
compared with 41.8% of the intra-MELA total. Variations are more apparent with th
professional and managerial group which is particularly over-represented in journe
between labour markets, accounting for 20.9% of the total but for only 12.4% of
journeys within labour markets, and with the semi- and unskilled manual SEG which
is under-represented in inter-MELA work travel. In other words, the intermediate
non-manual and skilled manual SEGs have the same proportion of inter-MELA journeys
as the total workforce (1 journey in 12), but for the professional and managerial
group this rises to 1 journey in 7 and for the semi- and unskilled manual workers
it falls to 1 in 16.

Just as there are differences between the social structure of inter-MELA and intra
MELA work travel in total, so inter-MELA journeys are themselves differentiated
according to the zone of destination. Journeys between labour markets which are
destined for core areas have above average professional and managerial components
(reaching a maximum of 27.4% of journeys from rings to cores), while the semi- and
unskilled manual group is over-represented in local journeys between outer rings.

Turning to journeys which are destined specifically for the Million City MELAs,
only for London is there clear evidence to suggest that the characteristics of
commuters into the conurbations differ from inter-MELA journeys in general. Thus
the non-manual SEG shares of the inflows to these other cities are similar to the
national inter-MELA total (50.2%), and indeed in Birmingham, Leeds and Glasgow are
actually below it. Commuting into London, however, is strongly biased towards the
non-manual groups, which together account for 68.5% of the total; the professiona
and managerial group alone accounts for almost one-third of the capital's inflow,
compared with only one-fifth nationally.

The same general pattern is repeated for journeys to Million City cores. Although
the non-manual proportion is higher in each case than for journeys into their MELA
the same is true for core-destined inter-MELA journeys in general (the proportion
being 59.3%). Only London is substantially above this level with 77.2% of its
core's inflow being in non-manual SEGs. It should be mentioned that this aggregat
level disguises a wide variation in the importance of the non-manual component in
the outflows of the labour markets around the periphery of London. This variation
has a marked spatial dimension, with the labour markets to the west displaying muc
higher levels than those to the east. In Guildford, the professional and managerial group alone accounts for a massive 60% of the outflow to London's core, while
at the other extreme only 10% of Thurrock's outflow is accounted for by this group

4.3.3 Modal Split Characteristics of Worktravel

Of all the characteristics of the journey to work which have been considered without a doubt the greatest change has occurred in the mode of travel. The five year
between 1966 and 1971 witnessed a massive shift from public to private motorised
transport. Of the two types of public transportation, train and bus, it is the
latter which has experienced the bulk of the decline. See Appendix for details
of the modal categories used in this study. It should though be mentioned that th
'bus' category includes private/works buses, but that in 1966 this sub-category
accounted for just 1.1% of the total intra-MELA worktravel, compared with the 30.3
share accounted for by public service buses. The number of journeys by train
(including tube) contracted by 73,000 (5.6%), a rate only slightly in excess of th
overall decline in intra-MELA worktravel (3.6%; Table 4.27). Consequently, the
share of the total accounted for by this mode was little changed (1966 6.0%,
1971 5.9%). In contrast, bus travel fell by 1.2 million journeys (17.7%), and its
share of the intra-MELA total slumped as a result from 31.4% in 1966 to 26.8% in
1971. The reverse side to this picture is that the number of journeys by car increased by 1.0 million (16.4%). The 'car' mode includes motor cycle journeys,
which in 1971 accounted for 1.5% of the intra-MELA total. Hence the term is used

TABLE 4.27   The Modal Split of Journeys within MELAs 1966-71
(thousands)

| Mode of Travel | 1971 | | Change 1966-71 | | |
	Absolute	Percent	Absolute	Change in Share	Rate of Change
Train	1,225.6	5.91	-73.2	-0.12	-5.64
Bus	5,568.3	26.83	-1,193.7	-4.58	-17.65
(public transport)	(6,794.0)	(32.74)	(-1,267.0)	(-4.70)	(-15.72)
Car	7,198.8	34.69	1,000.8	5.90	16.14
Walk/Cycle	5,407.0	26.06	-531.6	-1.52	-8.95
Other	1,350.8	6.51	21.5	0.33	1.62
Total	20,750.8	100.00	-776.34	-	-3.61

to cover private motorised transport in general. Between 1966 and 1971, the car mode's share of total intra-MELA worktravel increased by 5.9% (from 28.8% to 34.7%), and by the latter date the number of car journeys exceeded the total number of public transport journeys (7.2 million and 6.8 million respectively).

The other major mode of travel to work which will be considered here is walk/cycle, which declined by 532,000 journeys (9.0%). However, the two components of this group had different trends; the number of journeys on foot actually increased by 102,000 (2.3%), but pedal cycle journeys contracted by a massive 634,000 (41.2%). Consequently the latter's share of total intra-MELA worktravel fell from 7.2% to 4.4%, while journeys on foot increased their share from 20.4% to 21.7%. In view of the size of this component (in 1971 4.5 million journeys were on foot), it seems remarkable that so little attention has been given to the problems and requirements of pedestrian travel in urban areas. As Hillman and Whalley (1973) point out, planning measures which are designed to assist the flows of motorised traffic usually increase the lengths of journeys on foot. Since one in every five work journeys within labour market areas are made on foot, perhaps greater attention should be devoted to facilitating such movement.

Certain types of worktravel flow have distinctive modal split characteristics. The within-zone components have above average proportions of the walk/cycle and 'other, none, not stated' modes (which includes people working at home). Nevertheless, the modal split of within-core journeys is different from within-ring or within-outer ring journeys, due to the importance of public transportation in the former location. Thus in 1971, 40.8% of journeys within cores were by public transport and 31.3% were walk/cycle/other. For journeys within rings, however, the respective proportions were 17.4% and 46.9% (Table 4.28). The car proportion is less variable, though predictably it is lower for journeys within cores than within rings or outer rings; indeed, only 27.9% of within-core journeys are by car, lower than any other intra-MELA flow component.

Turning to the inter-zonal interactions, by 1971 the car mode had overtaken public transport in each of the flow types. Only in the reverse commuting flow from core to ring areas did car travel account for less than 50% of the total. Nevertheless, the highest public transport proportion (41.0%) is to be found in the largest inter-zonal component, the ring to core flow. Interestingly, whereas public transport can generally be regarded as synonomous with bus, the ring to core flow is characterised by having a high proportion of train journeys (14.6%, compared with 5.9% of

TABLE 4.28   The Modal Split of Flows Within and Between Urban Zones.   Intra-MELA Journeys, 1966 and 1971

1966

Mode / Urban Zone	C – C	C – R	C – OR	R – C	R – R	R – OR	OR – C	OR – R	OR – OR
Public Transport (1 + 2)	44.66	48.16	42.61	48.56	20.74	41.82	48.71	44.32	18.55
Car (3)	23.49	39.99	53.12	44.63	30.31	48.26	48.42	46.59	27.34
Walk/Cycle, Other (4 + 5)	31.80	11.80	4.22	6.76	48.89	9.87	2.82	9.04	54.05

1971

Mode / Urban Zone	C – C	C – R	C – OR	R – C	R – R	R – OR	OR – C	OR – R	OR – OR
Public Transport (1 + 2)	40.81	40.13	31.71	41.04	17.42	30.32	35.78	31.74	15.35
Car (3)	27.86	47.75	61.82	52.42	35.64	58.12	59.23	57.66	33.46
Walk/Cycle, Other (4 + 5)	31.28	12.09	6.41	6.50	46.89	11.50	4.95	10.53	51.15

total intra-MELA journeys). This reflects the importance of the suburban rail and tube networks in the London region, for train commuting is almost exclusively a London phenomena. For the same reason, the outer ring to core flow is also characterised by an above average proportion of train journeys (13.1% in 1971).

Changes between 1966 and 1971 in the modal split of the various flow components uniformly reflect the trend of public transport decline and the associated growth of car usage. This shift is greatest in relative terms in the small but fast-growing journey to work flows. The public transport share of the outer ring to core component, for example, fell from 48.7% in 1966 to 35.8% in 1971. The uniformity of the trend is even more striking in terms of absolute changes, for in each of the nine flow types public transport usage declined and car usage increased, regardless of whether that type of journey was expanding or contracting overall. At one extreme, for example, the number of persons commuting by public transport from outer ring to core areas fell by 11,000 (11.3%), while the number making this type of journey by car increased by 48,000 (47.8%). In just five years, then, the modal split of the outer ring to core flow was inverted; in 1966 there were more public transport than car journeys, but by 1971 there were 10 journeys by car for every 6 journeys by public transport.

At the other extreme attention should be placed on the massive decline in the number of journeys to work within core areas, a decline which characterises journeys by both males and females, and by all of the SEGs except for the professional and managerial group. Yet within-core journeys by car increased by 227,000 (8.7%) during this period, an absolute increase only slightly less than the increases in car commuting between rings and cores and within rings (241,000 and 238,000 respectively). Public transport usage, however, fell by 804,000 journeys (16.2%). Within urban core areas, not only is the total number of journeys declining as homes and jobs decentralise to the ring areas, but the share of this shrinking total captured by public transport is itself contracting rapidly. Within core areas in 1966 there were five journeys by car for every ten by public transport; by 1971 the proportion had risen to 7 for every 10.

There are substantial mode of travel to work differences between males and females. Males are characterised by high car usage, females by a high level of dependency on bus and walk modes. Thus in 1971 44.9% of male journeys were by car, compared with only 18.2% of female journeys. Meanwhile, 36.4% of female journeys were by bus and a further 30.0% were made on foot, the equivalent male proportions being 20.9% and 16.6%.

Despite these marked variations in mode of travel in 1971, the changes in the preceding five years were similar for males and females, these reflecting the national trend of a fall in public transport's share of the total and a commensurate increase in private motorised transport. This latter trend is particularly strong for female journeys to work, the car mode increasing its share of the total by 6.4% from a 1966 base of just 11.8% (the male increase in share being 6.2% on a much larger base of 38.7%). This represents a remarkable absolute increase in car usage by females. In 1966 the number of journeys to work by car within labour markets totalled 6.20 million, of which only 0.93 million were by females. Yet in the following five years, the number of car journeys by females increased by 0.51 million (55.2%), compared with the male increase of 0.49 million (9.2%). Thus the female component accounted for over half of the overall expansion in car commuting, even though its share of the mode total in 1966 was just 15%.

The basic differences between male and female mode of travel to work characteristics are repeated in each of the nine intra-MELA flow components (Fig. 4.10). In 1971 the car mode was more important than either public transport or walk/cycle/ other for all types of male journey to work except those within outer rings, where

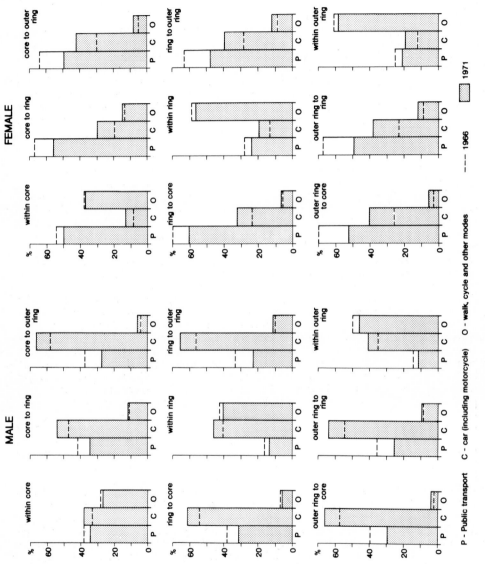

Fig. 4.10 Male and female modal split of flows within and between urban zones, intra-MELA journeys, 1966 and 1971.

the latter modal group was dominant.   Even for journeys within core areas then,
the car was more important than either of the other modal categories (accounting in
1971 for 38.1% of the male total), despite the fact that for within core journeys
as a whole, the car was a less important mode of travel than either public transport or walk/cycle/other (accounting for just 27.9% of the total). For journeys to
work between zones, the car mode completely dominates the male pattern with at
least 60% of the total in each flow type barring the reverse commutation from core
to ring areas.

For female journeys, public transport displaces car as the dominant mode in all of
the inter-zonal interactions, with the most unbalanced modal split being in the
ring to core flow. In 1971, 60.4% of such journeys were by public transport and
only 32.9% were by car, almost the exact inverse of the respective male proportions.
Of the intra-zonal interactions, it is clear that female journeys within rings and
outer rings tend to be highly localised, as over 55% of the total in each case is
in the non-motorised modal category, walk/cycle/other (with the 'other modes' category, mainly comprising those who work at home, accounting for about 10% of the
total in both rings and outer rings).

There are marked variations between SEGs in the modal split of journeys to work,
variations which centre primarily on the split between public and private motorised
transport, but which are also related to the relative importance of journeys on
foot and of people who work at home. Unlike many of the variations in patterns of
work travel, these modal variations cannot be satisfactorily explained in terms of
a simple non-manual/manual breakdown, due to the strong influence of male/female
differences on mode of travel.

This is best illustrated with reference to the two non-manual SEGs, the professional
and managerial group and the intermediate non-manual (Table 4.29). The only point
of similarity between them is the train mode proportion, which at approximately 10%
in each case is well above the manual group levels. The professional and managerial group has a particularly unbalanced split between the public and private forms
of motorised road transport; in 1971 only 8.6% of the group's journeys were by
bus while 58.0% were by car (compared with 26.8% and 34.7% for total intra-MELA
journeys). The intermediate non-manual group, on the other hand, displays above
average bus usage (30.7%) and average car usage (34.1%). Even in the non-motorised
modal categories, the differences between the two non-manual groups are substantial.
The former has a low walk/cycle proportion and a high 'other modes' proportion
(13.3% and 11.0% respectively), while the latter group has a slightly low walk/
cycle share and a low other modes (22.1% and 3.2%). On the basis of social class
alone the expectation is a higher emphasis on the car mode in the professional and
managerial group than in the intermediate non-manual group, but not that this difference would be so pronounced. The explanation would seem to lie in the sex composition of these non-manual socio-economic groups.

For this reason, the modal structure of the professional and managerial group is
much more akin to the skilled manual group than it is to the intermediate non-
manual group (the skilled manual workers are even more predominantly male; only
12.2% of the persons in this SEG are female). The skilled manual group thus has
below average bus usage and above average car usage (28.2% and 36.5% respectively).
It should nevertheless be noted that the deviation from the average modal split is
considerably less pronounced than in the professional and managerial group, even
though the male/female proportions are almost the same. Thus just as social class
differences cannot alone provide more than a partial explanation of variations in
the mode of worktravel within MELAs, neither too can a male/female division.

Modal structure of inter-MELA worktravel.

The most easily predictable difference between the modal structures of inter-MELA

TABLE 4.29 The Socio-Economic Group Modal Split of Journeys within MELAs; 1966-71

Mode of Travel / Socio-Economic Group	1971						Change 1966-71					
	Train	Bus	(Public Transport)	Car	Cycle	Other	Train	Bus	(Public Transport)	Car	Cycle	Other
Professional & Managerial	9.12	8.56	(17.68)	58.02	13.30	11.00	-0.42	-2.84	(-3.26)	3.48	0.65	-0.88
Intermediate Non-manual	9.89	30.73	(40.62)	34.09	22.13	3.15	-0.72	-5.52	(-6.24)	7.12	-1.25	0.37
Skilled Manual	3.36	24.41	(27.77)	42.34	22.41	7.48	-0.28	-3.81	(-4.09)	5.89	-3.50	1.70
Semi- and Unskilled Manual	2.97	35.78	(38.75)	21.03	36.68	3.54	0.00	-3.63	(-3.63)	4.05	-1.98	1.55
Residual	3.30	25.24	(28.54)	12.87	42.85	15.73	-0.55	-3.47	(-4.02)	2.58	8.82	-7.39
Total	5.91	26.83	(32.74)	34.69	26.06	6.51	-0.13	-4.56	(-4.69)	5.90	-1.54	0.33

journeys is that in the former, the non-motorised modes (walking and cycling) are
insignificant due to the greater distances involved. As for the relative importance of public transport, the distinction between bus and train travel has to be
emphasised because buses are generally used for short journeys they are under-
represented in inter-MELA work travel, accounting for only 18.3% of the total in
1971 compared with 26.8% of the intra-MELA total. The train mode, on the other
hand, is almost exclusively a London phenomenon and caters for very different types
of commuting, frequently over long distances. As such it is overrepresented in
inter-MELA worktravel (13.5%, compared with only 5.9% of intra-MELA journeys).
The effect of these two counteracting variations is that the combined public transport proportion is almost identical for both intra- and inter-MELA journeys. The
decline in public transport usage between 1966 and 1971, however, is much stronger
in the inter-MELA case, its share of the total falling by 10.4%. Car travel substantially increased its share of this total, and by 1971 accounted for 58.3% of
inter-MELA work travel (compared with only 32.7% of the intra-MELA total).

The influence of London on the national inter-MELA figures is reflected in the
modal split of the various zonal origin/destination combinations. Journeys destined for cores, for example, display above average train usage, reaching a maximum
of 30.0% for journeys from one core to another. As a consequence, this essentially
long distance movement has the lowest bus and car proportion of the inter-MELA flow
types (13.4% and 49.3% respectively). It should be stressed, however, that in all
of these flow types, the car is more important than the combined public transport
modes and would completely dominate the overall structure of work travel between
labour markets were it not for the enormous level of commuting into London's core
area (a quarter of a million journeys).

Even journeys into the other Million City MELAs, which also have levels of public
transport provision well above the average, are dominated by the car mode; only
in Glasgow does public transport account for a larger proportion of the total inflow than private motorised transport, and this is due to the importance of the
train mode rather than bus. At the other extreme, the modal split of the inflow
to the Birmingham labour market, which of the Million Cities has made the strongest post-war effort to plan for the motor-car, is four car journeys for every one
by public transport.

The degree to which different types of work journey are linked to different modes
of travel is amply demonstrated by London. Long distance commuting into its core
area is dominated by the train mode, for bus usage is almost non-existent and car
usage is only half of the national inter-MELA level (the shares accounted for by
these three modes being 63.8%, 3.1%, and 28.9% respectively). For more local
journeys into London's ring this structure is completely reversed; train usage is
insignificant (8.5%), bus usage is more important than for core-destined journeys,
though it is still a minor component of the total (11.4%), while the car takes
over as the major mode of travel (72.6%).

Clearly, then, the interrelated trends of more dispersed patterns of employment and
increasing car ownership are going to decrease even further the importance of public transport's contribution to inter-MELA work travel. Even in London, despite
the expansion of office employment in its central area and a rail commutation network ideally suited to moving large numbers of people into this centre, car commuting to the core increased at a faster absolute rate than did rail commuting
(31.0% and 21.9% respectively). In other parts of the country, of course, the
changes in mode of travel have been much more clear-cut, with the bus mode becoming
in just five years of minor importance in inter-MELA commuting, the result of the
rapid increases in non-local travel and in car usage with which such types of
movement are inextricably linked.

Spatial variations in mode of worktravel

The conurbations and the other industrial centres in the main axis of urban Britain
are characterised by high levels of public transport usage, particularly so the
Million Cities group which has an average public transport share of 42.4%. The
other industrial centres (Major and Secondary) and the Lancashire/Yorkshire group
have levels of public transport usage of approximately 30%, while the remaining
groups all have levels below 20% (with the lowest being 13.7% in the Southern Freestanding towns). It might be expected that levels of car usage would simply be the
inverse of those of public transport, but the situation is not this simple. While
it is true that the established industrial towns display relatively low car mode
proportions, they also tend to display low proportion of 'walk, cycle and other'.
Variations in the importance of the non-motorised component of intra-MELA work
travel are pronounced, with a range from just 27.1% in the Million Cities to 44.0%
in the Southern Freestanding towns (compared with the range in the car component's
share from 27.7% in the Lancashire/Yorkshire group to 42.6% in the New Towns).

The modal structure of the New Towns group is interesting for it has been suggested
that the physical segregation of employment and residential areas, which is one of
the characteristics of post-war New Town planning, leads to a high dependence on
the private automobile and constrains the possibilities for walking to work (Thomas
and Potter, 1977). It is certainly true that the New Town group exhibits a lower
walk, cycle and other proportion than might be expected; at 37.9% it is much higher than in the major cities, but it is lower than in the other comparable labour
market groups, such as the London Peripheral and Southern Freestanding towns (42.5%
and 44.0% respectively). However, the bulk of the difference is produced by the
other modes component (mainly people working at home) being lower in the New Towns
than in the comparison group, rather than variations in the walk proportion itself.

Changes in the mode of travel to work reflect the strength of national trends, for
in each of the groups public transport and walk/cycle/other journeys have contracted in relative importance while car journeys have increased. The largest declines
in public transport's share took place in the groups with high public transport
usage (the Million Cities, Major Industrial, Secondary Industrial and Lancashire/
Yorkshire towns). Each of these groups recorded declines in excess of 5.0% in the
public transport share, while at the other extreme the New Town group decline was
only 1.5%. The positive shift in the car component was substantial in all cases,
again with the New Towns recording the smallest change (4.4%). Declines in the
walk/cycle/other component were lowest in the conurbation and industrial cities,
in which the component was already of below average importance.

Three main features can be identified in mode of travel proportion in 1971 and in
the changes in these proportions in the preceeding five years:

(a) The older-established industrial urban areas are distinctly different from
     the other groups, particularly in their emphasis on public transportation.

(b) Groups with high public transport shares tend to have relatively low depend-
     encies on non-motorised modes of travel (walk, cycle and other).

(c) There is an inverse relationship between the level of each mode and the sub-
     sequent change in that level (e.g. groups with the highest levels of bus usage
     had the largest declines in this component, and groups with the lowest car
     usage had the largest increases). In other words, there was a tendency for
     variations between groups to converge in the 1966-71 period.

These features can be examined in more detail at the scale of individual labour
market areas.

(i) Public Transport - The importance of public transport usage for intra-MELA journeys to work is clearly differentiated in space and by size of labour market. High levels of usage are associated with the largest cities; thus five of the seven Million Cities are in the top ten while only Birmingham is not in the top 20. The highest level of all is found in Glasgow (52.3%), this being the only labour market in which more than half of total journeys to work are by public transport. Size of city is not the only relevant criteria however, for as Fig. 4.11 shows there are regional effects operating. Of the forty MELAs with the highest public transport percentages, only two (London and Brighton) are to be found south of a line running from the Wash to the Severn estuary. More specifically, it is the cities in depressed regions which exhibit the highest dependence on public trans-portation especially including much of Lancashire and Yorkshire, the North East, and the central lowlands of Scotland.

The MELAs with the lowest levels of public transport usage are also clearly differ-entiated; they are invariably freestanding towns with large rural hinterlands, such as Kings Lynn, Taunton and Hereford (each of which have less than 10% of their totals journeying to work by this mode).

Changes in the level of public transport usage between 1966 and 1971 are inversely related to the 1966 level. The correlation coefficient between the percentage of intra-MELA journeys which were public transport in 1966 and the subsequent change in that percentage is -0.72. This suggests that labour markets with high levels of usage at the beginning of the period were likely to experience the largest de-clines. However, the areas with the largest negative shifts in public transport's share were not those with the largest shares at the end of the period. The top ten in 1971 is dominated by the Million Cities, but none of these cities feature in the change ranking. Rather than the size of labour market, regional factors seem the most identifiable characteristic of those labour markets recording the largest negative shifts in the public transport percentage; of the ten largest declines, five are from Scotland, (with the worst being -11.3% in Motherwell) and three from Wales.

(ii) Car - In many respects of course the pattern of car usage is the reverse of public transport's (the correlation between the two percentages in 1971 was -0.77). Thus high car usage is confined to the southern half of the country. Fig. 4.12 shows that the top twenty labour markets (represented by the darkest shading) fall into two distinct clusters. Labour markets in East Anglia have uniformly high levels of car usage, and this belt extends down as far as Stevenage on the northern edge of the London labour market area. The second cluster occurs to the west of London and includes a wide variety of labour market types, ranging from big cities such as Bristol (48.0%) and Southampton, through free-standing rural towns such as Yeovil and Gloucester, to the expanding town of High Wycombe on the western fringe of London.

The towns with the lowest car travel percentages are far less diverse, being mainly small and medium-sized towns adjacent to the conurbation of northern England and Scotland. In particular, an almost unbroken chain of these labour markets extends from the east of Liverpool across the northern edge of Manchester to West Yorkshire, and includes Leigh, St. Helens, Bolton, Dewsbury and Rochdale. The lowest car travel percentages though are found in Sunderland (22.9%) and Greenock (22.8%), which had the second and third highest public transport shares respectively. In view of the strong negative relationship between public transport and car percent-ages, it might have been expected that the Million Cities, which have some of the highest levels of public transport usage, would have low levels of car travel. However, the only Million City in the bottom twenty labour markets is Glasgow, which at 24.3% is ranked 122 in terms of the car mode's share of total intra-MELA work travel. The Million Cities' levels of car usage would appear to reflect their

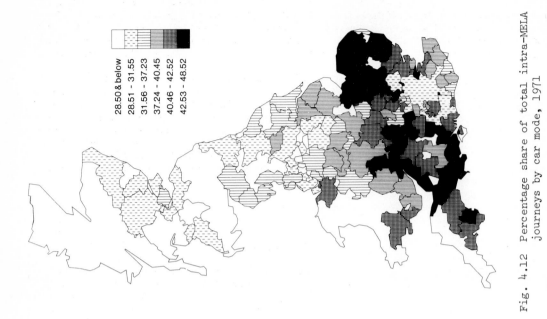

Fig. 4.12 Percentage share of total intra-MELA
journeys by car mode, 1971

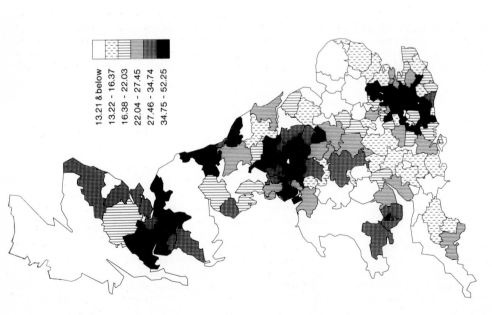

Fig. 4.11 Percentage share of total intra-MELA
journeys by public transport, 1971

regional locations rather than any factor particular to big cities; thus Liverpool
and Manchester have low levels of car usage in accordance with the labour markets
surrounding them, while Birmingham has almost 38.0% of its journeys made by this
mode, reflecting the more prosperous situation of the West Midlands. The exception
to the rule is London, which contrasts sharply with the rest of the region, having
the lowest level of car commuting in the southern half of the country (29.9%).

Although there is an inverse relationship between the 1966 level of car usage and
the 1966-71 change, it is considerably weaker than for public transport (the correlation coefficient being -0.27, compared with -0.72). Consequently the changes
in car usage are more difficult to interpret. The ten largest increases, for example, include four labour markets in Scotland which all had low levels at the beginning of the period (in Kilmarnock, the car mode's share of total work travel increased by 11.1% from a 1966 base of just 20.4%), and yet also includes labour
markets such as Kings Lynn and Norwich which even in 1966 had levels of car usage
well above the average.

In spite of the lack of a clear inverse relationship between the 1966 percentage
and the subsequent change, some specifically regional features are of interest.
Firstly, London and many of its immediately surrounding labour markets had low
levels of increase in the importance of the car mode. London itself is ranked 120
with an increase of 3.2% while the New Towns of Harlow, Crawley and Basildon record
even lower levels. And yet in 1966 London had a level of car usage well below average, while the aforementioned New Towns had amongst the highest levels in the
country. Secondly, there is a marked contrast between labour markets in the North
West region and in the Yorkshire and Humberside region. At the beginning of the
period, both regions had consistently low levels of car travel; in the following
five years, however, the labour markets in the North West recorded above average
increases, while those in Yorkshire experienced uniformly below average increases.
These regional variations in changes in car usage will be returned to later when
household car ownership changes are considered.

(iii) <u>Walk, cycle and other modes</u> - The non-motorised modes of transport have very
different locational characteristics. They do have one feature in common, however,
in that they are all relatively unimportant modes of travel in the conurbations and
largest cities. This is of course hardly surprising, for although major urban areas
have dense concentrations of population and employment, the spatial separation of
homes and work places tends to be much greater.

4.3.4 <u>Household Car Ownership and Worktravel</u>

The scale of the shift from public to private motorised transport in the second
half of the 1960s is made far more comprehensible when placed in the context of the
rapid increase in car ownership. The number of intra-MELA journeys made by persons
in non-car owning households fell by 2.10 million (21.1%), while the number in
households owning one or more cars grew by 1.45 million (13.1%); Table 4.30.
Within the car-owning category, it is the number of persons within households owning two or more cars that has displayed the most rapid rate of change, increasing
by 0.69 million (37.1%). The number of persons in one-car households increased
by a slightly larger amount but at a much slower rate (0.75 million, 8.2%). The
result of these changes is that by 1971, 60.3% of people making intra-MELA journeys
to work were members of households owning at least one car, compared with only
51.4% five years previously. The share of the total accounted for by persons in
households owning at least two cars increased from 8.7% to 12.3%.

As would be expected, a cross tabulation between socio-economic groupings and
categories of household car ownership reveals a strong association (Table 4.31).
It was noted previously that variations in mode of travel reflected both social

TABLE 4.30　　Number of Persons in Household Car Ownership
Categories.　Intra-MELA Journeys, 1966-71 (thousands).

| Household Car Ownership | 1971 | | Change 1966-71 | | |
	Absolute	Percent	Absolute	Percent	Percent rate of change
Non-car owning	7,828.8	37.7	-2,098.9	-8.4	-21.1
1 car	9,960.1	48.0	752.8	5.2	8.1
2 or more cars	2,556.5	12.3	692.1	3.6	37.1
1 or more cars	12,516.7	60.3	1,445.0	8.9	13.0
Non-private persons*	405.2	2.0	-122.4	-0.5	-23.2
Total	20,750.8	100.0	-776.3	-	-3.6

(* non-private persons refers to employed people who are not members of private
households, living in institutions, barracks, etc.)

class and sex characteristics.　In the case of car ownership variations, however,
sex differentiation does not appear important because of course it refers to households, not persons.　Consequently the simple non-manual/manual distinction is a
useful way of categorising variations in car ownership levels.　In 1971, 72.7% of
(intra-MELA) non-manual workers were in households owning one or more cars;　for
manual workers the car-owning proportion was only 53.5%.　Unlike variations in
patterns of work travel, however, the intermediate non-manual group and the skilled
manual group have more in common with each other than with the professional and
managerial and semi- and unskilled manual groups respectively.　Thus the two middle
groups have 67.1% and 62.0% of their respective totals in households owning one or
more cars, compared with 86.3% of the professional and managerial group and only
42.5% of the semi- and unskilled manual group.　In other words, a professional or
managerial worker is twice as likely to be a member of a car-owning household than
is a semi- or unskilled manual worker.　Of even greater contrast is that a worker
in the former group is five times more likely to be a member of a household owning
two or more cars;　in 1971, 29.3% of the professional and managerial group were in
this category, compared with only 5.6% of the semi- and unskilled manual group.

In spite of these substantial differences between SEGs in levels of car ownership
in 1971, the changes which took place in the preceding five years were similar.
Indeed, the shift to car ownership was so all pervasive that even in the semi- and
unskilled manual group (which declined overall by 0.74 million, 14.3%) there was
an absolute increase in journeys by persons in car owning households (by 73 thous-
and, 4.0%).　In terms of changes in share of each SEGs total, there is an interesting contrast between households owning one car and two or more cars.　There is an
inverse relationship between the 1966 level of one-car ownership and the subsequent
change in that level, whereas a positive relationship exists for two or more car
ownership.　Thus although the lowest level of one-car ownership in 1966 was recorded by the semi- and unskilled manual group, this SEG recorded the largest increase
in share between 1966 and 1971 (from 30.9% to 36.9%).　In contrast, the professional
and managerial group actually récorded a small drop in the share of its total persons which were in one-car owning households (from 58.5% to 57.0%).　In the case of
two or more car ownership, however, the semi- and unskilled manual group displays
both the lowest level in 1966 and the smallest increase in share (from 4.1% to
5.6%), while the professional and managerial group has the highest initial level
and the largest increase in share (from 22.7% to 29.3%).

TABLE 4.31 The Percentage of Persons in each Socio-Economic Group within Household Car Ownership Categories. Intra-MELA Journeys, 1966-71

(a) Percentages 1971

Household Car Ownership	Socio-Economic Group						
	Professional & Managerial	Inter. Non-Man	Skilled Manual	Semi & Unskilled Manual	Residual	Services*	Total
Non-car owning	13.75	32.94	37.98	57.49	38.21	(49.28)	37.73
1 car	56.96	53.73	51.28	36.91	32.84	(42.36)	48.00
2 or more cars	29.30	13.33	10.74	5.61	6.47	(8.35)	12.32
1 or more cars	(86.25)	(67.06)	(62.02)	(42.51)	(39.32)	(50.72)	(60.32)
Non-private persons	---	---	---	---	22.47	---	1.95
Total	100.00	100.00	100.00	100.00	100.00	(100.00)	100.00

(b) Changes in percentages 1966-71

Household Car Ownership	Socio-Economic Group						
	Professional & Managerial	Inter. Non-Man	Skilled Manual	Semi & Unskilled Manual	Residual	Services*	Total
Non-car owning	-5.03	-8.76	-8.61	-7.44	-1.07	(-5.61)	-8.38
1 car	-1.53	4.77	5.63	5.97	5.55	(4.23)	5.23
2 or more cars	6.57	3.99	2.99	1.48	1.47	(1.37)	3.66
1 or more cars	(5.03)	(8.76)	(8.61)	(7.44)	(7.03)	(5.61)	(8.89)
Non-private persons	---	---	---	---	-5.96	---	-0.50

(* services refers to the residual groups minus non-private persons)

Having considered the relationship between social class and household car ownership,
it remains to establish the differences between the mode of travel to work structures of those in different car ownership categories. As expected the aggregate
modal split of people in non-car owning households is completely different from
that of car owning households, due to the enforced dependence of the former on
public transport and on their own feet. In 1971, 52.8% of the non-car owning
group travelled to work by public transport, compared with 20.8% of the car owning
group (the train percentage is similar: it is bus usage which varies). The walk/
cycle proportion of the total is 35.7% for the former group and 19.3% for the
latter (Table 4.32). There are also differences between the car owning categories,
though of course they are far less marked than those above; workers in households
owning two or more cars have lower public transport and walk/cycle proportions than
those in one-car households, and a correspondingly higher car proportion (64.2%,
compared with 49.9%).

Changes in these proportions between 1966 and 1971 are interesting in that they
indicate the changing propensity to use a particular mode, with level of car ownership held constant. In the car owning categories, the propensity to travel to
work by car has increased (from 46.1% to 49.9% in the one-car owning category, and
from 58.8% to 64.2% in the two or more car category). Thus increases in car commuting can be attributed to the product of two components of change: firstly, a
shift towards higher levels of car ownership, which means that a car is available
to a higher proportion of the population; and secondly, an increase in car usage
among those with similar levels of car availability. On apportioning the total increase in car commuting to each of these components, the increase in levels of car
ownership accounts for a greater proportion of the total than does the increase in
propensity for usage (57.1% and 42.9% respectively).

Spatial variations in household car ownership

It is hardly surprising that those labour market groups with low levels of household car ownership are those with low levels of car travel and high levels of public transport usage (the Million Cities, Major Industrial, Secondary Industrial,
and Lancashire/Yorkshire towns). Both of the car owning categories have similar
distribution between the groups, though there are certain variations. The lowest
percentage of total journeys which are made by people in households owning one car
occurs in the Million Cities (43.9%), while this category accounts for 58.5% of
total journeys in the New Towns. The Million Cities fare comparatively better in
terms of the percentage in two-or-more car-owning households, with 10.1% of the
total in this category compared with only 8.0% in the Lancashire/Yorkshire towns.
The New Towns fare comparatively worse, having only the fourth highest two-car
percentage behind the London Peripheral group (17.9%) and the Southern Freestanding
and Resort/Retirement Area groups.

Changes in these levels of household car ownership between 1966 and 1971 display
little variation between the labour market groups, with both of the car owning
categories increasing their share of each group's total at the expense of the non-
car owning category. What little variation exists is concentrated in the change
in the proportion in households owning one car, which ranged from a 3.4% increase
in the New Town group to a 6.1% increase in the Peripheral Freestanding labour
markets. The range of variation in the two-or-more car increase was from 3.0% in
the Secondary Industrial group to 4.5% in the Southern Freestanding towns. In
this latter group, the two-or-more car proportion increased by a larger percentage
shift than did the one-car proportion, even though the former accounted for a much
smaller proportion of the total in 1966 (12.4%, compared with the one-car share of
50.1%). Indeed, relative to the size of the respective shares at the beginning of
the period, the increase in the two-or-more car component was much greater than the
one-car in all of the labour market groups.

TABLE 4.32   The Household Car Ownership Modal Split of
Journeys within MELAs: 1966-71.

(a) Percentages 1971

Modes of Travel

Household Car Ownership	Train	Bus	(Public Transport)	Car	Walk & Cycle	Other	Total
Non-car owning	7.40	45.36	(52.76)	6.80	35.72	4.72	100
1 car	5.16	17.70	(22.86)	49.90	21.09	6.16	100
2 or more cars	4.52	8.19	(12.71)	64.24	12.50	10.56	100
1 or more cars	5.03	15.75	(20.78)	52.83	19.33	7.06	100
Non-private persons	4.10	11.21	(15.31)	13.33	47.12	24.23	100

(b) Changes in percentages, 1966-71

Non-car owning	0.38	-0.64	-0.25	1.26	-0.20	1.70	
1 car	-0.08	-3.17	-3.23	3.84	-0.89	0.30	
2 or more cars	-0.66	-2.53	-3.19	5.47	-1.19	-1.07	
1 or more cars	-0.18	-3.41	-3.54	4.63	-1.27	0.22	
Non-private persons	0.77	-2.81	-3.58	1.71	29.42	-27.56	

Turning to the level of individual labour markets, Fig. 4.13 shows the 1971 pattern of variation in the percentage of journeys within each area made by persons in one-car owning households. The high values are concentrated in the southern half of the country, particularly in East Anglia, the South West, and in the small labour markets around the north-eastern edge of London. All of the New Towns are highly ranked, with Crawley recording the highest level in the country (60.6%) and Basildon and Harlow also in the top ten. The lowest values are clustered in Yorkshire, the North East and Scotland, with Greenock coming bottom with just 35.2%. Three of the Million Cities are to be found in the bottom ten (Glasgow, Newcastle and Liverpool), while London (47.8%) has the lowest one-car percentage in the southern half of the country.

The pattern of variation in the two-or-more car owning percentage (Fig. 4.14), is very similar to the one-car pattern, the main difference being in the labour markets around the periphery of London. The New Towns and the other towns to the north-east of London do not have particularly high levels of two-or-more car ownership, while the labour markets around the western and south-western periphery of London emerge with high levels. High Wycombe is ranked first in the country (22.2%), and Slough, Walton and Weybridge, Woking and Guildford are also in the top ten. The lowest levels of two-car ownership are found in the same areas in which one-car ownership was lowest, the depressed regions of northern England and Scotland, with Sunderland ranked 126 with just 5.0% of its intra-MELA journeys being made by people in this car-ownership category. There is one further difference between the two distributions, however, and that concerns the London labour market. The Million Cities in general tend to fare slightly better in terms of the two-car owning percentage than the one-car, but in London this is particularly apparent. Some 14.1%

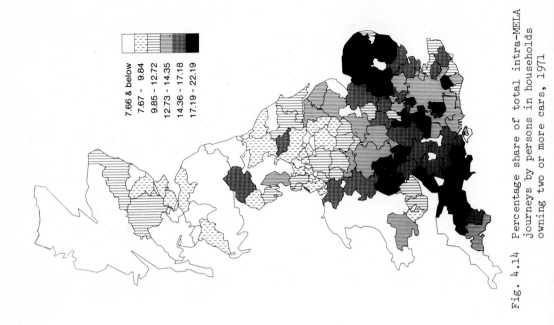

Fig. 4.14 Percentage share of total intra-MELA
journeys by persons in households
owning two or more cars, 1971

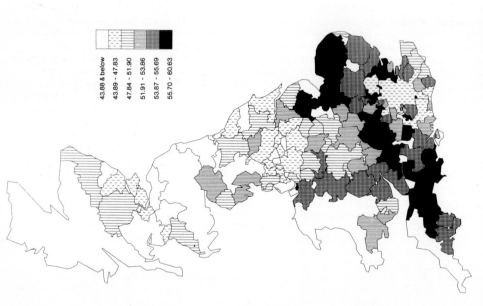

Fig. 4.13 Percentage share of total intra-MELA
journeys by persons in households
owning one car, 1971

of journeys in London are made by persons in this category, which ranks fifty-fourth out of the total of 126 labour markets; in terms of the percentage in one-car owning households, however, London is ranked 94th.

The pattern of change in the one-car and two-or-more car components is very different. Although there existed a strong positive relationship between the two percentages in 1971, changes in these two percentages during the preceeding five-year period were actually negatively related, the labour markets with the largest increases in the one-car percentage tended to have the smallest increases in the two-or-more car percentage. Rhondda, for example, had low levels of car ownership (both components) at the beginning of the period, yet during the next five years the one-car proportion of the total increased by a greater amount than in any other labour market (11.1%), while the increase in the two-or-more car proportion was the fifth lowest (1.8%). At the other extreme, the town of High Wycombe had initially high levels of car ownership, with the subsequent increase in the one-car component being the third lowest in the country (0.9%), and the increase in the two-or-more car being the highest (8.8%).

It has then been demonstrated that the relationship between the level of car ownership at a particular point in time and the change in that level is a complex one, due to the quite different pattern of change in the one-car and two-or-more car components. Although the highest levels in both components in 1971 were heavily concentrated in the southern half of the country, in the preceeding five-year period the largest increases in the one-car component occurred in the north while the two-car component increases were concentrated predominantly in southern labour markets.

In conclusion it would seem that the proportion of the employed population journeying to work by car is likely to continue increasing. As indicated car usage is much dependent on car ownership, and in spite of the effects of the energy crisis levels of car ownership are likely to continue increasing for many years to come. The Department of the Environment's revised estimates suggest that the saturation level of 0.45 cars per person will not be reached until 2000-2010. (Department of the Environment,1976). Increasing car availability does not, however, inevitably mean that car usage also increases, only that choice of mode of travel is possible. The car has a number of attractions compared with public transport, such as convenience and comfort - nevertheless, the modal choice which car owners can exercise becomes almost a necessity to use the car, for public transport is caught in a vicious circle of decline, in which falling patronage leads to service cuts and to fares increases, which feed back into a further decline in patronage by those who can exercise modal choice. The sizeable minority of the population which remain in non-car owning households bear the brunt of these changes. They are not able to exercise any other modal choice but public transport or walking; the first of these modes is beset by problems requiring huge subsidies just to arrest its decline, while the potential of walking as a journey to work mode is not helped by the drop in accessibility levels due to the general deconcentration of population and economic activity within urban areas.

PART FIVE

British Urban Systems Policy

5.1 BRITISH CITIES : CONCLUSIONS

Before considering some of the policy issues pertinent to the future development of the British urban system this last part of the study might first usefully review the empirical conclusions so far. It has already been explained that this research set its task to describe the principal patterns of socio-economic change using a funct-ional urban systems framework and, further, to illustrate the important features of migration and worktravel operating within such a framework. All this was set with-in a well surveyed context of total population and employment change, and net mig-ration and natural change available as <u>British Cities : urban population and emp-loyment trends</u> (Department of the Environment, 1976). A summary of this context together with summaries of similar contexts for the United States and Europe formed Part One of this study.

Population and employment in British cities

Part Two isolated some detailed aspects of trends in population and employment in the British urban system for further description. Beginning with employment, trends for males and females and trends for various occupational and industrial groups were all thought to add further perspective to the aggregate picture. For population changing socio-economic structure, age structure and birthplace structure all seemed to have the potential to illustrate and qualify the population trends considered in total. Thus these five aspects of socio-economic change provided the model which was repeatedly applied to the British urban systems framework specified at the nat-ional, regional and local spatial scales.

One of the most important changes in the space economy during the period reviewed by this study has been in the contribution of females to the remunerated workforce. During the 1950s female employment growth almost matched that of males in the nat-ion's urban cores, was more than twice as high in the rings and grew by one hundred thousand in the outer rings in contrast to a decline of the same magnitude for males All this is expressed in absolute terms, the relative change figures being even more impressive. And even more impressive still is the global picture for the 1960s. In the nation's cores, male employment declined by almost three quarters of a mill-ion, female employment grew by over a quarter of a million. In the rings, female job growth was two and a half times that of males. In the OMR, male job losses amounted to 136,000 while female employment grew by twice this amount. Again these are absolute values and the relative change figures are again more contrasting.

Basically what employment growth that has taken place has been for females. Even
in the urban cores of the nation, suffering markedly from employment decentralisation, increased employment opportunities for women have been seen. However not
unnaturally it is in the ring zones, the major receiving areas of employment decentralisation, that female job growth has been at its most dynamic.

All of these trends are reflected in the changing patterns of male and female activity rates. Male activity rates, although still usually twice as high as for
females, have declined almost everywhere, but especially so in the nation's cores,
and perhaps least so in the nation's ring zones. Female activity rates have increased everywhere, including the nation's cores, but especially in the nation's
rings and OMRs where in general they were not as high to begin with. The net effect has been a convergence of activity rates between urban zones.

Although a national view provides a useful summary some important sub national deviations are concealed. For example, it is a fact that even female jobs declined
(-132,000) in the cores of the nation's million cities such was the strength of the
decentralisation trends therein. For males, declines in the cores of million cities
have been more substantial, and growth in the rings of million cities less significant, than similar trends in these urban zones in the rest of the country. For
females the above mentioned job decline in the million city cores has to be placed
alongside a growth of some 400,000 jobs in the cores of the cities in the rest of
Britain. In the metropolitan rings of the rest of British cities female employment
growth far exceeded, in both absolute and relative terms, that in the rings of the
million cities. So there is a city size contrast apparent in the changing fortunes
of jobs for males and females, far more marked than was apparent when employment
was simply considered in aggregate.

Growth in job opportunities for women especially in the metropolitan rings must of
course be related to a number of other trends ongoing in the urban system. Population decentralisation is perhaps the major component, with women tending to
work near to home and frequently in occupations serving local populations. Trends
in the occupational and industrial structure of the economy (in all urban zones)
are the other major component in the explanation.

Substantial reorganisation of the occupational structure of employment occured
during the period 1961-1971 with marked differences for men and women. The chief
effect was of a shift from manual to non-manual occupations, especially a growth
in office employment. For Britain as a whole the key features are a high growth
in professional and technical jobs for both men and women. There was also a high
growth of service, sport and recreation workers, but these were mainly women, and
the same can be said, only even more so, for growth in clerical employment.
Administrators and managers on the other hand, traditionally a male preserve, focuses nearly all of its impressive absolute growth into male employment, although
in relative terms females also achieved important gains.

Office employment is highly localised in London and the South East region. Only
three cities outside these areas had a greater share of office employment than
total employment. The South East region also records the highest rates of growth
in office employment (but not London), although of course growth in this activity
has taken place in many other areas. Inter regional inequalities in opportunities
to take up office employment continue to be apparent. Not unexpectedly office
activities proved to have an urban-size focus, although concentration of office
employment in the large cities declined marginally between 1966 and 1971. However
it seems that the localisation of office employment is in fact more influenced by
regional factors. Major provincial cities in the North, for example Manchester
and Liverpool, have less office employment than might be expected on the basis of
their size. And over the period 1966-1971 most large cities had less office growth

than might be expected on the basis of their office employment structure in 1966. Most significant gains were by medium sized cities in the southern half of the country.

Much of the growth of office employment in towns in the South East can be attributed to office decentralisation from London. This dispersal has been widely spread over a large number of smaller towns up to 80 or so miles from the capital. Major cities, however, which are relatively close to London, such as Birmingham, seem to have benefitted less from such transfers, and this equally goes for the major provincial cities.

Using an industrial instead of an occupational categorisation of employment, it can be seen that almost ubiquitous manufacturing decline and service industry growth, save for transport, distributive and miscellaneous services, typifies the national change picture 1966-1971. Most of the largest cities which dominate the axial belt of urban England have been losing manufacturing jobs while smaller towns and cities have been growing. The net regional effect has been a dispersal of manufacturing activities from core to peripheral regions. A process of inter-metropolitan decentralisation from larger to smaller cities within each major region also seems to have reduced intra-regional concentration of manufacturing industry.

Nationally, all industries, except chemicals, financial, professional and administrative services, have declined in urban cores. In total the urban cores lost 600,000 jobs between 1966 and 1971, and it is important to record that around half of these were in decline-following, non-basic services. Conversely, most industries except those nationally in decline (which includes most manufacturing industries) have increased in metropolitan rings. Even those in decline, however, have had lower rates of losses in metropolitan rings. Likewise the service sector growth industries have increased most rapidly in metropolitan rings.

In the larger cities the decline in manufacturing employment in urban cores has not been compensated for by increases in office employment. Only higher level managerial office occupations have been achieving significant growth, while clerical jobs in urban cores of the million cities have been declining absolutely. In the smaller cities, office jobs of all types have been increasing more rapidly. Similarly a wide range of office occupations have increased in the nation's metropolitan rings and OMRs.

Given the commentary on the changing nature of employment it is no surprise to find that Britain during the sixties underwent significant changes in its socio-economic group composition. Major increases in managerial and professional and intermediate non manual groups and decreases in the skilled manual and the semi and unskilled manual groups were recorded. The changes were greatest at the extremes of the social structure. The most striking feature of the changes in the social groupings by urban zone is the way in which they have been dominated by these changes at the national level. The main difference between the changes in the extremes of the social hierarchy is that while the decline in the lowest status groups has been remarkably uniform for all zones, the increase in the highest status groups, though existing in all types of zone, has been concentrated in the rings. This has meant that although the professional and managerial groups have increased in the cores (the only major group to do so), in relative terms this group is decentralising from cores to rings. In general the relative changes in the intermediate groupings - the intermediate non manual and the skilled manual - were far smaller. Both of these groups declined relatively in the cores but increased in relative terms in the rings and OMRs.

Overall the profiles for the cores, SMLAs and MELAs in aggregate display the great-

est degree of similarity with the national pattern. The rings are of relatively
higher status than the cores with a greater proportion of their total employed
males in the professional and managerial grouping. Moving to the outermost limits
of commuting, in the OMRs the profile is of a lower socio-economic status with
much larger proportions in the skilled manual and semi and unskilled manual.
Clearly the inner ring zones incorporate more of the professional classes likely
to commute to the urban cores each day. In the outer ring zones the level of commuting is less and a more balanced social status profile ensues.

In national aggregate terms the simple statistics of change for urban zones do not
on the whole signify social polarisation. Despite the relative decentralisation
of the more affluent social groups from the cores, the profile for this zone is
remarkably close to the national average. Given the relatively small size of the
two extreme groups and this large scale spatial view, it is perhaps unrealistic to
expect any tendency for marked social polarisation to be illustrated. The rates
of change in these social groupings also do not suggest any increasing tendency
towards polarisation in the cores. It is of course probable that unemployment in
1971 was greatest for semi- and unskilled workers in the cores and this may have
served to accentuate the decline in this group. However it seems unlikely that
the extent of this factor could radically change the overall decline in the lowest
status social group in cores.

The higher status groups were increasing at the fastest absolute and relative rates
in the regions in which they were already concentrated namely the South East, though
to a much lesser extent also the West Midlands. The lower status groups were also
declining faster in those areas in which they were concentrated, but in general
these were outside the South East. Given the relatively high rate of unemployment
in 1971, and the fact that this is generally concentrated, in relative if not always absolute terms, in the peripheral regions in time of economic downturn, then
it seems likely that this has served to accentuate the decline or low relative
increase in the lower social groups outside the South East and West Midlands.
Nevertheless, it can be suggested that the extent of this factor was not sufficient
to override the main pattern of regional change in socio-economic groupings.

Superimposed on and working in conjunction with the regional effect is the second
basic element in the spatial pattern of socio-economic change - the effect of population size. Large cities may be expected to record larger absolute decreases in
the lower status groups but they are also amongst the extremes in relative terms.
Clearly then the middle income groups are declining within (and by implication
migrating from) the centres of the major British cities. These size and regional
effects combine to play an important role in the patterns of intra-regional change.
Thus within the South East those areas which rank highest in terms of relative change in the four main socio-economic groups are frequently new and expanded towns.
These include Basildon, Harlow, Stevenage, Crawley and Milton Keynes, but, in general, medium sized towns in the South East also figure prominently in the ranks of
relative change. In contrast only the high social groups increased in London.
Much of London's decline then in the various social groupings has been channelled
into the surrounding towns and cities in the region. These patterns also exist -
albeit at a smaller spatial scale - in the other major British conurbations.

In considering the changing social structure of the principal cities of the nation
the basic distinction is between London and the rest. Only in the London core does
the proportion of the economically active population in managerial and professional
occupations (17.7%) and in the intermediate non-manual occupations (22.7%) exceed
the national average for this zone. At the other extreme only in the capital does
the proportion in the core of unskilled manual occupations fall below the national
average. Changes since 1961 have tended to reinforce these contrasts with the
Manchester, Liverpool and Newcastle cores recording absolute decline in the manag-

erial and professional group. Nevertheless in the remaining cores also rate of increase of this group was well below the national average. Decentralisation has
clearly progressed further in London with the highest rates of increase in the managerial and professional group achieved in the OMR. Furthermore it was the only
MELA to record a decline of skilled manual workers and zero growth of intermediate
non manual occupations in its metropolitan ring.

Finally it may be useful to conclude this section with a reexamination of the notions of social polarisation. The fact that managerial and professional SEGs are
increasing in the urban cores of the nation contrary to a general decline of the
total economically active population and that the rate of decline of semi and unskilled groups is in line with aggregate trends is perhaps a possible indication of
a tendency towards social polarisation in urban cores. Shift/share analysis lends
some limited support to this notion. All groups suffered negative core shifts and
positive ring shifts. However professional and managerial groups achieved the
highest shifts in both zones and the semi and unskilled manual groups the lowest
shifts. The two intermediate SEGs showed similar but weaker decentralisation tendencies to the higher status group. So having taken into account the national trends the number of semi and unskilled manual groups in cores was largely unchanged
or marginally declining. But the other groups, again after accounting for national
trends, were in marked decline. This especially applies to the professional and
managerial group a feature counterbalancing positive actual growth. Therefore
there was relative decentralisation at similar rates as measured by differential
shifts of all groups except the lowest from urban cores. These groups achieved
associated growth at similar rates in the metropolitan rings. In this way social
polarisation may be thought to have increased in the core areas of the nation, par-
alleling the process that is almost certainly occurring in the much more tightly
defined inner cities. The intra urban differences in growth rates are however much
complicated, as is shown by the earlier contrary reference to polarisation, by the
national decrease in the lower status groups and increase in the higher status
groups. And there is still insufficient evidence at this scale of analysis to state
that the lowest status groups were more concentrated in the cores than the other
groups. However given the trends relative to those in the nation this seems unlikely to continue to be the case. Overall though, the issue of social polarisation
is far from clear cut and this also applies to the changing social fortunes of individual cities.

From themes of socio-economic change differentially affecting the components of the
British urban system, perhaps resulting in social polarisation in certain parts,
attention can next be usefully focussed on changing age structure raising the issue
of age polarisation. Nationally the sixties produced increases in the sizes of all
age groups except the 30 years to pensionable age group. The largest absolute increase was in the 15 to 29 years age group while the largest percentage increase
was in the above pensionable age group. With the exception of the 30 years to pensionable age group, all groups increased as a proportion of the total population
with the largest increase in the above pensionable age group.

Regionally there is a tendency for larger proportions in the 0 to 14 years age group in the northern regions and a tendency for larger proportions in the above pensionable age group in southern regions. As for growth and decline, most age groups
are increasing in the south and decreasing in the north, basically following the
patterns of total population change. The major exception to this pattern is the
above pensionable age groups which revealed a pattern of percentage changes with
no clear alignment along a north-south pattern.

These broad regional change patterns are replicated at the level of individual
cities. In the 0 to 14 age group the largest absolute increases tend to occur in
southern towns while northern systems tend to have decreases. London of course is

the major exception to this pattern with a large absolute decrease. The pattern
of absolute change in the 15-29 years age group is affected by large increases in
big cities, but of these those in the north tend to have smaller increases. The
30 years to pensionable age group has the largest absolute increases in a belt of
SMLAs surrounding London, but again, the north-south pattern is clear. The absolute
changes in the above pensionable age group are again dissimilar to the previous
groups in that they reveal no firm north-south pattern, but this group has large increases in the big cities, in alignment with the changes in the 15-29 years age group. The percentage changes in the age groups in individual SMLAs reflect the patterns of regional change observed previously.

The largest proportions in the 0 to 14 years age group tend to be in SMLAs which
are or include new or expanded towns. Additionally these SMLAs tend to have small
proportions in the above pensionable age group. The reverse pattern is displayed
by the southern retirement resorts - small proportions in the younger age groups
and large proportions of their populations above pensionable age.

Taken as a whole then the results of inter-urban change in age structure tend to
confirm and reinforce the importance of regional factors as an influence on population and demographic change in the British urban system. Nevertheless, superimposed on these broad patterns are a number of other influences. Many large SMLAs are
losing large numbers of their populations aged between 0 to 14 and 30 years to pensionable age, while at the same time increasing their numbers of persons aged between 15 to 29 years and above pensionable age. To the extent that these population
losses and gains are aligned with the north-south division, this reflects regional
patterns of change and in particular inter-regional migration.

However, it is also clear, especially involving the behaviour of the South East
region system, that powerful intra-regional processes are also in operation. Given
the importance of migration as a determinant of urban change, it is apparent that
many persons aged between 30 years and pensionable age (together with their families)
have been leaving London for the surrounding new and expanding towns in the outer
South East. This is one of the reasons of course for an increase in the proportions
of persons aged 15 to 29 years and above pensionable age in the capital.

Decentralisation has also influenced the distribution of the age groups. The proportion of each age group fell in the cores and increased in the rings and OMRs.
However there were variations in the changes experienced by each group. Those aged
15 to 29 or above pensionable age increased in all zones, the 0 to 14 group decreased in cores and increased in other zones and the 30 to pensionable age group had a
large decrease in cores and a small increase in rings. As a result there were changes in the age composition of zones. Those aged between 30 and pensionable age
decreased as a proportion of the total population in every zone; conversely the
other groups increased as a proportion in all zones. There is not a strong concentration of any one group in any zone. However both percentage changes and changes
in proportions between 1961 and 1971 suggest ongoing processes of age polarisation.
The 0 to 14 and 30 to pensionable age groups have become relatively more concentrated in the rings and the 15 to 29 and above pensionable age groups relatively
more concentrated in the cores. This suggests polarisation of older adults and
their young families, on the one hand, and young adults and the elderly on the
other hand. As to cause, it must be apparent that these changes in age structure
correspond well with the main patterns of migration.

The study of birthplace characteristics identified two major types of immigrant
group. The first composed of the Irish, the Other Commonwealth and Other Migrants
have similar patterns to the British born. For the latter two types of immigrant,
although the differences between regions and between urban zones are small compared to the British born, there are much larger increases in all areas. The second

cluster of immigrant types – the Indian sub continent,African and West Indies –
have markedly different patterns with respect to the British born, especially with
respect to intra urban variations.

Nationally all birthplace groups increased at a faster rate than the British born
population. These increases were especially great for the Indian sub continent,
African and West Indies birthplace groups. However mostly the high rates depend
on low absolute bases, but the total increase of all immigrants was about a million
between 1961 and 1971 or about one third of the total population increase.

There were considerable intra-urban differences in the distribution of the immigrant
groups. The British born experience a decrease in cores and an increase in both
rings and OMR in line with well established patterns of decentralisation. Approximately 50% lived in cores and this proportion fell between 1961 and 1971. The
first cluster of immigrant groups were in some ways similar to the British born.
There were decreases or small increases in cores and relatively large increases in
the other zones. The proportion resident in cores also fell during the decade.
However the proportion resident in cores did remain greater than for the British
born. The second cluster of immigrant groups were far more differentiated. The
Indian sub continent and African groups had larger increases in cores than rings
and the proportion resident in the inner zone increased. The West Indies group had
larger increases in the rings and the proportion resident in cores fell. However
even in 1971 over 90% of this group lived in urban cores. In aggregate then the
mainly coloured immigrant groups seemed to be increasing their share of core population at a time when most groups including the British born were reducing theirs.
Definite polarisation of birthplace groups is occuring, certainly in the cores but
also in some metropolitan rings.

The national changes were composed of distinct regional patterns. The largest absolute and percentage increases were in the urban-industrial axis composed of the
South East, East Midlands, West Midlands, North West and Yorkshire and Humberside.
The smallest increases were in the peripheral regions and in East Anglia and the
South West. Principal relative growth has then taken place in regions where concentrations were already apparent in 1961. Lack of job opportunities in the peripheral regions and competition from migrating British born population in the growth regions of East Anglia and the South West seem to offer plausible explanations.
Similarly a replacement hypothesis in which immigrants are taking jobs left by
migrating British born population seems appropriate (Peach, 1968) in the areas of
high growth of immigrants. Such a process might reasonably be expected to be operating at both an inter-regional and intra-regional scale.

Broadly similar patterns existed for the urban zones within regions. The largest
numbers in both 1971 and 1961, for both clusters of immigrant groups were in the
South East. The largest proportions in all groups were also in this region. For
the second cluster of immigrant groups there were also large proportions in the
urban axis already described. Change rates had different patterns however. The
largest changes for the first cluster of groups were in the south, and the largest
changes in the second cluster were in the urban axis, excluding the South East.
In terms of concentration these patterns indicate polarisation of the second cluster
of immigrant groups in the cores of all regions. The change rates were less uniform
for there was a tendency towards increased polarisation in the cores of all regions
only for those born in the Indian sub continent. The African and West Indies group
had tendencies towards increased polarisation in the cores in some regions but tendencies towards increased polarisation in the rings in other regions.

Finally the examination of individual cities revealed that regional patterns may be
considerably influenced by the patterns in a few large cities. This is particularly
true of London in the South East, Birmingham and Coventry in the West Midlands and

Leicester in the East Midlands. The largest cities however were less influential in other regions with smaller increases in number of immigrants. The rankings of individual urban zones of cities show a similar pattern. The largest cities dominated the rankings of absolute numbers of immigrants in 1961 and 1971 and the largest absolute changes in these zones. For the largest percentage changes and proportions of total population however regional location rather than city size seems to be the important factor. The large percentage increase of the Indian subcontinent group in the North West and Yorkshire and Humberside for example, reflects large increases in the belt of towns stretching from Bolton to Wakefield. In the bottom ranks of changes and proportions again regional location rather than city size appeared to be important.

To conclude, the changing distribution of birthplace groups presents a most dynamic aspect of social change. However the patterns of change are much less predictable than for say the socio-economic groups. This largely reflects the fact that immigrants are an injection of persons into the system rather than merely the outcome of the rearrangement of the system's internal structure.

Migration and British cities

Part Three considers residential population redistribution - one of the most fundamental aspects of change operating in the subnational space economy. Analysis of migrant characteristics falls naturally into two sections. First, analysis of the principal patterns of movement within and between British cities and emphasising volume and direction was undertaken. Second, analysis of the age and socio-economic group structure, together with immigration status, of migrants was considered.

Migration is of course a dynamic process and comprehension of such phenomena using cross-sectional data is consequently limited. This study was restricted to the 1966-1971 and 1970-1971 periods because of data availability and comparability. Movements during these periods were clearly related to earlier migrations of individuals (as well as to changing distributions of investment and economic activity). Similarly population trends since 1971 (and other labour market trends) will, in part be a result of the movements described here. Nevertheless, a detailed analysis of migration characteristics can provide hypotheses concerning the nature of the process across wider-time spans and this was a secondary objective of the research.

Results from an assessment of the relative importance of movements between a hierarchy of places showed that the use of the MELA system allowed many more migrants to be 'captured' than in the more usual regional net. About 40% of all migrants were directed between MELA zones, whereas only one in eight were exchanged between planning regions. But even so the majority of migrations are still not encapsulated by this spatial system. Most of these were between local authority areas for which there is no comparable information. Whilst the majority of intra-local authority relocations will be made for 'life-cycle' reasons this is not always the case. (Harris, 1966; Hyman and Gleave, 1978). Equally, it is not accurate to define all inter-MELA migrants as those simultaneously changing home and workplace or labour migrants.

The analysis of net migration trends for the 1966-71 and 1970-71 periods supported in aggregate the analysis for the 1961-71 decade. Urban cores mostly suffered net migration decline and, nationally, each of the other three urban zones; the metropolitan ring, the outer metropolitan ring and unclassified areas experienced net in-migration. Whilst the biggest gains accrued to the metropolitan rings, inflows into the unclassified areas reverse the traditional trends of rural depopulation, suggesting a spatial expansion of the urban system.

Due to differential migration propensities among population subgroups, areas with

high rates of net out migration are likely to be ageing. Commensurately, areas
with rapid rates of inflow are likely to attract the footloose (younger and white
collar) groups. In aggregate zonal terms it did appear that urban core populations
were 'growing older' due to specific migration and metropolitan rings were 'becoming younger' by disproportionate inflows of young adults. For outer rings and
certain city types the generalisation did not operate. Older groups, particularly
those of pensionable age were attracted to the OMR, and despite high rates of population inflow the resorts were clearly acting as primary destinations for retirement migrants.

In the same way, analysis of exchanges between urban Britain and unclassified areas
did not provide a simple picture of population deconcentration. Inflows of migrants
mainly consisted of those over forty-five years and were disproportionately biased
toward white collar workers. Net outflows of those between 15 and 29 were still
directed to the urban system.

The exchanges above refer to interactions between aggregate urban zones. It is
difficult to develop these arguments and clearly separate inter and intra-urban
processes in the complex British urban system. Nevertheless a difference in the
emphasis of population redistribution could be suggested. The growth of the metropolitan ring was primarily attributable to intra-MELA increases, whilst the OMR
gained more migrants from inter-labour area exchanges. Despite a smaller population base, inter-MELA gains by the OMR exceeded similar net shifts to the metropolitan ring. Moreover, both within and between MELAs, the metropolitan ring incurred
deficits by exchanges with the OMR. Thus while in absolute terms the inner commuting belt areas were the most rapidly growing areas, increasingly the outer ring
has been growing by net shifts of predominantly older, relatively wealthy white
collar populations. Since these populations are prepared to commute longer distances, this supports the suggestion that daily urban systems were expanding in the
1960s.

It is important to underline how widespread net outward redistribution was between
1966 and 1971. For example, net decentralisation between cores and rings was pervasive even over the longest distances (i.e. between non-contiguous planning regions). However, the relative strength of decentralisation (measured by the ratio
of in-movers) did decline as distances increased.

But whilst undoubtedly decentralisation was the most important process operating
it is easy to ignore other important trends. When inter-zonal migration stresses
are considered on an origin/destination basis, those movers from rings to urban
cores in fact comprised the second largest of sixteen flows. On a proportionate
basis, the percentage of cores' population moving to metropolitan rings was only
fractionally higher than the proportion of the rings' population moving to cores.

The labour markets with fastest rates of internal decentralisation tended to be the
conurbations and the major industrial cities. Thus a city typology is able to reflect greater variation in performance compared with regional divisions. Whilst
nowhere does the absolute level of decentralisation to the OMR match gains by the
rings within city systems, relative increases are the most rapid in the largest
systems.

The peripheral systems revealed lowest levels of net decentralisation and in some
cases continued to centralise. Thus although each planning region presents an apparently uniform pattern of city decline and hinterland growth there are still some
daily urban systems with growing cores and declining hinterlands. These areas represent the last vestiges of traditional rural depopulation. Additionally, they
will continue to lose their most vigorous young economically active populations by
inter-MELA migration. This might result in problems that are no less severe than
those more commonly experienced by the 85% of the urban systems suffering patterns

of <u>urban</u> population decline.

Analysis of internal migration flows supports the model of a city life-cycle. Each
city is postulated to have an initial phase of growth to urban status. This is
followed by a period of consolidation, involving centralisation of people and jobs
in the urban core <u>vis-a-vis</u> the outer metropolitan ring. On from this the process
of decentralisation begins. This takes place initially from the urban core to the
metropolitan ring, during which it is likely that centralisation is still proceeding from the outer ring. After a period the decentralisation movement spreads even
to the outer metropolitan ring. The analysis of migration seems to suggest a further stage, reached by the largest cities, whereby MELAs lose populations from both
core and ring zones to the outer ring and further, beyond its boundaries, into neighbouring systems.

Whilst the Million Cities' most important outward migration streams were directed
as a whole to their satellite MELAs, a greater proportion of the major centres'inflows were received from other large areas, including other Million Cities. This
suggests that the mean distance of inter-MELA outflows from the major centres was
shorter than their migration inflows. A similar inference may be made for cores
in general. MELAs on the edge of the urban system (like Hereford and Shrewsbury)
are again exceptions as they attract urbanising populations from neighbouring unclassified areas and direct outmigrant streams to labour markets at higher tiers in
the urban hierarchy, principally their regional capitals, or London. Despite the
huge inter-MELA losses made by the capital, London continues to receive net inflows
from many peripheral systems and unclassified areas. The importance of London's
migration field - or indeed other Million Cities - should be emphasised.

Despite the apparent rejuvenation of population totals in many outlying or rural
areas, as has been shown the indigenous young adult population still failed to find
sufficient opportunity in their home areas and moved out mainly to their regional
capitals or London. It is tempting to develop this theme as part of an ongoing
process whereby young adults move from rural areas to cities to find work and cheap
accommodation. Later, in their early or mid-twenties with a better job, they might
move further out of cities, buy a house and get married, and later still return home
on or about the time of retirement. Whilst this model might have intuitive appeal
for a number of reasons it is very much a simplification. One major shortcoming is
that it relies heavily on migration between labour markets, whereas the vast majority of moves are of very short distances. To provide further evidence to support
or reject these models longitudinal, or lifeline studies are needed for samples of
migrants.

Disproportionately high numbers of migrants directed from the million city cores
into neighbouring labour markets tended to relocate in their destination's core.
Thus while population is deconcentrating between MELAs it is not necessarily decentralising, in terms of constituent zones, by inter-MELA migration from the largest
areas.

Although the Million Cities' satellite MELAs are among those growing most rapidly
in terms of population and employment, they are doing so solely because of the
decline of their dominant neighbour. The satellites in fact often incur migration
deficits by exchanges with the rest of the nation excluding the major cities.
(For example the New Town group incurred losses by inter-regional migration in all
age cohorts except the young economically active group.) Analysis of flows suggests
that population is moving further and further from conurbation centres in the form
of a 'wave' or 'ripple' process.

In this light, it is not surprising to find that inter-MELA per capita inflows and
outflows are positively associated such that the higher the rate of population

turnover the higher the net surplus. Thus it appears that turnover is stimulated
by healthy local economic environments and suppressed by those under duress. Of
the nine functional groups only the Million Cities lost population in aggregate
terms to the rest of Great Britain. The New Town, Resort, London Peripheral and
Southern Freestanding city types were strongest gainers by inter-MELA population
redistribution.

Because of the notions concerning population turnover, it was suggested that vigor-
ously growing MELAs will tend to lose a high proportion of their populations. These
will principally be among the young adults because of their higher migration propensities. (Available data for age and occupation specific migration were not good
enough to support this contention.) The implication from these issues is that a
subtle shift in perceived opportunities could lead to a dramatic fall in in-migratic
rates (which are far more variable than outmigration levels). Thus these labour mar
kets could rapidly become areas of population decline. Since New Towns have the
highest in <u>and</u> out migration rates per capita, it is possible to perceive them as
being particularly vulnerable to such shifts.

Despite employment decentralisation, one aspect of outmigration from cities might
be an overall increase in journey to work lengths (suggested by the research on
worktravel). Consequently not only is the urban system extending further into
rural Britain, but individual labour markets are becoming increasingly interwoven
with a rise in cross-MELA commuting. It is also possible to hypothesise a reduction of labour migration rates during the late sixties and early seventies. If the
levels of per capita inflows and outflows are lowest for depressed local labour
markets, it would seem reasonable to associate an overall decline in the economy
with lower propensities of labour migration.

Against this should be set the apparent increase in <u>assisted</u> labour migrations.
Government aided moves via the Employment Transfer Scheme reached an annual level
of 26,000 during 1977-78 (to which the employees' families should be added). The
steady increase of response to the Government scheme might be interpreted as a
result of the economy's problems. Similarly, with the increase of multi-plant
firms, private initiatives to move workers between branch plants have rapidly assumed importance. So too, have the number of workers asking to be moved between
plants which diminishes the risk of moving to a new location since a job is guaran-
teed. (Johnson and Salt, 1980). Interestingly, patterns of government assisted
moves via the Employment Transfer Scheme appear to be taking net flows of population into London and the South East and away from peripheral regions. One of the
objectives of the Employment Transfer Scheme is to allow workers access to jobs
which sheer distance, through the cost of moving, might have prohibited. Doubts
have been cast on the scheme's rate of success, (Beaumont, 1976 and 1977), but
there are doubts too concerning the relative importance of migration in changing
an area's social structure. (Hamnett, 1976; Dugmore, 1975). While age selective
movement is the fundamental cause of variation in age structure, occupational mobility has been regarded as being of equal, if not of greater importance, than the
migrational component of social change. Unfortunately, data are too poor to be
able to test this proposition for the hierarchy of areal units used here. What is
clear is that an analysis of social change cannot be regarded as fully completed
until occupational mobility has been considered.

This research has confirmed that migration propensities and decentralisation rates
are lower for the manual groups when compared with white collar workers. It has
been suggested that in part, the longer distances moved by the managerial and professional groups may be the result of these workers having greater difficulty in
exchanging occupations and therefore having to use a wider field, possibly the
whole nation, in job searches. (Gleave and Palmer, 1977). On the other hand, it
is argued that unskilled workers may change their occupations relatively easily.

This coupled with other constraints on mobility (such as living within the council housing tenure sector, and lower awareness of job opportunities elsewhere and finances to reach them) may severely reduce migration propensities over longer distances.

Higher levels of decentralisation from cities by the managerial and professional groups are a result of the much greater mobility levels. In terms of the proportion of _migrants_ decentralising, the manual workers reveal more efficient levels of out migration than the white collar groups. Because of the distribution of jobs in the research and development, corporate and office sectors, the South East has acted as a magnet for the higher income groups. Even Greater London reported inflows of female professional workers between 1966 and 1971 (although this was easily offset by outflows of males in this group).

The New Towns stand out in the South East as places with particularly marked inflows of skilled manual workers, as a result of planned decentralisation. Million City MELAs lost workers in each socio-economic category, whilst in the Major Industrial cities the managerial and the professional workers were the only two groups to show decline. This suggests that the deconcentration of population into contiguous labour markets is being pioneered by the wealthy, a hypothesis consistent with the standard invasion and succession models.

The extension of the outmigration fields from the cities has resulted (and will continue to result) in an important change in the status of the smaller settlements peripheral to the largest cities. Many are developing as significant employment centres in their own right. In summary, the effect of outmovement from the large cities, which still contain forty per cent of the nation's population, has been a net shift of population into intermediate and smaller sized settlements in parts of the country which previously had lower proportions of the population most notably in East Anglia and the South West.

It is upon these relatively recent inter-urban trends that the long established southward shift of population and economic activity has been superimposed. Thus many of the problems of Britain's traditionally declining regions now also appear to be exacerbated by changes in the intra-regional distribution of population.

Worktravel and British cities

Part Four was concerned with the implications of the changing distribution of population and employment for patterns and characteristics of worktravel. Indeed this typology into pattern and character of the journey to work forms the basic structure of the research. After a consideration of the changing patterns of worktravel within and between British cities, the study focusses attention on the sex, socio-economic group, and modal split composition of the journey to work, as well as taking a brief look at variations in household car ownership.

The 1966-71 period was characterised by a sharp rise in unemployment. The slow-down in the economy which this trend reflects had important implications for changes in the zonal redistribution of employment. In the 1961-66 period, the cores experienced almost static employed population and employment totals while the rings grew rapidly in both components. In the following five years, the cores experienced substantial absolute declines while the rate of ring growth was much reduced. In general terms there was thus a shift from relative to absolute decentralisation. Of greater importance for journey to work changes, however, was that in the second half of the period the zonal shifts in employed population and employment began to display marked divergence, resulting in an increasing net surplus of jobs in core areas and an increasing net deficit in rings. Clearly the late 1960s were characterised by greater home/workplace separation.

Journeys between areal units (be they local authorities, urban zones or MELAs) grew

absolutely and relatively at the expense of journeys within areal units during the
1966-71 period. Although there is no explicit measure of journey distance in this
analysis, these changes must again lead to the conclusion that home/workplace separation increased in aggregate terms. It should nevertheless be stressed that even
in 1971 more than 60% of the nation's employed population did not cross a local
authority boundary in their daily journey to work.

The changes in work travel within labour market areas also reflect these locational
shifts of homes and jobs. In general terms, the overall pattern of work travel
became less centrally dominated, with the number of journeys within cores declining
by almost 1 million. At the same time, however, the functional inter-dependencies
between urban zones increased; although employment in ring areas expanded by over
100 thousand jobs, the resident labour force increased by a larger amount and consequently commuting from ring to core areas grew substantially in importance.

Despite wide variations between the nine-fold classification of labour market areas
in terms of their overall growth/decline performances, all exhibited the trend of
increasing net job surpluses in core areas and net deficits in ring and outer ring
areas. Variation in the strength of this trend and in the stage it had reached,
however, suggested the efficacy of a simple typology of labour market groups according to the nature of the zonal shifts in journey origins and destinations. The
least advanced stage in the typology was represented by the New Town group, in
which both homes and jobs were still centralising strongly into the urban cores
and commuting hinterlands were barely established. At the opposite extreme, the
Million City labour markets exhibited massive decentralisation and very strong commuting dependencies between their core areas on the one hand and their rings and
outer rings on the other. Nevertheless, the increases in core-ring dependencies
in the 1966-71 period were most marked in the less advanced labour markets with
lower initial levels, and consequently there was a clear tendency for convergence
between the different groups in the period under examination. It was hypothesised
that the next stage in the sequence is one in which ring-core dependencies actually
begin to decline in relative terms in the most advanced areas, due to the continued
decentralisation of employment (as indeed was the case in the Major Industrial
group).

The extent of the decentralisation trend in the British urban system is indicated
by the within-core component of work travel, which declined absolutely in all labour
market groups with the exception of the New Towns, reaching a maximum of -0.7 million journeys in the Million City group. The nature and scale of this contraction
has important policy implications, for the core areas of the major cities contain
the bulk of the public transportation infrastructure.

Changes in the pattern of total intra-MELA journeys to work disguise substantial
differences between the male and female components of the labour market. Although
intra-MELA work travel declined by 0.8 million journeys, the number of journeys by
females actually increased slightly. The relative decentralisation of the workforce and especially of jobs into the urban ring areas is in net terms almost entirely a function of rapid growth in the female component in this zone. Nevertheless, in one important respect male and female zonal changes were similar. For
both sexes in core areas, the number of employed residents declined at a faster
rate than the number of jobs, while the reverse was found in the outer zones with
employed residents faring better in relative terms than employment. Consequently
net zonal commuting interdependencies increased for both males and females.

The pattern of commuting flows within labour markets suggests that on average
journeys by females are shorter than those by males, in that a greater proportion
of the former are contained within urban zones. Thus males display a higher degree
of commuting interdependency between zones; for example, 40% of males residing in

ring areas work in cores, whereas the equivalent female level is only 33%.

Changes in the home and workplace locations of the various socio-economic groups are largely determined by their overall growth or decline in the labour force as a whole. Both of the non-manual SEGs increased absolutely in total (particularly so the professional and managerial group), while both of the manual SEGs declined (particularly the semi- and unskilled group). As a result, the share of total intra-MELA work travel accounted for by manual workers fell by 3.8% to 49.5% in 1971. The strength of these shifts is such that professional and managerial group origins and destinations grew substantially in each zone type, whereas the semi- and unskilled manual group universally declined. The overall growth in employment in ring areas was in net terms confined to female jobs, and the analysis of SEG variation indicates that it was even more strongly confined to non-manual jobs (the two are not of course unrelated).

There are substantial variations between the SEGs in the zonal shares of journey origins and destinations. The professional and managerial group has a particularly unbalanced structure due to an extremely decentralised workforce, with the result that the group displays a very strong level of net commuting dependency between urban cores and the outer zones. The intermediate non-manual group also reveals an unbalanced structure, but in this case it is due to a very high degree of job centralisation. For both of the non-manual groups, therefore, employment is considerably more centralised than the employed population, resulting in substantial centripetal commuting flows (47% of non-manual ring residents work in the core areas, compared with only 31% of manual residents).

The manual groups have more balanced zonal commuting structures, due mainly to their residential locations being more strongly centralised than average. This low level of residential decentralisation, which characterises semi- and unskilled workers particularly, reflects in part the locational structure of the housing market; the owner-occupied sector, which has a low level of entry from this group, is overrepresented in ring areas while the public and private rented sectors are concentrated particularly in the urban cores.

Despite these different structures, there are clear similarities between the SEGs in terms of relative changes in the importance of the various journey to work flow components. Thus for each SEG, the within-core component declined and the ring to core, within-ring and outer ring to core flows increased their shares of the respective group totals. It should, however, be stressed that this uniformity when changes in share are examined does not extend to absolute changes; for example, the number of manual workers commuting from rings to cores contracted during the period, but at a slower rate than the contraction in the group as a whole.

Changes in the mode of travel within labour markets in the late 1960s were even more remarkable in scale than the alterations to patterns of movement. The five years between 1966 and 1971 witnessed a massive shift from public to private motorised transport. Bus travel within labour markets declined by 1.2 million journeys (17.7%), while car journeys increased by a commensurate amount. In 1966, the bus accounted for 31.4% of the intra-MELA total and the car for 28.8%; by 1971 the shares were 26.8% and 34.7% respectively. The third major mode of travel, walking, increased slightly during the period inspite of the growing complexity and length of the average journey to work, and in 1971 journeys on foot amounted to 4.5 million (21.7% of the total). In view of the numerical importance of this component of intra-urban movement, it is surprising that so little attention has been devoted to examining and facilitating pedestrian accessibility within urban areas.

By 1971, the only type of journey which continued to have a greater number of public transport than car journeys was the within-core component. Nevertheless, even for this type of trip the modal split had altered markedly in the preceding five years. Journeys by car within core areas increased by almost ¼ million, but journeys by public transport fell by more than ¾ million. These figures highlight the enormous problems of public transport; not only is the <u>total</u> number of within-core journeys declining as homes and jobs decentralise to the ring areas, but the <u>share</u> of this shrinking total captured by public transport is itself contracting rapidly.

There are substantial differences between the mode of travel structures of males and females. Males are characterised by high car usage, females by a high level of dependency on bus and walk modes. Although these differences were still strongly apparent in 1971, the 1966-71 period had been characterised by a remarkable absolute increase in car usage by females (0.5 million journeys). The female component accounted for over half of the overall expansion in car commuting, even though its share of the mode total in 1966 was just 15%.

Variations in mode of travel between the different SEGs do not reflect a simple manual/non-manual division (unlike the variations in patterns of travel above). Although as would be expected car usage is high in the professional and managerial group, the other non-manual group (intermediate) has a lower level of car usage than does the skilled manual. The explanation lies in the male/female composition of these groups, for the professional and managerial and the skilled manual groups are predominantly male, while the intermediate non-manual group is predominantly female.   The emphasis on private and public motorised transport then is strongly differentiated by sex.

The shift from public to private motorised transport should be placed within the context of rapidly growing levels of car ownership. By 1971, 60.3% of people making intra-MELA journeys to work were members of households owning at least one car, compared with only 51.4% five years previously. The two-or-more car owning category increased particularly rapidly, and its share of the total grew from 8.7% to 12.3%.

There is a strong relationship between social class and level of car ownership. 86.3% of professional and managerial workers are in car-owning households, compared with only 42.5% of the semi- and unskilled manual group.   In terms of changes between 1966 and 1971, the manual groups recorded substantial increases in the percentage of their total in households owning one car, while for the non-manual groups the increase in two-or-more car ownership was the dominant relative trends. Although the gap between the SEGs in the percentage of their respective totals in households owning at least one car narrowed slightly between 1966 and 1971, the trend towards increasing two-or-more car ownership in the non-manual SEGs suggests that in terms of persons rather than households the 'mobility gap' betweem SEGs may have actually have widened.

As would be expected, the mode of travel structure of people in non-car owning households is completely different from those in car owning households. In 1971, for example, 52.8% of the non-car owning group travelled to work by public transport, compared with only 20.8% of the car-owning group. Similarly, the non-motorised travel mode (i.e. walk and cycle combined) accounts for 35.7% and 21.1% of the respective group totals.

However some 40% of intra-MELA journeys to work are made by people in non-car owning households, and thus for a large segment of the population the only modal 'choice' they are able to exercise is between the bus and walking. The first of these modes is caught in a spiral of falling patronage, declining levels of service and increasing fares, while the potential of walking as a journey to work mode is not enhanced by the general deconcentration of population and economic activity within urban labour markets. Non-car owners, then, are faced with the problem of declining relative (and frequently absolute) levels of accessibility to job locations. Although

the proportion of the population in non-car owning households declined markedly
between 1966 and 1971, the group will not simply decline into insignificance; the
Department of the Environment's own estimates suggest that by the end of the century some 30% of households will still not own a car. On economic and social grounds, therefore, it is clear that one of the major objectives of transport policy
must be to maintain, and hopefully improve, the level of mobility of those without
access to a car.

There are substantial variations between different types of labour market area in
the relative importance of each of the travel to work modes. The conurbations and
other large cities are characterised by high levels of public transport usage; in
the Million City group the average share of total work travel accounted for by public transport was 42.5%, compared with the national intra-MELA figure of 32.7%.
In addition to labour market size, variations in the importance of public transport
have a strong regional component, with high levels in the industrial areas of northern England and Scotland. In the 1966 to 1971 period, the relative importance of
public transport declined in all but four MELAs (of which two, Crawley and Stevenage,
are New Towns).

As would be expected, the pattern of variation in car usage is generally the inverse
of the above. The highest levels are found in southern England, particularly in
East Anglia and in the labour markets to the west of London, while London itself
has the lowest level in the southern half of the country (and one of the smallest
increases in this level in the 1966-71 period).

Unlike public transport and car usage, the other major journey to work mode, walking, displays no apparent regional variation in its importance. Labour market size,
however, is an important determinant, with very low levels of walking to work in
the major cities; London (17.5%) has the lowest level in the country. In these
largest MELAs, home-workplace separation is such that non-car owners are very strongly dependent upon public transportation.

Variation in the percentage of journeys within each area made by persons in car
owning households display a strong regional pattern, with the highest levels occurring in East Anglia, the South West and in the small labour markets around the
edge of London, while the Million Cities have generally low levels. Although the
one car owning and two-or-more car owning percentages reveal a similar pattern of
variation in 1971, the same cannot be said for changes in these components in the
preceding five year period; the largest increases in the level of one car ownership were found in those areas which had the lowest levels at the beginning of the
period (i.e. northern England) while the largest increases in the two-or-more car
percentage characterised labour markets with already high levels in 1966 (i.e.
southern England). As a consequence, regional variation in overall levels of household car ownership (i.e. both categories together) narrowed only marginally during
the second half of the 1960s, even though the 'base level' was substantially raised.

Although there is a strong positive relationship between the percentage of each
MELA's workforce in one-or-more car owning households and the percentage of total
work trips which are made by car, this does not mean that the relationship is cau-
sally deterministic. In London, for example, car usage is considerably lower than
would be expected on the basis of its car ownership level, due presumably to a well-
developed public transportation system (particularly rail) and congested roads.
These features are themselves closely related to spatial structure and to the density of development. Policies which affect the spatial distribution of people and
jobs within urban areas (and between different types of urban areas), together with
policies which directly affect the cost and operation of public vis a vis private
transportation, can be expected to modify significantly the modal split of work
journeys.

Although in 1971 inter-MELA journeys to work accounted for only 8.1% of the national total, in certain types of labour market such journeys are considerably more impor- tant. In the New Town, London Peripheral and the Lancashire/Yorkshire groups, jou- rneys destined for other MELAs account for more than 20% of total origins. In all of the groups, the relative importance of inter-MELA inflows and outflows increased between 1966 and 1971.

The principal destination for inter-MELA work travel is of course London, which has a daily net inflow of a quarter of a million journeys. Indeed, the importance of the capital's jobs is such that in much of the South East it is unrealistic to talk of discrete labour market areas, as indicated by the fact that twenty separate MELAs have in excess of 10% of their respective workforces commuting to London (and in all but two of these MELAs this percentage had increased between 1966 and 1971).

The greater average journey lengths of inter compararared to intra-MELA worktravel is reflected in differences in male/female and social class composition. Male journey are overrepresented in journeys between labour markets, as are journeys by profess- ional and managerial group workers. The modal split between private and public transport is also different, with the car mode being relatively more important in the inter-MELA case. Indeed, were it not for the scale of long-distance rail comm- uting into the core of the London labour market, the car would completely dominate the national inter-MELA modal structure. The example of London amply demonstrates the extent to which different types of work journey are linked to different modes of travel. Journeys destined for its core are predominantly by rail (64% of the total, compared with 29% by car), whereas for more local, and frequently non-radial journeys destined for London's ring the structure is completely reversed (8% by rail and 73% by car).

5.2 BRITISH URBAN SYSTEMS POLICY

To do justice to this title would doubtless entail the researching of another vol- ume of equivalent length. Nonetheless some of the basic themes of such a piece of research, were it to be undertaken, can be pointed to in these concluding remarks. Three themes in particular have been isolated for brief attention here. First, this study, like others of its type undertaken in different national settings, has been short on explanation. More attention will have to be given to answering ques- tions of why the urbanisation trends as detailed in this study are as they are be- fore truly efficient policies can be designed. Second, more research is needed into the nature and scope of possible interventions in the development of urban and regional systems. And third, the real value of an integrated, urban systems view of sub-national development needs to be grasped. This view has implications for both research, not least in the monitoring of urban change, and policy, not least in terms of coordination between various agencies. A short statement relev- ant to each of these themes will conclude the study.

The changing role of large cities in the British urban system.

This study began by developing an international context of urban systems evolution in which it was indicated that the trends towards a decentralised and deconcentra- ted form of urban living now characterise many advanced industrial nations. (Vining 1977; Vining and Kontuly, 1978; Vining and Pallone, 1980; Hansen, 1976). The extent of the shifts towards decentralisation call into serious question the pleth- ora of theories which justify the economic and social advantages of metropolitan concentration, so much so that Vining has argued that these theories should be th- rown away and research effort focussed as here, on describing and monitoring what is happening to and within cities. He argues that on this basis a new and empir- ically valid urban development theory can be based.

Now, although very far from a theory, the principal argument that will be developed here is that the economic and demographic problems of the inner parts of large cities are a symptom of more general processes of economic change which in the long term will lead to the re-structuring of the national urban hierarchy. The key notion in this argument is that the previous regional hegemony of the provincial conurbations has been undermined by relatively recent changes in the corporate organization of industrial production. In essence the nation is left with a number of large cities whose functions within the national urban system no longer correspond to their size.

An historical perspective is essential if the forces bringing about these changes are to be fully understood. Consideration also needs to be given to the relationship between the twin processes of regional and urban development - for example the changing nature of the links between major cities and their tributary regions and the impact of these changes on the internal structure of city regions. What follows is an attempt to summarise some of these ideas in a general way. Some of the arguments are difficult to substantiate empirically, although fragmentary evidence is available to support some of the themes.

Excepting Greater London and the West Midlands, it is not without significance that all of the conurbations are to varying degrees focal points of less prosperous regions. These urban agglomerations emerged at a time when the respective regional economies of the North West, Yorkshire, the North East and West Central Scotland were booming. Their growth was inextricably linked with that of the surrounding regions they served as well as their own indigenous industry. Historically, large urban agglomerations offered external economies to small scale manufacturing industry, both within the urban area and the surrounding region.

The past twenty years or so have seen dramatic changes in the organization of industrial production. The reorganisation of production into large corporations may have reduced the importance of intra-urban and inter-urban linkages and hence the attraction of the large urban agglomeration for new industrial investment emanating from the corporate sector. Thus corporations organized on a national and international scale will obtain many inputs from other parts of their corporation and not necessarily from the local area. Service linkages might also be internalized and directed elsewhere, especially to London. Similarly, the declining importance of small-scale industry in the hinterlands of large cities may also have contributed to their declining significance as regional centres. Although such centres may have a continuing role in providing population orientated services, their significance as a focus for industrial, business and professional services may be declining. At the same time the declining functional significance of the provincial centres induced by changes in the corporate sector may have had indirect effects on small scale industry both within and outside the centre by reducing the supply of essential service functions.

Thus the employment problems of the inner city cannot be attributed solely to environmental problems of the inner city per se but to broader changes in the organisation of industrial production. The demise of the small firm and the decline in the birthrate of new industrial activities has been a response to many factors. The problem is that small firms have been generally more important in the employment structure of the inner parts of many conurbations than elsewhere.

Of course, these changes have been reinforced by general environmental policies whereby new investments, for example, in road transport and industrial estates, have made locations away from the conurbations and other large urban centres more attractive. New corporate investment has therefore occurred in the hinterlands of large cities and in free standing towns elsewhere, often areas previously lacking an industrial base. The increasing service functions of such settlements may also have acted as a stimulus to local industrial expansion outside the corporate sector. Conversely, problems of congestion in the inner areas of the conurbations coupled with comprehensive redevelopment with an emphasis on renewing the residential fabric may have dampened down the traditional function of inner urban areas as a seedbed for new industry.

If this view is correct, the changes in the organisation of production that have been described will have had a profound effect on the occupational and industrial structure of employment in large urban areas. These areas will have experienced an increasing share of employment in declining industrial sectors and, when compared with national trends, an increasing proportion of the work force employed in unskilled and semi-skilled manual occupations. In particular, the declining importance of locally based manufacturing industries will have resulted in a decline in the number of jobs requiring managerial and professional skills. Similarly office jobs in the professional and business service sector outside the corporate hierarchy will not have grown as fast as nationally. In contrast, smaller cities and non-urban areas will have increased their share of growth industries and employment in skilled manual and professional occupations while other areas previously closely integrated with the conurbations will have shared in their decline.

These changes will be closely reflected in linkage patterns within and between cities. Much industry, especially in the corporate sector, in the regional hinterlands of large conurbations may no longer look to them for services. These provincial centres, at least in the private sector, may be relatively unimportant in linking the regional economy into the national economy. Organisational ties will be directed via corporate head offices located in London or overseas.

Linkages reflected in labour migration flows may also be increasingly steered by the changing occupational structure of different urban labour markets. The lack of skilled manual and professional job opportunities will have resulted in migration away from the larger cities of the occupationally mobile. At the same time migration in search of better living conditions will have created an attractive environment for new industrial activities in previously less industrialised areas. Residential migration in search of amenities will therefore have been both a cause and a consequence of the rapid growth of new employment in previously non-industrialised areas.

The key message of this description is that the functional organisation of the urban system may be out of line with its current spatial organisation. The present urban hierarchy consists of a number of large centres lacking a contemporary functional role in the organisation of <u>private</u> production. The organisation of the <u>public</u> system may however be more closely in line with the hierarchical structure of the urban system. Thus the conurbations may still act as major provincial centres for certain public functions: what growth these areas have experienced in managerial and professional occupations may be largely attributed to the public sector.

If this diagnosis is correct, the policy problem is essentially to find a role for the conurbations that will justify the fixed investment in urban infra-structure that they represent and provide greater opportunities for the substantial human resources resident there. Insofar as self-sustained regional economic growth depends on growth in established indigenous industries and upon new locally-based entrepreneurship, the question is to identify the types of function and spatial organisation for the conurbations and the regional urban hierarchy that can provide the economic and social environment that will engender these processes.

The processes of inter-urban change that have been described have clearly been superimposed upon the related forces for intra-urban change, principally populat-

ion and employment decentralisation from the cores of cities. Population decentralisation, engendered by rising personal incomes, higher personal mobility and not
least urban containment policies, has been followed by job decentralisation. Again,
the employment shifts need to be related to secular changes like increasing female
activity rates and increases in employment in population orientated service sector
jobs. The important point is that decentralisation is a process that has come
to characterise most British cities despite their age, region or relative location.
What does vary is the rate at which this process is operating and the stage it has
reached. Generally the less dynamic growth of population and employment in the
assisted areas which has been associated with a smaller managerial and professional
group in the labour force, a group which has elsewhere led the outward movement of
population, has led to lower rates of decentralisation. Where decentralisation has
occurred it has been to the benefit of previously declining smaller settlements
(e.g. mining settlements around Tyneside or mill towns in Lancashire) and been
reinforced by regional policies directing industry to suburban locations (e.g.
Washington New Town).

In spite of these regional differences, it is clear that as a result of both intra
and inter-urban forces for change it has been the smaller urban centres close to
the conurbations or peripheral to the main axial belt of urban England that have
been growing most rapidly and are likely to exhibit the greatest growth potential
in the future. In many instances the growth of such settlements has been dependent
upon the conurbations, not least because they continued to provide important service functions both regionally and nationally. Indeed, a new pattern of settlements
seems to be emerging of rapidly growing settlements which are either satellites of
declining urban centres or free-standing towns outside the highly urbanised parts
of the country.

In order to produce realistic policies for the inner city, the nature of the relationship of the urban area of which they are part with other cities in the regional hinterland and elsewhere in the country need to be more fully understood.
And since cities are largely a product of economic forces of agglomeration the
essence of the problem is to develop a deeper understanding of the relationship
between processes of change in the production system and its implication to the
functioning and spatial organisation of the urban system. (Pred, 1977).

Dispersal policies and inner city rejuvenation

Much has been written on the current urbanisation trends in this and other studies
but what has been the planning response to these trends? First, of course, in
Britain the traditional separation of urban and regional policy formulation has to
be noted. Regional policy, traditionally the preserve of the Department of Industry
and economically based, has been concerned with the balance of population and employment between the major regions of the country. This has involved in particular
the rejuvenation of the declining nineteenth century industrial areas in the north
and the arresting of population growth in and around London in the south. The
major instruments of policy are mainly economic measures of grants and subsidies
applied across wide areas to encourage industrial mobility and dispersal. Urban
policy, traditionally the preserve of the Department of the Environment and land
use based, has been concerned with the structure of individual urban areas and the
development of separate spatial strategies for each individual planning region.
The major instruments of policy are mainly land use designation and development of
transport infrastructure, with the new and expanded town programme assuming a
special importance.

More recently however, there have been a number of changes in this U.K. policy
context, while still maintaining its broad structure. (Chisholm, 1976). There has
been a changing economic and demographic environment with continuing high levels of

unemployment and low or zero population growth. As the recession has deepened unemployment levels of development area proportions have been found in hitherto prosperous areas. There has been a national priority for increased industrial efficiency. There has been a growing awareness of the openness of regional economies associated with the increased significance of multi-plant national and international corporations. And there has been the rise and development to crisis proportions of the urban (inner city) problem in all its social and economic manifestations. In the light of all of these developments, and others not mentioned, there has emerged a consensus of the need for more selective and place-specific regional policies and their integration with urban policies at the national level. (Frost and Spence, 1981). Certainly regional policies have become more selective as the recent review of areas eligible for assistance shows (Frost and Spence, 1981, forthcoming). Certainly urban policies have become more selective, as the partnership scheme and enterprise zone developments indicate. (Frost and Spence, 1980). But this seems to fall short of an integrated approach which specifies a detailed national settlement strategy.

In the absence of a detailed social and economic evaluation of the desired settlement strategy for Britain it is possible to proceed on the grounds that policies for inner city rejuvenation are based on sound political judgement. They are naturally a response to the decaying social and physical environment of central cities. But it is sensible to remember that many of the trends currently visible were once thought desirable and can thus be viewed in terms of success as well as failure. It is not so much that planning objectives have changed, rather that the demographic and economic context has shifted. Urban and regional planning still aims to match people with jobs in satisfactory environments bearing in mind national efficiency and levels of welfare.

Britain is entering a phase of low or zero population growth. Planners are no longer concerned with the location of major new urban centres to meet the demands of an ever increasing population but rather with careful propogation and resuscitation of some towns and certain parts of large cities. In such a no-growth situation it is of even greater importance to get the overall settlement strategy right. Generalised or 'blanket' responses, such as those of the fifties and sixties when spatial problems were considered in terms of a simple dichotomy between congested core areas and declining peripheral regions are no longer appropriate.

With low rates of natural increase of the population, net migration becomes an even more important factor in creating differences between places in rates of overall population change. (For example the entire London labour market area - much more extensive than the Greater London Council area - lost close on one million people through net migration in the period 1961-1971). Migration becomes more significant in a low birth rate future because it heightens the disparities between demographically old and demographically young communities. Population will continue to grow in places which have experienced strong immigration in the past - generally the smaller to medium sized towns. Nevertheless, the sheer size of the largest cities, in spite of their ageing population, will still mean that they will account for most of the natural increase of the urban population. For example in the sixties the London labour market area alone gained half a million people through natural increases; Birmingham gained a quarter of a million; Glasgow 140,000; Manchester 112,000 and Liverpool 110,000.

It is clear that metropolitan decentralisation of population is a long run process continually extending over a wider and wider area and has also come to affect cities other than the very largest. During the sixties 101 of the 126 city regions in Britain were experiencing relative or absolute population decentralisation from their urban cores to their metropolitan rings. The 1930's suburbs are now experiencing population decline in favour of satellite town growth. It is not just the localised inner city areas of physical deprivation that are experiencing population decline but rather a broader central city zone. This process may give cause for alarm in the future. Much of this decentralisation has of course been planned and can be properly viewed as a planning success. But to think that by ceasing such policies decentralisation would stop, would be to ignore the voluntary movement which has been matched in roughly equal terms by planned movement. Such a strategy might be disadvantageous to big cities in that the lower social economic groups usually involved in planned moves would remain even more localised in inner areas. Furthermore, especially in the development areas, planned decentralisation from provincial conurbations has revitalized many previously decaying settlements. While decentralisation has occurred from large cities in the development areas, the rate at which this process has operated has been slower than in more prosperous parts of the country, suggesting that economic growth and decentralisation are inter-related processes.

Superimposed on the principal decentralisation theme is the emergence of a new pattern of urbanisation in Britain. Declining urban cores have generated growth in small, often still dependent, towns satellite to them (e.g. places like Guildford, Kidderminster and Harrogate). Further, the decline in the conurbations has been in favour of the small to medium sized free standing towns outside the main axial belt of urban Britain (e.g. places like Hereford, Shrewsbury, Yeovil, Norwich and Lincoln). In policy terms it is much more difficult to discourage growth in such diverse situations than it was to contain London's expansion in the 1950's and 1960's.

The role of amenity consideration in these population movements needs to be emphasized. In the United States where many of these processes are more advanced, amenity has become one of the most important decentralisation factors. In this country it is reflected in the success of planned decentralisation, the voluntary push by the higher social economic groups to outer metropolitan areas and, most important, in the pattern of retirement migration. In policy terms the amenity values of central city location need to be emphasised; there are after all considerable benefits in terms of access to services to be gained from a central location.

The continuous process of population decentralisation already described has clearly lead employment decentralisation, the latter dramatically following suit in the sixties. It has been the sudden switch from job centralisation in the fifties to job decentralisation in the sixties which has accentuated the problem of the changing economic base of inner urban areas. It appears that the motor of employment growth in the suburbs is not so much physical job movement but rather an in situ growth of population orientated service functions. This is a response to two fundamental trends in the British economy - the shift to the service sector and the increase in female activity rates. Female participation in the labour force is crucial to the understanding of urban growth on account of the economic sectors to which women are chiefly attracted and the fact that women choose or are constrained to live near their work. Of course some employment change is due to physical movement. Office decentralisation, often to high amenity areas, is one such component, as is the particular success of long distance manufacturing relocation which has been directed at the commuting hinterlands of larger provincial conurbations rather than to their urban cores.

Manufacturing growth has in the main been switched to small and medium sized settlements peripheral to the conurbations and to smaller places elsewhere with consequent disproportionate decentralisation of skilled manpower. This has policy implications for both the sending and the receiving areas. Employment policies always attempt to match the skills supplied by a local population with those demanded by the employers in an area. The rejuvenation of inner

urban areas through the relocation of manufacturing industry paradoxically may run
into skill shortages without careful manpower planning. The long term implication
for the manufacturing growth towns is that some may become too dependent, because
of their size, on single plants and thus vulnerable to individual industry misfor-
tunes. In this context, the strength of the conurbations needs to be emphasised.
Their size facilitates diversity and hence resistance to cyclical economic fluctuations. In response to the changing skill requirements of industry size provides
opportunity for occupational mobility without geographical mobility.

High unemployment in inner urban areas has been an important facet of the current
cause for concern. The present recession has hit a wide range of occupations but
as always the unskilled manual group has been the worst affected. Although the unemployment problems of the unskilled can be tackled through training programmes the
occupational mobility that such training facilitates is difficult in unstable economic environments especially in small towns. Job choice in big cities should be
greater ceteris paribus; transport policy may hold the key to an even wider search
area within the city.

The social balance of cities is being changed mainly through migration. The process is not a simple one-way decentralisation. Large cities articulate a continuous
turnover of population. Example, London's urban core, although losing 800 thousand
people through outmovement during the 1966-1971 period also gained some 350 thousand
through in-movement. Similar situations exist for other big cities. This turnover
of population must be recognised and planned for. The problem population of the
inner urban area may not be the same population from year to year. Policy may therefore have to focus on the residual population - that is those groups that become
trapped in the inner parts of cities largely through the operation of the housing
and labour market. The tendency towards spatial social polarisation is the result.
The range of housing and assisted labour mobility policies that are already available clearly have a role in reducing such differentials. Area based policies therefore have to be complemented by person orientated policies which have spatial manifestations.

There are changes in the composition of urban zones which suggest age polarisation,
although there is not a strong concentration of any one group in any zone. The 0
to 14 years and 30 years to pensionable age groups are becoming relatively more concentrated in the suburban rings and the 15 to 29 years and above pensionable age
groups concentrated in the urban cores. This suggests polarisation between older
adults and their young families on the one hand and young adults and the elderly
on the other with clear implications for social provision and retirement migration.

In the context of a falling birth rate among the British born population the higher
birth rate of the overseas born population will play an increasing role in shaping
the characteristics of British cities. During the sixties the overseas born population of British cities increased by almost one million people, representing over
a third of the total population increase for the period. Two types of immigrant
groups can be identified. The Irish, other Commonwealth and other migrants follow
patterns of change and distribution similar to the British born. The Indian sub-
continent, African and American (Caribean) groups on the other hand have different
patterns with large percentage and in many cases absolute increases in core areas,
totally contrary to the trends of the British born population. These patterns clearly indicate that there is some polarisation of birth place groups in the inner
parts of British cities.

In the context of the previous discussion it is clear that a range of both place
and person-orientated policies will be needed to deal with inner urban problems.
The foremost requirement is one of commitment to inner areas from all of the agencies involved. In part the problems of inner urban areas stem from a loss of con-

fidence especially by the business community. Programmes aimed at improving the
physical environment may chiefly bring benefits through upgrading the image of
inner urban areas. A small amount of investment could bring significant improvements in business images and investment patterns. Environmental improvement schemes
are also labour intensive and suited to the relatively unskilled who live in urban
areas.

Public transport improvements have been suggested as one of the means for facilitating greater integration of the labour market areas of larger cities particularly
by creating opportunities for people to travel from inner to outer areas. The
chief drawback of such policies, apart from their expense, is the fact that most
suburban jobs are highly dispersed. Past decentralisation of population and employment has given rise to a massive increase in the volume of journey to work trips
which both begin and end in the urban rings of cities. It may therefore be cheaper
and more effective to subsidise the travel of individuals by private transport to
enable them to gain access to dispersed suburban jobs from inner urban residential
areas.

Transport also has a significant role to play in an inter-urban context. The development of the motorway network has been of primary importance in making smaller
settlements more attractive for new industrial investment. It is difficult to see
how this situation can be reversed, even through the building of expensive urban
motorways.   Substantial reductions of the price of industrial land compared with
alternative locations outside the cities would also have to be affected. Only
office-type functions continue to be attracted to central locations although again
planning policies have tended to encourage dispersal both within and between urban
areas. In the case of office development, inter-urban and intra-urban transport
considerations converge. Public transport is ideally suited to bring in large
numbers of workers to the city centre, while inter-city rail transport is orientated towards the needs of the business traveller and also focuses on the urban core.

With respect to office-type employment and the range of other considerations the
position of the provincial conurbations is fundamentally different from London.
The share of total office employment in the major cities declined over the period
1966-71, largely due to a net shift away from London in favour of smaller towns
elsewhere in the South East. The increasing dominance of large corporations in
the economies of the assisted areas has meant that the traditional business service
role of the provincial conurbation is being undermined. If the public sector is
excluded, office employment growth in the provincial conurbations is less significant than it might seem at first sight. Most of the growth has been confined to
clerical jobs. Some devolution to the English regions coupled with active use of
the powers available under the 1972 Industry Act to encourage manufacturing concerns to decentralise decision-making functions to their branches in the regions
could contribute significantly to restoring the traditional role of some of the
provincial conurbations. Some modification of the 1972 Industry Act may also be
necessary to assist business service firms which are at present not eligible for
support. While such strategies will not solve the problem of loss of manufacturing
jobs from inner urban areas in the short term, in the long term benefits could be
considerable through providing new opportunities for inter as opposed to intra
generational occupational mobility. It will also be economically beneficial in
providing some returns for the large investments the provincial conurbations represent not least through providing a better business climate for regionally-based
industrial enterprises.

The negative effects of emphasising the office service role of the provincial conurbations on London would probably be small. The London labour market area is already in a completely different position from the provincial conurbations with a
much higher professional and managerial component in its economically active work

force. Towns which could afford to export office functions to the provincial conurbations are chiefly in the outer South East where previously low female activity
rates have now reached a high peak; these towns also have the advantages of significant numbers of commuters to London. The national capital role will ensure that
London continues to have a much more viable economic base than any of the provincial
conurbations.

From a regional point of view it will be difficult to discriminate too heavily in
favour of attracting manufacturing industry to the inner urban areas of the provincial conurbations simply because many other settlements have equally justifiable
needs. Places like Skelmersdale, Cumbernauld and Peterlee are still significant in
regional industrial development strategies. If all inner cities were given enhanced
development area status it is highly likely that London would be the chief bene-
ficiary. Sheer size suggests that the best strategy for London would be comprehensive urban development programmes of the New Town type - for example in docklands.
Nevertheless, there will be problems of matching the build-up of jobs and people
in areas which would then be vulnerable to population and employment leakages to
the rest of the London labour market area.

The problem of attracting industrial employment back to the inner urban areas needs
to be seen in the light of the Government's industrial strategy, chiefly those parts
of the strategy which involve backing selective industries. Locational considerations, be they inner urban or development areas, are likely to be of secondary importance. The extent to which industrial winners are concentrated in the urban areas
certainly needs to be established.

Strategies for the inner city clearly need to be seen in the light of other policies
for example for industrial regeneration, regional development and regional devolution. It would be a mistake to approach the inner urban problem with the same set of
arguments and policies that led to the establishment of development areas. The situation is totally different. All that is comparable is that the nature of the problem requires a long term strategy involving the integration of social, economic
and infrastructural policies. The economic demise of large urban areas is a function of very fundamental changes in the organisation of production and transport
technology which is resulting in a transformation of the entire urban system. In
the light of continuing high levels of unemployment in the nation as a whole and
low population growth, there is a vital need to reconsider the complex range of
policies designed to influence the distribution of population and economic activity
in Britain. Any short term prescriptions for inner urban areas need to be seen as
a first plank in building national spatial policies for the 1980's.

An integrated urban systems approach

The real conclusion of this research is the recognition of the inadequacy of traditional approaches to policy formulation. It is apparent that demographic and
economic change operates through an integrated urban framework. The urban system
clearly differentiates between the performance of towns and cities in different
parts of the country, between towns and cities of different size, and internally
within these urban areas. However what is more important is the perspective which
the comprehensive national urban view permits. But the urban systems view not only
indicates differentials as above it also specifies integration. Change performance
in one component of the system invariably means a reaction elsewhere within the
system or elsewhere in another separate urban system depending on the nature of the
migration and change component. In policy terms, issues relevant to local problems
need not necessarily be themselves local.

There have been several recent comparative reviews of urban systems views of national settlement strategies. (Goddard, 1973; Bourne, 1975). In one of these

reviews covering countries of the European Free Trade Area, Goddard concludes:

> It is fully appreciated that numerous public and private decisions
> like those relating to the location of homes, workplaces and trans-
> portation facilities interact with one another in a very complex
> fashion. The chief function of corporate planning is to manage
> this 'urban system' in such a way as to balance the needs of all
> sections of the community, both firms and households. What is
> less widely appreciated is that the system of all settlements
> within a nation operates in a similar way to the single urban unit;
> each unit is but one sub-system within an independent system of
> urban units.

Such an urban systems view is of course not new (Berry,1961). What is new and
important is the call for its translation to policy. Once a national urban systems
view of policy is accepted a number of difficult, but vital, questions need to be
tackled concerning its nature, its goals and its policy instruments. It is perhaps
reasonable to say that nowhere is such a system fully worked out although some
attempts have been made to formulate national urban policy in this way in Australia,
Canada and Sweden. Interestingly, in the second of the comparative reviews previously mentioned, Bourne concludes his section on British spatial policy as follows:

> This raises the interesting question of whether the current set
> of policies adds up to a national development strategy. It can
> be argued that Britain has an emerging national regional policy
> and a regional urban policy, but no national urban policy. Nor
> does it appear that the national urban system approach has much
> political sympathy given the complexity of regional economies
> and the strength of regional over urban interests and politics.
> This leads to an intriguing point for speculation concerning the
> degree to which the established and well-tested policies of reg-
> ional planning and industrial location on the one hand, and the
> land use and new town components or urban planning policies on
> the other hand, are converging on a focus which is both urban and
> national. That is, a focus explicitly based on the interdepend-
> encies of location decisions between cities and regions.

The lack of a national urban systems approach, often associated with a lack of policy coordination, also infers a lack of understanding of the policy options and
their implications. Take the prime issue of what reaction to take to the fundamental
process of metropolitan decentralisation. In both the United States and Britain the
recent response has been the same, to attempt to rejuvenate the inner areas of the
nation's major cities. (U.S. Department of Housing and Urban Development, 1978;
Department of the Environment, 1977). Now this might well reflect, as stated previously, sound political judgement and be totally justified within a democratic form
of government. But has the judgement been made with the full benefit of an understanding of its potential implications for the urban system as a whole? How does
such a policy relate to the future role of new and expanded towns? How does such
a policy relate to the future of the development areas? How does such a policy relate to the economic efficiency of small to medium sized towns currently achieving
high growth rates? All of these questions remain unanswered. At least one American
observer begs to question and to debate the nature of the official policy response
in the United States (Vining, 1979). Another American researcher poses the problem
as the counter urbanisation conundrum - social trends moving one way and planners
wanting them to move in the opposite direction. (Berry, 1978). Berry asks if this
oppositional quality prevails elsewhere. In Britain perhaps it does.

Postscript

Purely fortuitous timing between writing the preface and checking the proofs
permits this short postscript on the provisional results of the 1981 Census of
England and Wales. The 1970s was a decade of very low population growth amounting
to only a half a percent,in contrast to the five percent growth in the fifties and
sixties covered by this study. Yet during the seventies the counter urbanisation
trends continued to gain momentum. Generally, the population of large cities and
conurbations fell, with the larger the city the larger the population loss. The
reception areas were again the metropolitan fringes, the small to medium sized
towns and, increasingly, the rural periphery. London suffered one of the largest
rates of loss and its population now totals less than seven million for the first
time since 1901. It was primarily the inner Boroughs of London which made the
principal contributions to this population loss - Kensington and Chelsea losing a
quarter of its 1971 population during the decade. So although the details are yet
to be fully worked out, and the statistics checked, the indications are that the
trends discussed in depth in this research are the same as those currently ongoing
operating in the same directions and at similar strengths. The implications of
this research and the lessons learned thus have considerable contemporary relevance

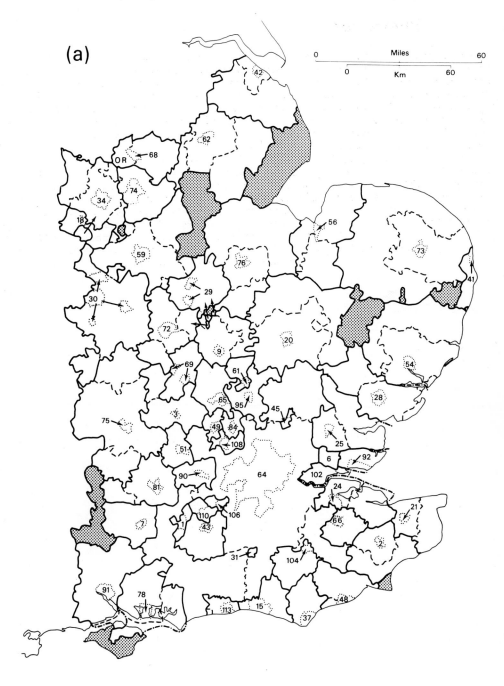

Appendix : Constituent zones of Metropolitan Economic Labour Areas, 1971
         (For numbered placename key see below Fig. 1.1)

(b)

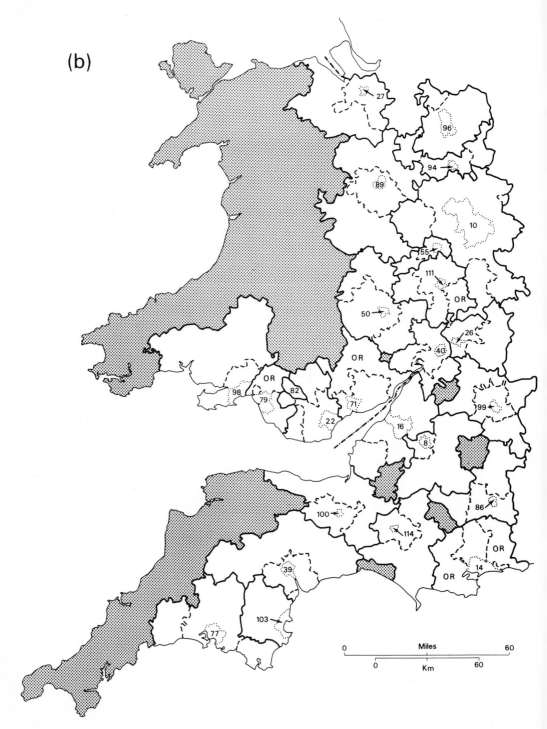

Appendix : Constituent zones of Metropolitan Economic Labour Areas, 1971
         (For numbered placename key see below Fig. 1.1)

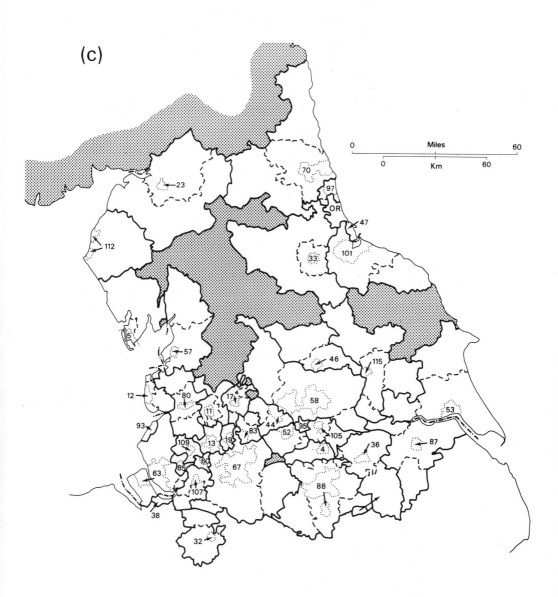

Appendix : Constituent zones of Metropolitan Economic Labour Areas, 1971
         (For numbered placename key see below Fig. 1.1)

(d)

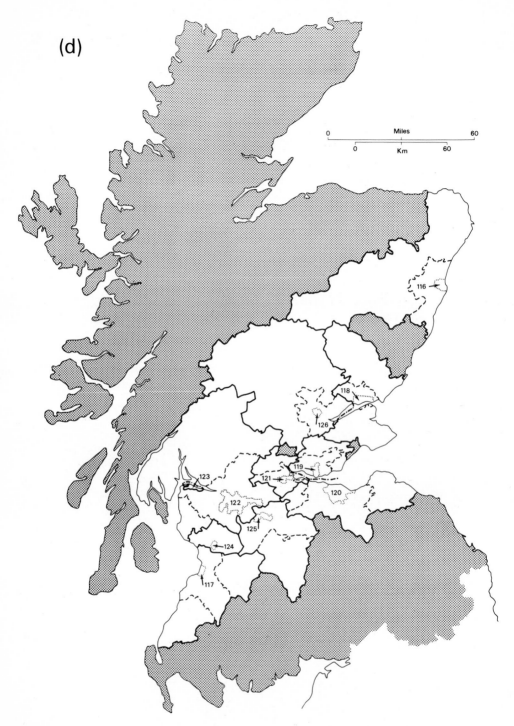

Appendix : Constituent zones of Metropolitan Economic Labour Areas, 1971
(For numbered placename key see below Fig. 1.1)

Appendix : Socio-Economic Group Classifications

In both 1966 and 1971 some 17 socio-economic groups (SEGs) were used in the
Census. These are as follows:-

1   Employers and managers in central and local government,
     industry, commerce, etc. - large establishments

2   Ditto, small establishments

3   Professional workers - self-employed

4   Ditto - employees

5   Intermediate non-manual workers

6   Junior non-manual workers

7   Personal service workers

8   Foremen and supervisors - manual

9   Skilled manual workers

10   Semi-skilled manual workers

11   Unskilled manual workers

12   Own account workers (other than professional)

13   Farmers - employers and managers

14   Farmers - own account

15   Agricultural workers

16   Members of armed forces

17   Inadequately described occupations

For analysis of SEG change in Part 2 of the study these 17 classes were aggregated
to four major groups. These are as follows:-

A   Managerial and professional (SEGs 1-4, and 13)

B   Intermediate non-manual (SEGs 5 and 6)

C   Skilled manual (SEGs 8-9, 12 and 14)

D   Semi- and unskilled manual (SEGs 7, 10-11, and 15)

Furthermore a residual grouping E was formed from SEGs 16 and 17 but only rarely
used.

For analysis of migration change by SEG in Part 3 of the study two of these four
major classes were subdivided further in order to discriminate better mobility and
housing tenure characteristics. The classes are as follows:-

A   Managerial (SEGs 1-2, and 13)

B   Professional (SEGs 3 and 4)

C   Intermediate non-manual (SEGs 5 and 6)

D   Skilled manual (SEGs 8-9, 12 and 14)

E   Semi-skilled manual (SEGs 7, 10 and 15)

F   Unskilled manual (SEG 11)

G   Armed forces and inadequately described (SEGs 16 and 17)

In 1971 the SEG data on the journey to work files of the Census was provided for some 8 groups. These are as follows:-

1   Employers (SEGs 1-2, and 13)

2   Professional (SEGs 3 and 4)

3   Manual - high (SEGs 8 and 9)

4   Manual - low (SEGs 10-11, and 15)

5   Own account (SEGs 12 and 14)

6   Services (SEGs 7, 16 and 17)

7   Intermediate (SEGs 5 and 6)

8   Agricultural (SEGs 13-14 and 15)

Note - Socio-economic group 8 (Agricultural) includes Census socio-economic groups that have already been included in the previous 7 groups.

For analysis of worktravel change by SEG in Part 4 of the study these 8 groups have been further aggregated to 5 major groups. These are as follows:-

1   Professional and managerial (SEGs 1-2, 13, 3 and 4)

2   Intermediate non-manual (SEGs 5 and 6)

3   Skilled manual (SEGs 8-9, 12 and 14)

4   Semi- and unskilled manual (SEGs 10-11, and 15)

5   Residual (SEGs 7, 16 and 17)

Note that these 5 major groups are not identical to those used in Part 2 of the study. This is due to the 'group 5' problem. In the previous analyses the semi- and unskilled manual class has included SEG 7 (Personal service workers). This is not possible with the data as provided on the journey to work files.

Appendix : Journey to Work Mode of Travel Categories

In both 1966 and 1971 the mode of travel normally used for the longest part, by distance, of the journey to place of work is tabulated in the journey to work files of the Census. However, a number of differences do exist between 1966 and 1971 in the mode of travel categories used. These are as follows:-

1966   1   Train

        2   Private/works bus

        3   Tube

        4   Public service bus

        5   Car (including motor cycle combination)

        6   Goods vehicle

        7   Motor cycle

        8   Pedal cycle

        9   On foot

       10   Other, none, and not stated (e.g. horse, ferry, working at home)

1971 1 Train (including London Transport tube)

     2 Bus (both private and public)

     3 Car (including van)

     4 Motorcycle (including motor cycle combination)

     5 Pedal cycle

     6 On foot and none (i.e. including people stating 'none' but whose usual residence and workplace addresses are different)

     7 Other (e.g. lorry, horse, ferry)

     8 Public transport (so described, despite request for clarification)

     9 Not stated

For the analysis of worktravel change by mode of travel in Part 4 of the study these problems of classification change have been reduced by combining the Census categories into some 6 major modes of travel. These are as follows:-

Mode 1 - Train (and tube)

In 1966, these were separate modes of travel, but in 1971 they were combined into a single category. By combining the two 1966 categories, therefore, direct comparability is achieved.

Mode 2 - Bus

In 1966, 'private/works bus' and 'public service bus' were separate modes of travel, but in 1971 they were combined into a single category. In addition, in 1971 there is a separate 'public transport' category for those Census returns which did not qualify whether bus or train was used. This residual accounts for less than 1% of total work journeys, and for the purposes of the present study has been combined with the Bus category (which is numerically far larger than Train).

Mode 3 - Car (including motorcycle)

In 1966, 'cars' and 'goods vehicles' were separate modal categories, but in the 1971 definitions the 'car' mode included vans while lorries were assigned to the 'other modes' category. For the purposes of the present study, the 1966 'car' plus 'goods vehicle' is taken to be equivalent to 1971 'car'. It should be noted, however, that this combination includes lorries in 1966 but not in 1971.

It was also decided to include the 'motorcycle' mode in with the Car category for both dates. It could alternatively have been included with Pedal Cycle or the Other Modes categories. Frequently in the study, Walk and Cycle modes are combined to produce a non-motorised travel component, and consequently it was felt that motorcycle journeys were more appropriately combined with car journeys. The second alternative was similarly rejected, as the Other Modes category is mainly comprised of people living and working at home. A further reason for including motorcycle journeys with the Car category is that it avoids an inconsistency concerning motorcycle-combinations, which were included with the 'car' mode in 1966 but with 'motorcycles' in 1971.

Mode 4 - Walk

In 1966, people stating 'none' but whose normal address of residence was different from their normal address of workplace were tabulated as 'not stated', but in 1971 they were included in the 'on foot' category. For the purposes of this study, however, the Walk mode is taken to be 'on foot' in 1966 and 'on foot and none' in 1971.

Mode 5 - Pedal Cycle

Directly comparable.

Mode 6 - Other, None, Not Stated

This category includes lorries in 1971 but not in 1966 (See Mode 3 above), and people stating 'none' but whose normal residence and workplace addresses were different, in 1966 but not in 1971 (See Mode 4 above). Its main component at both dates, however, is people living and working at the same address.

References

Barabba, V.P. (1975). The national setting: regional shifts, metropolitan decline and urban decay, in Sternlieb, G. and Hughes, J.W. Post Industrial America. pp. 39-76. Rutgers - The State University of New Jersey, The Centre for Urban Policy Research.

Beaumont, P. (1976). Assisted labour mobility policy in Scotland, 1973-74. Urban Studies, 13, 75-79.

Beaumont, P. (1977). The assisted spatial mobility of unemployed labour in Great Britain. Area, 9, 1, 9.

Berry, B.J.L. (1961). Cities as systems within systems of cities. Economic Development and Cultural Change, 9, 573-578.

Berry, B.J.L. (1968). Metropolitan area definition: a reevaluation of concept and statistical practice. United States Bureau of the Census, Working Paper, 28.

Berry, B.J.L. (1973). Growth Centres in the American Urban System. Ballinger: Cambridge, Mass.

Berry, B.J.L. (1976). Urbanisation and Counterurbanisation. Urban Affairs Annual Reviews, 11.

Berry, B.J.L. (1978). The counterurbanisation process: how general?, in, Hansen, N.M., Human Settlement Systems. Ballinger: Cambridge, Mass.

Bourne, L.S. (1975). Urban Systems: Strategies for Regulation. Clarendon Press: Oxford.

Chisholm, M. (1976). Regional policies in an era of slow population growth and higher unemployment. Regional Studies, 10, 201-213.

Cordey-Hayes, M. and Gleave, D. (1973). Migration movements and the differential growth of city regions in England and Wales. Centre for Environmental Studies, Research Paper, 1 : London.

Cordey-Hayes, M. and Gleave, D. (1974). Dynamic models of interaction between migration and the differential growth of cities. International Institute of Applied Systems Analysis, Conference on Urban Development Models.

Davis, N. and Walker, C. (1975). Migrants entering and leaving the U.K., 1964-74. Population Trends, 1. HMSO: London.

Deakin, N. and Ungerson, C. (1977). Leaving London: planned mobility and the inner city. Centre for Environmental Studies, Heinemann: London.

Department of the Environment, (1976). British Cities: Urban Population and Employment Trends, 1951-1971. Research Report 10: London.

Department of the Environment, (1976). Transport Policy: consultation document II. HMSO: London.

Department of the Environment, (1977). Inner Area Studies: Inner London, Policies for Dispersal and Balance. Shankland Cox, HMSO: London.

Department of the Environment, (1977). Policy for the Inner Cities. Cmnd. 6845.
    HMSO: London.

Dugmore, K. (1975). The migration and distribution of socio-economic groups in
    Greater London: evidence from the 1961, 1966 and 1971 Censuses. Greater
    London Council, Research Memorandum, RM 443.

Flowerdew, R., and Salt, J. (1979). Migration between labour market areas in
    Great Britain, 1970-1971. Regional Studies, 13, 211-231.

Frost, M. and Spence, N. (1980). Employment and Worktravel in a Selection of
    English Inner Cities. Department of the Environment, Inner Cities Directorate
    Reprinted in Geoforum (1981 forthcoming)

Frost, M. and Spence, N. (1981). Unemployment, Structural Economic Change and
    Public Policy in British Regions. Progress in Planning, 16.

Frost, M. and Spence, N. (1981 forthcoming). Urban and regional policy responses
    to recent socio-economic change in Britain. Royal Geographical Society,
    Technical Meeting. Forthcoming in Geographical Journal.

Gilje, E.K. (1975). Migration patterns in and around London. Greater London
    Council, Research Memorandum, RM 470.

Gillespie, A. (1977). Journey to work trends within British Labour Markets,
    1961-1971. London School of Economics and Political Science, Department of
    Geography.

Gleave, D. and Palmer, D. (1977). The relationship between geographic and occup-
    ational mobility in the context of regional economic growth, in, Hobcraft, J.
    and Rees, P. Regional Demographic Development, pp. 188-210. Taylor Francis:
    London.

Goddard, J.B. (1973). National Settlement Strategies: A Framework for Regional
    Development. European Free Trade Association: Geneva.

Gray, P. and Gee, F.A. (1972). A quality check on the 1966 ten percent sample
    Census of England and Wales. Office of Population Censuses and Surveys: Londc

Hadjifotiou, N. (1972). The analysis of migration between Standard Metropolitan
    Labour Market Areas in England and Wales. University College, London, Depart-
    ment of Geography, Housing and Labour Mobility Study, Working Paper, 4.

Hall, P., et al. (1973). The Containment of Urban England: 1945-1970. Allen and
    Unwin: London.

Hall, P. and Hay, D. (1980). Growth Centres in the European Urban System.
    Heinemann: London.

Hamnett, C. (1976). Social change and social segregation in inner London, 1961-71.
    Urban Studies, 13, 261-271.

Hansen, N. (1976). Systems approaches to human settlements. International Institut
    for Applied Systems Analysis, Human Settlement Systems Study, RM-76-3.
    Laxenburg, Austria.

Harris, A. (1966). Labour Mobility in Great Britain, 1953-63. Government Social
    Survey, March.

Harris, M. (1973). Some aspects of social polarisation, in, Donnison, D.V., and
    Eversley, D.E.C. London: Urban Patterns, Problems and Policy. Heinemann:
    London.

Hillman, M. and Whalley, A. (1975). Land use and travel. Built Environment
    Quarterly, 105-111.

Hyman, G. and Gleave, D. (1978). A reasonable theory of migration. Transactions,
    Institute of British Geographers, 3, 2, 179-201.

Johnson, J. and Salt, J. (1980). Employment transfer policies in Great Britain.
    The Three Banks Review, 126, 18-39.

Kennett, S. (1978). Census data and migration analysis: an appraisal. London
    School of Economics and Political Science, Department of Geography.

Kennett, S. and Randolph, W. (1978). The differential migration of socio-economic
    groups, 1966-71. London School of Economics, Graduate School of Geography,
    Discussion Paper, 66.

Lowry, I.S. (1966). Migration and Metropolitan Growth: Two Analytical Models.
    University of California: Chandler.

Peach, C. (1966). Under enumeration of West Indians in the 1961 Census. The
    Sociological Review, 14, 73-80.

Peach, C. (1968). West Indian Migration to Britain: A Social Geography. Oxford
    University Press: London.

Peach, C. et al. (1975). The distribution of coloured immigrants in Britain.
    Urban Affairs Annual Reviews, 9, 395-419.

Plessis-Fraissard, M. (1975). Age, length of residence and the probability of
    migration. University of Leeds, School of Geography, Working Paper, 107.

Pred, A. (1977). City Systems in Advanced Economies. Hutchinson: London.

Redcliffe-Maud, Lord. (1969). Royal Commission on Local Government in England,
    1966-69. III Research Appendices. Cmnd. 4040: HMSO: London.

Rees, P.H. (1976). The measurement of migration from census data and other
    sources. University of Leeds, School of Geography, Working Paper, 162.

Rees, T.L. (1978). Population and industrial decline in the South Wales coalfield.
    Regional Studies, 12, 69-78.

Sternlieb, G. and Hughes, J.W. (1975). Post Industrial America: Metropolitan
    Decline and Inter Regional Job Shifts. Rutgers - The State University of
    New Jersey, The Centre for Urban Policy Research.

Thomas, R. and Potter, S. (1977). The future of non-motorised transport. Built
    Environment Quarterly, 286-290.

U.S. Department of Housing and Urban Development. (1978). The President's
    National Urban Policy Report. Washington, D.C.

Vining, D. (1977). Post Industrial America: review article. Journal of Regional
    Science, 17, 141-146.

Vining, D.R. (1979). The Presdient's National Urban Policy Report: issues skirted
    and statistics omitted. <u>Journal of Regional Science</u>, 19, 69-77.

Vining, D.R. and Kontuly, T. (1978). Population dispersal from major metropolitan
    regions: an international comparison. <u>International Regional Science
    Review</u>, 3, 1, 49-73.

Vining, D.R. and Pallone, R. (1980). Population dispersal from core regions: a
    description and tentative explanation of the patterns from 17 countries.
    University of Pennsylvania, Department of Regional Science.

Walker, C. (1977). Demographic characteristics of migrants, 1964-75. <u>Population
    Trends</u>, 8. HMSO: London.

Ward, J.H. (1963). Hierarchical grouping to optimise an objective function.
    <u>Journal of the American Statistical Association,</u> 58, 236-244.

Willis, K. (1974). <u>Problems in Migration Analysis</u>. Saxon House/Lexington Books:
    Farnborough, Hants.